Approaches to Teaching Shakespeare's *Hamlet*

Approaches to Teaching
World Literature

Joseph Gibaldi, series editor

For a complete listing of titles,
see the last pages of this book.

Approaches to Teaching Shakespeare's *Hamlet*

Edited by

Bernice W. Kliman

The Modern Language Association of America
New York   2001

© 2001 by The Modern Language Association of America
All rights reserved. Printed in the United States of America

For information about obtaining permission to reprint material from
MLA book publications, send your request by mail (see address below),
e-mail (permissions@mla.org), or fax (646 458-0030).

Library of Congress Cataloging-in-Publication Data

Approaches to teaching Shakespeare's Hamlet / edited by Bernice W. Kliman.
   p. cm. — (Approaches to teaching world literature, ISSN 1059-1133 ; 72)
      Includes bibliographical references (p.) and index.
      ISBN 0-87352-767-4 (cloth) — ISBN 0-87352-768-2 (pbk.)
   1. Shakespeare, William, 1564–1616. Hamlet. 2. Shakespeare, William,
   1564–1616—Study and teaching. I. Kliman, Bernice W. II. Series.
                  PR2807.A954 2001
            822.3'3—dc21   2001034297

Cover illustration for the paperback edition: Simon Russell Beale as Hamlet,
in the Royal Shakespeare Company production of *Hamlet*,
London, 2000. Photo by Clare Park.

Set in Caledonia and Bodoni. Printed on chlorine-free paper

Published by The Modern Language Association of America
26 Broadway, New York, New York 10004-1789
www.mla.org

CONTENTS

Preface to the Series xi

Preface to the Volume xiii

PART ONE: MATERIALS *Bernice W. Kliman*

Introduction 3
Editions 3
    Single-Play Editions for Students 4
    Single-Play Editions for Instructors and Advanced Students 6
    Complete Works 7
    Anthologies 9
The Student's and Instructor's Library 9
    References and Guides 10
    Criticism 11
Aids to Teaching 12
An Annotated and Chronological Screenography: Major *Hamlet*
    Adaptations and Selected Derivatives 14
    Kenneth S. Rothwell

PART TWO: APPROACHES

Introduction 31

Introducing Verse and Meter

Hearing the Poetry 41
    George T. Wright

Dancing the Meter 48
    Ellen J. O'Brien

The Multiple-Text *Hamlet*

"The Play's the Thing": Constructing the Text of *Hamlet* 52
    T. H. Howard-Hill

An Editing Exercise for Students 57
    Randall Anderson

Teaching with a Variorum Edition 62
    Frank Nicholas Clary

Teaching *Hamlet* through Translation 66
    Jesús Tronch-Pérez

Performance Approaches

Exploring *Hamlet*: Opening Play Texts, Closing Performances   73
  Edward L. Rocklin

To Challenge Ghostly Fathers: Teaching *Hamlet* and Its
    Interpretations through Film and Video   77
  Stephen M. Buhler

Critical Practice through Performance: The Nunnery *ophelia*
    and Play Scenes   81
  Mary Judith Dunbar

Teaching the Script: The "Mousetrap" in the Classroom   86
  Michael W. Shurgot

Narrative, Character, and Theme

Hamlet's Narratives   *fictions*   90
  Arthur F. Kinney

From Story to Action: A Graduated Exercise to Teach *Hamlet*   95
  Nina daVinci Nichols

A World of Questions: An Approach Indebted to Maynard Mack   97
  Robert H. Ray

"That Monster Custom": Highlighting the Theme
    of Obedience in *Hamlet*   102
  Joan Hutton Landis

Teaching *Hamlet* as a Play about Family   107
  Bruce W. Young

Ten Questions Basic to Interpreting *Hamlet*, with
    Special Focus on the Ghost   113
  Roy Battenhouse

Comparative Approaches

The "Encrusted" *Hamlet*: Resetting the "Mousetrap"   118
  Graham Bradshaw

Teaching *Hamlet* in a Global Literature Survey:
    Linking Elizabethan England and Ming China   129
  Paula S. Berggren

Hamlet in a Western Civilization Course: Connections
    to Montaigne's *Essays* and Cervantes's *Don Quixote*   134
  Ann W. Engar

The Pyrrhus Speech: Querying the Uses of the Troy Story   138
  Lisa Hopkins

From Elsinore to Mangalore and Back: *Hamlet* between Worlds 141
Ralph Nazareth

Modern and Postmodern Strategies

The Gertrude Barometer: Teaching Shakespeare with
Freud, Eliot, and Lacan 146
Julia Reinhard Lupton

"She Chanted Snatches of Old Tunes": Ophelia's Songs
in a Polyphonic *Hamlet* 153
Nona Paula Fienberg

Decentering *Hamlet*: Questions and Perspectives
Concerning Evidence and Proof 157
Terry Reilly

More than Child's Play: Approaching *Hamlet*
through Comic Books 161
Marion D. Perret

Hamlet and Sylvia, Shakespeare and Bambara:
Reading *Hamlet* as Context 165
Mary S. Comfort

Focus on Scenes

Act 1, Scene 3: An Introduction to *Hamlet* 170
Michael J. Collins

Act 2, Scene 1, 75–120: Psychoanalytic Approaches 174
H. R. Coursen

The Closet-Scene Access 180
Maurice Charney

Language, Structure, and Ideology: Act 4, Scene 5 184
John Drakakis

The Fencing Scene 191
Laurie E. Maguire

Shaping Our Ends: A Workshop on the Last Scene 197
Arthur Kincaid

Hamlet Online

The Prince of Punk in the Festive Classroom 201
James R. Andreas Sr.

An Interdisciplinary Approach to *Hamlet* in a
Distance-Learning Classroom 206
Anthony DiMatteo

E-Mail to Facilitate Discussion   211
  Eric Sterling

Short Takes

Hamlet Refracted through Three Definitions of Tragedy   214
  David G. Hale

Francis Bacon's "Of Revenge"   216
  Margaret Maurer

Introducing Students to Effective Refutation   216
  Joanne E. Gates

Believing and Doubting Ideas about *Hamlet*   218
  Meta Plotnik

Students as Characters, Speaking in Character   219
  Christine Mack Gordon

Two Ways to Use Film for Student Writing   219
  Rob Kirkpatrick

Hamlet Is Not Mad   221
  D. Buchanan

Defamiliarizing Hamlet: Hamlet with and without His Soliloquies   222
  Barbara Hodgdon

Helping Chinese Students Study *Hamlet*   223
  Luo Zhiye

Oral Reports on Criticism   224
  Edna Zwick Boris

Teaching Text and Performance through Soundscripting   226
  Michael W. Young

More Matter (but Not Necessarily Less Art): Using My
  Coloring Book to Introduce Seventh Graders to *Hamlet*   227
  Denise M. Mullins

Priming Questions for the "Mousetrap"   230
  Bente Videbaek

Puns and Wordplay in *Hamlet*   231
  Paul J. Voss

Leaping into the Text: Teaching Stage Directions in Act 5, Scene 1   232
  Hardin L. Aasand

Groups Debating Issues   233
  David George

Existential Questions   234
  Alan R. Young

Writing to Make Personal Connections   235
    Mike Sirofchuck

Words, Words, Words: Comparing, Cutting, Explaining   235
    Nathaniel Strout

Hamlet and Subjectivity   237
    Dympna Callaghan

Epilogue

Cheating Death: The Immortal and Ever-Expanding
        Universe of *Hamlet*   239
    Maria M. Scott

Notes on Contributors   245

Survey Participants   253

Works Cited and Materials for Further Study
    Editions   255
        Single-Play Editions   255
        Complete Works   256
        Anthologies   256
    References and Guides   257
    Criticism   262
    Aids to Teaching   273
        Works on Teaching   273
        Shakespeare on Screen   275
        Special Editions, Comic Books, School Guides,
            Audio Performances   278
        Journals   279
        Web Sites   279
        Resources for Comparison and Illustration   280

Index of Names   283

Index of Scenes in *Hamlet*   289

Index of Characters in *Hamlet*, Other Than Hamlet   291

PREFACE TO THE SERIES

In *The Art of Teaching* Gilbert Highet wrote, "Bad teaching wastes a great deal of effort, and spoils many lives which might have been full of energy and happiness." All too many teachers have failed in their work, Highet argued, simply "because they have not thought about it." We hope that the Approaches to Teaching World Literature series, sponsored by the Modern Language Association's Publications Committee, will not only improve the craft—as well as the art—of teaching but also encourage serious and continuing discussion of the aims and methods of teaching literature.

The principal objective of the series is to collect within each volume different points of view on teaching a specific literary work, a literary tradition, or a writer widely taught at the undergraduate level. The preparation of each volume begins with a wide-ranging survey of instructors, thus enabling us to include in the volume the philosophies and approaches, thoughts and methods of scores of experienced teachers. The result is a sourcebook of material, information, and ideas on teaching the subject of the volume to undergraduates.

The series is intended to serve nonspecialists as well as specialists, inexperienced as well as experienced teachers, graduate students who wish to learn effective ways of teaching as well as senior professors who wish to compare their own approaches with the approaches of colleagues in other schools. Of course, no volume in the series can ever substitute for erudition, intelligence, creativity, and sensitivity in teaching. We hope merely that each book will point readers in useful directions; at most each will offer only a first step in the long journey to successful teaching.

Joseph Gibaldi
Series Editor

PREFACE TO THE VOLUME

Why *Hamlet* should be the focus of an Approaches volume seems clear: it is an enduring classic, taught in secondary schools and at every college level—to first-year students and to advanced graduate students, to English majors and non-majors. *Hamlet* has been an ideal text for the issues that were important to the discipline from its beginnings as well as for ideas that have become central in the last twenty years. Lewis Theobald's *Shakespeare Restored*, often cited as the first work of literary criticism of an English text (1726), concentrated on *Hamlet*. The play stimulated Romantic theory (in the work of Goethe, Schlegel, Coleridge, and Bradley), a heritage that still affects our perceptions of *Hamlet* and its characters. It was the site for early psychoanalytic theory (Freud; Ernest Jones) and continues to interest psychoanalytic theorists through the work of Jacques Lacan and others. Feminists, materialists, and historicists all find in the play ample ground for speculation and contestation that enrich our understanding of the play's 1,600 contexts and our ways of grappling with its mysteries now. In addition, the length of the play (about four thousand lines), the vast number of works written about the play, and the myriad problems of its interpretation make it a particularly challenging play to teach well.

Over eighty instructors responded in rich detail to MLA's *Hamlet* survey; all have helped shape this collection. From the pool of those who offered to contribute essays, I selected the majority of the essays that appear, and, because of their particular interests, I urged others to contribute. My own bias is toward textual study and performance criticism, and obviously that bias has affected my selection of essays. However, I have tried to include representative essays of all the types that the respondents offered as well as a few other types.

Contributors write at every stage of their careers, the enthusiastic beginning as well as the seasoned middle and beyond. All contributors exhibited generosity of spirit, creativity, and thoughtfulness while progressing through the lengthy process of completing the volume. The format of this volume follows that of other Approaches books, with, in part 1, a discussion of materials derived from responses to the survey and from the essays, including a detailed screenography by Kenneth S. Rothwell. Part 2 consists of an introduction based on the survey, followed by the essays, including "Short Takes." Many of the essays resist classification, treating, say, film and e-mail, textual criticism and performance, cross-disciplinary studies and a focus on a particular scene, and so on. The short takes are similarly varied in approach. Though categories overlap, I have classified the longer essays to reflect their main concerns.

I owe the largest debt to those who responded to the MLA survey and who wrote the essays for this volume. Others who have edited Approaches volumes, particularly Robert H. Ray (*King Lear*) and Maurice Hunt (*The Tempest* and other late romances), provided valuable models. In addition, I am grateful to the Modern Language Association (esp. Joseph Gibaldi, the series editor, who set the high standard for this series with his *Approaches to Teaching Chaucer's Canterbury Tales*); to the readers of the proposal, prospectus, and manuscript for their invaluable suggestions; and to Michael Kandel for carefully copyediting and for helping with the indexes. Andrew McLean some years ago undertook this project, but exigencies forced him to relinquish it; I thank him for his gracious good wishes and for supplying the Roy Battenhouse essay. Barbara Bowen, Kent Cartwright, Edwin DeWindt, Michael P. Jensen, Dave Kliman, Merwin Kliman, and Thomas Pendleton read drafts and made helpful suggestions, and Roger Shabazz helped clarify some issues. The National Endowment for the Humanities has generously supported the work on the new variorum *Hamlet* edition, and the program officers (esp. Helen Agüera, the senior program officer) urged us to consider the role of the edition in teaching. Their concerns led me to this Approaches project. Finally I dedicate this volume to my colleagues in the Nassau Community College Writing Group: Toby Bird, Joe Dowling, Kathryn Feldman, Barbara Horn, Patricia Owen Irwin, Hedda Marcus, and Meta Plotnik. We have spent years talking and writing together about teaching and learning, and their example has kept up my spirits in the face of some difficult teaching tasks.

Part One

MATERIALS

Introduction

With over four hundred new editions, books, and essays on *Hamlet* appearing annually, the voluminous materials obviously can only be hinted at here. Since standard editions are also selective, instructors will want to seek out their own materials: reviews of editions, books, and essays from *Hamlet Studies*, *Shakespeare Quarterly* and its annual *World Shakespeare Bibliography*, *SEL* (*Studies in English Literature*), *Shakespeare Bulletin*, *Shakespeare Newsletter*, *Shakespeare Survey*, *Shakespeare Studies*, and the *MLA Annual Bibliography*. Many other periodicals include detailed descriptions and evaluations of important texts (see the "Journals" section in "Works Cited and Materials for Further Study" at the back of this volume). "Materials" presents the judgment of those who responded to the MLA survey. Their choices offer graduate students a reading plan; they can help instructors who are not Shakespeareans but who, in their survey courses, bear the main responsibility in many colleges for introducing Shakespeare to general students; and possibly they can remind seasoned Shakespeareans of work that could reinvigorate their teaching. Included are editions, an instructor's library, and aids to teaching. The organization of "Works Cited and Materials for Further Study" follows the sections of "Materisls": editions (single plays, complete works, anthologies), the student's and instructor's library (reference works and guides, criticism), aids to teaching (works on teaching, Shakespeare on screen, and more). Although some items fit easily in more than one category, I have limited them to the one that seems most suitable for this volume.

Editions

Respondents to the survey frequently allow students to select their own texts of *Hamlet*, a strategy that allows students to discover that editors' choices vary. These spontaneous realizations afford instructors the opportunity to discuss the three original texts (the 1603 First Quarto or Q1, the 1604 Second Quarto or Q2, and the 1623 First Folio or F1) and their use by editors. Many instructors are keenly aware of textual issues. Most agree that knowing the three early texts is indispensable to the instructor and that some acquaintance with textual variants is mind opening for students, letting them glimpse the editors' premises behind the curtain of their textbooks' infallibility. By incorporating, as helpful adjuncts to edited texts, facsimile versions of the quartos (Allen and Muir) and folio (Hinman; Kökeritz) or texts with modern fonts (Bertram and Kliman; Kliman, *Enfolded*), instructors can encourage students to enter the scholarly conversation about text and textual issues. Scholarly and student editions have included textual variants since the Cambridge (1866 [Clark, Glover, and W. A. Wright]) and Furness (1877) editions of *Hamlet* (anticipated by Jennens in 1773). Textual scholars (Honigmann; Maguire; Mowat; Urkowitz; Warren; Werstine; and others) have turned their lenses on *Hamlet*, *Lear*, and other multiple-text plays. Many modern editions provide histories of editions and argue for their approach and against those of other editors; Stanley Wells and Gary Taylor have a helpful overview.

Single-Play Editions for Students

For multipurpose courses like Literature and the Law (reported by Howlett), Literature and Medicine (reported by Belling and by Oakes), an introduction to literature for sophomores, freshman composition, and other courses that range widely, instructors favor single-play editions. In courses devoted to Shakespeare, many instructors prefer the small texts for their light weight, which is important if students stand up to perform. Several series vie for primacy.

The Signet edition (271 pp.) is selected by a majority of instructors because of the breadth of its introductory and secondary materials and the succinct yet inclusive performance history by general editor Sylvan Barnet (including in the third edition films through Branagh). As editor of the third edition, Barnet resists objections to the conflated Second Quarto and First Folio and discusses (and counters) the arguments—from the Oxford and Cambridge editors—against conflation. The small paperback contains a generous seven essays (in whole or in part), including the often cited Maynard Mack essay ("The World of *Hamlet*"; see Ray's essay, this volume) and a fourteen-page list of suggested readings. Notes at the bottoms of pages are reasonably easy to read; minimal textual notes, gathered near the end, are visually well organized and lucid. The second edition, edited by Edward Hubler, is also a frequent choice.

The compact, 197-page Bantam Classic (Bevington) contains a long, modernized excerpt from the English translation of Belleforest, "The History of Hamlet," originally published in 1608. David Bevington includes an appendix, "Memorable Lines"; these might provide an opening for teaching the play. The introductory essays are brief, with several pages on performance; a respondent remarks that this Bantam edition has the best notes for actors. The commentary footnotes are succinct, the textual notes compressed into four pages, followed by a listing of words and passages found only in Q2. As in his *Complete Works* edition, Bevington numbers only lines that have footnotes. The annotated bibliography is brief and undivided. The one illustration, on the inside back cover, is of Kevin Kline as Hamlet.

The Folger edition (Mowat and Werstine) is a favorite with students, who like the commentary on facing pages, with room for their own comments. Its illustrations from the Folger Shakespeare Library Collections, its scene summaries, and its brackets alerting students to variants from the Q2 copy text and Q2-only lines are also attractive features. Students will probably find the textual apparatus thorough but densely presented (289–306). In its well-arranged, annotated bibliography (corresponding to the divisions of the introductory essay), performance studies—except for a listing on Shakespeare's theater—are absent. The single additional essay, by Michael Neill, is an overview of the play. The 337-page volume ends with a list of famous lines.

The New Penguin (now not so new) has an entirely different emphasis. T. J. B. Spencer's expansive commentary notes follow the play (205–361). Nothing in the text signals the presence of notes, but if students turn to the back of the book, they will find notes that are kind to the eyes and occasionally comprehensive, without, as one respondent noted, being overwhelming. The textual notes are also readable, each on a line in eight pages. One has to guess that editors of some other editions did not expect students to read textual notes and so saved space by compacting them into a dense lump. For those who value textual studies, variant notes that are easy to decipher are clearly an advantage. So is the ample, forty-five page introduction by Anne Barton.

The Bedford edition, using the *Riverside Hamlet* text, serves instructors who want to acquaint students with recent critical trends—with five essays discussing specific approaches (feminist, psychoanalytic, deconstructionist, Marxist, and new-historicist) and with the editor's, Susan L. Wofford's, helpful introductions to and selected bibliography for each essay. A glossary of critical and theoretical terms completes the volume. As more plays become available in this series, instructors who want to present a variety of current critical perspectives may select these volumes over the complete works, whose critical apparatus is necessarily both more broad and more limited. They may want to supplement these essays with other, traditional essays so that students can compare them with other approaches. Martin Coyle, for example, reprints both traditional and newer analyses. Instructors may also want to read Brian Vickers (*Appropriating*) for his objections to the five approaches.

In popularity among respondents, the Bedford replaces Cyrus Hoy's Norton Critical Edition, which, however, remains useful for its wide range of materials, including textual commentary, intellectual backgrounds (with short pieces from Bright, Lavater, Montaigne, and others), excerpts from Saxo Grammaticus and Belleforest, selections of criticism from the eighteenth century through 1958, and a classified bibliography. Like the Bedford, it scants performance studies.

The Everyman text, edited by John F. Andrews, though influenced by the Folger format, is the most idiosyncratic single-play edition among this group in that it retains readings of its control text, Q2, rejected by other editors (even those who use Q2) and capitalizes words for emphasis, emulating but not duplicating upper cases in the folio. This edition provides textual notes before rather than after the text and classifies them helpfully. Because Andrews presents the textual notes in list form rather than in paragraphs, they are easy to read and use. Like the Folger, the Everyman has commentary notes that face the text pages, but its scene summaries are collected in one place. A short concluding essay summarizes critical perspectives on *Hamlet*. The volume's reading list features critical anthologies, critical and background studies. The volume scants performance studies, except for a brief foreword by Derek Jacobi, about half of which he devotes to his theory that Hamlet says his "To be" speech directly to Ophelia. Parallel time lines list events in Shakespeare's life and a chronology of his times.

Since some students may turn to Sidney Lamb's Complete Study Guide (a Cliff's Notes publication), instructors would do well to know what is in it. An edition with commentary, the study guide contains much that will be helpful to students, sometimes overinterpreting but often asking questions for students to ponder. The three-column format allows them to turn, when they need help, to the left of the text for discussion and to the right for glosses. The introductory material has standard discussions of Shakespeare's life, plays, and theater; an introduction to *Hamlet* specifically; and a very short bibliography. Instructors can recommend it to students who need a lot of help, and it may be preferable to Alan Durband's modernization in the series Shakespeare Made Easy. The translation is flat-footed but perhaps purposely so, because Durband urges students to turn to the original (on facing pages) as soon as possible. Students should be able to see what the play loses in translation, and with the pony at their sides they may gain confidence in their ability to understand Shakespeare's language; they will see how much more Shakespeare says. The book contains, along with the typical general introduction and introduction to *Hamlet*, simple questions. This is remedial Shakespeare.

Illustrated *Hamlet*s (a.k.a. comic books) also have a place, and these can be objects worth studying in themselves for their interpretations of design, blocking, and casting (see Perret, this volume).

Single-Play Editions for Instructors and Advanced Students

The Arden edited by Harold Jenkins is the choice of many instructors for their own study and for advanced students. The extensive notes—textual notes below the text and commentary footnotes as well as longer endnotes—make the Arden the most complete single-volume resource for the play. The forthcoming Arden (2002) will publish three texts, Q1, Q2, and F1, each separately edited. In the meantime, Jenkins's authoritative voice and forceful erudition will make students feel they are in safe hands. He provides a very full discussion of the three early texts, with strong arguments for the primacy of Q2. He does not tolerate what he calls actors' interpolations (62–63) and ruthlessly excises even "Oh Vengeance!" from Hamlet's second-act soliloquy (2.2.577). Jenkins summarizes the sources more fully than most other editors and discusses issues thoroughly in his longer notes, but he provides no index and no bibliography, both of which would have enhanced this densely annotated edition.

Respondents cite less frequently similar scholarly editions, the Oxford and Cambridge, the former with F1 as its copy text and the latter a conflated, eclectic text, with Q2-only passages bracketed. G. R. Hibbard, the Oxford editor, devotes about half his introduction to textual concerns, writing persuasively for F1 as deriving from a revised manuscript. (It is well to remind students that textual hypotheses are not facts but theories amenable to further questioning.) Oxford's commentary and textual notes are in very small type. One of the five appendixes contains eighteen fully annotated (and cleverly edited) Q2-only passages excluded from the main body of the play; the third appendix is a discussion of *Der Bestrafte Brudermord*, the German script that shows some connections to Q1 *Hamlet*. The Oxford volume concludes with a twenty-two-page index.

The Cambridge edition, edited by Philip Edwards, pays more attention than the other scholarly editions to performance issues, using them to help shape textual choices and including in its introduction a discussion of the play's action, with C. Walter Hodges's graceful pictorial representations of staging and with illustrations of actors. The short reading list contains a section on stage history (but not film or television) as well as sections on bibliographies, criticism, and anthologies of criticism. Textual notes are too small for any but a very persistent reader; students are apt to skip over them. There is no index.

A possible option for students who do not require glosses (particularly if the legibility of the Cambridge edition's font were improved) is Robert Hapgood's *Hamlet Prince of Denmark* in the Cambridge series Shakespeare in Production, which uses Edwards's text but, instead of interpretive commentary notes, provides instances from performances; in addition, Hapgood's introductory overview summarizes the development of interpretation from Garrick to Branagh.

The Kittredge edition of *Hamlet*, though published in 1939, is still valuable to instructors because of its intelligently crafted commentary notes (131–298) and full though perhaps outdated textual notes (299–332). The play itself appears with no adornments beyond line numbers. This edition, like the 1936 *Complete Works of Shakespeare*, edited by Kittredge, and the revision of 1971, edited by Irving Ribner and Kittredge, is a folio-based text.

Complete Works

The *Riverside*, in its 1997 incarnation (Evans et al.), still holds the primary position among the one-volume editions of the plays and poems, but not as decisively as it did when Robert H. Ray surveyed instructors of *Lear* for his MLA Approaches volume. The second edition is not very different from the first; it retains its extensive apparatus: thorough introductions, brackets to indicate variants from the Q2 copy text, and fine illustrations (thirty-nine plates and fifty-three illustrations in the text). The "Note on the Text" that precedes the textual variants discusses the "dangerous premise" that an acting text like F1, which might change from performance to performance, is preferable to a "literary text" like Q2 (1234). Obviously, others disagree with this view. One advantage of the *Riverside* is that Marvin Spevack's concordances are keyed to its numbering system and many scholarly articles use *Riverside* numbering. The text of the 1997 edition is very slightly changed from the 1974 edition; Larry Weiss reports variations in *Hamlet* at 2.2.73, 2.2.541, and 3.2.223. Heather Dubrow's essay "Twentieth-Century Shakespeare Criticism" (27–54), a concession to developments in criticism since 1974, is a helpful overview for students and instructors. The essay "Chronology and Sources" links Shakespeare's works with probable sources. The editors wisely retain Charles Shattuck's lively "Shakespeare's Plays in Performance from 1660 to 1971," continued by William T. Liston: the Riverside gives stage (including the new Globe Theatre at Bankside) and screen their due weight. "Records, Documents, and Allusions" and "Annals" (1951–2019) contain a rich stock of material for students' explorations. A classified selected bibliography, several indexes, and glossary complete the volume.

The 1997 *Complete Works* (ed. Bevington), also with Q2 as copy text, has fluent notes that explain difficulties and suggest variants. Students will find the textual notes at the end of the volume rather than after each play as in the other editions. Bevington divides the bibliography helpfully, with literary criticism through the 1930s, the 1970s, and the 1980s and 1990s, with separate bibliographies for each genre and for almost every play. For the updated fourth edition, Bevington adds *The Two Noble Kinsmen* and "A Funeral Elegy for Master William Peter" but not *Edward III* or *Sir Thomas More*. A colorful gathering of illustrations, several from films, brightens the clear introduction, which covers everything from Shakespeare's life to brief synopses of recent critical developments. A glossary and an index, with personages identified, complete the volume.

The 1997 one-volume Norton (Greenblatt et al.), based textually on the Oxford edition (i.e., with folio as control text) but with many helpful deviations (such as marking with brackets the editors' additions), is the choice of some instructors who want a theoretically grounded apparatus. The Shakespearean backgrounds and foregrounds occupy sixty-five pages. Some respondents expressed disappointment with the apparatus and with the bleed through caused by thin paper. Headings, however, are lively and likely to entice students: "The Playing Field," "From Foul to Fair: The Making of the Printed Play." The Norton arranges plays chronologically, providing also a table of contents by genre. An appendix by Andrew Gurr, the Globe Theater expert, discusses Shakespeare's stage and theatrical practices (but not film, television, or stage performances beyond Shakespeare's time), and another contains over thirty early documents. The Norton single-column text supplies glosses in the margin in addition to textual and interpretive footnotes. "A Shakespeare Chronicle" offers the same type of material as the Riverside's "Annals." The bibliography follows the design of the introductory material, with the addition of strong sections on literary criticism, arranged in three periods, and on performance. There is no general index—only one for first lines of poems. In *Hamlet*, the volume italicizes the Q2 passages, emphasizing rather than minimizing them (as did the Oxford editions, relegating them to an appendix). Because it numbers these Q2 segments separately, its system strays far from that of the other conflated editions; thus this text might be difficult to use in a class where students are invited to make their own choice.

Anthologies

Publishers, of course, design anthologies for particular courses: for a Shakespeare course there is a selection of plays, such as Bevington's *Four Tragedies*; for an introduction to literature (Western or world) there are many contenders, each with perhaps only one or two Shakespeare plays; and there are a few anthologies for an introductory course in classical to modern drama (see Worthen; Coldewey and Streitberger). There are also some anthologies for composition courses, such as Lee Jacobus's editions. Anthologies by particular editors or publishers can be counted on to switch plays every few years. Most of the anthologies listed in "Works Cited and Materials for Further Study" contain *Hamlet*. See "Comparative Studies" in part 2 of this volume for ways that anthologies might be used.

The Student's and Instructor's Library

The diversity of resources that respondents say are essential for the instructor's own library has been illuminating. Since many works are mentioned by only one respondent, the list is larger than one might expect in a survey answered by about eighty instructors. This state of affairs suggests that the idea of one standard of scholarship has disintegrated (if there ever was such a thing). It also may explain why so many instructors think that students need not read critical studies but rather should concentrate on the play itself. If there is no agreement on the one or ten main resources that one *must* read, why read any?

Most respondents who teach undergraduates do not assign outside readings beyond the introductions and critical essays in the editions—and sometimes not even those. Otherwise, students might fasten on a critical essay as a substitute for "bearing down on the text of the play" (Maurer, from the survey). The problem for instructors who do not assign readings is how to harness the explosive energy from critical essays—without relying too heavily on what Paulo Freire calls "banking education," the depositing of information into students' minds without giving students any sense of the instructor's or the writer's work to bring the ideas to life (see 57–74).

As for the Cliff's Notes, to which students may turn robotically, one instructor requires students to compare its commentary with that in a standard edition.

Another preempts it by "teaching how the play is built and how themes emerge out of language and action" (Nichols, from the survey). John Doyle and Ray Lischner's *Shakespeare for Dummies* is another elementary aid. Charles Boyce and Norrie Epstein are other contenders. A possible exercise for students might be to find textual evidence to complicate these books' assertions. Some students may think they need these aids, and thus instructors should not spurn them—but co-opt them creatively.

References and Guides

When an edition does not include enough source material or historical background and when instructors prefer not to lecture on these topics, they may recommend companion volumes—Isaac Asimov's *Guide*, John Andrews's three-volume collection *William Shakespeare*, Richard Corum's *Understanding* Hamlet, David Kastan's *Companion to Shakespeare*, Thomas MacCary's Hamlet: *A Guide*, Russ McDonald's *Bedford Companion to Shakespeare*, and Gerald Pinciss and Roger Lockyer's *Shakespeare's World*. McDonald's book, for example, contains biographical materials; illustrations (maps, illustrations by C. Walter Hodges, De Witt, Hollar); theatrical links (Edward Alleyn, Henslowe, Marlowe); facsimiles from primary texts; historical, religious, and dramatic sources and analogues; literary theory (Aristotle, Sidney, Rhymer); language and rhetoric (Hoskyns, Puttenham, T. Wilson); society (Coke, Queen Elizabeth). Pinciss and Lockyer have excerpts from DuLaurens, Montaigne, church homilies, *Thirty-Nine Articles of the Church of England*, Hooker, Reginald Scot, John Dee, Machiavelli, Duplessis-Mornay, Bodin, James I, Fortescue, Coke, Castiglione, Thomas Wilson, Puttenham, Elyot, Ascham, Thomas Smith, Camden, Queen Elizabeth, letters of the earl of Essex.

The sections on reference works list both primary and secondary sources mentioned in the survey and essays. Among the often cited resources for students that instructors also find profitable are Geoffrey Bullough's source materials, Marvin Spevack's concordances, and the *OED* and other dictionaries. Students can supplement Spevack's concordances with online concordances (see "Web Sites" in "Works Cited and Materials for Further Study"). The *OED* is available on CD and online.

Other dictionaries could benefit students and instructors (Abbott; Coye; *Early Modern English Dictionaries* [in "Web Sites"]; Onions; Schmidt). The 1877 New Variorum Edition of *Hamlet* (Furness) is a rich store of verbal choices and commentary notes on lines in the play (see Clary, this volume); a new variorum edition, forthcoming, will extend the history of ideas about *Hamlet* to the end of the twentieth century. See "References and Guides" in "Works Cited and Materials for Further Study."

Criticism

Though many instructors do not assign early, standard critical works to their students, many respondents turn (and return) to them for their own reading; among these works are Mack's analysis (*Everybody's Shakespeare*), A. C. Bradley's character study, and Ernest Jones's psychoanalytic study. Many instructors rely on Roland Mushat Frye, Northrop Frye, E. M. W. Tillyard (to see what is wrong, according to new historicists, with Tillyard's view of Shakespeare's worldview and what is usable, see Landis, this volume), Harley Granville-Barker (*Prefaces*), Harry Levin, John Dover Wilson, and other early- to mid-twentieth-century writers. For the full set of essays and books suggested in the survey and essays, see "Criticism" in "Works Cited and Materials for Further Study."

Several of the trendier books of the last twenty years or so do not have much to say about *Hamlet*—perhaps an indication of this play's resistance. To select a few at random: Jonathan Dollimore's *Radical Tragedy* has no reference to *Hamlet* in its index. The almost four hundred pages of *Subject and Object in Renaissance Culture* (de Grazia, Quilligan, and Stallybrass) contain, on *Hamlet,* only two incisive pages, by Peter Stallybrass (314–16). Stephen Greenblatt mentions *Hamlet* on one page (87) of his *Renaissance Self-Fashioning* (but now he has written a book on the play, *Hamlet in Purgatory*). Students might test these books' templates by applying them to *Hamlet.* The exercise affords students opportunities for interpretive or analytic originality; they can gain practice in the skill of using critical literature without swallowing it whole.

However, many recent collections of essays and books contain significant commentary on *Hamlet* that may inspire both students and instructors. There are, to mention a very few, Jean E. Howard's *Shakespeare's Art of Orchestration*; Lisa Jardine's *Reading Shakespeare Historically*; Bert O. States's Hamlet *and the Concept of Character*; Ellen J. O'Brien's "Mapping the Role," which deals with a useful postmodern concept of character, focusing on Gertrude; Julia Reinhard Lupton and Kenneth Reinhard's *After Oedipus*, an erudite analysis of psychoanalytic approaches; and Graham Bradshaw's bracing books *Shakespeare's Scepticism* and *Misrepresentations.*

With current interest in cultural studies, some instructors turn to nonliterary resources. Laura Bohannon's essay "Shakespeare in the Bush" is beguiling, with its proof that culture affects apprehension of meaning, and instructors can compare her ideas with more recent works on global interpretation. In *Chushingura,* a traditional Japanese revenge play, the hero takes a year to exact retribution, but no one appears to consider that he delays (see also Nazareth, this volume). Many philosophers, cultural and social historians, and other intellectuals have written on existentialism, materialism, skepticism, and other topics that will be helpful to instructors. This volume's "References and Guides" is a start toward gathering a bibliography of non-Shakespearean texts that interest Shakespeareans. For understanding Renaissance contexts, familiarity with iconography is useful (see this volume's "Resources for Comparison and Illustration"). Instructors can also awaken students' awareness of cultural interpretations through theatrical and film illustrations (see Ashton; Mander and Michenson; A. Young; Rosenberg; Rothwell, "Akira Kurosawa").

The essays on meter, text editing, comparative literature, interdisciplinary studies, and any one of the other approaches suggest further reading.

Aids to Teaching

Instructors can seek information about teaching from a wide variety of resources. *Shakespeare Set Free* (O'Brien, Roberts, Tolaydo, and Goodwin) is the commendable result of years of experimentation in schools. The *MLA International Bibliography* has a section on pedagogy. Journals such as *Shakespeare Magazine* and *Shakespeare and the Classroom* publish plans for all kinds of classrooms. The "Aids to Teaching" section in "Works Cited and Materials for Further Study" lists some individual scholars who have written about teaching the play (e.g., Coursen; Hirsh; Howlett; Marcus; Potter; Robinson; Rozett; Voss; Wheeler). Some respondents refer to basic pedagogic texts (like those of Elbow; Freire; Ponsot and Deen; Wiggins) that do not discuss *Hamlet* but that propose a philosophy of teaching.

Since more frequently than ever instructors are flicking on VCRs in their classroom, they will find an indispensable resource in Kenneth S. Rothwell and Annabelle Henkin Melzer's guide to film and video, with full details on the *Hamlet* films most frequently cited by instructors: Laurence Olivier's (1948), Franco Zeffirelli's (1990), Kenneth Branagh's (1996), and dozens of others. Rothwell and Melzer provide full credits and generous appraisals. Michael Almereyda's 2000 film is likely to be useful for the classroom (see Sirofchuck, this volume). The present volume contains an annotated screenography by Rothwell listing the films and videos cited in the volume's essays and a selection of others of general interest, with abbreviated credits and thumbnail criticism, and an essay by Stephen Buhler. To gather resources and to attend to performance issues, instructors also consult works that are listed in the "Criticism" and "Shakespeare on Screen" sections of "Works Cited and Materials for Further Study" (on stage, Beckerman, Cartwright, Dawson, Goldman, Styan, and others; on screen, Davies, Donaldson, Jorgens, Kliman, and others; on audio recordings, Behrens; and on the comparison of the media, Coursen, Crowl).

Since obsolescence is a daily event, the "Works Cited and Materials for Further Study" sketches only lightly CD-ROM (the fading technology) and Internet (the new wave) materials (see Andreas, this volume). Norton offers a CD-ROM with film clips, concordances, and bibliographies; it received a mixed reception from respondents. Other publishers also feature adjunct materials on CD-ROM; each publisher and every university has a Web site. MIT is developing an interactive Web archive of *Hamlet* illustrations, texts, and commentary (Donaldson). Searching the Web for *Hamlet* resources supplies one with too many possibilities. Because attention to the play is instructors' main concern, they do not want electronic debris to distract them. It's important, then, to seek out the sites that will further a course's aims and also to know which sites students are exploring. Filtering sites, such as *Mr. William Shakespeare and the Internet* and *Shakespeare: A Magazine for Teachers and Enthusiasts*, have links to the MIT project, the Tufts University *Perseus Project* (classical texts with Shakespearean connections), and much more. *Shakespeare Magazine*'s Web site offers guidance to instructors, including teaching strategies. The National Endowment for the Humanities' *Edsitement Websites* is an attractive entry point for Internet explorations. The *Surfing with the Bard* Web site seems appropriate for high school students, while the splendid University of Virginia *Shakespearean Prompt-books* Web site is for specialists interested in early texts and performances. The Folger Shakespeare Library Web site builds on the experience of teaching institutes. Since URLs change and sites cease to be supported, some of the URLs given in "Works Cited and Materials for Further Study" may not remain current. But *Folger Shakespeare Library*, *Perseus Digital Library*, and *Edsitement* are likely to be available for the long term.

Above all, respondents declare that the play's the thing: any resource that helps students to focus on the play is to the good. Anything else may subtract from the time available for studying the play, which could be as little as four hours during a quarter. Even a year-long course devoted to *Hamlet* cannot do it all. Since it is impossible for us to know—let alone to read or see—everything about *Hamlet*, we want to select carefully among the materials to make working with the play as stimulating as possible to mind and spirit—our own and our students'.

An Annotated and Chronological Screenography: Major *Hamlet* Adaptations and Selected Derivatives

Kenneth S. Rothwell

This chronological compilation includes major Shakespearean adaptations and a few derivatives such as Chabrol's *Ophelia* (1962) but omits most educational documentaries and bypasses the countless *Hamlet* references in feature films such as Katharine Hepburn's recitation of the "To be or not to be" soliloquy in *Morning Glory* (1933) or Danny DeVito's teaching army recruits about the play in *Renaissance Man* (1994).

So-called *Hamlet* films and videos and DVDs come in many guises, ranging from full-scale adaptations like Kenneth Branagh's 1996 *Hamlet* down to passing references to the play (as in Steve Martin's 1991 *L.A. Story*), to documentaries such as *The Great Hamlets* (1985). Luke McKernan, British Film Institute archivist, has informally counted nearly 250 titles bearing on *Hamlet*, but even that unpublished listing is incomplete. Commentaries on and credits for most screened *Hamlet*s can be found in Bernice W. Kliman's Hamlet: *Film, Television, and Audio Performance*, which is abbreviated here as "Kliman, Film," and Kenneth S. Rothwell and Annabelle Henkin Melzer's *Shakespeare on Screen*, which is cited here as *SoS*. Of critical importance also is Luke McKernan and Olwen Terris's *Walking Shadows: Shakespeare in the National Film and Television Archive*. For silent film versions of *Hamlet*, which for the most part are omitted here, there is no substitute for Robert H. Ball's 1968 *Shakespeare on Silent Film* (cited here as "Ball"), which lists twenty-six entries for *Hamlet*, though many are of questionable status, sometimes having only borrowed the title for other scenarios. Updated commentary is also in my *History of Shakespeare on Screen* (1999). In addition, references at the close of each entry suggest other readings. Abbreviations in the screenography follow MLA and British Film Institute guidelines:

bw = black and white
col = color
mins = duration, though run times vary depending on the condition of the print and the speed of projection. Allow for some leeway especially for older films.
sd = sound
st = silent
tv = television or nonterrestrially transmitted video

Hamlet. Dir. Clément Maurice. Perf. Sarah Bernhardt (Hamlet), Pierre Magnier (Laertes). Phono-Cinéma-Théâtre. St/bw, with supplementary Edison sound cylinders. France, 1900. 3 mins.

The inaugural example of *Hamlet* in moving images and the second ever Shakespeare "movie," this fragment showing the great Bernhardt in the duel scene followed closely on the heels of the first Shakespeare movie, the Sir Herbert Beerbohm Tree *King John*, produced in 1899 by British Mutoscope and Bioscope. References: *SoS*, entry 74; Ball 23–28; Taranow 129 (see also Taranow's 13 frame enlargements, 231–34).

Hamlet. Dir. E. Hay Plumb and Cecil Hepworth. Perf. Sir Johnston Forbes-
    Robertson (Hamlet), Gertrude Elliott (Ophelia). Hepworth Manufacturing
    Company. St/bw. UK, 1913. 59 mins.
The first feature-length adaptation of *Hamlet*, which even though employing the Drury Lane London cast moves beyond theatricality into a cinematic grammar, as shown, for example, in the Méliès-like special effects of the ghost scene and the ambitious outdoor sets constructed on location at Dorset's Lulworth Cove. Sixty-one-year-old Forbes-Robertson had made a career of playing Hamlet on stage. Clips from the film appear in a 1984 documentary narrated by Trevor Nunn, *The Great Hamlets* (see below). References: *SoS*, entry 82; Kliman, *Film* 247–74; Ball 186–92; Rothwell, *History* 21–25.

Hamlet, the Drama of Vengeance. Dir. Svend Gade and Heinz Schall. Perf.
    Asta Nielsen (Hamlet), Mathilde Brandt (Gertrude). Art-Film. St/bw. Germany, 1920. 117 mins.
If it were not for the awkward fact that the movie considerably departs from the *Hamlet* text by turning the prince into a cross-dressed woman and by raiding the Saxo Grammaticus legend for numerous plot elements, this gender-bending movie would have to be unequivocally declared the best of the silent *Hamlets*. Even so, postmodernist theory licenses indulgence for a film with a great actress, a protofeminist agenda, and the indubitable cinematic virtues of the Weimar expressionist school. Since Bernhardt's foray, the casting of women as Hamlet has gained considerable cachet, though Asta Nielsen departs from the Bernhardt formula somewhat by playing the prince not so much as a cross-dressed woman as a woman disguised as a man, actually more in the British "breeches" tradition than in the French *travesti*. References: *SoS*, entry 86; Ball 272–78; McKernan and Terris 47–48; Guntner 90–102; Rothwell, *History* 3; Thompson.

Hamlet: Test Shots. Dir. Robert Jones. Perf. John Barrymore (Hamlet), Irving
    Pichel, Reginald Denny, Donald Crisp. RKO Studios. Sd/col. USA, 1933.
    10 mins.
Test shots of the fabulous John Barrymore as Hamlet for a film that never materialized include the "O what a rogue and peasant slave" soliloquy and the ghost scene in act 1. They suggest how he appeared in his sublime performances on the Broadway and London stages during the 1920s at the peak of a brilliant career. An interesting sidebar for any student of the play, when it can be located. References: *SoS*, entry 89; Kliman, *Film* 316.

To Be or Not to Be. Dir. Ernst Lubitsch. Perf. Jack Benny, Carole Lombard,
  Robert Stack. United Artists. Sd/bw. USA, 1942. 99 mins.
This backstage pic, directed by Ernst Lubitsch, one of Hollywood's Weimar exiles, is a clever derivative of *Hamlet* that has stood the test of time and remains
useful for stirring up the interest of lethargic students in Shakespeare's play.
Ask them, for example, how the scenario of Lubitsch's movie logically fits the
play. References: *SoS*, entry 93; Willson, *"To Be."*

Strange Illusion. Dir. Edgar G. Ulmer. Perf. James Lydon (Paul Cartwright and
  Hamlet), Warren William (Brett Curtis and Claudius), and Mary McLeod
  (Lydia and Ophelia). A PRC Picture. Sd/bw. USA, 1945. 80 mins.
A modernized *Hamlet*, like Kurosawa's *The Bad Sleep Well* (qv), *Strange Illusion* is the film noir work of a German exile, Edgar G. Ulmer, who struggled
on Hollywood's Poverty Row making B horror movies until, in the 1950s, he
was magically declared by the French critics to be an auteur. Some students
with a keen eye for film may enjoy comparing it to *Hamlet*. Reference: *SoS*,
entry 94.

Hamlet. Dir. George More O'Ferrall. Perf. John Byron (Hamlet), Sebastian
  Shaw (Claudius). BBC. Tv/bw. UK, 1947. 180 mins, transmitted in two parts.
Now of course unavailable, because before Kinescope there was no handy
technology for recording these early transmissions, this ambitious *Hamlet* with
a cast of seventy filling forty-eight roles was broadcast live from the BBC's
Alexandra Palace studio (actually a derelict ex-resort) to the handful of Lon-
doners then owning television sets. It has special interest also for, anecdotally
anyway, having influenced the deep-focus camera work in the subsequent
Olivier *Hamlet*. Reference: *SoS*, entry 97.

Hamlet. Dir. Laurence Olivier. Perf. Olivier (Hamlet), Jean Simmons (Ophelia), Eileen Herlie (Gertrude). Two Cities Films. Sd/bw. UK, 1948. 152
  mins.
So famous a movie as this one hardly needs additional commentary here,
though worth mentioning again is the consistent and beautiful camera work
that tirelessly escorts the spectator through the vast rooms of Elsinore and, almost literally, even into the innermost recesses of Hamlet's being. References:
Davies 40–64; Jorgens 207–17; Kliman, *Film* 23–36.

Hamlet. Dir. George Schaefer. Perf. Maurice Evans (Hamlet), Sarah Churchill
  (Ophelia). Hallmark Greeting Cards. Tv/bw. USA, 1953. 98 mins.
In the early days of television, sponsors like Hallmark Greeting Cards actively
sought to bring culture to the lobotomized masses, though the perpetual qua-
vering of Maurice Evans, famous for his World War II "GI *Hamlet*," left mil-
lions with the impression that Shakespeare was more unpalatable than
palatable. References: *SoS*, entry 101; Griffin; Kliman, *Film* 117–29.

Hamlet. Dir. Kishore Sahu. Perf. Mala Sinha, Venus Bannerjee. Hindustan
   Chitra. Sd/bw, in Urdu. India, 1953. 80 mins (?).
Listed here simply as a reminder that nonanglophone Shakespeare movies, including *Hamlet*, are a worldwide reality. From all accounts, Olivier's *Hamlet*
heavily influenced this film, which opened with much fanfare in Bombay but
received merciless reviews from local critics. References: *SoS*, entry 104; Rothwell, *History* 169.

Hamlet. Dir. Ralph Nelson (CBS) and Michael Benthall (Old Vic). Perf. John
   Neville (Hamlet), Barbara Jefford (Ophelia), Frederic March (Host).
   DuPont Show of the Month and CBS. Tv/bw. USA, 1959. 90 mins.
An abbreviated version of an Old Vic production, imported for the DuPont
Show of the Month on television at a time when corporate sponsors had not yet
reserved most of their advertising budgets for professional athletics. In Re-
gency costumes, the production features a thin, rather neurasthenic John
Neville as the prince and a compelling Barbara Jefford as Ophelia. It manages
some brilliant camera work in the chaos and confusion capping the play-
within-the-play scene. References: *SoS*, entry 107; Kliman, *Film* 130–38.

The Bad Sleep Well. Dir. Akira Kurosawa. Perf. Toshiro Mifune (Nishi and
   Hamlet), Kyoko Kagawa (Kieko and Ophelia). Toho Films. Sd/bw, Japanese
   with subtitles. Japan, 1960. 135 mins.
A nonanglophone *Hamlet* derivative that recontextualizes the play into contemporary Japan. Despite the gap between the cinematic and Shakespearean
text, Kurosawa's epistemological anxieties strike a chord reminiscent of Shakespeare's own obsession with the interplay between illusion and reality. References: *SoS*, entry 107; Perret; Rothwell, "Akira Kurosawa."

Hamlet: Prinz von Danemark. Dir. Franz Wirth. Perf. Maximilian Schell
   (Hamlet), Hans Caninenberg (Claudius), Dunja Mobar (Ophelia). Bavaria
   Attelier. Tv/bw, dubbed-in English. West Germany, 1960. 127 mins.
It was originally filmed for Austrian television, then later brought to America
by Edward Dmytryk and screened theatrically with dubbed-in English. Schell
makes a precise, Teutonic Hamlet whose perturbed spirit lends power even to
the minimalist set. References: *SoS*, entry 110; Kliman, *Film* 139–53; Coursen,
"A German *Hamlet*"; Wilds.

Ophelia. Dir. Claude Chabrol. Perf. André Jocelyn (Yvan and Hamlet), Juliette
   Maniel (Lucie and Ophelia). Boreal Pictures. Sd/bw, English subtitles.
   France, 1962. 150 mins.
A derivative from *Hamlet*, not an adaptation, but so incredibly resourceful and
compelling in its exploration of the interplay between what seems and what is
that it effectively mirrors the quandaries of Hamlet himself. Like other serious derivatives, it offers a sounding board for discovering fresh possibilities of

interpretation. References: *SoS*, entry 111; Kliman, "Chabrol's *Ophelia*"; Newman.

Hamlet at Elsinore. Dir. Philip Saville. Perf. Christopher Plummer (Hamlet), Michael Caine (Horatio), Robert Shaw (Claudius), Donald Sutherland (Fortinbras), Lindsay Kemp (Player Queen). BBC and Danmarks Radio. Bw/tv. UK and Denmark, 1963. 170 mins.

At the time a critic rhapsodized over Plummer's portrayal as the embodiment of Goethe's romantic idea of the prince of Denmark as "a gentle spirit broken by a burden too heavy for him to bear," which tells part of the story. What needs to be added is mention of Plummer's wit and resourcefulness in capturing the full flavor of Hamlet's intricate personality, though the use of the castle at Elsinore as location actually does not embellish the production much at all. This memorable performance with a remarkable cast rivals the nearly contemporaneous Burton *Hamlet* and should not be allowed to go gently into the night. References: SoS, entry 118; Kliman, *Film* 154–66; Coursen, *Watching Shakespeare* 62–63.

Gamlet. Dir. Grigori Kozintsev. Perf. Innokenti Smoktunovsky (Hamlet), Anastasia Vertinskaya (Ophelia), Elza Radzin-Szolkonis (Gertrude). LenFilm. Sd/bw, English subtitles. USSR, 1964. 148 mins.

Grigori Kozintsev thought that the secret of filmic success lay in the ability "to point a cine camera," a creed that he practiced as successfully as he advocated. Searing, explosive images fill the screen as the late Innokenti Smoktunovsky unforgettably places Hamlet's story into a Russian context against harsh images of stone, water, and iron. Ophelia straitjacketed in an iron farthingale becomes the ultimate icon for female subjugation, while Boris Pasternak's translation and Dmitri Shostakovich's score lend even more interest. Legal tangles have unhappily prevented this wonderful film from being recorded on videocassette, though it is available on 16mm film from Corinth Films, 34 Gansevoort Street, New York City, NY 10014. For rates, phone 800 221-4720. References: *SoS*, entry 116; Jorgens 218–34; Kliman, *Film* 87–113.

Hamlet. Dir. John Gielgud. Perf. Richard Burton (Hamlet), Hume Cronyn (Polonius), Alfred Drake (Claudius), Eileen Herlie (Gertrude), Linda Marsh (Ophelia). Electronovision Theatrofilm. Sd/bw. USA, 1964. 199 mins.

Acted in "rehearsal clothes" (whatever that means, as some actors wear sweaters and others coats and ties) at New York's Lunt-Fontanne Theatre, this stage production was later, by a now obsolete technology called electronovision, simultaneously released on film throughout the hinterlands nationwide to give provincial folk a taste of Shakespeare live on Broadway. Burton's raw power as a virile Hamlet prevents the endeavor from teetering over into disaster. Long out of circulation, it recently reemerged in the UK on PAL, then in the USA on NSTC VHS formats, and in 2000 on a shiny new DVD. References: *SoS*, entry 117; McKernan and Terris 55–56; Sterne.

Enter Hamlet. Dir. Fred Mogubgub. Perf. Maurice Evans (Narrator). Janus New Cinema. Sd/animation. USA, 1965 or 1967 (?). 10 mins.
An animation of the "To be or not to be" soliloquy with Maurice Evans as the offscreen narrator that is distinguished for an intricate fugue of visual and verbal puns paralleling Shakespeare's words. Reference: Kliman, "Enter Hamlet."

Shakespeare Wallah. Dir. James Ivory. Prod. Ismail Merchant. Screenplay by Ruth Prawer Jhabvala and James Ivory. Perf. Shashi Kapoor (Sanji), Felicity Kendal (Lizzie Buckingham), Madhur Jaffrey (Manjula), Geoffrey Kendal (Mr. Buckingham), Laura Liddell (Mrs. Buckingham). Sd/col. India, 1965. 115 mins.
An early Merchant-Ivory production about a British acting troupe touring in India, based on the lives of the Kendal family, featuring an East-West love story as well as scenes from Shakespeare plays, including *Hamlet.* No one should miss this wonderful brew of heartache and humor, which measures the height and depth of the human spirit against the exquisitely refined interplay between British and Indian culture. Reference: Wayne (takes a position at variance with the above comments).

Hamlet. Dir. Tony Richardson. Perf. Nicol Williamson (Hamlet), Judy Parfitt (Gertrude), Anthony Hopkins (Claudius), Marianne Faithfull (Ophelia). A Woodfall Production. Sd/col. UK, 1969. 117 mins.
Nicol Williamson's Hamlet is closer to a seismic upheaval than to the neo-Victorian representation of the prince as a sensitive young fellow. He doesn't just act, he gyrates and wheels and spins and spits out his anger against stuffy bourgeois values so energetically, one fears he will self-destruct. His stage performances as Hamlet in London and in North America had already made him famous for tantrums, which linger on in this hastily made movie shot in the claustrophobic cellars of London's Roundhouse Theatre. The decision to film almost entirely in close and mid shot deprives the actors of legs, but authentic feeling emerges anyway in the elegant portraiture of the tight shots. An excellent film for showing students how *Hamlet* resists stereotypes, it was probably also produced as a small-screen experience with residual television rights in mind. References: *SoS*, entry 123; Kliman, *Film* 167–79; Manvell 127–30; Mullin.

Hamlet. Dir. Peter Wood. Perf. Richard Chamberlain (Hamlet), Michael Redgrave (Polonius), John Gielgud (Ghost). Hallmark Hall of Fame and NBC. Tv/col. UK, 1970. 115 mins.
A drastically cut made-for-television version in Regency period costumes, filmed on location at Raby Castle. This was an early example of the Master-

piece Theatre syndrome, by which highbrow American tastes, largely ignored by commercial networks, were catered to by British television. Jay Halio saw Chamberlain's Hamlet as a rather high-minded young man whose worldview was underwritten by a notable use of Christian iconography. Kliman thought the visual codes splendid but Chamberlain too "bland" for the mercurial role. References: *SoS*, entry 126; Halio; Kliman, *Film* 180–87.

Hamlet. Dir. David Giles and Robert Chetwyn. Perf. Ian McKellen (Hamlet), John Woodvine (Claudius), Tim Pigott-Smith (Laertes), Susan Fleetwood (Ophelia). BBC-2 and Prospect Theatre. Tv/col. UK, 1972; USA (CBS), 1982. 115 mins.
In this London stage play adapted to television, a youthful Ian McKellen was allowed an opportunity to show his considerable talents in a production later televised in the United States. Despite McKellen's impressive performance, a limited budget undercut him with sparse sets and a propensity to cramp him with excessive close and mid shots. References: *SoS*, entry 129; Kliman, *Film* 188–94.

Hamlet. Dir. Celestino Coronado. Perf. Anthony Meyer and David Meyer (Hamlet and Hamlet's Father), Helen Mirren (Gertrude and Ophelia), Vladek Sheybal (First Player and Player Queen and Lucianus). Cabochon Films and Royal College of Art. Tv/col. UK, 1976. 67 mins.
Coronado's two transgressive Shakespeare movies (this and *Midsummer Night's Dream*, 1984) eagerly ferret out the subtext's darkest, most hidden secrets (usually sexual) and are therefore not recommended for beginning students. This *Hamlet*, however, is caviar for the cognoscenti who can tolerate a split vision of Hamlet (played by the Meyer brothers) that dissects the psyche of a human being torn by conflicting attachments to father, mother, and girlfriend. Shot on video in one week by enthusiastic young people and later transferred to 16mm film, this is not a movie for persons unacquainted with the play. References: *SoS*, entry 132; Holderness 63–74; McKernan and Terris 58–59; Rothwell, *History* 202–03.

Dogg's Troupe Hamlet. Dir. Ed Berman. Perf. Jane Gambia, Katina Noble, John Perry. Inter-Action and Hornsey Coll. of Art. Sd/col/16mm. UK, 1977. 15 mins.
Tom Stoppard's fifteen-minute version of *Hamlet* performed on the steps of the National Theatre. See also his 1995 version below. Reference: Terris 4.

Hamlet. Dir. Rodney Bennett. Prod. Cedric Messina. Perf. Derek Jacobi (Hamlet), Claire Bloom (Gertrude), Patrick Stewart (Claudius), Lalla Ward (Ophelia). BBC and Time-Life's The Shakespeare Plays. Tv/col. UK, 1980. 210 mins.
One of the productions in the Shakespeare Series made by the BBC with United States financing that was partially designed to please "purist" American

classroom teachers but neglected to use any American actors. The result is a splendid reading of *Hamlet* by distinguished actors like Derek Jacobi and Patrick Stewart (Captain Jean-Luc Picard of *Star Trek* fame), but not much in the way of visual excitement. When it is assigned for library study, students tend to read the text as they screen the video, which suggests that they'd be better off with a plain audio rather than an audiovisual experience. This is not to say that there aren't grand moments, especially the play-within-a-play when Jacobi as the prince and Stewart as the corrupt king come to their moment of truth. References: *SoS*, entry 140; *Shakespeare Plays*; Coursen, *"Hamlet"*; Kliman, *Film* 195–201; Rothwell, *"Hamlet"*; Taylor.

Hamlet Act. Dir. Robert Nelson and Joseph Chang. Perf. Dick Blau (Hamlet), Bob Whitney (Polonius). Univ. of Wisconsin Film Dept. Sd/col (?). USA, 1982. 21 mins.

An avant-garde postmodernist exploration of the epistemological puzzles in *Hamlet*, built around the metadrama of Hamlet's advice to the players. As the scene is enacted through the use of an on-site video camera, the play becomes nested in other plays, until Hamlet begins to become the spectator for his own play. This is an interesting essay but probably more bewildering than enlightening for the novice student. References: *SoS*, entry 144; Birringer; Kliman, *Film* 317.

The Great Hamlets, Parts 1 and 2. Dir. Derek Bailey. Perf. Trevor Nunn (interviewer) and interviewees playing themselves and Hamlet: Laurence Olivier, John Gielgud, Richard Burton, Maximilian Schell, Jean Louis Barrault, Vittorio Gassman, Mandy Patinkin, Innokenti Smoktunovsky, Nicol Williamson, and Ben Kingsley. Tv/col. Thames. UK, 1982. Part 1, 53 mins; part 2, 56 mins.

In this most absorbing educational documentary, the RSC director Trevor Nunn interrogates famous twentieth-century Shakespearean actors about their interpretations of *Hamlet*. They comment not only on their own performances but on their colleagues' as well, Laurence Olivier's contrasting his Hamlet with John Gielgud's being a case in point. Backing up the talking but passionate heads are clips from all their films, which highlight differences among the mercurial Burton, diffident Kingsley, meditative Olivier, decisive Schell, and so forth. There is even a clip or two from the Sir Johnston Forbes-Robertson 1913 silent *Hamlet*, which adds a detritus of historic richness. It's full of interesting tidbits, such as the revelation from Olivier that his *Hamlet* was in black and white because he was having fights with Technicolor, Inc., about the color of the *Henry V* prints, and that Olivier got his much-contested summary sentence about the work being about "a man who could not make up his mind" from a Gary Cooper film (probably *Souls at Sea,* 1937). References: Mahon, *"Hamlet"*; Writing Company Catalogue (1999) 30.

Playing Shakespeare. An eleven-part program originally aired on UK Channel
4 Television, now available from Films for the Humanities (qv). Written and
dir. John Barton. Perf. RSC actors, including Ben Kingsley, Ian McKellen,
Michael Pennington, Judi Dench, and others. Tv/col. UK, 1984. c. 50 mins.
each.
A skillfully directed series by John Barton that really aims more at acting students than at typical undergraduates, but it does have three or four absorbing
segments from *Hamlet,* particularly in programs 1, 3, and 6. More directly concerned with *Hamlet* is *The Great Hamlets,* above. References: *SoS,* entries
723–34; Huffman.

To Be or Not to Be. Dir. Alan Johnson. Perf. Mel Brooks (Frederick Bronski),
Anne Bancroft (Anna Bronski), Tim Matheson (Lieutenant Andre Sobin-
ski), Charles Dunning (Colonel Erhardt), Christopher Lloyd (Captain
Schultz), José Ferrer (Professor Siletski). Sd/col. USA, 1983. 108 mins.
A remake of the 1942 Jack Benny version, which lacks the sparkle of its predecessor, though so gifted a comic as Mel Brooks should never be underesti-
mated. References: *SoS,* entry 147; Willson, *"To Be or Not to Be* Once More."

Den tragiska historien om Hamlet, prinz av Danmark. Dir. Ragnar Lyth. Perf.
Stellan Skarsgaard (Hamlet), Mona Malm (Gertrude), Frej Lindquist
(Claudius), Pernilla Wallgren (Ophelia). SVT 1. Tv/col. English subtitles.
Sweden, 1984. 160 mins.
Ragnar Lyth never flags in his feverish quest for originality from the opening
sequence, which shows an Elsinore steeped in domesticity, to the macabre
burial of poor Ophelia in a cheap wooden coffin, to the prince's wild revenge,
when a demonic Skarsgaard turns the duel scene with Laertes into a grotesque
but lethal farce. Here is a Hamlet who progresses from an unkempt hippie into
a vicious skinhead and who benefits from the imaginative settings, which turn
a nineteenth-century Nobel explosives factory into a bizarre ambiance for dire
events presided over by a caged crow. A daring and intelligent translation of
Shakespeare's words into images. References: *SoS,* entry 148; Kliman, *Film*
202–24; Rothwell, *History* 173–76.

Hamlet. Dir. Roland Kenyon and Rod MacDonald. Perf. Tricia Hitchcock
(Ophelia), Melanie Revill (Gertrude), Richard Spaul (Claudius), entire cast
(Hamlet). Cambridge Experimental Theatre. Tv/col. UK, 1987. 96 mins.
Like the Coronado *Hamlet* unapologetically experimental, this offbeat production turns the entire cast into Hamlet, with masked actors speaking separately,
simultaneously, and contrapuntally. It thereby underscores how Hamlet sub-
stantially reflects or mirrors the play's other characters. We are all Hamlet, in
a sense. Not for beginners, this highly choreographed production with overtones of rock video will provide the basis for spirited discussion by people who
know the play. References: *SoS,* entry 154; Crowl, "Fragments"; Maher, "Stage

into Film"; Spaul, Ritchie, and Wheale. In 1987, the videocassette was available for $195.00 from Audio-Visual Unit, Cambridgeshire College of Arts and Technology, East Road, Cambridge CB1 1PT.

Hamlet Goes Business. Dir. Aki Kaurismäki. Perf. Pirkka-Pekka Petelius (Hamlet), Kati Outinen (Ophelia), Elina Salo (Gertrude), Esko Salminen (Klaus), Kari Väänänen (Polonius), Hannu Valtonen (Simo), Mari Rantasila (Helena). Finnkino and Villealfa. Sd/bw. Finland, 1989. 86 mins.

Another postmodernist take on *Hamlet,* along the lines of the Cambridge Experimental Theatre production described above, only this one is possibly more a destruction than a deconstruction of the text. In a film noir mode, its modern-day characters closely follow the *Hamlet* story line, which has been reshaped to echo an old Warner Brothers thriller. Screened at the seventeenth Norwegian Film Festival, it kept the audience "wide awake." Reference: Kell.

Hamlet. Dir. Kevin Kline and Kirk Browning. Perf. Kline (Hamlet), Peter James (Horatio), Dana Ivey (Gertrude), Diane Venora (Ophelia). New York Shakespeare Festival and WNET. Great Performances. Tv/col. USA, 1990. 150 mins.

Kevin Kline accomplishes the double feat of simultaneously directing and acting in this *Hamlet,* which was originally produced for the New York Shakespeare Festival and subsequently transmitted on public television. His special niche was to explore the potential madness of Hamlet, so that he was constantly walking a fine line between jocularity and a lunatic behavior spiced with razor-edged wit. Besides Kline's obvious talents, I found Peter James's Horatio one of the best ever, in the way James makes this static character kinetic. References: Maher, "American *Hamlet*" and "Kevin Kline"; Pall.

Hamlet. Dir. Franco Zeffirelli. Perf. Mel Gibson (Hamlet), Glenn Close (Gertrude), Alan Bates (Claudius), Helena Bonham Carter (Ophelia), Paul Scofield (Ghost), John McEnery (Osric). Carolco. Sd/col. USA, 1990. 134 mins.

Although technically credited to the United States, this Shakespeare movie — with an Italian director, Australian star, British supporting players, and an American like Glenn Close sprinkled in here and there—obviously reflects the internationalization of the cinema industry that has long abandoned the "classical Hollywood cinema" of the 1930s and 1940s. Nowadays the stars do not inhabit storybook homes in Beverly Hills like Pickfair but jet in from everywhere. True to his belief in popularizing art for the masses, Franco Zeffirelli brilliantly chose the unlikely Mel Gibson, macho survivor of shoot 'em, slash 'em, blow 'em up action movies, for his prince of Denmark. And why not? Hamlet is a one-man exercise in cultural diversity who can be tweaked into virtually any kind of behavior, but Gibson confounded his critics by playing the role with sensitivity and imagination—almost too much so, one critic argued, finding the production "dour." So powerful is the aura projected by Glenn Close that Hamlet's paternal obsession gets overshadowed by his passion for the maternal. The scenarists further redirected the script into cinematic idiom, dropping Fortinbras (who is often sacrificed both on stage and screen to the exigencies of time) and adding a highly inventive opening scene of King Hamlet's burial. Gone also are the vivid colors of Zeffirelli's Italian films, to be replaced by a kind of blue-gray haze, but the supporting cast, the location settings in crumbling British castles like Dover, and the movie's surging energy reassert the timeless appeal of Shakespeare's great tragedy. References: Quinn; Romney 48–49; Impastato; Skovmand; Rothwell, *History* 137–42.

L.A. Story. Dir. Mick Jackson. Prod. Mario Kassar and Steve Martin. Screenplay by Martin. Perf. Martin (Harris K. Telemacher), Victoria Tennant (Sara McDowel), and Rick Moranis (Gravedigger, uncredited). Rastar Productions. Sd/col. USA, 1991. 95 mins.

Steve Martin's witty spoof on the gravedigger scene from *Hamlet* becomes a memento mori from late medievalism displaced into a mawkish Hollywood cemetery. Moments like this prove once again the essentialist nature of Shakespeare's obsession with human mortality. References: Buhler, "Antic Dispositions"; Floyd.

Rosencrantz and Guildenstern Are Dead. Dir. and screenplay by Tom Stoppard. Perf. Gary Oldman (Rosencrantz), Tim Roth (Guildenstern), Richard Dreyfuss (Player). Brandenberg Intl. Cinecom Entertainment. Sd/col. USA, 1991. 118 mins.

In the tradition of Luigi Pirandello's *Six Characters in Search of an Author*, Stoppard turns two minor characters from *Hamlet* loose to blunder into a web of intrigue and inevitable doom. Their fate underscores the fallout from Hamlet's strange behavior, though what happens to them is absurd but not funny. References: Aspden; Wheeler.

Shakespeare: The Animated Tales: Hamlet. Screenplay Leon Garfield. Dir. Natalia Orlova. Designers Peter Kotov, Natasha Demidova. Soyusmultifilm et al. Sd/col. Moscow and Cardiff, 1992. 30 mins.

Generations of literature teachers have railed against the subversion of academic standards when indolent students swap the printed text for a comic book. If it were done, though, " 'twere well / It were done [well]," as it is in this ingenious animation. Reference: Osborne.

Last Action Hero. Dir. John McTiernan. Prod. McTiernan et al. Written by Zak Penn. Perf. Arnold Schwarzenegger (Jack Slater and Himself), Charles Dance (Benedict), Tom Noonan (Ripper and Himself), Robert Prosky (Nick), Austin O'Brien (Danny Madigan), Joan Plowright (Teacher), Apollo Dukakis (Polonius). Sd/col. USA, 1993. 130 mins.

A metadramatic treatment of *Hamlet* that offers yet another insight into the play from a fresh perspective. The distinction between illusion and reality blurs as a little boy watches his modern hero take on some of the coloration of the prince of Denmark—with allusions to Olivier's *Hamlet*. Reference: Mallin.

The Lion King. Dir. Roger Allers and Rob Minkoff. Perf. (voices only) James
  Earl Jones, Nathan Lane, Whoopi Goldberg. Walt Disney Productions.
  Sd/col. USA, 1994. 88 mins.
The obvious parallels to *Hamlet* in this elaborate animation provided quite a stir when it was released several years ago, some parents even worrying about its being too traumatic for children. Since then it has been staged by Julie Taymor, the director of the 1999 film *Titus*, with Anthony Hopkins as the emperor Titus. References: Klass; Myers.

The Fifteen-Minute Hamlet. Dir. Todd Louiso. Prod. Gina Belafonte et al.
  Based on play by Tom Stoppard. Perf. Austin Pendleton (Hamlet), Ernest
  Perry Jr. (Claudius and Polonius), Angie Phillips (Gertrude), Todd Louiso
  (Ophelia). Cin-cine 19. Sd/col. USA, 1995. 22 mins.
In this Tom Stoppard spoof, the main gag has Shakespeare throwing away sheets of his work so that *Hamlet* can be squeezed into a fifteen-minute and then a two-minute film. Transmitted recently on cable television. Reference: www.imdb.com/title?0125746.

In the Bleak Midwinter (USA: *A Midwinter's Tale*). Dir. Kenneth Branagh.
  Screenplay Branagh. Prod. David Barron et al. Perf. Michael Maloney (Joe
  Harper and Hamlet), Richard Briers (Henry Wakefield and Claudius and
  Ghost, and Player King), Hetta Charnley (Molly), Joan Collins (Margaretta
  D'Arcy), Nicholas Farrell (Tom Newman and Laertes and Fortinbras),
  Mark Hadfield (Vernon Spatch and Polonius and Marcellus and First
  Gravedigger), Julia Sawalha (Nina and Ophelia). Rank and Midwinter
  Films. Sd/bw. UK, 1995. 98 mins.
A group of down-at-the-heels actors assemble in an abandoned church to rehearse and produce *Hamlet*, a play that to them is not just larger than life but life itself. In its Chekhovian nostalgia for a lost past, Branagh's low budget movie reminds me of *Shakespeare Wallah*, in which there are also tears for things in the midst of not just bleak midwinter but a redemptive life force. Reference: Jays.

Hamlet. Dir. Kenneth Branagh. Perf. Branagh (Hamlet), Derek Jacobi
  (Claudius), Julie Christie (Gertrude), Brian Blessed (Ghost and Old Ham-
  let), Michael Maloney (Laertes), Nicholas Farrell (Horatio), Kate Winslet
  (Ophelia), Charlton Heston (Player King), Rosemary Harris (Player Queen),
  Rufus Sewall (Fortinbras), Billy Crystal (First Gravedigger), Gerard Depar-
  dieu (Reynaldo), Robin Williams (Osric), Jack Lemmon (Marcellus), John

Gielgud (Priam), Judi Dench (Hecuba). Castle Rock Entertainment. Sd/col. UK, 1996. 242 mins.

Kenneth Branagh achieved the unachievable in managing to produce, direct, and star in an uncut, four-hour *Hamlet* with a cast of big-name stars filmed on wintry location at Blenheim Palace and indoors on a Shepperton set opulent enough for Sigmund Romberg's *Student Prince*. Branagh's prince emerges as an activist, aggressive young man, who ends the picture by literally swinging on a rope like a circus acrobat, though the energy, supported by a swooping, swirling, almost dizzying camera, tends to erase the prince's more thoughtful side. Branagh's supporting cast of famous actors is a daring exercise in code switching, a device that some critics stigmatized as "stunt casting" but that others praised as a clever scheme to ensnare the audience's attention. Who ever paid any attention to Marcellus until Jack Lemmon played the role? Taken all in all, this is a dazzling film of *Hamlet* that will delight students even when some of their teachers are hunting for ways to find fault with it. References: Branagh; Pendleton; Mahon, "Editor's View"; Felperin; Buhler, "Double Takes"; Crowl, *"Hamlet"* (1997); Rothwell, *History* 253–58.

Shakespeare in Love. Dir. John Madden. Written by Marc Norman and Tom Stoppard. Perf. Joseph Fiennes (Will Shakespeare), Gwyneth Paltrow (Viola de Lesseps), Judi Dench (Queen Elizabeth), Ben Affleck (Ned Alleyn), Colin Firth (Lord Wessex), Geoffrey Rush (Philip Henslowe), Rupert Everett (Christopher Marlowe), Imelda Staunton (Nurse). Miramax Films. Sd/col. UK, 1998. 122 mins.

Nothing much to do with *Hamlet*, everything with *Romeo and Juliet*, but listed here simply because it's the most popular Shakespeare movie of recent times, one that is guaranteed to stir the interest of even the grumpiest student. Historically accurate? Of course not, but then neither were Shakespeare's history plays. Reference: Rothwell, *"Elizabeth."*

Hamlet. Dir. Michael Almereyda. Perf. Ethan Hawke (Hamlet), Kyle MacLachlan (Claudius), Sam Shepard (Ghost), Diane Venora (Gertrude), Bill Murray (Polonius), Casey Affleck (Fortinbras), Julia Stiles (Ophelia). Miramax. Sd/col. USA, 2000. 111 mins.

This bold modernization set in New York City with much of the text intact intrigued a sophisticated preview audience at the April 2000 Montreal convention of the Shakespeare Association of America. It's full of witty surprises, including Hamlet's discovery while airborne on a jet en route to England of a laptop with Claudius's message on the hard drive ordering the executions of Rosencrantz and Guildenstern. As Hamlet, Ethan Hawke manages to be contemporary cool and yet passionate; as Claudius, jut-jawed star Kyle MacLachlan radiates corporate power; as Gertrude, Diane Venora is both wary and ravishing; as Ophelia, Julia Stiles goes wonderfully mad in the Guggenheim Museum; as the Ghost, a chilling, frozen-faced Sam Shepard almost steals the show; and as Polonius, Bill Murray seems properly bewildered. Undergraduates will probably love it. References: *The Internet Movie Database* (www.imdb.com); Crowl, *"Hamlet"* (2000).

Where Do I Buy or Lease These Films?

To the question of how to obtain these films there is no simple answer, because ownership and availability are as unstable as the soil on a California hillside. The best strategy is to get on the telephone and begin calling or to get on the Internet and begin surfing. For that reason there has been no attempt, with a few exceptions, to give definitive information about dealers and distributors of specific films. Silent movies are, when not entirely lost, generally unavailable except in such archives as the NFTVA at the British Film Institute in London; the Folger Library and Library of Congress Motion Picture Division in Washington, DC; and the Museum of Modern Art in New York City. But at times *Hamlet* segments appear in anthology collections such as *The Great Hamlets* (see above). Prolix video distributor lists are available in such easily accessible annual paperback publications as *VideoHound's Golden Movie Retriever* (New York: Gale Research, 1998). It may, however, be worth trying the following retailers that have shown a special commitment to Shakespeare on video.

Poor Yorick CD and Video Emporium, 89a Downie Street, Stratford, Ontario Canada N5A 1W8. Phone 519 272-1999; fax 519 272-0979; yorick@ bardcentral.com. Web site: www.bardcentral.com/category. html.

The Writing Company, 10200 Jefferson Blvd., PO Box 802, Culver City, CA 90232-0802. Phone 800 421-4246; fax 800 944-5432; access@ writingco.com. Web site: writingco.com.

Facets Multimedia Incorporated, 1517 West Fullerton Avenue, Chicago, IL 60614. Phone 800 331-6192; fax 773 929-5437; sales@facets.org. Web site: www.facets.org.

Films for the Humanities, PO Box 2035, Princeton, NJ 08543. Phone 800 257-5126.

The Web site of the *Internet Movie Database*, www.imdb.com/ Credits?/>, can also be extremely useful.

NOTE

The author is grateful to Neal-Schuman Publishers for permission to use here updated and revised material from his (with Annabelle Henkin Melzer) *Shakespeare on Screen: An International Filmography and Videography*.

Part Two

APPROACHES

Introduction

Hamlet *in the Classroom Now*

To paraphrase Rosalind at the end of *As You Like It*, a good collection of essays on teaching, which I trust readers will find here, needs no prologue. But perhaps an overview not only of the essays but also of the Modern Language Association survey, which over eighty teachers answered, fifty in great detail, will clarify where we are now in teaching *Hamlet*. (I often do not name survey respondents. All are listed in "Survey Participants." In this introduction only, many respondents' names are given in parentheses, while "see" indicates reference to an author in "Works Cited and Materials for Further Study.")

Few respondents stopped to theorize their approach but plunged directly into descriptions of what they do. The writers' critical tenets certainly shaped their answers—their perception of their role (often as the director of a decentered classroom), their desire that students participate actively in the classroom. They want students to discern the varied possibilities that the text allows, but they also want students to grasp that implicit and explicit stage directions shape the play. Instructors join with students in the exciting game of making meaning and at the same time help students historicize their own readings (see Boris, this volume; Callaghan, this volume; see Rozett). Deconstruction may be moribund in recent theoretical discussions—perhaps because its legacy, the argument for verbal slippage, has been so thoroughly integrated into our understanding of Shakespeare. Every attempt to discover the coherent center is doomed—an exciting enticement to turn and twist the gem to see light flashing out. Is there a theory in this classroom that tends toward iron readings? If so, it speaks sotto voce (examples of essays in this volume that demonstrate theory in action are Bradshaw, Drakakis, Lupton).

A Hook for Students

In teaching at all but the highest levels, instructors sometimes have to move their scholarly interests to the rear and deal first with fundamental barriers to their students' pleasure and perception. The prospect of introducing students to *Hamlet*'s characters, ideas, language, to its mystery, complexity, and bounteousness, inspires instructors to reach beyond the routine, but the prospect can also be daunting. Many consider *Hamlet* to be Shakespeare's foremost play and thus the world's foremost play. As Graham Bradshaw notes, "Its critical credibility depends upon our [. . .] explaining why [. . .] his most popular play has continued to enthrall audiences in different periods and different cultures." Beyond the responsibility to the play as world-famous cultural icon—which many would gladly forget—respondents express their sense of its value in their lives as students, teachers, critics, and scholars. Instructors want to make the experience of

Hamlet in their students' lives at least approach its richness in their own. They ponder ways to connect the play with students who may not know much about it beyond the name (such students are perhaps an instructor's best collaborators in the classroom), with those who are intimidated or eagerly expectant, or, worst of all, with those whose previous exposure has been a turnoff. Students unprepared by prior literary experience for reading the play appear in many courses. The respondent Catherine Belling teaches the course Shakespeare's *Hamlet* and Renaissance Medicine in the School of Medicine at the State University of New York, Stony Brook, and her medical students sometimes have limited grounding in the humanities. Joan Landis, a humanities teacher in a conservatory of music, is challenged by bright students whose primary interest is practicing music. For all these students a demythologizing jolt can be a valuable first step, with a showing or reading of Tom Stoppard's *Fifteen-Minute* Hamlet or a screening of Fred Mogubgub's *Enter Hamlet* (see Rothwell's screenography, this volume).

Instructors as well as students need a little lightheartedness, because their responsibility toward the text may weigh them down. But the text can also make instructors search for ways that foster their students' affection for the work—for the play itself and for the tasks they do to understand it. Particularly in lower-division survey courses, instructors may face students who respond more directly to *The Last Action Hero* than to Laurence Olivier's *Hamlet*, the focus of the Arnold Schwarzenegger film's affectionate disdain—to say nothing of the play on the page. For students to whom revenge is simple and quick— all one needs is an Uzi—Hamlet's self-doubt can be mystifying. Students without a sense of class and gender roles in Renaissance England may not notice Hamlet's royal graciousness or understand Ophelia's obedience to her father or the impediments to her relationship with Hamlet. Students with little interest in reflection may find Hamlet's musings on life and death completely beside the point. They see differences between Protestantism and Catholicism through a glass darkly (Hopkins). Instructors devise creative ways to leap over the gaps in their students' knowledge (A. Young).

Some instructors assign personal writing on focused topics to help students connect with the play (Plotnik, Sirofchuck). After students write for five to ten minutes on, say, their experience of remarriage, brotherly advice, or friendship and treachery, they share whatever they wish within small groups of four or five students, and each group may select one piece to read aloud to the class. The complexity in everyone's lives rushes into view. Students can link the family drama enacted in the play to their experience, personal or vicarious (B. Young). Though Shakespeare's characters are not real, most students and instructors, too, respond to the play because of its characters, through the willed perception that they *are* real, perhaps more real than anyone they know, and that what happens to them matters. One instructor invites students to "create both convincing human characters in a convincing human context and a web of relationships among the characters and events through which the story of *Hamlet* can be understood. They complete a story that the play leaves incomplete" (Collins). Students might, for example, fill out potential details about the Polonius family, about Yorick's role in Hamlet's life, or about the relationship of Hamlet to his father. Others ask students to take on the persona of a particular character, during class or in journals, inferring what the character knows and what he or she guesses (Gordon, Kirkpatrick). Playfully exploring characters' "lives" is a beginning; talented actors are able to convey their characters' lives between the scenes because they have engaged in just such play. Most instructors, however, focus on the scenes and words in the play as expressing all that can be known about the characters.

Language Issues

Once students become aware of the play's human issues, the language remains a formidable barrier for many. American students often face the same difficulties experienced by Luo Zhiye's Nanchang University students. Whatever the students' native language, testing key lines in translations of *Hamlet* could helpfully expose the multiplicity of possible meanings (Tronch-Pérez). Beginning with the students' experience, one respondent has them write about their first encounter with Shakespeare, as reader or spectator. Their responses, read aloud, tease out their fears about the language but also their pleasure in its sensuous richness—even in language they do not understand. One instructor distributes an Old English version of the Lord's Prayer; the exercise demonstrates that *Hamlet* is written not in Old English (as they think) but in Early Modern English. Some instructors start with the basic sentence pattern, subject-verb-object, its permutations and combinations, and unthread Shakespeare's syntax. Others pay particular attention to pronouns and urge students to follow them back to their (sometimes ambiguous) antecedents. Even a short session on sentence sense can make a great deal of difference. Instructors find it helpful to work with small segments apt to capture students' imaginations, such as the Ghost's words to Hamlet, Hamlet's to Ophelia, Hamlet's to Gertrude, Polonius's to Laertes and Ophelia, and Hamlet's to the Gravedigger.

Some instructors have students memorize speeches to encourage ownership of the language. Others have students paraphrase a soliloquy in a (parodic) style of their own choosing (perhaps based on pop culture). *OED* and other dictionary studies can be productive. Concordance work is popular among instructors and students; many students respond to the concept of imagery and patterns of imagery. One instructor has each student pick an often repeated word (*revenge, mother, who, time*, etc.) and follow its use in the play and in other plays: the challenge is to make something of the permutations and variations. Some editions list famous lines, and since many of those lines may be familiar to students who do not know they come from *Hamlet*, they can provide a way into the play's language (see Beck). Hamlet's bawdy usually delights students. From there to puns generally is an easy step (Voss). One instructor has students paraphrase a segment in writing, then explain by specific citations "where Shakespeare's language says something more than or different from the paraphrase" (Cummings), an exercise particularly useful for students using a pony.

Respondents are almost unanimous in citing students' difficulty with meter and rhetorical tropes, but most do not hesitate to lecture on these topics, especially about a speech under discussion. Students might compare the verse patterns of *The Murder of Gonzago* to that of the other verse passages in *Hamlet*, dance the rhythm (O'Brien), start with sonnets, or write in the varying rhythms of the play. George T. Wright has contributed for this collection a worksheet that will help interested students understand the play of meter. Instructors usually tackle rhetorical tropes and the dynamic of images as a by-product of looking carefully at one of the soliloquies. One instructor has students apply parts of Orwell's "Politics and the English Language" to the king's rhetoric in the first court scene.

Students benefit from listening to an audio recording. Though an audio performance, like a stage or screen version, makes limiting decisions about what remains broadly potential in the script, for most students what reaches the ear is not so likely as visual images to imprint itself as the one true interpretation. Listening while reading can make all the difference between bewilderment and enlightenment.

Performance Strategies

Language becomes clearer to students who work out performance choices in small groups. Though this method is well known, having been written about for years, many survey respondents surprisingly said, "Never," to the question about having students perform. But those who do try performance say that the task of reading, paraphrasing, or performing a segment meaningfully forces students to interpret what they might have overlooked while reading alone. A compelling reason (their performance before the class) to search out the meaning and uncover the implicit stage directions motivates their work. Instructors who are reluctant to spend time with performance but who want to reap the benefits of that method have groups of students focus on a line or two: one person approaches another across a circle of students and asks, "Who's there?" The person spoken to answers, "Nay answer me" (Folio 4–5 [see Bertram and Kliman]) and then moves to another person to reask the question, and so on, until many people have tried the line in many different intonations. Other useful short pairs are "Looke too't, I charge you; come your wayes" with "I shall obey, my Lord" (601–02); "Mother, mother, mother" with "Ile warrant you, feare me not" (2381–82); the king's and queen's responses, one of the most troubling exchanges in the play, to Laertes's question "Where's my Father?": "*King*. Dead. *Qu*. But not by him" (2873–75); and "The Queene Carowses to thy fortune, *Hamlet*" and "*Gertrude*, do not drinke" (3758 and 3760). The exercise takes a few moments and immediately underscores what the script does not specify and how even small moments can affect the play's meaning. Another possibility is asking students to bring in appropriate props or their facsimiles: How long is a truncheon? What does Ophelia try to hand Hamlet? Does she carry real flowers? Putting these props into action can introduce students to the play beyond the words. Steven Doloff describes David E. Jones's "spectogram" technique: students playing a character in a given scene are asked first to explain the feelings of their character *in character* and then to position themselves in space in relation to the other characters according to those feelings (see Howe and Nelson). Even a few moments away from lecture and discussion (which is sometimes good talk between the instructor and one or two students) can enliven an entire class. Actors in the classroom from visiting companies like the Shenandoah Shakespeare Express and Actors of the London Stage (formerly ACTER)—their URLs are in "Web Sites"— and performances on stage for students to attend are other resources readily available (Andreas).

Shakespeare on screen, at times in tandem with performance in the classroom, is a frequent resource. Since students are seldom jolted into attention by a TV monitor, instructors design sessions for active response. They usually confine in-class viewing to video bits, selected short segments of two or more versions; the juxtapositions can excite awareness of choices and sharpen analytic skills (Bradshaw). A compilation of scenes, such as the cannily edited *The Great Hamlets* (1982), not only exposes students to many great stage and screen productions of the play but also shows actors talking about their choices, which are often completely divergent from one another (Collins). Instructors can require students to view one or more versions of *Hamlet* outside class; many community and college libraries are now well supplied with tapes. Prompting questions help: What effect does the response of the players to Hamlet's advice have on your perception of particular Hamlets? (the BBC *Hamlet* [1980], the Branagh *Hamlet* [1996]). Do you believe that this Hamlet and this Ophelia love each other? (the Zeffirelli *Hamlet* [1990], the Schell [1960]). Is this Gertrude as culpable as Hamlet accuses her of being? (the Olivier *Hamlet* [1948], the Richardson *Hamlet* [1969]; see Lupton, this volume). Deviations in film scripts from the play text can galvanize students' understanding of Shakespeare the director as opposed to, say, Zeffirelli the director. Zeffirelli, like many other film directors, substitutes his own prologue for Shakespeare's first scene: What does the first scene do for Shakespeare? What does Zeffirelli's substitution do for Zeffirelli? Comparison helps students notice details and reflect on their effect.

Other useful classroom aides are audiotapes and illustrations. Comparing two or more audiotapes of a soliloquy focuses attention on intonation, pace, and pauses without the distraction of stance, expression, costume, and setting; audiotapes allow students to draw inferences without swamping them with information, as any film does. Illustrations from Renaissance texts can also contextualize the play's images. Some instructors are designing lectures that take advantage of the computer's ability to present stills, videos, and sound recordings. Among the respondents, the purpose of supplements is to promote attentive observation and critical thinking.

Electronic Media and Teaching

Electronic media are beginning to influence teaching. Some instructors offer distance courses with interactive phone links (DiMatteo). Many use e-mail, with an electronic discussion list for the class, encouraging conversation among students (Andreas, Sterling). One instructor requires three students per class to complete online discussion work sheets and to distribute them for peer review before the class discussion (Clary). Students like to write questions, comments, and journal entries online and to elicit online comment and discussion. Many instructors do not have the time or inclination to explore Internet resources, but they can sometimes enlist students to search for attractive sites and critique them for the class (see M. Scott, who recommends working with students). Several respondents have students create Web pages for the class or course—sometimes for extra credit, sometimes in lieu of a paper. Some instructors worry about plagiarism from Web sources (for help against student plagiarism, see Hale), but, as usual, thoughtfully crafted assignments often obviate the problem (see, e.g., Plotnik, this volume).

Courses

Respondents teach the play in a wide array of courses, and each one affords its own challenges. When they teach *Hamlet* in a Shakespeare course, instructors may launch discussions based on comparing plays: Prince Hal related to Hamlet; Claudius to other usurpers such as Bolingbroke, Antonio in *The Tempest*, Richard III—or to that other regicide, Macbeth. *Midsummer Night's Dream*, *Taming of the Shrew*, *Tempest*, and the mock play in *Henry IV, Part 1* can be useful for discussing the play within and Shakespeare's metatheatrical concerns. Comparisons of *Hamlet* with any of the history plays highlight political issues of authority and corruption. To emphasize gender politics, which many instructors declare is the most interesting topic for them and for their students, students can contrast Ophelia and Gertrude to female characters in almost all the other plays. Other "and" possibilities are Brutus in *Julius Caesar*, Troilus in *Troilus and Cressida*; revenge in *Titus Andronicus*, *Romeo and Juliet*, and *Othello*; madness and pretended madness in *Lear*. Deborah T. Curren-Aquino asks students to look at the first lines of all the tragedies in their Riverside edition to consider how *Hamlet*'s first lines differ from all the others.

If *Hamlet* is the sole Shakespearean play in a survey course, it may be compared to the *Iliad*, *Oedipus the King*, the *Aeneid*, Montaigne's works, Castiglione's *Book of the Courtier*, *Don Quixote*, the classic Chinese drama *An*

Orphan in Zhao's Family (Chuanxiang), Tourneur's *The Revenger's Tragedy*, Kyd's *The Spanish Tragedy*, Stoppard's *Rosencrantz and Guildenstern Are Dead*, Shiga Naoya's 1912 story "Kurôdiasu no Nikki" ("Claudius's Diary"), Chinua Achebe's *Things Fall Apart*, and numberless other works from ancient, Renaissance, and current literature (see, in this volume, Berggren, Bradshaw, Comfort, Nazareth, Zhiye; see DiMatteo, "*Hamlet*"). Lisa Hopkins writes, "*Doctor Faustus* provides opportunities to relate both plays to Wittenberg and to discuss differences between Protestant and Catholic theology." Deborah T. Curren-Aquino, recommending Brower, says, "Hamlet as a combination of Achilles and Aeneas [is] an excellent way to tackle the play's and the central character's matrix of contradictions." Focusing questions help students think about correspondences and differences among disparate literatures: "Which narrators or characters seem most like the Hamlet who broods and philosophizes in the soliloquies?" "Who besides Hamlet deliberates about the rightness of action?" (Gates).

Instructors in advanced courses try to move students from a subjective impression toward more sophisticated responses. To open up the play to wider concerns, instructors rely on any number of approaches and resources—and shift from one to another as their own experience with the play changes, grows, and deepens. One respondent declares, "Nothing kills a discussion faster than a reference to a work that most students haven't heard of" (Strout). To invite students to become experts in unpacking allusions, instructors might, as an opening gambit, assign the story of Jephtha in Judges 11 and ask students to speculate on its relation to the ballad Hamlet sings in the second act (Berggren). How to introduce outside readings that encourage critical thinking is the topic of several essays in this collection (Boris, Clary, Engar, Fienberg, Hale, Hopkins, Maguire, Reilly, Scott, Strout). To ground a psychoanalytic approach, H. R. Coursen provides a detailed list of readings, which are mainly for instructors but some of which might be assigned to students. When the critical essay is the introduction in a textbook, instructors want to bring in contrasting views to help students overcome the awe they might feel about the ideas of their book's editor.

Creative assignments are at the heart of successful classes: in other words, what instructors have students *do* rather than what they themselves *say*. Don Foster tells students to ask themselves, "What can I do with this text?," rather than, "What does this text mean?" Some specific questions of doing are "How can I fit parts of the text together?" and "How can I compare the arguments of critics to expose weaknesses and discover strengths?" Several instructors brainstorm questions and problems with their students before starting discussion (Battenhouse, Hirsh, B. Young). To draw out the best from their students, instructors invite them to keep journals with questions, opinions, interpretations, and more; to make a coloring-book version of the play for children (especially good for students who will be teachers; Mullins, this volume); to reduce the length of the play by twenty-five percent or more (Strout), shaping the play to focus on the interpretation the student would like to advance (and perhaps discussing gains and losses of the cut version or performing the cut version); to present group arguments for and against a critical interpretation (Plotnik); to create a storyboard for a film version of a scene; to cast a scene and justify choices; or to write a dialogue between them and a character, between characters, or between an actor and a director of a production. These activities are the means to one end: close attention to details in the play for an interpretive, analytic purpose.

Since what instructors want students to know varies as greatly as responses to the play, no one classroom will answer all the questions about *Hamlet*. From the vast possibilities, instructors select what will work for their own engagement and for their students. All the respondents seem keenly aware that no formula can encompass the play and its eponymous character and that its ambiguity is part of its appeal to students. The respondent James Hirsh notes, "The point of teaching the play is not to give students the final word about the play but to get them hooked on it so they will keep returning to it and exploring new features of it for the rest of their lives." Most of us are drawn into teaching Shakespeare because the plays move us, and drawn to *Hamlet* because its richness renews us. My own first experience of responding to *Hamlet* came not from a classroom but from seeing Olivier's film and, later, Bernard Beckerman's stage production at Hofstra University. Looking back at those experiences, I realize how little I grasped of the play's complexities and yet how deep an attachment I formed to this imperfectly understood entity. Even now it remains mysterious to me. One excellent experience with *Hamlet* in our classrooms—though necessarily incomplete—may similarly inspire students to seek further encounters.

The Essays

Many instructors accommodate the multiplicity and open-endedness of *Hamlet* by concentrating on one or at most a few aspects of the play and on one or two approaches. Some contributors demonstrate the fruits of their own studies and their techniques for sharing these with students (DiMatteo, Drakakis, Howard-Hill, Kinney, O'Brien, Ray, Wright). Several compare the play with alternative texts, including films, offshoots, and illustrated books (Anderson, Andreas, Buhler, Perret, Rocklin). Several have a performance orientation (Andreas, Collins, Dunbar, Hodgdon, Kincaid, Shurgot, M. Young). The performances might be thought experiments rather than actual (Aasand, Charney, Maguire, Videbaek). Some instructors show students how to stand up to critics (Gates, Plotnik). Many outline specific class sessions and assignments (among them, Buchanan, George, Landis, Nichols).

Several essays in this collection and many survey respondents in their teaching concentrate on small moments that radiate through the play—the Ghost and Hamlet's encounter with it in the first act (Battenhouse), the advice and commands to Ophelia in the third scene, the "Mousetrap" (Bradshaw, Shurgot, Videbaek); Hamlet's first and only private encounter with his mother in the third act (Charney), the reports of Ophelia's death by Gertrude and by the gravediggers, the gravedigger's conversation with Hamlet, and the fencing match in the last act (Maguire, Kincaid). Instructors have students fasten on one area of the play in the expectation that they will be able to apply what they learn from this focus to other aspects of the play or to other plays. Most abjure the potentially deadening chore of going through the play line by line.

What Moves Students and Instructors

This introduction began with the resistance to *Hamlet* that some teachers encounter. Perhaps it would be good to end with the aspects of the play many students respond to immediately. Among them are the Ghost and the idea of ghosts; revenge and obligations; the love affairs; the rebellious child; the duel; Hamlet's intelligence, brutal wit, friendship, treachery, and festive energy. Instructors build on these points of entry and help their students become proficient thinkers about the play and an alert audience for further encounters with Shakespeare. The plot, the psychology, the spectacle enacted in the mind— these are aspects of the play most accessible to students. Using them as a springboard, instructors leap into the specifics of language. Many care about the poetry because that's where Shakespeare's genius lies; they want students to hear the supple variety and expressive aptness of the verse and prose. The essays and the short takes that follow the essays are meant to encourage instructors to find, rediscover, or affirm their creative exuberance and to use it to kindle a like creativity in their students. Over time, instructors will change the ways they teach the play, responding to what they hold to be true about the play, about students, and about teaching. The energy and joy that inform the descriptions of teaching that follow will remain, I hope, to inspire future teachers.

Students in the classrooms of those who contributed to this volume will not be pipes to be played on. Instead the students will learn how to analyze the play: observe details, draw inferences, and argue for and against their own and others' perspectives. They will join the line of all those who have put their shoulders to this task, ready to make delightful, painful, maddening discoveries about this ever-generative *Hamlet*.

Hearing the Poetry

George T. Wright

I've retired from teaching, but when I taught *Hamlet* in undergraduate Shake-speare courses, there were so many other issues to discuss that we couldn't spend much time on matters like meter, imagery, or language. Still, as a way of getting students to inspect Shakespeare's wording closely and unfold its subtle meanings, I always asked them to write detailed paraphrases of puzzling passages that the footnotes didn't entirely clarify. It was in another course that I usually dealt with meter in English poetry, and there I sometimes set, as a passage to scan on the final exam, part of the Ghost's wonderful narrative of his murder, the queen's description of Ophelia's death, or Claudius's confessional meditation on his guilt (though my favorite speech, and the one that most brought out my students' insights into meter and euphony, was Claudio's "Ay, but to die" in *Measure for Measure* [3.1.117–31]).

But even in Shakespeare courses where we read six plays a quarter, I would spend an hour in the first week on sonnet 30, hoping to get students to notice the subtle imagery and hear how various and expressive the meter was. Then, eager to move on to the plays and other matters, I would distribute handouts like the one below, with examples drawn from plays we would read that term. Here I have taken all the quotations from *Hamlet* and combined the notes on meter with those on pronunciation. As the quarter went on, there would be opportunities to enlarge on some of these points, and sometimes interested students would enroll in my course in meter and form or in another course (less often taught) in diction, imagery, syntax, and rhetorical tropes and figures. Despite the strong lure of other approaches, some of which occupied most of the hours we spent on Shakespeare, the technical details of his versecraft will still be of interest to many.

Shakespeare's Meter:
A Handout for Students

Shakespeare wrote most of his verse lines in iambic meter. This means that what we usually hear is an alternating rhythm: a lightly stressed syllable (often marked ˘) is followed by a stronger one (ˊ), and this pattern or "foot" (˘ˊ) is repeated throughout the line. It usually appears five times in a line, so the lines are known as iambic pentameter. It looks and sounds like this:

      ˘   ˊ   ˘   ˊ   ˘ ˊ   ˘   ˊ   ˘ ˊ

1. The King doth wake to-night and takes his rouse   (1.4.8)

      ˘   ˊ   ˘   ˊ   ˘ ˊ   ˘   ˊ   ˘ ˊ

2. For who would bear the whips and scorns of time   (3.1.69)

You can hear that every second syllable in these lines is spoken more strongly than the one it follows. Accented syllables of nouns, many adjectives and adverbs, and most verbs (but not usually auxiliary verbs or forms of *to be*) fill most of the stressed positions (2nd, 4th, 6th, 8th, and 10th), because in our speech we tend to accent those kinds of words more than most monosyllabic pronouns, prepositions, conjunctions, and articles. But there are many exceptions. Minor words often turn up in stressed positions, partly because we do sometimes emphasize them in our speech, either lightly (as in 3) or for contrast (as in 4), and partly to give the lines variety (as in 5). In these and the following examples the emphasis is mine:

3. And *with* them words of so sweet breath compos'd   (3.1.97)

4. Had *he* the motive and the cue for passion
   That *I* have   (2.2.561-62)

5. He took me *by* the wrist, and held me hard   (2.1.84)

In 5, *by* doesn't need as heavy a stress as *took* or *wrist*, but iambic meter follows English speech in often giving a little emphasis to the middle one of three successive minor syllables. After all, to have five equally strong syllables in every line would make the verse dull. To ensure variety, Shakespeare sometimes writes lines that encourage a reader or actor to focus on only three or four strongly stressed syllables:

6. That *beetles* o'er his *base* into the *sea*   (1.4.71)

7. The *slings* and *arrows* of out*rageous fortune*   (3.1.57)

Even in such lines we are likely to hear an alternating rhythm as we read them quickly; once the iambic rhythm establishes itself in our minds, we will proba- bly hear a lighter beat on the minor syllables in stressed position: *o'er, -to*, and *of*. Skillful readers may manage these differences in various ways. But even in normal lines the strongly stressed syllables are almost never stressed *equally* strongly. They also usually avoid falling at exactly equal intervals. For good poets, verse is almost never as precisely timed as even the most flexibly timed music is. No one can direct a good actor exactly how long to pause between the phrases of a line like this:

> 8. To be,   or not to be,   that is the question   (3.1.55)

But even after a lengthy pause (or two) we can usually hear that the line we just heard had five beats, that it was iambic pentameter.

Variations

To vary the iambic meter, Shakespeare uses three other kinds of feet, pyrrhic, spondaic, and trochaic. The pyrrhic foot puts less-than-expected emphasis on a syllable in strong position ($\smile\smile$), as in 4, 5, 6, and 7 above. The spondee puts more-than-expected stress on a syllable in weak position ($\smile\diagup$):

> 9. *All saws* | of books, | *all forms*, | *all pres* | sures past   (1.5.100)

And the trochee does both, thereby reversing the usual iambic pattern ($\diagup\smile$). Trochees usually appear at the beginning of a line or after a mid-line phrasal break:

> 10. *Sée* what | a grace was seated on this brow   (3.4.55)

> 11. *Gó to* | their graves like beds, | *fíght for* | a plot   (4.4.62)

Sometimes these patterns combine with each other. Here is a trochee- spondee:

> 12. Would harrow up thy soul, | *fréeze thy* | *young blóod* (1.5.16)

The three italicized words will probably not receive equal stress: *freeze* and *blood* carry the line's fourth and fifth beats; *young* and possibly even *thy* get due emphasis but not quite as much weight as *blood* or *freeze*.
  Another frequent combination is the pyrrhic-spondee:

> 13. *In my* | *heart's core*, | ay, in my heart of heart   (3.2.73)

Shakespeare and his contemporaries would probably have heard the line's first beat falling on *my* (or even on *In*) and the second on *core*, but many modern readers are tempted (mistakenly—i.e., anachronistically—in my view) to lurch past the first two words and give equally strong stress to both *heart's* and *core*. Some other examples:

14. *In the* | *most high* | and palmy state of Rome   (1.1.113)

15. Is sicklied o'er | *with the* | *pale cast* | of thought   (3.1.84)

The Play of Phrase and Line

The pyrrhic, spondee, and trochee are the principal variations Shakespeare uses to give interest to his lines, so that we almost never find two successive lines patterned alike. His system is essentially very economical: a basic pattern, with three variant subpatterns, that can be used to accommodate the various stress patterns of English phrasing. But sometimes short lines occur, and sometimes long lines, and there are many lines with weak endings (they used to be called feminine), that is, with an extra unstressed syllable (as in 4, 8, and 16):

16. The present death of Hamlet. Do | it, Eng*land*   (4.3.65)

Sometimes, too, the extra syllable turns up at the end of the first half of a line, especially if there is a pause in the phrasing (usually indicated by punctuation). This pattern (used much more by Shakespeare than by other poets and playwrights) is known as an epic caesura:

17. And by oppos | ing, end *them*. | To die, to sleep   (3.1.59)

Poetic lines that are as long as ten syllables usually include more than a single phrase, and the musical character of a verse line depends not only on the way metrical variations change the steady alternating progress of unstressed and stressed syllables but also on where the line's phrasal break occurs. The crucial oddity of a five-foot line is that it can never divide into equal halves. Any division into two phrases must give more of the line's five stresses to one phrase, which means that iambic pentameter lines can never become singsong. Even if the language in the lines is a bit elevated, as Shakespeare's usually is, the five-foot line sounds more like natural speech than verse in other meters.

Still, five thumping iambic feet will not sound very natural. Shakespeare and other poets tried to make successive lines sound different from one another. One way to do this is to vary the place where the phrasal break occurs—early in the line or late, and after a stressed (even) or unstressed (odd) syllable. So in two lines the Ghost can say:

18. Thus was I, sleeping, by a brother's hand
    Of life, of crown, of queen, at once dispatch'd   (1.5.74–75)

Ending a phrase in mid-line, especially late in mid-line, means that the poet has to find a short phrase for the second half of the line or run the sense over the line ending. Running it over is especially tempting when there is no rhyme at line's end, when the verse is blank verse. During his long career, Shakespeare often found it natural or expressive to carry the sense of a blank verse line over into the next one, and in his middle and later plays the sentences often run from mid-line to mid-line:

19.   but know, thou noble youth,
    The serpent that did sting thy father's life
    Now wears his crown.   (1.5.38–40)

Variations on this pattern are frequent, too, and you may find many passages of similar but slightly different arrangement in *Hamlet*. You will also find many examples of a character's ending a speech in mid-line only to have it picked up metrically and finished by another character. In the conversation, for example, between the king and Laertes (4.7, especially from about 102 to 148), not only do both men conspire against Hamlet but most of their speeches conclude with short lines that the other man finishes, a pattern of shared lines that indicates perhaps how deeply they are in league with each other.

Scansion

Scanning verse means to assign marks that indicate whether the syllables are weak (ᵛ) or strong (´). See, for examples, 1, 2, and 9, above. As we have seen, it's convenient to use an intermediate mark (ˎ) to show a rather strongly stressed syllable in an unstressed position or a rather weakly stressed syllable in strong position. Foot divisions (as in 9) are also useful, not to suggest that in speaking the lines we actually pause after every two syllables but just to make it easier to see graphically how the metrical patterning of one line differs from that of another. There is often room for different views of how a line might be scanned, just as different actors will prefer different readings of the line on the stage. Scansion and metrical analysis generally can help our understanding of how dramatic lines sound and draw our attention to their emotional interest and excitement. They should not be a pedantic exercise.

Some modern critics have developed other systems of scansion or metrical analysis that are variously useful but also have disadvantages. The traditional system described above still seems to me the one most closely connected to any expressive speaking of the lines.

Pronunciation

To hear lines accurately, we need to be aware of differences between our pronunciation and Shakespeare's, especially the following examples:

Some words have changed their accent, like *revenue* and *commune* in the following lines:

20. That no | reve | nue hast but thy good spirits   (3.2.58)

21. Laertes, I | must com | mune with your grief   (4.5.203)

An *-ed* suffix that is silent in our speech, but that Shakespeare and his contemporaries apparently regarded as an optional pronunciation, is given full value in many lines:

22. It waves you to a more remo | ved ground   (1.4.61)

23. And with such maim | ed rites? | This doth betoken   (5.1.219)

If the *-ed* is not to be pronounced, modern editors usually indicate that by using an apostrophe:

24. Hath op'd | his ponderous and marble jaws   (1.4.50)

In the interests of speedy delivery on stage, syllables may sometimes be contracted, especially (a) in combinations of minor words: *in the* becomes *i' th'* (4.7.126); *Is it* becomes *Is't* (5.2.25); (b) when two vowels fall together in adjacent words or are separated only by an *h* (elision): *I am, I have, you are, he is, th' event* (4.4.41); or when they fall together in the same word (synaeresis): *hideous, being, bestial, violent, influence, Polonius*; and (c) immediately after the accented syllable (syncope): *either, even, ever, never, power, heaven, seven, having, over, spirit, marry, Sirrah, warrant, natural, general, flattering*. Syncope may occur even in words like *medicine* (5.2.314), *emulate* (1.1.83), *imminent* (4.4.60), *pestilent* (4.5.91), and *particular* (1.3.26, 1.4.23, 1.5.19, but see also 2.1.12).

Some words may be expanded (though this is rare in *Hamlet*), for instance, words that end in suffixes like *-tion*:

25. This present object made proba | tion   (1.1.156)

26. By their o'ergrowth of some complex | ion   (1.4.27)

A few words like *soldiers* (1.5.141 but not elsewhere), *business* (2.2.82), and *convenient* (1.1.175) may sometimes be treated as having more syllables than we usually give them.

Exercises

1. Try different ways of reading some of the example lines above, to bring out the slight differences between strong and intermediate stresses (*blood* and *young* in 12) and between intermediate and weak stresses (*me* and *by* in 5), and to indicate the metrical value (of *up* in 12 or other weak syllables in strong position).

2. Try scanning other lines and passages (like those suggested below), especially to bring out how variously Shakespeare has placed the syllables he wants to emphasize and has arranged the pauses and the run-on lines or shared lines to make his characters' speeches more rhythmically interesting or more dramatic. Remember that while scanning helps make clear a line's relation to the basic standard metrical pattern, it should always serve, not inhibit, an effective dramatic reading.

Make thy two eyes like stars start from their spheres   (1.5.17)

We should do when we would; for this "would" changes   (4.7.119)

Why thy canoniz'd bones, hearsed in death   (1.4.47)

As day does to your eye.
              Let her come in   (4.5.153)

Rest, rest, perturbed spirit! So, gentlemen   (1.5.182)

Having ever seen in the prenominate crimes   (2.1.43)

That hurts by easing. But to the quick of th' ulcer   (4.7.123)

Some longer passages for scanning are the Ghost's speeches to Hamlet (1.5), Laertes's advice to Ophelia (1.3.10–44), Hamlet's dialogue with the queen (3.4), Claudius at prayer (3.3.36–72), and Hamlet's soliloquies.

3. Why does Shakespeare use prose rather than verse for some scenes or passages?

NOTE

Hamlet quotations are from Evans et al. See Wright for a fuller account, book-length (*Art*) or chapter-length ("Hearing") of Shakespeare's meter.

Dancing the Meter

Ellen J. O'Brien

Verse is, at its root, a physical phenomenon: though metrical analysis is an activity of the brain, rhythm belongs to the body. For this reason, I teach iambic pentameter as a dance, in the hope of putting meter into students' bodies as well as their brains, encouraging a response to verse that is both visceral and intellectual. My goal is to help students develop the ability to sense meter in "normal" lines without conscious analysis, to analyze what they cannot immediately sense, and to appreciate the dramatic possibilities of different metrical constructions and alternate scansions.

Introduction to the Dance

We begin on our feet—if conditions permit, without shoes. In order to focus students on visceral understanding of the energies in the line, I encourage them to note and articulate the feel of each stage of the process: the sense of weight, of potential for forward movement, and so on. (To minimize distraction from that focus, I also assure them that dancing ability is not required and that none of us will look graceful.)

Exploration 1: We move around the room on the balls of our feet, rigorously avoiding bringing the heel in contact with the floor. Here, students usually comment on a feeling of lightness, quickness, and potential for forward motion. This "ball" step will become our equivalent of the unstressed syllable.

Exploration 2: We then switch to walking so that the full foot comes in contact with the floor simultaneously on each step (no rolling down from the heel or the toe). Now students notice such things as a sense of slowness, ponderousness, deliberateness, and lack of spontaneity. This "flat" step will be our stressed-syllable step.

Exploration 3: Finally, we switch back and forth between ball steps and flat steps, varying the speed and weight of the step in each mode and observing the effect. When students seem comfortable with this, we add sound. Students create individual sounds, to last exactly as long as each step and to reflect the difference in feel between ball steps and flat steps. Usually, the variety of sounds in the room suggests a good range of the possible dramatic uses of stressed and unstressed syllables in iambic pentameter. This variety is helpful with later stages, when we begin to explore meter as a shaper of meaning.

The Basic Step

Now we're ready to master the iamb, the basic dance step in the iambic pentameter two-step. So we try moving across the floor in repeated units of ball step + flat step, keeping our sounds going as we dance.

The Iambic Pentameter Line

To give the dance more shape, we put the iambs into lines, five ball-step units across the floor, turning on the final step to begin the next line. Suddenly what the students see around them looks more like art and less like chaos. To enhance this effect, I often organize them into two facing lines that move toward each other for five iambs, then turn away for five, and so on. Side coaching is important here to help them take the iambic feel into their bodies clearly. Keeping the movements precise is essential: sounds and steps should exactly coincide, and the swing into the next line should not add an extra step or create a big pause. What that swing will do is lift the voice in a way that marks the end of the line without breaking the sense. I can then tell the class that they have mastered the basic iambic pentameter line. To prove the point, we switch from nonsense sounds to words (sonnet 106),

> Of hand,| of foot,| of lip,| of eye,| of brow|

and take one step on each syllable, still dancing the ball-flat (iambic) units across the floor: ball-flat| ball-flat| ball-flat| ball-flat| ball-flat. Lightbulbs usually start to go on at this point.

Variations on the Basic Step

By now, the dance is probably becoming a bit boring: a good point at which to discuss the importance of variation in iambic pentameter. After all, just as box stepping all night would take the joy out of the waltz, an unbroken string of iambs would put us all to sleep. So I ask them to invent variations on the basic step, using only ball or flat and working in two-step units like the iamb. They will quickly come up with the flat-ball (trochee), the ball-ball (pyrrhic), and the flat-flat (spondee). Then we play with the feel of a line that begins with a trochee and continues with iambs, working again with nonsense sounds. Asked to describe what they feel and hear, students note things like an abrupt or energetic start to the line, a quick skip from first to fourth step, giving unusual power to the fourth, and so on. Similarly, we'll explore the impact of throwing in a pyrrhic or a spondee, and finally the impact of a pyrrhic followed by a spondee. They are usually surprised by how much meaning (particularly in terms of possible emotional states) they can feel in these nonsense-syllable rhythms when the whole body is engaged in the act. Now we are ripe for marrying sound and sense.

Dancing *Hamlet*: Beginner's Level

At this point, I will toss them lines from Hamlet's act 2, scene 2, soliloquy (502–58: "O what a rogue and peasant slave am I [. . .]"), selected to exemplify the variations we have been talking about. I work first with lines that contain no elisions, feminine endings, or other elements we have not discussed.

O, what| a rogue| and pea|sant slave| am I!   (502)

Is it| not mons|trous that| this play|er here   (503)

Upon| whose pro|perty| and most| dear life| (522)

The students work out the dance of each line, and we discuss how the variations on the iamb help shape the meaning of the line and suggest character interpretations to the actor—beginning with the energies of the trochee in "O what a rogue." Having taken the trochee-iamb rhythm into their bodies, students are quick to notice the weight thrown on "O" and "rogue" and the sense of frustration or disgust that may emerge from that. Someone may then notice that in the next line, "monstrous" may be given similar weight if we begin with a pyrrhic. In the third line, someone else will probably discover the extra impact of a spondee on "dear life." Wherever there are two (or more) legitimate choices in scansion, I try to draw them out of the class and discuss their differing impact, to make clear that scanning is an interpretive act, not a mathematical science. Although we can agree on certain metrical characteristics of the soliloquy, no two speakers would dance it—much less Hamlet's entire role—identically.

Advanced Steps in *Hamlet*'s Dance: Dancing Three Syllables as Two and Related Moves

As students grow confident with this process, I'll begin to throw in lines that seem to have fewer or more than ten syllables, and when they notice the complications, I introduce elision and expansion as ways of creating more sophisticated iambs.

Prompted| to my| revenge| by heaven [heav'n]| and hell| (537)

That I| the son| of the| dear mur|dered   (536)

The Three-Step Moves

With the two-step moves strongly established, we're ready to add three-syllable feet to our dance:

Double (feminine) ending:

But in| a fic|tion, in| a dream| of passion| (505)

Epic caesura (here also with elision and double ending):

With most| mira|culous órgăn.| I'll have| these plăyers| (547)

Here, as with trochees, our discussion includes where in the line the variants tend to appear. After a few comments on double onset, headless lines, and missing syllables, I can tell the students that they know all the steps they need for Shakespeare's iambic pentameter dance.

The Dance of the Rogue and Peasant Slave

Now the real fun begins. The entire soliloquy is divided up among the students (working in groups of at least two), and they are charged with choreographing performances of their sections—finding both the required variations on the purely iambic line and as many legitimate choices as possible. As we work through the lines, an energetic discussion of the dramatic impact of the variations develops with little prompting. Even more energy can emerge as they defend their choices among several possibilities. And, of course, as we put the soliloquy together, the sense of the lines begins to interact more strongly with the metrical choices.

The whole process can be completed in a couple of 75-minute sessions. Working through variations on the basic step and a few very regular lines of the soliloquy makes a good first day. If students have a few more of these simple lines to work on at home, they will come back better prepared to tackle advanced steps and the whole soliloquy in the next session. Different classes move at different speeds, of course, but I find the more often I teach the dance, the more quickly it goes.

Only after the students have taken the dance of iambic pentameter into their bodies do I give them a handout on the iambic pentameter line and Shakespeare's normal variations, summing up what they have already danced. Presented this way, ink and paper becomes a reminder of something students already possess as visceral knowledge rather than a new construct to be absorbed by the brain alone.

NOTE

Hamlet quotations are from Edwards. The principles of iambic pentameter that I teach are drawn primarily from *Shakespeare's Metrical Art*, by George T. Wright, to whom I am deeply indebted.

"The Play's the Thing": Constructing the Text of *Hamlet*

T. H. Howard-Hill

In *Hamlet*, we see Hamlet himself revising an old play, adapting it for performance at court. The presence of the traveling players directs attention to the questions, Where do plays come from? How did we get *Hamlet*? However, in my experience, students never ask such questions; like hungry guests at a feast, they are content to eat unquestioningly what is put before them. Nevertheless, instructors often feel the need to explain the origins of the texts on which so much time and attention are lavished by both undergraduate and graduate students. Frequently, teachers are more comfortable with critical theory and techniques of literary criticism than with bibliography and textual criticism, which are even less often a part of graduate education in English than they were in the heyday of Fredson Bowers and the "new bibliography." (This essay is not directed to bibliographers.) Further, the constraints of the curriculum are always pressing: there is never enough time available to teach all that should be taught, or to teach it in adequate detail. Something added means that something else is scanted. These are substantial reasons to query whether bibliography (used here comprehensively for analytical bibliography, textual criticism, and editing) should or could be incorporated in the classes devoted to *Hamlet* that are predominantly and properly given over to literary criticism.

For many years I believed that bibliography was such a large subject that one could not do justice to it by casual attention given during the discussion of a single literary work, even in a course devoted exclusively to *Hamlet*. The bibliographer and editor Bowers at the University of Virginia and the literary historian Jerzy Limon at the University of Gdańsk have each given semester-long courses on *Hamlet,* but it takes longer than a semester even to tell students about bibliography. Nevertheless, students persisted in their painful indifference to the origin and construction of the sources of their literary experiences, apparently believing that someone at W. W. Norton and Company or the Oxford or Cambridge university press had copied out *Hamlet*, say, from Shakespeare's original manuscript — or whatever. The point became not whether I could do justice to bibliography but whether I could do justice to the students. The goal was, I eventually appreciated, to teach students the relevance of bibliography to the texts they were studying in order to enhance their literary understanding of the individual works.

For undergraduate survey classes my bibliographical presentation is no more than a prosaic lecture on the conditions of dramatic authorship in Shakespeare's time. (If I had the opportunity, I should like to show clips from the film *Shakespeare in Love*, even though it is centered on *Romeo and Juliet*, because it depicts playwrighting in the context of the early theater with zest and conviction.) The introductory lecture is larded with analogies to television and other popular entertainments and illustrated with facsimiles of early plays. The Shakespeare First Folio, even in unprepossessing facsimile copies, receives attention on account of its major contribution to the Shakespeare canon and opens up the Pandora's box of modern compositorial analysis leading to textual criticism and editing, but this temptation can be resisted. Students invariably bring up the authorship question and enjoy learning of mad Delia Bacon and the Reverend Mr. Thomas Looney, but discussion can be turned back to the passage in the manuscript of Anthony Munday's *Sir Thomas More*, more likely than not in Shakespeare's handwriting. There is no limit to such bibliographical show-and-tell, but it can all be directed toward contextualizing the literary qualities of the Shakespearean texts at point. I do not focus this discussion on a single play but use many titles to illustrate the general lecture.

For graduate survey courses, however, I have used *King Lear* with its valuable facsimile teaching aids. Now *Hamlet* occupies the bibliographical center of the students' attention. At my university in recent years students in Shakespeare courses rarely have any graduate studies background in medieval or Renaissance literature, or more than minimal knowledge of Shakespeare's plays or their historic situation. Their academic careers are not largely governed by their knowledge of Shakespeare; for most students, Shakespeare is a distribution requirement. Consequently, I concentrate on a play, *Hamlet*, of which many of them have heard beforehand, and endeavor to provide, particularly in the bibliographical component, knowledge that will be useful for every literary course they may take.

All texts are constructed, even bookless texts on the Internet. I usually do not require students to use the same anthology or single-text edition of the plays, unless an exceptional amount of attention is to be given to a single play. Therefore, students often pose challenges in the form "My edition says . . ." It is instructive then to consider why different modern editions of the same play are indeed different, not merely in the apparatus (e.g., the introductions, the arrangement of textual collations, the notes and commentary) but in the text itself. Students should understand that they hold in their hands just one representation of the work among many and that representations may be constructed from different materials and for different purposes. Frequently, of course, differences among modern editions mirror the variety of materials that their editors have drawn on. My point is simply that, instead of having descended from the English equivalent of Parnassus, pure and perfect, Shakespeare's plays are constructed, work in progress as it were, and that students eventually participate in the construction. Shakespeare's works were constructed in his time (to name the most obvious agents) by himself, by his scribes, by the theatrical bookkeepers, by the master of the revels as censor, by the theatrical company as the initiators of revisions, by the editors and compositors of the contemporary editions—and then by the modern editors, general editors, and publishers of the plays that students bring to class in order to embark on their own work with the aid of their teachers. All things being equal, this constructedness is true of every literary work studied in universities, and it is a point worth reinforcing during the study of a canonical work that illustrates it so well.

To illustrate this fundamental point within my survey course on Shakespeare's tragedies, and to demonstrate its relevance to the study of *Hamlet*, I chose a crucial passage in the play. There are many crucial passages in *Hamlet*, and any of them may be examined in the way I describe here. However, I chose the "Mousetrap" scene because, first, its understanding is fundamental to what viewers and readers make of Claudius's guilt and thence Hamlet's situation; second, productions and films often do not present it fully or clearly; and third, modern editors represent it differently in their editions.

After Xeroxing the relevant portions of Harold Jenkins's new Arden edition (1982), Philip Edwards's New Cambridge edition (1985), and George Hibbard's Oxford edition (1987), with cutting and pasting onto legal size paper I produced not a parallel-text *Hamlet* (cf. Bertram and Kliman) but a parallel-edition text. The first column gives the Arden text, from 3.2.133 (*"The trumpets sound. A dumb-show follows."*) to line 268 after the exit of the king and the court. One can go on as far as one chooses, of course, but stopping just after the trap has been sprung results in a manageable handout of nine leaves. The text is accompanied by the Arden textual collation and commentary at the foot of the page, and the Arden's "Longer Notes" to the passage are provided as an appendix to the handout. The third and fourth columns are occupied by the commentary alone of the Cambridge and Oxford editions. This arrangement gives a graphic illustration of the different amounts of annotation the editions supply and reduces the complexity of the illustrative materials. However, the students are directed toward the significant differences among the texts of the three editions in the second column, which gives my collation of them. On the assumption that the Arden edition's textual collation records the important variations among the primary documents (First Quarto [1603], Second Quarto [1604–05], and First Folio [1623]) from which all the editors constituted their texts, students can quickly perceive where the editors have preferred different authorities. For instance, at Arden 3.2.133sd9, where Jenkins prints *"They seem to condole with her,"* both Edwards and Hibbard print *"seeming"* for *"They seem,"* but only Hibbard prints the First Folio's *"lament"* for *"condole."* (This observation can lead to a discussion of the principles of copy text and eclectic editing and why Hibbard chose the Second Quarto reading in one case but not in the other.)

The collation of the editions in the second column also records that some lines of text appear in one edition but not another. What is the status of the omissions or insertions? The three editions differ significantly in their treatment of passages such as Hamlet's fourth soliloquy (*"Now all occasions do inform against me"* [Arden 4.4.32–66]). Basing his edition on the Second Quarto, Jenkins nevertheless includes "anything preserved in F which I take to have been lost from Q2; but all words and phrases in F which I judge to be playhouse additions to the dialogue [. . .] I omit" (75). Overall, this conflated text gives a version of the play most familiar to readers. But, wishing "to keep the different shapes of the second quarto and the Folio in front of the reader as much as possible," Edwards marks with square brackets "all the second quarto passages which are cut from the Folio" (32). Hibbard, however, relegates passages peculiar to the Second Quarto to an appendix at the end of his edition. Accordingly, readers of these editions will have different reading experiences of *Hamlet*. Such varying editorial treatments have practical implications as well as theoretical interest and deserve (and receive) discussion by professional readers, that is, graduate students.

In order to appreciate some of the factors that influence editorial choices, students need a guide to the relations among the early witnesses to the text of *Hamlet*. I distribute Kathleen Irace's figure showing the "Conjectural Relationship between Q1, Q2, and F" ("Origins" 119). Any recent diagram (such as on Edwards 31) is useful, for rather than teach received opinion, the instructor can use the diagram to illustrate the complexity of the problem and to identify and define such basic concepts as foul papers, memorial reconstruction, and theatrical abridgment. The stemma usually prompts discussion of the conditions of dramatic authorship in the early period, particularly the relations among the playwright, his company, and theater in general.

Whether discussion is driven by students' questions and observations or by the teacher's, the display of different editorial treatments of the same passage of text invariably leads to a fuller understanding of the materials of literary scholarship and criticism and of the play itself. The pedagogical success of such an exercise as this depends on the amount of time that can be devoted to it as well as on the knowledge and enthusiasm of the instructor and students, but they are not obliged to be bibliographers. I distribute the handout beforehand to allow students to brood over it. Success also depends on the selection of the passage illustrated in the handout: if the students do not come to recognize that their appreciation of the literary work is to a measure contingent on the edition they use, then the instructor has failed. Usually, however, students acquire a more thorough knowledge and appreciation of at least a part of Shakespeare's play by having considered where it came from and not only what to make of it. Understanding what to make of it, of course, follows.

In summary, assign your students the following:

1. In a scholarly edition, select a textual crux in *Hamlet*.
2. From Horace Furness's New Variorum edition, copy his discussion of the crux.
3. Using conventional bibliographical aids, compile a checklist of discussions of the crux that were published in a suitable period (e.g., 1961–70).
4. Identify (as available) one linguistic, stylistic, metrical, theatrical, bibliographical, and critical argument in favor of the reading you would prefer as an editor.
5. Do the same for a reading you would reject.
6. Write a paragraph to show how the chosen reading may affect literary criticism of the play.

For time, some steps may be omitted.

An Editing Exercise for Students

Randall Anderson

> Conjecture has all the joy and all the pride of invention,
> and he that has once started a happy change, is too much
> delighted to consider what objections may rise against it.
> —Samuel Johnson, "Preface to Shakespeare"

It is no small feat to cultivate in undergraduates an appreciation of, not to mention an interest in, the work of the textual critic. While it takes substantial vigilance to read a play with one eye on the swelling scene and another on the nearby (or distant) collations, a few choice examples of the kind of editorial decisions that go into assembling a version of *Hamlet* ought to challenge the students' assumptions that today we read the same text that was available four centuries ago.

As a preliminary exercise to the written assignment, we look at a separate passage in class that gives the students a taste of a challenging editorial choice. At the end of the apology Hamlet extends to Laertes—an apology supposedly urged by Gertrude ("The queen desires you to use some gentle entertainment to Laertes before you fall to play" [5.2.206–07])—the folio offers a tantalizing alternative to Hamlet's apparent contrition over Polonius's death (Allen and Muir 660; Kökeritz 770; Bertram and Kliman 256-57):

Second Quarto (N3r-v)
Giue me your pardon sir, I haue
done you wrong
[. . . . .]
Free me so farre in your most
generous thoughts
That I haue shot my arrowe ore
the house
And hurt my brother.

First Folio (pp6v)
Giue me your pardon Sir, I'ue
done you wrong,
[. . . . .]
Free me so farre in your most
generous thoughts,
That I haue shot mine Arrow o're
the house,
And hurt my Mother.

Most texts of *Hamlet* let this moment pass with little comment. The newest competitor in the textbook market, *The Norton Shakespeare*, merely reports "F's reading is 'mother'" (Greenblatt et al. 1752n), and this is by far the most direct attention the line receives (some texts with abbreviated collations do not bother to include the alternative reading at all). Based on Laertes's chilly response to Hamlet's apology, "I am satisfied in nature, [. . .] But in my terms of honour / I stand aloof" (5.2.244–47), it is not wholly impossible to imagine Hamlet turning away from Laertes at 5.2.243–44 and looking at Gertrude when referring to the "hurt" he has inflicted. But contrary to the nameless lord's indication of Gertrude's concern (5.2.206–07), it is significant to note that Claudius openly initiates the peacemaking between Laertes and Hamlet (5.2.225) while Gertrude remains silent; her position onstage and her expressions are a matter of production, rather than editorial, choice, but the door remains open to the director who may opt for the folio's reading of the passage. Regardless of the choice finally made, the act of considering such alternative readings—here and elsewhere— demands that we learn to see the value of some conflicting possibilities.

The Handout for Students

This exercise is designed to make you more aware of the subtleties and responsibilities of close, careful reading. In addition, I want you to become sensitive to another type of intervention which determines—or predetermines—the interpretive moment.

Attached are four passages from *Hamlet* that were chosen for their textual, as well as contextual, interest:

2.2.549–605 ("O what a rogue and peasant slave am I")

    Q1 (E4v–F1r); Allen and Muir 596

    Q2 (F4v–G1r); Allen and Muir 633

    Bertram and Kliman 114, 116, 118

3.1.89-161 (the nunnery exchange)

    Q1 (E1r–2r); Allen and Muir 592–93

    Q2 (G2v–3r); Allen and Muir 635

    Bertram and Kliman 124–29

4.5.74-153 (Laertes's return from France)

    Q1 (H1r–v); Allen and Muir 604–05

    Q2 (K4v–L1v); Allen and Muir 649–50

    Bertram and Kliman 196-203

5.2.280-360 (the death scene)

    Q1 (I3r–v); Allen and Muir 610–11

    Q2 (N4v–O1v); Allen and Muir 661–62

    F1 (qq1r); Kökeritz 771

    Bertram and Kliman 260–67

In every instance I have provided you with the text from the Second ("Good") Quarto (1604), which has furnished the basic foundation for most modern editions of *Hamlet*. In addition I provide parallel passages from the First ("Bad") Quarto (1603) and, in one case (5.2), a portion of the passage from the First Folio (1623). The *Hamlet* that we read—in the *Riverside* and elsewhere—has been assembled from these three texts, but in Shakespeare's time the play was never available in the version that we hold in our hands today.

Each passage presents several important interpretive moments. Your task is to examine your passage for ambiguity, tension, and paradox (old, but still invaluable, points of entry into the text). Why is the passage you've chosen especially appropriate? Could we present *Hamlet* without the scene (or with a condensed version of the scene)? How does it connect with earlier scenes or prepare us for later scenes? What do we learn about the characters involved? Do any particular words, images, or themes from the passage resonate elsewhere in the play (the concordance would be helpful for this purpose)? What do the words mean? Are you absolutely sure? What else might they have meant in 1603? (Consult the *OED*!) Are there any puns? Are any crucial words changed from one version of the passage to another (here you might refer to the list of substantive variants)? If so, do all variant readings make sense? What validates one alternative more than the others? In terms of dramatic effects, think about what action or what gestures may be appropriate to the scene (Renaissance drama has notoriously meager stage directions). To whom—or about whom—are lines spoken? Can we always determine the referent of pronouns? In terms of poetic effects, does it make a difference whether the passage is in prose or verse? Some characters speak in both prose and verse; what, then, can we determine about the circumstances of the scene? (In other words, what evidence—psychological or interpersonal—is revealed or concealed by the mode of presentation?)

Pick any one of these four scenes and play the editor: assume you are engaged in preparing an edition of *Hamlet*, identify your target audience, make the necessary choices, and then defend them to me in four to six pages.

Four Scenes

While there are other candidates for this assignment in textual criticism, the four scenes I list for the students offer a high density of variant readings that provide not only textual but also dramatic cruxes; in return I often get versions of the scenes that have more in common with a director's promptbook than with a scholarly text, but that result can be a happy by-product of the assignment. While some may think that students will be intimidated by this exercise—I am, after all, asking them to do what is supposedly reserved for trained professionals—my experience shows that nearly every one rises to the challenge (and at term's end many remark that this was their favorite assignment). If nothing else, those students who feel overwhelmed by open-ended paper assignments are here firmly anchored to the text. For proof, witness a small sample of observations made by four different students in my 1998 Shakespeare class:

2.2.559–66

The lines in which Hamlet considers what the player might do if he had experienced Hamlet's loss are quite fascinating. In both Q1 and Q2 Hamlet suggests that the player would respond to his loss in similar ways—ways that would demonstrate his extreme pain—and Hamlet uses strong, even terrible, words and images to describe these responses (which vary between editions). In both Q1 and Q2 Hamlet says that the player would weep, but in Q1 the player would weep "droppes of blood." In both Q1 and Q2 the player would amaze the crowd with his words, but in Q2 these words are emphasized as "horrid." Both Q1 and Q2 have the same phrase, "Confound the ignorant," but Q1 then mentions the "iudiciall ears" of the audience. It is possible that here "judicial" was meant to suggest "generall eare," as written in Q2. But "iudiciall" is actually more powerful, as it implies that the audience is judge of the guilty murderer. This would also tie into an alternative reading of the Q2 line indicating that the player would make "mad the guilty, and appale the free." In the Q3 and Q4 editions of this line, the word "appeale" is substituted for "appale." This interpretation seems valid, and would add another twist to the line, for the player (and Hamlet, in commissioning *The Murther of Gonzago*) could indeed be seen as appealing to the free, in the sense of the innocent, to recognize the fault of the guilty.

3.1.92–95

Speech patterns and diction give strong clues within the scene to the shifting balance of power between the two characters and for those characters' individual motivations. In Ophelia's first speech, Q1 reads "when givers grow unkind" as opposed to Q2's "when givers prove unkind." I have chosen "grow" instead of "prove" because "grow" suggests an actual change in Hamlet's behavior over time rather than a change in Ophelia's perception; in contrast, the word "prove" would suggest that Ophelia is approaching Hamlet defensively. Ophelia does not seem to believe in the first lines of the scene that she has been deluded about Hamlet's love for her; she is perplexed when he denies giving her "ought," but she immediately defends her own memory and understanding.

5.2.287–92

Q2 includes Gertrude's motherly gesture of trying to give her handkerchief to wipe off Hamlet's sweat and her request a few lines later, "Come let me wipe thy face," both of which are absent from Q1. These touches in the Second Quarto give more evidence of Gertrude's dotage on Hamlet; however, they contrast a bit with her more impersonal reference to herself as "the Queen" instead of as "thy mother," as in Q1. [. . .] Q2's use of "carouse" to mean "drink" is slightly problematic, because "carouse" has the connotation of drinking to the bottom (*OED*), and if Gertrude really did this, there would be no poison left for Horatio to refer to when planning suicide. It could be argued that she felt the effects of the poison before she was able to drink the whole cup, but in that case she would probably drop the cup. There is more time in Q2 to feel the potential tragedy in Gertrude's drinking of the poison; while in Q1

Claudius tries to stop her too late and tells us that it is the poison after she drinks, in Q2 the dialogue with Claudius before she drinks actually heightens the tension.

5.2.358

F1 includes an interesting last gasp by the dying Hamlet that effectively elaborates his character. When he dies in the F1, Hamlet does *not* conclude, stonily, "The rest is silence," as he does in Q2. He trails off, instead, saying "The rest is silence. O, o, o, o" (F1). When this short groan is added, Hamlet stays in character by not even *dying* quickly or decisively; he says that there will be silence, and yet he continues to make noise. This addition is a rather fitting end to the prince of Denmark.

These examples reveal how a simple compare-contrast assignment, when disguised as a sophisticated editorial exercise, can yield impressive results. Students often have difficulties considering how Shakespeare may be transferred from the page to the stage, but the close reading enforced by this assignment liberates their imaginations in a way Dr. Johnson no doubt could appreciate.

NOTE

Quarto references are to Allen and Muir, folio references are to Kökeritz, other *Hamlet* references are to Evans et al.

Teaching with a Variorum Edition

Frank Nicholas Clary

The New Variorum *Hamlet* that Howard Horace Furness prepared in 1877 was the latest in a line of editions that sought to make possible a fuller understanding of the play by providing detailed collations of the text as well as informative annotations. Although other kinds of *Hamlet* editions provide brief glosses for difficult words and obscure references, which allow readers to move through the play with a degree of confidence, a variorum edition encourages them to examine particular details, to assess the interpretive implications of textual variants, and to consider the relative merits of alternative commentaries. Because the textual situation is so complicated and the histories of commentary and performance so varied, the apparatus Furness provides enriches the study of *Hamlet* in a variety of ways. Students in my undergraduate Shakespeare course, in a research exercise designed to show them the usefulness of this variorum edition, have made important discoveries in their investigations of *Hamlet*.

During the semester, my students read the plays as they appear in *The Riverside Shakespeare*, second edition (Evans et al.). I regularly assign readings from the supplementary apparatus and point out particulars in the appendices from time to time. Throughout the course I remind my students that Shakespeare's plays have been published as well as performed in a variety of ways and that most of the plays are rooted in stories available in other forms. I also screen clips from different productions, which trigger interest in the plurality of interpretations.

During the *Hamlet* unit I make a point of calling attention to G. Blakemore Evans's "Note on the Text," which provides basic information about the three early editions of the play. Evans summarizes the debate over the authenticity of the First Quarto (1603) and assesses the relative merits and independent authority of the Second Quarto (1604–05) and the First Folio (1623). Students also learn that three other quartos appeared before the closing of the theaters and that several players' quartos were printed after the Restoration. Evans gives no further information about these publications, however, and does not mention other editions published after the seventeenth century. Furthermore, though the appendices on stage history and on plays in performance allude to a number of memorable *Hamlet* performances, they provide few details about the versions of the text employed in specific productions. "Textual Notes" identifies sources for modern emendations adopted in the *Riverside* text, but students get no clear impression of the editions from which these emendations come. Furthermore, unless I call specific attention to an emendation during class, it is unlikely that any but the most zealous students will take the time to examine the textual notes. The Furness variorum edition, however, locates the textual collations and the commentary just beneath the text on each page. With this arrangement students may readily check the variants at any time. In addition, because variorum editors provide more detailed information about the many permutations that the text has undergone, students not only get a stronger impression of the variables but also may be led to consider them in relation to the commentary.

By having students work with a variorum edition, I can create opportunities for them to discover a number of important things about the instability of the text, the practices of editors, and the controversies that have arisen over the centuries among Shakespeare's commentators. For example, in the course I have been describing, students are assigned a research-and-analysis exercise (between five and eight typed pages) that involves comparison between their *Riverside* edition of *Hamlet* and the Furness variorum *Hamlet*. After we have read and discussed the play in class, I give them an array of crux passages for closer inspection. First, they examine the *Riverside* annotations and notes on the text. Afterward they study the corresponding collations and commentary in the Furness variorum to assess the differences and to estimate the interpretive consequences of what they discover. For the purposes of this assignment, I have scanned sections of the Furness variorum and made them available to the students as an electronic database, which they can reach through a link on my course Web site (http://academics.smcvt.edu/clary_class). I also place copies of the two-volume variorum on library reserve. In this assignment the students are required to explain how Furness's management of text, collations, and commentary for a brief passage they have selected differs from what they find in the *Riverside* edition. Next they illustrate from the variorum *Hamlet* where and how, in this particular instance, editors have deviated from one another in their representations of the text or in their commentary. After the students have analyzed the specific interpretive consequences of the deviations they have pointed out, they go on to consider broader implications and to assess the pluralism they have discovered as it bears on their understanding of *Hamlet* as an enduring work in the canon of English literature.

One of passages available for this study occurs in the closet scene. Here Hamlet instructs his mother after the Ghost has departed (3.4). At this point Hamlet offers a bit of proverbial wisdom and a directive. The grammar of the lines as they appear in the *Riverside* edition indicates that a word has been omitted in line 169:

> For use almost can change the stamp of nature,
> And either [. . .] the devil or throw him out
> With wondrous potency.   (168–70)

Evans generally employs square brackets to indicate that the enclosed matter represents a departure from the copy text; here, ellipsis signals a gap in the line. He explains in a footnote: "A word seems to be wanting after *either*: for conjectures see the Textual Notes." The textual note in question lists a small number of interpolations that have appeared in editions subsequent to the Q2 copy text (1604): "master (*Q3–4*), curb (*Malone*), quell (*Singer*), shame (*Hudson*), etc. C. J. Monro (*in Cambridge*) *suggests reading* entertain *in place of* either, *a reading strongly argued for by A. S. Cairncross in* SQ, IX (1958)." Evans does not indicate that the *Riverside* emendation (the gap) is not original. In the variorum edition, however, Furness adopts the reading initially proposed by Charles Jennens (ed. 1773) and later embraced by George Steevens (ed. 1785): "And either master the devil, or throw him out." Furness properly attributes this emendation and also identifies the Globe edition (1864) as the point of origin for the editorial solution employed in the *Riverside* text. Furness also notes correctly that the early quartos did not interpolate *master* between *either* and *devil*, which might mistakenly be inferred from the *Riverside* note, but rather printed *Maister* instead of *either*. Furness lists several other conjectural emendations, identifying the edition in which each first appeared. He also lists and attributes emendations not adopted in a published edition.

The *Riverside* editor does not indicate what principle may have guided his selection of suggested emendations, nor does he choose among them. Though his arrangement of alternatives is simply chronological, Evans appears to privilege Munro's by citing a "strongly argued" essay that endorses it. Even though *entertain* is clearly antithetical to the four other suggested emendations, the editor does not comment on the interpretive implications of choosing one over another. Unless I call attention to this particular passage, students typically overlook this textual crux entirely. The *Riverside* editor, by foregrounding a perceived omission while not adopting one of the conjectural emendations, appears both responsible and unintrusive. However, he has not provided readers with a rationale for filling the gap he has opened up.

Furness, however, assembles several excerpts of the arguments made by commentators who have proposed or defended one or another reading. At a glance, students can see the line in question, the variants listed below the text, and the opening section of the commentary, which runs an additional page and a quarter. Beginning with the editorial annotations of Malone and Steevens, students can read the arguments for *curb*, based on the requirements of meter as well as sense and supported by a parallel passage in *The Merchant of Venice*. They can also consider the cases made for other interpolations, at least two of which speculate that a sound effect may have led the compositor to omit a particular word. Most explanations, however, wrestle with the question of whether the omitted word, in combination with *either*, is to be thought of as antithetical to *throw him out* (as *aid*, *throne*, or *lodge* are) or simply conjunctive (as *foil*, *thwart*, and *rouse* are). Among the solutions to this problem, students notice that Furness includes Munro's emendation but only as a friendly and "half-serious" suggestion made to Clement Mansfield Ingleby for inclusion in *Shakespeare Hermeneutics* (1875). Furness, in fact, concludes his note on Ingleby's general assessment of the controversy:

> We can hardly say that conjecture has yet determined the best reading here, though it cannot be said that sufficient indications are wanting for

its guidance. Unfortunately, it is in the very nature of the case that some doubt should continue to vex this passage, after conjecture has done its work.   (1: 304–05)

Though Furness does not openly advocate for the emendation he has chosen ("And either master the devil, or throw him out"), any more than Evans does for his, the variorum commentary puts readers in an excellent position to understand a number of important things: about the possibility that errors may exist in an otherwise authoritative version of the text, about the ways editors and commentators reason toward conjectural emendations, about the assumptions held by some commentators concerning printing-house practices, and about considerations that editors as well as noneditorial commentators have entertained in their various efforts to "restore the original text."

Students in my Shakespeare class have provided ample evidence that variorum readership is not limited to advanced scholars but is designed for all readers, including students, willing to take *Hamlet* and all its difficulties seriously. One student's recent assessment of an editorial conjecture that one brief passage traditionally assigned to Hamlet (4.4.24–28) originally belonged to the Norwegian captain was a model of close reading and careful analysis. More meaningful than the fact that there have been controversies over line assignments in *Hamlet*, this narrowly focused hands-on exercise led this student to discover for herself the interpretive consequences of textual emendation.

The Furness variorum, used in conjunction with *The Riverside Shakespeare*, serves very nicely for the exercise I have described. A New Variorum *Hamlet*, however, is currently in preparation and will be published by the MLA (the editorial team includes Bernice W. Kliman, Eric Rasmussen, Frank Nicholas Clary, and Hardin Aasand). This new edition will offer more details from a longer editorial history and survey a broader array of commentaries. It will also include information on the history of *Hamlet* acting editions, which will enable readers to investigate the relation between page and stage and to appreciate the way these editions occupy an important theoretical space between text and performance. The team that is preparing this print version of the New Variorum *Hamlet* is also constructing an electronic version of considerably larger proportions. This electronic variorum, for example, will contain full-text transcriptions of commentaries that are summarized or excerpted in the print version. A full transcription of the first Restoration acting edition of *Hamlet* as well as a collation of passages omitted or marked for omission on the stage in an array of other representative acting editions will be included as well. Linked and searchable, the electronic database will also be expandable after its initial release. Until these two versions of the newest variorum *Hamlet* are available, teachers may use the resources currently accessible. Exercises like the one I have briefly illustrated make it possible for young scholars not only to make discoveries about *Hamlet* for themselves but also to appreciate the fact that this play, as a site of countless realizations and reproductions, remains open for their further investigations.

Teaching *Hamlet* through Translation

Jesús Tronch-Pérez

Many would agree that teaching *Hamlet* to students for whom English is a second language would benefit from approaching the play in its original language. How otherwise could students fully appreciate its verbal texture, rhythms, ambiguities, puns, and other artistic exploitation of language? Yet this paper proposes ways in which the use of translation into the students' first language alongside the original can be an approach to the teaching of *Hamlet*, especially the teaching of its formal aspects (verbal, stylistic, dramatic), since focusing on translation entails concentrating on the manipulation of language.

By the use of translation I mean both the students' analysis of translations and their active translating of Shakespeare's play text. On the one hand, published translations can be compared in order for students to perceive different interpretations of the original, especially in cases of ambiguity. The differences among translated versions may prompt students to find out why they have come about, to describe and evaluate the effects of those differences in terms of poetic intensity, a character's attitude, and construction of character or scenic building. On the other hand, the challenge of translating Shakespeare, or any literary work of art, drives students into a more conscious appreciation of the way every word, sentence, speech, and dialogue sequence was wrought. That a translation is as good a critical exercise as an explication de texte is an opinion I have often heard from my mentors and one my own teaching experience has confirmed. I hope the following examples will convince the reader also of this.

One of the main features that students discover on comparing translations is that some appear in prose (such as the well-known Spanish translations by Luis Astrana Marín and by José M. Valverde, both of the complete Shakespeare canon), while others are in verse (such as Alvaro Custodio's version and the one produced by the Instituto Shakespeare, a team of translators based in Valencia). This prose-verse difference may prompt students to discuss the value and uses of verse as a formal mode of dramatic speech in Shakespeare and Elizabethan drama in general, and in *Hamlet* in particular. Prose translations do not allow the pleasure of hearing highly patterned speech and subtle changes in rhythm; they cannot reproduce the shifts from prose to verse and vice versa as devices for characterization; for emphasis; and for changes of tone, attitude, and style. In act 2, scene 2, Hamlet, after speaking in prose, delivers his soliloquy in blank verse. In Ophelia's speech beginning "Oh what a noble mind is here o'erthrown!" (3.1.144), a passionate but smooth and controlled utterance of lament is expressed in formal, regular blank verse that contrasts with the violent and convulsed prose of the "nunnery scene"—or, as Philip Edwards sees it, the speech shows Ophelia's sanity "against the disordered prose of Hamlet's madness" (151). Leandro Fernández de Moratín's and

Valverde's prose translations, however, render in unrhymed verse the high-pitched lines of the speech on Pyrrhus's story and the couplets of the play within the play.

With verse translations, students may observe that metrical pattern is not the same. Some translations keep to a rigid eleven-syllable-per-line pattern (Macpherson, Custodio) in an attempt to follow the pentameter scheme of blank verse, while others use a kind of free verse or loose verse (Instituto Shakespeare, Molina Foix). These solutions may lead students to discuss the nature of blank verse in *Hamlet* and how it may be transposed into Spanish. Since ten syllables in English usually give more information than ten or eleven syllables in Spanish, translations adopting a strict eleven-syllable pattern need to increase the number of lines per speech. In order to keep the same number of lines in a speech, the translated line usually must stretch to twelve, fourteen, or sixteen syllables. Such expanded lines present a more irregular pattern than blank verse does, but if the play of line is important in the building of a dramatic verse speech (Wright, *Metrical Art* 213–28), this system has the advantage of preserving the flexibility of the original speech structure, its enjambment, its end-line and mid-line pauses, and the changes of mood and pace that fit into its overall rhythm.

If it is stylistically important to observe in Ophelia's verse speech (3.1.144–55) that all lines are end-stopped except

> That unmatched form and feature of blown youth
> Blasted with ecstasy.   (153–54)

a verse translation may achieve a similar effect if it preserves the same number of lines. Students may compare Custodio's translation—that renders the twelve original lines in fifteen lines, five of which are not end-stopped—with the twelve-line version of the Instituto Shakespeare.

And if it is important that "blown youth" be placed on the emphatic final position of the line, and that the enjambment create a certain suspense out of the slight pause after "youth" only to fall heavily on "Blasted" as a culminating participle that sums up the description of Hamlet's state, a verse translation may re-create this subtle effect by leaving equivalents to "blown youth | Blasted" in these positions. Students may observe this re-creation in the Instituto Shakespeare version:

> Aquellas formas incomparables de su florida juventud
> se han marchitado con el delirio.   (363)

but not in Custodio's translation:

> ¡Aquel rostro y figura incomparables
> de juventud en flor ahora marchitos
> por el desvarío!   (206)

Through translation other verbal features of *Hamlet* come to the fore, such as wordplay, unusual and nonce words, repetition of keywords and echoes.

Puns are always a challenge in translation. Students may be prompted to suggest translating solutions to moments such as Hamlet's first interventions in the play:

A little more than kin, and less than kind.   (1.2.65)

Not so my lord, I am too much i'th'sun.   (1.2.67)

The task of translating these lines leads students to think of what they mean, in what context they appear, why Hamlet replies in this particular way, the ambiguity of *kind* in the senses "Affectionate, loving," "nature in general," and "family" (Onions 148), and the question of whether Hamlet's words at line 65 refer to the king or to himself (see Furness 1: 33–34 for the controversy over this). Students are also led to appreciate stylistic aspects such as the repetition of *k-n*, the syntactic parallelism, the antithesis "more than / less than" and the homophonic play on *sun = son*.

Published translations can be looked at in order for students to assess how translators have dealt with these problems. The first quoted line Fernández de Moratín translates into "Algo más que deudo y menos que amigo" (7), a literal rendering except for the last word, which is "friend," thus emphasizing the sense of *kind* as benevolence. Guillermo Macpherson's "Más que deudo tal vez; deudor en nada" (282 [1909]) ("More than kin, in nothing debtor") reproduces the alliteration with "deudo" and "deudor" but creates a new idea with "in nothing debtor," which suggests that Hamlet is implicitly refusing to have anything to do with the king.

Astrana Marín's "Un poco menos que primado y un poco más que primo" (33) ("A little less than prelate, and a little more than cousin") preserves the play on the repeated sounds with "primado" and "primo" and takes *kind* in the sense of "family." Because Astrana Marín has chosen to reproduce the alliteration, he has had to find a word similar to "primo" and to justify the presence of a word ("primado") that has nothing to do with kinship. He alters the previous line spoken by the king to "Y ahora Hamlet, primado de mi trono, y mi hijo [. . .]" ("And now Hamlet, prelate to my throne, and my son [. . .]"), thus anticipating the king's declaration that Hamlet is "the most immediate to our throne" at line 109.

Valverde's version is "Un poco más que pariente y menos que padre" (12) (a literal rendering, except for the last word, which means "father"), which retains the alliteration *pariente = pa*dre but implies that this riddling sentence refers to the king and not to Hamlet himself.

The play of sound seems to have been Custodio's main option "Parentesco un tanto pintoresco" (160) ("A rather picturesque kinship"), which overlooks the enigmatic antithesis "more than kin [. . .] less than kind" and maintains the ambiguity about the addressee of these words. The Instituto Shakespeare's

"Algo más que deudo y menos que hijo" (a literal translation, with the last word meaning "son") has not paid much attention to the repetition of sounds in the line, although there is repetition inasmuch as Hamlet reiterates the king's words in the previous line:

Y tú Hamlet, deudo mío y también hijo [. . .]   (121)

But now my cousin Hamlet, and my son—   (1.2.64)

For two pairs of correlative but different words in English, *cousin* and *kin* —cousin in the sense of "a kinsman or kinswoman, a relative," as the *OED* defines it (def. 1)—and *son* and *kind*, the Instituto Shakespeare maintains the first two words, *cousin* and *son*, thus creating an echo that reinforces Hamlet's wry and provocative words—as Hamlet's "inky cloak" shows a "defiant mourning brought to a Council called for the attesting of his [the king's] marriage" (Granville-Barker, *Hamlet* 56). Repeating the words of one's interlocutor is an efficient rhetorical device for tart replies and jests, and Hamlet makes use of it throughout the play.

In "Not so my lord, I am too much i'th'sun" (1.2.67), the pun *sun* = *son*, which J. D. Wilson judges as "direct, defiant and (to Elizabethan ears) unambiguous" (*What Happens* 32–33), is impossible to reproduce. Most translators have opted for the basic sense of *sun* (*sol* in Spanish), which maintains the enigmatic character of the phrase "I am too much i'th'sun" (see Furness 34–35; Jenkins 435–36). English and Spanish speakers belong to cultures close enough to understand the values of brightness, sunshine of the royal favor, and sun as royal emblem. The punning reference to "the son" can only be, and has been, accomplished by means of a note.

Multiple interpretations spring not only from wordplay. In act 1, scene 1, "What, has this thing appeared again tonight?" (21), there is an interesting moment, to which the issue of textual variation is added. Students may observe that Fernández de Moratín's translation's

MARCELO. Y que, ¿se ha vuelto a aparecer aquella cosa esta noche?
(3 [1977])

differs from Astrana's

MARCELO. Y qué, ¿se ha vuelto a aparecer eso esta noche?   (23 [1922])

They differ in the rendering of "this thing": "Aquella cosa" (lit. "that thing') and "eso" (lit. "that"). But they agree in assigning the line to Marcelo, unlike the Instituto Shakespeare's rendering:

HORACIO. Decidme, ¿volvió a aparecerse eso esta noche?   (87)

The divergence in the speech prefix ultimately derives from the fact that the Second Quarto assigns this line to Horatio, while the First Folio and the First Quarto give it to Marcellus.

Students may be asked to comment on the different effects of these lines and their prefixes, first bearing in mind the dramatic situation of each character. On the one hand, Horatio will show certain skepticism toward the Ghost. As Edward Capell observed, "The levity of the expression, and the question itself, are suited to the unbelieving but eager Horatio." The German scholar Benno Tschischwitz remarked that Horatio's allusion to the ghost as "the thing" showed "contempt and doubt." On the other hand, Marcellus is "more forward in his zeal to convince Horatio of the truth of his story" (Elze; Capell, Tschischwitz, and Elze are all qtd. in Furness 6), so that the line assigned to him becomes an "anxious enquiry" (Edwards 76).

Taking these interpretations into account, students may be asked to provide their own translation for act 1, scene 1, line 21, and compare it with the ones they know. The translation of "this thing" is an interesting point of discussion. If spoken by Horatio, it may be interpreted as showing "skeptical mockery" (Hibbard 144). Students may then seek a Spanish expression conveying this particular attitude, for which the demonstrative pronoun "eso" is a pertinent word. For literally minded translators, the closest equivalent to "this thing" in Spanish would be "esta cosa." The use of *cosa* may indicate disdain, but the repetition of the demonstrative *esta* at the end of the sentence in "esta noche" ("tonight") would advise against its adoption on euphonic grounds. *Eso* is employed, among other usages, when referring to something, or even someone, that is unpleasant, raises suspicions, is looked down on, or is not very welcome. Moreover, its neuter gender suits the reference to the "apparition"—a term that is heard a little later (line 28)—as well as the use of "it" to refer to this "spirit" (except in the Second Quarto in line 43).

If spoken by Marcellus, "this thing" may be taken as expressing his apprehension, his reluctance to call the Ghost or spirit as such. He will later refer to it as "this dreaded sight" (line 25). We have seen that translating "this thing" into "esta cosa" does make the sentence cacophonous, and the use of *cosa* would sound rather too strong to convey a sense of dread. The neuter demonstrative *esto* is a possibility, since it does not carry the negative connotations *eso* does, and leaving the sentence without a subject—perfectly possible in Spanish—could also be a valid alternative, as in

MARCELO. Y qué, ¿se ha vuelto a aparecer esta noche?

There is no explicit subject in this sentence; only the verbal ending makes it clear that it is in the third person and singular. The speaker's omission of the subject may indicate an anxious reticence about referring to the dreaded apparition.

Students may then evaluate published translations that have Marcellus as the speaker. Fernández de Moratín's version "aquella cosa" ("that thing"), with the demonstrative *aquella* indicating the most distant thing and toning down the reflex sense of contempt that *cosa* has, may be seen as suitable to Marcellus's state of mind. Custodio's translation reads

>   MARCELO. ¿Ha aparecido otra vez esa cosa?   (154)

with no indication of "tonight" and with "esa cosa," which would be more appropriate, in my opinion, to Horatio, although an actor can equally convey anxiety and apprehension by saying "esa cosa."

It is interesting to note that, while the same wording "What, hath this thing appeared again tonight?" (the Folio version with "has" instead of "hath") can yield different interpretations depending on the character speaking them, the same wording in Spanish may be assigned to different characters. Both Astrana Marín and the Instituto Shakespeare use the term *eso*, but their character speaking is different.

The use of translation could also be valuable for native speakers of English, inasmuch as they can observe how differently a single reading in English (a double reading, in the Marcellus/Horatio line) can be interpreted. The variations will suggest to them the multiple possibilities for the line in English, as we have seen in "A little more than kin, and less than kind" (1.2.65).

More specific examples could be given, but I hope this selection has illustrated an approach to teaching *Hamlet* by prompting students to consider a variety of stylistic and pragmatic aspects of the original through a discussion of how a fragment of text can be and has been translated.

NOTE

Line numbers are from Edwards. Bibliographic information for references to translations is given in the appendix to this paper.

Appendix
Translations into Spanish

Astrana Marín, Luis, trans. *Hamlet*. Madrid: Calpe, 1920, 1922. S.A. de Promoción y Edición, Club Internacional del Libro, 1992.

Custodio, Alvaro, trans. *Hamlet*. 1968. Tarragona: Tarraco, 1977.

Fernández de Moratín, Leandro, trans. Hamlet. *Tragedia de Guillermo Shakespeare. Traducida é ilustrada con la vida del autor y notas críticas por Inarco Celenio*. Madrid: Villalpando, 1798. Ibérica, 1965. Buenos Aires: Porrúa, 1977. Cincel, 1980.

Instituto Shakespeare, trans. *Hamlet*. Valencia: Fundación Instituto Shakespeare, 1989. Madrid: Cátedra, 1992.

Macpherson, Guillermo, trans. *Hamlet, príncipe de Dinamarca*. Cádiz: Imp. y Litografía de la Revista Médica de D. Federico de Joly, 1873. *Shakespeare: Obras dramáticas*. Vol. 3. Madrid: Perlado, Páez y Cía, 1909.

Molina Foix, Vicente, trans. and adapt. Hamlet. *William Shakespeare*. Madrid: Centro Dramático Nacional, 1989.

Valverde, José M., trans. *William Shakespeare: Teatro completo*. Barcelona: Planeta, 1967. *William Shakespeare:* Hamlet *[and]* Macbeth. Clásicos Universales Planeta, 1980.

Exploring *Hamlet*:
Opening Play Texts, Closing Performances

Edward L. Rocklin

Prologue: Primary Objective and Key Practice

Perhaps the most concise way for me to introduce this suite of activities for teaching *Hamlet* is to note some facts about my class, articulate the primary objective, and describe the key practice through which students achieve that objective. In my upper-division Shakespeare courses, I have twenty-five to thirty students, meeting for two 110-minute classes each week for ten weeks, for a total of slightly over thirty-six hours. The primary objective is for students to learn to translate between the two languages of drama. One language is the text of the play, what Susanne Langer has called the *"commanding form,"* which mandates what must happen, what must be said, and in what order, thereby defining what is left open to the inventions of the actors and director (385). The second language is the medium of action, embodied in the disciplined engagement of actors and directors with that commanding form, who experiment in order to invent elements not specified by the text. I initiate the process by which students become more fluent in these languages and in translating from one language to the other by teaching them to ask the key question, "What does x do?," where x is any element of the play.

What Does a Beginning Do? Segmenting a Scene

In the traditional literary study of drama, the opening of a play is called the exposition, and students learn to ask, "What is the exposition of this play?"

Framing this as a "What is *x*?" question, however, perpetuates a static model of reading that runs counter to the dynamics of drama and to the spectator's experience of the play as a temporal event. If students learn to ask, "What does the beginning do?," they can develop better analyses of the opening. Thus I start by asking that students segment the opening scene of *Hamlet*, noting that typically people find from four to twelve segments. I call these audience segments, to indicate that this type of analysis focuses on how spectators might divide the scene, not on the "beat" that actors often use in analyzing scenes. As the students share segmentings, we discuss what seems to make a group of speeches a unit, what each unit does, and what signals a shift from one unit to another. And as they lay out contrasting segmentings, students engage in a discussion that enables them to produce detailed analyses of what the beginning of *Hamlet* does.

Reexploring the Play's Design: Examining the Act-Scene Divisions

Reexploring the play's design offers a chance to examine some larger temporal patterns. As the "Note on the Text" in *The Riverside Shakespeare* (1235) informs us, the first quartos have no act-scene divisions, and the folio marks only 1.1 through 1.3 and 2.1 through 2.2; all other act-scene divisions are supplied by later editors. The *Riverside* text follows the divisions suggested by Edward Capell (1235), but Capell's work is hardly sacrosanct and in fact creates problems. The assignment, therefore, is to reexamine the text in order to suggest other possible act divisions. I start this activity by focusing on the way the traditional editing begins "act 4" at a point where there may be no need for an exit by Gertrude, let alone a scene or act division. This work can set up other activities that examine the play as a completed rather than an evolving event, with its patterns fully visible. It also opens the door to examining how Shakespeare's plays in general and this play in particular have been, are being, and should or should not be edited.

Exploring Speech as Action and Action as Speech: Opening Act 1, Scene 2

Next, we focus on what happens when we witness the opening scenes of a play that is new to us and on the way we learn who the characters are and what their speeches mean by what they do. Responding to a prompt developed by Miriam Gilbert, students explore 1.2 by reducing the first part of Claudius's opening speech (1.2.1–16) to a telegram (605–06). Once they discover the skeleton of the speech through sharing telegrams, students move into a more precise analysis of what Claudius is trying to do through the semantics, syntax, and pragmatics of his speech. Conversely, we look at Hamlet's entrance and dress as his first "speech" in the scene, functioning as his silent attack on the king, queen, and court of Denmark. In short, students work to master the essential task of analyzing speech as action and action as speech.

Showing and Telling: The Dramatist's Choices in Act 2, Scene 1

Intriguingly, as 2.1 unfolds, it forces spectators to recognize that in a sense they have witnessed two scenes, because even as Polonius is directing Reynaldo to spy on Laertes, Hamlet, we soon learn, is visiting Ophelia in her closet. When she appears, Ophelia's twenty-two line speech compels us to imagine that encounter in our mind's eye. For this activity, I ask one student to read Ophelia's part while two others mime the action described. We do this straight through and then begin to invent stagings in order to imagine different meanings the scene might have for Ophelia and Hamlet. Next, we perform the Ophelia-Polonius scene itself, concentrating on the choices students can imagine Ophelia making. Overtly, Ophelia obeys her father's orders, but as feminist critics have insisted, she may not be the "chaste, silent, and obedient" woman Elizabethan conduct books extolled (Hull 142, see also 31, 81, 125, 135). For example, students will discover that Ophelia's choices might manifest themselves in how she does or does not obey her father in something as simple as her responses to his repeated command "Come" (98, 114, 117).

Staging the Duel: Opening Play Texts, Closing Performances

From the beginning of the course, I suggest that one reason to consider questions of performance is that the choices made by the performers create the experience from which the spectators re-create an imaginative vision. In the last scene of a play, these choices complete patterns enacted in that performance and thereby prompt the spectators to create a whole from what has been an emerging gestalt. For *Hamlet*, students analyze 5.2 from the moment the court assembles to the end of the play. In particular, they are to locate the major choice points and to suggest primary production options for each choice point. In class we enumerate choice points, survey choices, invent new combinations, and explore what meanings these imagined stagings might prompt spectators to articulate. Reflecting on these choices, students also consider the play's universe as it manifests itself in alternative performances. They thus begin to delineate possible productions that the text as blueprint makes possible. Articulating this range of producible interpretations, in turn, offers them a useful vantage from which to reflect on literary interpretations of the play.

What If the Ghost Came Back?

This exploration of choice points becomes the ground for examining another option the dramatist had in completing the play's design, namely, to bring back the Ghost. "Imagine that, as the body of Hamlet is borne off, followed by Fortinbras, Horatio, and the Danish court, the Ghost of Hamlet's father reappears. He turns upstage and stands motionless, watching the procession. What would his final appearance do?" Students often start by suggesting that the Ghost would seem to return in triumph, and he might make some gesture that would indicate that his command has been honored. Furthermore, he might exit upward or to the second level—an ascent to "heaven" which might imply that the son's action has finally freed the father's spirit. But students also see that an unresting Ghost might be disturbing, suggesting that the destruction of the Danish royal family and the Danish court, embodied in the family of Polonius, was too high a price to pay for revenge. Indeed, we might be prompted to ask, "Is the Ghost also a victim of ironic reversal?" In discussion, students realize that if the Ghost came back he would underline the mystery about the design embodied in the play's universe. To complete their exploration, students reflect on the choice Shakespeare did make, asking, "What do the final actions of Fortinbras do?"

Epilogue: Reading Differently

When I share these activities with colleagues, they sometimes ask how I respond to students who suggest wild or implausible stagings. One of my responses is that what interests me when students make "wild" leaps is precisely the way in which thinking about performance opens up a play for them and, moreover, the way in which, like actors, students can only delimit the boundaries by sometimes exceeding them. Students may indeed imagine stagings we think of as unproducible or as producible but invalid, but as they begin to translate between the two languages, they are mastering a type of engagement with a Shakespeare play different from that proposed by a more literary model of reading. When their mastery of both languages develops, their engagement with the performance text enriches and sharpens their interpretation of the literary text. And as they learn to speak more fluently in the languages of the page and the stage, students become better able to accept the invitation to disciplined creativity that a play text offers all its readers.

NOTE

Hamlet quotations are from Evans et al.

To Challenge Ghostly Fathers: Teaching *Hamlet* and Its Interpretations through Film and Video

Stephen M. Buhler

In recent years, my students and I have enjoyed great success and fun in the classroom with film depictions of the Ghost in *Hamlet*. What prompted me to have students join in examining this "ghostly father" more closely was a presentation by Peter S. Donaldson at the 1993 Shakespeare Association of America meeting in Atlanta. As Donaldson demonstrated the capabilities of the Shakespeare Interactive Archive, then in development, he focused on Laurence Olivier's and Franco Zeffirelli's very different cinematic realizations of *Hamlet* 1.5. The overt purpose of screening these excerpts was to show the archive's potential in linking an edited text with folio and quarto versions and with film or video performances thereof; the audience was justifiably impressed with the connectivity at work among these digitized renderings. There was, in addition, a ghost in the machine: I found that I was most deeply impressed by Donaldson's interest in the ontological issues raised—and the dramatic dilemmas temporarily resolved—by the directors' competing visions. (For another teacher's response to Donaldson, see Saeger 274–76.)

What kind of supernatural being is presented by Shakespeare's play texts to the reader, the viewer, the auditor? An answer to that question almost necessarily affects a number of related problems. How seriously are we to take Hamlet's anxieties over the Ghost's honesty: are his suspicions that the apparition (apparently of a "pleasing shape" [2.2.578]) is a disguised demon merely an excuse? Or is the Ghost's fulfillment of Hamlet's deepest fears and desires ("O my prophetic soul! Mine uncle?" [1.5.41]) grounds sufficiently relative for skepticism? How do Catholic pieties toward souls in purgatory strike a post-Reformation—indeed, a post-Wittenberg—sensibility? Donaldson's compelling contrast between Olivier's threatening presence and Zeffirelli's mournful revenant led me to consider other realizations of the Ghost and prompted me to use the old mole as an opportunity for students to discover these issues and grapple with them. In class I've shown excerpts from Tony Richardson's 1968 filmed stage version, from Kenneth Branagh's 1996 full-text rendering, and even the related scene from the Disney Studios' 1994 animated feature *The Lion King*, along with the Olivier and Zeffirelli versions.

As students come to Olivier's 1948 exercise in Shakespeare as film noir, they have to surmount a series of cultural obstacles. I have never experienced in the classroom the immediate derision aimed at this version that we see depicted in *Last Action Hero*: despite an impassioned introduction by the young protagonist's English teacher (as played by none other than Joan Plowright, Olivier's widow), most of Danny's classmates howl at what they see as the artificial acting, the primitive production values, and—most unforgivable of all—the absence of color in the film. Several of my students have, however, shared in some of the prejudices that can prompt such a contemptuous response. The presentation of the Ghost, especially, can strike today's filmgoers as amateurish in conception and execution. That resistance, though, can lead to strong insights. By fore-grounding the possible differences between the representational and the illu-sionistic, one can open up the discussion to include issues of what is being represented by means that viewers might initially find unconvincing. These means include the pulse of Olivier's sound track and throbbing camera work; the fog that blurs distinctions between castle and air, between self and other; the dis-passionate voice of the Ghost, supplied by Olivier himself and unconnected with any movement from the apparition's mouth. Even when some students see these elements as failed attempts at realism, they can entertain the possibility that something else is being represented by them: in response they have suggested that the scene portrays a troubled relationship between Hamlet and his father and that it raises the possibility that the Ghost is far more psychological than real.

In contrast to such modernist takes on Freud and such Protestant skepti-cism, a tender piety pervades the presentation of the Ghost in Zeffirelli's 1989 film version. A physical presence is established in part by having a recognizably authoritative actor, Paul Scofield, in the role. His rueful, weary, almost resigned delivery of the lines adds to the poignance conveyed by the Ghost's age and frailty: Hamlet Senior remains vulnerable, even in death. Students have commented on how such a depiction makes it easier to accept the idea that this is indeed a spirit subject to purgatorial sufferings. One classroom exchange built upon this insight to consider whether a less doubtful and uncer-tain view of the Ghost would put Hamlet's later indecision in a more negative light. Students acutely noted that inaction would hardly be a serious concern with Mel Gibson, Zeffirelli's choice as prince of Denmark.

Tony Richardson diminished the Ghost's presence even more than Olivier had done. Here the spirit is almost *manes absconditus*: a horrid clanging, a whispered voice, and a bright light reflected on the faces of his auditors. In this version, the response to Hamlet's father signifies far more than his father's words and (semi)appearance do. Classroom discussion has explored the cul-tural contexts of the production—notably the fateful year 1968, with its student uprisings—and their possible role in removing the father as much as possible. Other observers have drawn interesting comparisons between the polarities established by Olivier's and Zeffirelli's treatment of the Ghost and those sug-gested by Richardson's version and that of Kenneth Branagh. For his 1996 film, Branagh follows in Zeffirelli's tradition but intensifies the physicality of the Ghost. This is achieved, to no small extent, by borrowing from *Don Giovanni* and having a heroic statue of Hamlet Senior come to life for his first visitations. It is also achieved by casting Brian Blessed, the formidable Exeter of Branagh's *Henry V*, in the role. Despite the certainty the audience has concerning the Ghost's existence, Branagh introduces elements of doubt as to what Hamlet does with its story. Olivier's camera explicitly enters the prince's skull: the visual depiction of the murder that follows the words is therefore marked as Hamlet's own imaginative response. One student contrasted this device with Branagh's more open, less determinate use of flashbacks throughout his film. She wondered if we ever know whether these are independent versions of events or whether they are always limited by one character's (and which one's?) recollection. In this case, does Branagh present us with an objective record, with Hamlet Senior's own memory (and posthumous reconstruction), or with young Hamlet's construction of the deed? Unlike the credit and trust granted to Zeffirelli's Ghost, more than a hint of doubt and danger often impinges on Branagh's understanding of the character—sentiments reinforced, at the end of the film, by the dismantling of Hamlet Senior's statue, a visual echo of the end of the Stalinist cult of personality.

No such doubt registers in Disney's *The Lion King*: here we have an unambiguously "honest ghost" (*Hamlet* 1.5.142). Simba, the film's leonine protagonist, is even more reluctant to take action than the conventional view of Hamlet's character suggests. Far from bemoaning that the time is out of joint and that he was born to set it right, he rejects his role as scourge and minister for some time. A major factor in this refusal is Simba's sense of guilt for his father's death. The Disney version of events has sanitized the Freudian response to *Hamlet*: while Claudius can be seen as inspiring oedipal guilt and envy in the prince of Denmark, *The Lion King* has its villain intentionally deflect guilt upon the hero. In the play, the appearance of his father's ghost sends Hamlet into utter turmoil and toward his tragic end; in contrast, the spirit that appears to the newly mature Simba initiates the resolution of his problems and hastens him toward the obligatory happy ending. Mufasa, the murdered father, does not urge, "Remember me"; rather, the ghost insists that Simba "remember" who he is, repeating the word not only at the end of his apparition but again after Simba's struggle with Scar, the feature's Claudius figure. Instead of the fatal scene which "cries on havoc" (5.2.308) even to martial Fortinbras, we are witness to a renewed "Circle of Life" (as the Elton John and Tim Rice song puts it) under the reign of a supernaturally sanctioned monarch.

During the summer of 1995, I led a graduate seminar entitled Shakespeare, Performance, and Pedagogy at the University of Nebraska, Lincoln. The group was almost evenly split between English department graduate students and active secondary school teachers, with one middle school and one community college instructor also in attendance. As we went through these "ghostly fathers" excerpts and discussed their possible applications to high school and college classrooms, the Disney sequence threatened indeed to take the lion's share of the discussion's focus. This was not due to any consensus that *The Lion King* would appeal widely to students; several teachers noted that a perception of childishness or of being "taught down to" might work against the exercise. Instead, what intrigued many of the seminar's participants was the clarity provided by what the Disney version scrupulously left out. As one observed, the adapters didn't misunderstand *Hamlet*—they understood it very well and wanted to avoid many of the complexities, ambiguities, undercurrents, and ambivalences the play's texts offer.

That insight, I think, can be applied to all performance versions of this play, including its many film and video versions. Performances are interpretations: some are more open or wide-ranging than others, but all are engaged in the act of answering at least some of the questions posed by the play. As each performance embodies certain answers, it casts a shadow composed of the alternative answers not acted upon. Such are the ghosts—figures both of presence and of loss—that attend any performance, any interpretation. Since my own focus on the ghostly father in film versions could avoid considerations of Gertrude, the vital mother in *Hamlet*, I devote another class session to her character and Hamlet's complicated responses to her; I also try to foreground the processes by which one interpretive emphasis downplays or obscures other approaches. With time, most students can admit their fascination with this strange, spectral world of shifting perspectives and, as a stranger, give it welcome.

NOTE

Hamlet quotations are from Greenblatt et al.

Critical Practice through Performance:
The Nunnery and Play Scenes

Mary Judith Dunbar

Scholarly study of Shakespeare in performance, especially since the 1960s, has given fresh stimulus and rigor to teaching Shakespeare through performance. Performance work, like critical reading, requires close attention to language and involves interpretive acts. Students who explore short segments of *Hamlet* through performance intensively can develop keen awareness of the play's crucial conflicts and inquire into complex problems.

Performance work, if pursued rigorously, prompts inquiry into scholarship and criticism. Students become aware that since any modern text of *Hamlet* is an edited version of a script written for performance, they need to evaluate selected editorial choices, editorial stage directions, and folio and quarto variants, including significant differences in wording and punctuation. Making performance decisions, students also begin to see what is at stake in questions related to Elizabethan staging, dramatic conventions, Shakespearean stagecraft, and stage history. And students begin to see how dramatic poetry or prose offers cues for action, blocking, timing, gesture, speech, pause, and silence. Patrick Stewart, as associate artist of the Royal Shakespeare Company, said of teaching Shakespeare that he wants to help students perceive "everything that is contained within a script [. . .] verse form, rhythm, meter, construction, style and imagery, punctuation. All of these are not simply poetical abstractions, but actors' aids, tools, to help us."[1]

It is important to clarify for the students in an English department the aim of this kind of performance work. They are not evaluated on acting ability; they are challenged to become more astute readers, listeners, speakers and more critically informed viewers. Engaged in critical practice through performance, students become alert to differences between dramatic language and poetry or prose not written for theatrical performance; to specific, changing rhetorical contexts of language in moment-to-moment dramatic situations; and to the language's performative possibilities. In such critical acts, students become makers as well as discoverers of richly layered potential meaning. In their learning through the process of performance, there is an atmosphere of rehearsal, of trial and error, of investigating the play. Sharp focus on short units of action respects limits of time and student experience and allows language to be explored in detail, close textual comparisons to be made, and alternative versions of the same segment to be presented during a class session with opportunity for discussion and trying new options. Evaluative questions include the following: With what quality of commitment did particular students work? To what extent did the work sharpen their awareness of language and their grasp of crucial interpretive and textual debates? How perceptively could they discuss important ideas about the play and justify their performance decisions from the text in postperformance discussions and in subsequent essays?

While time can be given to in-class performance workshops (usually with students in pairs or small groups), students can choose performance work as an option for small group presentations, working outside class time to prepare their scenes and, as I often request, the written scene analysis outlines that they use, after their in-class performances, to guide discussion of their interpretive discoveries and decisions. I frequently work outside class with groups who are preparing in-class presentations, sometimes with two groups on the same scene, encouraging contrasts in the approaches being developed by each group. Student groups normally decide on their own casting. Some (especially for the play scene) use a student director; in others, the actors together determine the direction of their scene. Students memorize lines; if they cannot be off book completely, they may (but it happens rarely) carry a photocopy of the scene for reference if needed. Students bring in necessary hand properties stipulated in the script and use appropriate adaptations of ordinary dress, not elaborate costumes.

The nunnery and play scenes are rich sites for discussion in class of textual, theatrical, and critical debates focused on problems students need to be aware of in the allied acts of critical reading and performance work. Prior to Hamlet's "Soft you, now, / The fair Ophelia!" (3.1.90–91),[2] if Ophelia has been on stage during the "To be, or not to be" soliloquy, where might she be placed, and how does Hamlet become aware of her presence? At any point in the nunnery scene, does Hamlet suspect or know that Claudius and Polonius are spying on him and Ophelia? Unlike Harold Jenkins (283), Harley Granville-Barker (*Hamlet* 78–79) argues that Hamlet has a sudden awareness of their presence which prompts his line to Ophelia: "Where's your father?" (3.1.130).

Audiences need to see not only the play within the play (3.2) but, simultaneously, to see Claudius, Gertrude, Hamlet, Ophelia, and Horatio as these characters watch the play and one another. Which positions in the acting area might be strong or weak, and which positions allow maximum opportunity for sight lines and movement? To whom might a character direct particular lines? Which lines might be public (spoken by an actor to the whole onstage audience) and which private (spoken in intimate dialogue or to himself or herself)? These questions are important to representing conflicts between Hamlet and Ophelia as well as the struggle for political power. Is Hamlet the strong, controlling force (e.g., as in the Olivier film [1948] and, differently, in the Branagh film [1996]), or is Claudius ultimately the stronger force in this scene (e.g., as played by Stewart in the BBC television production [1980])? Toward the end of the play scene, exactly when, and how, might Claudius rise (243), move, say his final line (247)? Exit? What does Hamlet do in relation to each move of Claudius? Which of them, if either, is in control at the end of this cat-and-mouse game? Or is it a counterbalancing of mighty opposites? When might Gertrude rise? How might Polonius react? How exit? What is, indeed, his final line? In the Second Quarto, Polonius's last line (3.2.281)[3] is "Lights, lights, lights." But in the First Folio, the equivalent line ("Lights, Lights, Lights.") is given to *"All"* (Hinman 2141). How, according to the suggestions of either text, does the court exit? Students bring to these debates their experience of seeing two versions of *Hamlet*, normally the BBC television production and the Kenneth Branagh film, outside class time as a required part of the course, on which they have written brief response papers focused on interpretive differences, including those resulting from uses of the media of television or cinema compared to stage and from representations of gender.

Problems in textual scholarship, criticism, and theatrical practice acquire fresh relevance when students must try to suit the action to the word. To clarify and explore possible meanings of words, they use library reference room copies of C. T. Onions's glossary, Alexander Schmidt's lexicon, and the *OED*, among other reference works, and copies on reserve of major scholarly editions of *Hamlet*.[4] The significant textual variants discussed in class can also be explored later in performance. Resisting Hamlet's denial that he ever gave her gifts, Ophelia says to him, according to the Second Quarto (3.1.96), "you know right well you did," but according to the First Folio (Hinman 1752), "I know right well you did."

Wrestling with possibilities for performance suggested by language heightens students' perceptions of gendered conflicts between Hamlet and Gertrude, Hamlet and Ophelia. It is a challenge to give distinct nuance to each of the five times (within 3.1.122–48) Hamlet speaks variations of line 139 "To a nunnery, go," with differing plays on the double meanings of convent and brothel. Contending with such a challenge makes vividly clear that Ophelia, in Janet Adelman's words, "becomes contaminated in his [Hamlet's] eyes, subject to the same 'frailty' that names his mother" (14). Furthermore, what conflicts between Hamlet and Ophelia are suggested by shifts to short exchanges (3.1.104–08), then by shifts from verse to prose (esp. beginning at about line 3.1.109) and from prose to her verse soliloquy (149–60)? It helps readers as well as performers to be alert to such shifts, which can be part of a scene's smaller subunits, or beats, each of which begins with a significant change of direction in the actor's thought, feeling, or movement.

Can readers and performers see, in the spectrum of possibilities the text offers, space for a resistant Ophelia? Could her responses to Hamlet in the play scene allow her to resist Hamlet's sexual innuendos, fully conscious of their implications? What consciousness does Ophelia bear, in the nunnery scene, that she is a decoy for her father and Claudius? Could an actor suggest that Ophelia's submission to their manipulation is not willing? Could an actor perform an Ophelia who resists Hamlet's misogynist language by the way she delivers her reply: "Could beauty, my lord, have better commerce than with honesty?" (3.1.111-12). Might Ophelia show anger, as well as pain, on her line (121) "I was the more deceived."? Watching Glenda Jackson's defiant Ophelia (in the *Hamlet* directed by Peter Hall, Royal Shakespeare Company [1965]) alerted me to these and other possibilities (cf. Wells, *Royal Shakespeare*, 31–32; Dawson 144–45).

What is at stake in representations of gender and power becomes clearer to students when their performance work helps them critically interrogate film and television productions. Questions that arise in viewing the nunnery scene include: What are the effects of Olivier's and Zeffirelli's drastic cuts to Ophelia's lines? How does the submissive Ophelia of Lalla Ward (BBC) compare with the reserved, then passionately distraught Ophelia of Jean Simmons (Olivier)? How, and exactly on what lines, despite Zeffirelli's cuts, does Helena Bonham Carter convey a subtle but persistent resistance to Hamlet (Mel Gibson)? Initially the encounter of Kate Winslet's Ophelia with Branagh's Hamlet suggests intimacy and pain that is partially mutual; precisely when, how, do their emotions become sharply gendered—he violent, she shocked and far more in sorrow than in anger? Alerted by such questions to feminist issues, students examining Ophelia's role can study what Elaine Showalter calls the "*history* of her representation.*" Becoming aware of their own critical positions in "exposing the ideology of representation" (Showalter [Parker and Hartman] 79, 92), students can also explore the question: To what extent does the play reveal the tragic consequences of the dominant cultural norms imposed on Ophelia, that she be silent, chaste, and obedient?

Reading and performance are related interpretive, critical acts. Both stimulate further analysis in writing. Students can connect detailed dramatic analysis of a scene's language to the play's central ideas and problems, as well as to exact details of a scene as it was or could be performed. For longer papers, intensive scene analysis involves research in textual studies, criticism, stage history, intellectual and cultural history. Awareness of performance issues can help students in their writing to gain specificity, avoid broad-brush generalizations about themes, focus on close examination of language, and bring independent critical thought to bear on scholarship and criticism. Perception and analysis of *Hamlet* through performance encourages strong and detailed engagement with complex critical problems.

NOTES

[1]I interviewed Stewart at Santa Clara University, 9 November 1979, during an educational program developed by Actors in Residence, based at the University of California, Santa Barbara. Later known as ACTER (A Center for Theatre, Education, and Research), then as Actors from the London Stage, the program was moved to the University of North Carolina, Chapel Hill, then in 2000 to the University of Notre Dame. For certain ideas about teaching Shakespeare in performance I am indebted to this program, founded by Homer Swander; to the 1982 Institute on Shakespeare in Performance sponsored by the NEH and the Folger Institute for Renaissance and Eighteenth-Century Studies at the Folger Shakespeare Library, directed by Bernard Beckerman and Cary Mazer; and to the work of Michael Warren, Audrey Stanley, and

Paul Whitworth of the University of California, Santa Cruz. Two sessions on 13 April 2001 of the Shakespeare Association of America annual meeting intersected with this essay. For minor revisions to my paper, I am indebted to the title of the session, "Performance as Critical Practice," chaired by Katherine Rowe. My essay was written before I was invited to join Miriam Gilbert's workshop, "Teaching through Performance: *Hamlet* 3.1," but I here record the questions she posed to participants, because they are so useful to students: "Write down as many specific interpretive questions about this scene [the nunnery scene] as you can think of—questions that directors, actors, designers would have to answer." For example, "What are the 'remembrances' that Ophelia has with her? And where are they? Is she carrying them? Wearing them? Are they wrapped up? If so, how?"

[2]*Hamlet* quotations, unless otherwise noted, are from *The Norton Shakespeare* (Greenblatt et al.). Like *The Complete Oxford Shakespeare* (Wells and Taylor), on which it is based, the *Norton* uses the First Folio as the control text for *Hamlet*. The *Oxford* reprints in an appendix passages from the Second Quarto that are not in the First Folio, whereas the *Norton* facilitates comparison by inserting such passages in the body of the text, clearly identifying them by indentation and a different typeface.

[3]Line references to the Second Quarto of *Hamlet*, 1604–05, are to the Shakespeare Quarto Facsimiles, introduced by W. W. Greg, who added in margins line numbers of the 1891 Globe edition. Line references to the First Folio are to Charlton Hinman's collated edition.

[4]To support class discussion, performance work, and student essays, it is useful to put the following editions on library reserve: Hinman; Bertram and Kliman; Greg (First and Second Quartos of *Hamlet*); Wilson; Edwards; Jenkins; Hibbard. Among recent works of criticism, I suggest Parker and Hartman; Wofford. To capture earlier debates about the play scene, Granville-Barker's preface to *Hamlet* can be contrasted to Wilson. Among recent works on *Hamlet* in performance I recommend Kliman, *Hamlet*; Dawson.

Teaching the Script: The "Mousetrap" in the Classroom

Michael W. Shurgot

Attention to the performance options inherent in Shakespeare's plays can be immensely useful for both high school and college-level students. With some of Shakespeare's most complex scenes, such as Hamlet's "Mousetrap," students can learn more about Shakespeare's theatrical art by examining performance options at Shakespeare's Globe Theatre than they can by thinking only about modern performances of the plays. While we obviously cannot haul the Globe (old or new) into our classrooms, we can use some simple teaching devices to encourage students to "see" how one of Shakespeare's most theatrically challenging scenes might have created meaning on the Globe stage. Herewith is a brief discussion of one such device.

First, some crucial points about the "Mousetrap" that are relevant to any examination of it in the Elizabethan theater. Bernard Beckerman explains in *Shakespeare at the Globe* that 2.2 and 3.2 of *Hamlet* are the only scenes in Shakespeare's Globe plays that require more than five characters (229; appendix C). Given that the "Mousetrap" requires far more than five characters on stage, one can reasonably argue that it is among Shakespeare's most theatrically challenging scenes. One can further infer that, despite the prevailing critical wisdom that Elizabethan or Jacobean companies did not rehearse as assiduously as modern companies do, a scene as complex as the "Mousetrap" must have required some rehearsal, especially given the complex relation between the two sets of actors on stage: those playing Claudius's court, including Hamlet himself, and those playing the actors of *The Murder of Gonzago*. Further, students must understand that, unlike modern proscenium theaters, Elizabethan public theaters allowed no single, dominant visual perspective. By its design, the Globe, with its spectators surrounding the stage on three sides, reinforced among its spectators *in performance* a prominent feature of the "Mousetrap": the phenomenon of multiple perspectives on dramatic action. Stephen Orgel writes of Elizabethan popular drama that it is essentially fluid and disjunctive in nature and that "its elements fit together only so far as a viewer interprets and understands them" (44). Scott McMillin, discussing act 3, scene 1, of *Henry IV, Part 1*, writes that "the confidence of the writing is actually the confidence in a theater company. I take this scene as a sign that Shakespeare's company was very certain of itself and its audience by the late 1590's" (8). The complexity of the "Mousetrap" and the ensemble abilities that Shakespeare's company must have developed by the time Shakespeare wrote *Hamlet* suggest that studying this scene in its original theatrical setting could teach our students much about Shakespeare's theatrical art, especially in relation to the script of *Hamlet*.

I begin this class exercise at 3.2.90, and the questions I explore with my students are: Where do all the characters go on stage? How might their movements and placement suggest the placement of the other actors on stage? And finally, what might the placements or blocking arrangements that one proposes for this scene teach us about the relation between a Shakespearean script and its performance on the stage for which it was written? (See Shurgot.)

The only handout I use is a piece of paper with a scale drawing of the Globe stage, 27' x 43', with posts (simple squares) situated three-fourths of the way from the stage facade and showing space for spectators on all three sides of the thrust stage. With this drawing in hand, and with Shakespeare's script of the "Mousetrap" in front of them, I urge students to begin placing the various characters about the Globe's nearly thousand square feet of acting space. I ask them to note carefully where the script at least suggests movement and placement of characters. Hamlet sends Horatio to find his own "place," whereas Hamlet's line to Gertrude upon her invitation to "sit by me" indicates that he sits near Ophelia: "No, good mother, here's metal more attractive" (108). Polonius's quick response, "Oho! Do you mark that?" (109), seems to confirm that Hamlet does sit next to Ophelia (perhaps as the Arden stage direction for line 110 suggests, " at Ophelia's feet"), while also indicating that Polonius must be near the king when he says this line. I then ask students to visualize the next movements onto the stage: Gertrude and Claudius have entered and must also be placed on the stage, and they are soon followed by the Players, whose position in this scene is also crucial. Where do the Players play? Are they downstage, upstage, to one side of the Globe's wide stage, and what kinds of sight lines would be established by any of these stage groupings? Given Hamlet's directions to Horatio, what is Horatio's probable position on stage while the players enact both the dumb show and *Gonzago*, and where is he in relation to Hamlet? Is it necessary that they be widely separated on stage? If so, why; if not, why not? And what is Hamlet's place? Presumably, both he and Horatio must be able to see Claudius during the playing by the actors, but do they move about at all during the scene? Hamlet speaks to Ophelia after the dumb show, and his words signify increasing anxiety as his play, with those puzzling dozen or so lines he has supposedly asked the first player to add, careens toward enactment. In addition, there is John Dover Wilson's famous (and I think dramatically potent because unanswerable) question about whether or not Claudius sees the dumb show, and especially *Gonzago*, and what his reaction or lack thereof may signify about his character and this scene in performance. (Robson's book *Did the King See the Dumb Show?* is an excellent examination of some of these questions in performance.) Finally, students should consider the crucial moment when Hamlet leaps into his own drama and identifies Lucianus as "nephew to the King" (239), and they should ask themselves what has just happened on stage and how Hamlet's words affect movement for the remainder of the scene. Ophelia cries, "The King rises" (259), after Hamlet bursts into Lucianus's role, and thereupon the scene dissolves, but as M. R. Woodhead demonstrates, it is probably Hamlet's commentary on the play, suddenly turning Lucianus into a "nephew to the King" (i.e., Hamlet's uncle) that frightens Claudius, not the actual plot of *Gonzago*, which after all involves a duke whose murderer's relationship to his victim is never indicated (159).

In their effort to arrange all this movement in relation to Shakespeare's script during a Globe performance, students will produce an image of the scene itself, that is, multiple perspectives on how this scene might have been produced on the Globe stage and how well various approaches might have communicated the theatrical complexities of the scene. Presumably, judging from Hamlet's "Get you a place" to Horatio (91), Hamlet and Horatio saw the scene from different places—that is, perspectives—on the stage, yet neither Hamlet nor Horatio, as Woodhead observes, seems to realize that it was Hamlet's "talk of poisoning" that frightened Claudius, not Lucianus's. Why? And did neither see Claudius react earlier in the scene? Did Hamlet and Horatio see the same scene? Depending on where students place the characters on the Globe stage, would any one section of the audience, seated in tiers on three sides of the stage or standing anywhere around it, have seen the stage action from the same perspective and thus have had a comprehensive view of it? If not, to what extent would the experience of the Globe spectators have mirrored the experience of the court characters, especially Hamlet, Horatio, Claudius, and Gertrude, whose only line after the beginning of the dumb show is "The lady doth protest too much, methinks" (225)? Why does Shakespeare have her say so little, especially since, as Robson suggests, the whole episode may have been planned by Hamlet more as an attack on his mother than on the king? What has been her perspective on the play, and how might it be different from Claudius's? And how might this difference have been represented by blocking on the Globe stage?

This in-class exercise, which encourages students to lead discussions based on their own staging of the scenes, asks them to think visually, that is, to imagine a performance of one of Shakespeare's most complex scenes in the theater for which it was intended, a theater of multiple perspectives in which no one sight line dominates, much less dictates, spectators' experience of a play. By placing the characters of the scene upon the Globe stage, students can see how the "Mousetrap" could have embodied in a Globe performance, in the actual bodies of the actors, one of the scene's central theatrical ideas: that no one single experience of the scene, rife as it is with acting by two sets of player kings and queens, could possibly be complete. Not Hamlet's, not Horatio's, not Claudius's, not Gertrude's, and not any single spectator's. As spectators surrounding the stage on three sides watch one group of actors watch another group of actors, those spectators in any one section of the Globe are in turn watched by other spectators, who are watched by still others. As the levels of reality in this scene replete with acting both multiply and recede, the enactment of the entire spectacle superbly demonstrates the theatrical insight that all the world is indeed a stage and all the men and women merely players. For at a performance of this scene at the brilliantly named Globe, who, on stage or among the spectators, could claim certainty about the reality of his or her experience?

In an essay essential to all teachers of Shakespeare, Homer Swander writes:

> No playwright of genius could fail to include in his plays, in a most basic way, the theatre space and the actor-audience relationship that he knew were a given for him. To the extent that we now exclude such elements, we exclude something Shakespearean, something important. We accept a certain blindness to possibilities that are right before our eyes in the scripts.   (539)

This simple exercise, which asks students to place not only Shakespeare's actors but also themselves somewhere in his theater during one of his most fascinating scenes, should encourage students to begin to appreciate the theatrical possibilities inherent in the actual structure of the Globe. It should also help them to see, as Swander insists, how compelling the study of Elizabethan public theaters can be in the contemporary classroom.

NOTE

Hamlet quotations are from Jenkins.

Hamlet's Narratives

Arthur F. Kinney

At the climax of *Hamlet*—dead center in the play—Shakespeare pairs Hamlet's well-known advice to the players visiting Elsinore with the actual production of *The Murder of Gonzago*; in the brief interval between them, Polonius tells Hamlet that he once played Julius Caesar, just as Shakespeare's first actor no doubt did, in repertoire with *Hamlet* at the Globe in 1601. Such a sharp focus on drama, along with the asides, the soliloquies, and the staged encounters and duels, has long made this Shakespeare's most apparently metatheatrical play. As I introduce the play this way to my class, we note repeatedly how the play uses drama to test the possibilities and boundaries of drama, so that soliloquy, for instance, is a necessary way to dramatize interior thinking, just as swordplay enacts the conflict at the heart of everything that we call dramatic.

Oddly enough, then, the play begins with Marcellus's anxious request of Horatio to tell the story of Denmark's need for military preparation (1.1.70–79) and ends with Hamlet's anxiously commanding Horatio to tell his own: that is, the drama begins and ends in narrative. Moreover, these are stories that stretch backward to the antecedent causes of the play and forward to what will live in the memory after the final lines are delivered. The play seems to be surrounded by and encompassed with fictions, as Barbara Hardy has suggested. Once I raise this matter of narrative and we return to the text, we notice how very often key scenes are reports or accounts rather than the encounters that constitute the very stuff of drama. Why might this be so? Why does Shakespeare's play that most examines playing seem to undermine the usefulness and forcefulness of playing itself? Briefly, we think of other ways of expressing events—from current magazines to subjects like history or economics—only to find that, as cultures formulate records, they convert them into narrative forms. It is narrative, not necessarily drama, that always puts things into sequence, supplies causation, and implies (or examines) intention. As a culture, we too, like Shakespeare's playgoers, want to make narratives of what we see and what we hear. When Hamlet questions the practice speech of the Player ("What's Hecuba to him, or he to Hecuba?" 2.2.569), he seeks the answer in the story of the *Iliad*; when he confronts the purpose of his own life ("To be, or not to be," beginning 3.1.56) a short time later, extrapolating on Priam and comparing himself to him and perhaps to Hecuba, he turns his question ("that is the question") into a narrative of what dying might be like and so—through projected narrative, not through drama—judges his dramatic situation. The major conflict in *Hamlet*, I suggest as one basic premise for class discussion of the play, is the conflict not between Claudius and Hamlet, or King Hamlet and his son, or Hamlet and Laertes, but between the desirability and even the adequacy of drama and those of narrative. Shakespeare imports one form to judge another, one genre to expose the strengths and limitations of another.

This observation always requires some discussion, and I let the students choose those passages—perhaps their favorite, perhaps the most salient—that seem to address (or seem not to address) the question of the superiority of the dramatic versus the narrative: King Claudius's first appearance, perhaps, in 1.2; Hamlet with the Ghost in 1.5; Hamlet before the kneeling Claudius in 3.3 or the cornered Gertrude in 3.4; or even the jests with the gravediggers in 5.1. But the more we examine these passages, the more they turn into implied or even explicit stories. Claudius establishes rule through a sequence of events— a peace mission allowing him to earn a reputation and position of king and a farewell to Laertes and welcome to Hamlet that allow him to understand, then constitute a new family. While the speech is dramatic, the significance can only be put in the declarative and sequential sentences of narrative. The image of Claudius's kneeling in prayer is unwrapped by Hamlet into a narrative that establishes Claudius's penitent state and then plans (plots) the subsequent events this penitence causes that will work out the assassination of the king at a more suitable time. The confrontation with Gertrude relies on a narrative comparison of a good king followed by a bad one; the confrontation of the gravediggers leads to the autobiographical narrative of the child Hamlet playing with Yorick, now only a skull, a theatrical property. In each of these instances, to unwrap meaning—from commands, images, conversations, and props—demands a narrative response on the part of the audience. Playgoers do this so quickly, they may not know they are doing it; but the play doesn't make sense unless and until they do it.

Usually, for my students this approach is a whole new way of conceiving drama, and while all plays permit it, *Hamlet*, with its reliance on tales told by Horatio, seems to demand it. We return, then, to the one example of the five I have given that is explicitly a story to begin with: King Hamlet's account of his own murder. We read this story through, from "I am thy father's spirit" (1.5.9), establishing the narrator's credentials, to "Remember me" (1.5.92), punning on "memorialize me" by "re-membering" or reconstructing me. This speech, as an entity, as a speech act, turns the Ghost's story from history to legacy and from event to eternal life through memorialization. The story for Hamlet is "prophetic" (1.5.40) and serves his own desires and purposes, for it "May sweep [me] to my revenge" (1.5.31). But I point out that this line may make the story not merely a story, or a report, but a command; and the command itself has some troubling features. For one thing, can a man asleep see a person stealing toward him with poison? And if poison—literally and figuratively—might be applied through the ear most effectively, how is that application related by this self-conscious playwright of this self-conscious play to the words entering young Hamlet's ears: are they poisonous too? Are they encouraging King Hamlet's revenge at the expense of young Hamlet's very soul? If King Hamlet wants a murderer to die—and we have only his accusation to go on at this point—what does he anticipate will happen to young Hamlet as murderer? Will this second murder end his lineage and bring turmoil on Denmark? In time, the play will seem to confirm this account, but it is left to Horatio's final story, as Horatio absents himself awhile from felicity, to judge the merits of its premises and propositions. By 1.5, all we can say is that King Hamlet is explaining his essential innocence, ignoring the fact that a good king is one aware of potential enemies, such as his very own brother. The story, then, whatever else it is, and whatever function it may hold, is self-serving.

Such a class discussion troubles and complicates other stories, such as the first one by Horatio, which turns out to be a narrative way of explaining the need to keep the guards on the ramparts of Elsinore. It prepares us for Polonius's story—made up or not—of Hamlet's love for Ophelia, a story that issues into narrative when Polonius and Claudius later spy on the two from behind an arras (3.1.29–191). It suggests other motivations for storytelling besides revenge: Polonius may hope to put together various facts and observations about his daughter and Hamlet, or he may be assembling a tale that will strengthen his importance (and court position) with the new king Claudius, or he may even fear for his daughter's safety. We know Polonius sees storytelling as a way to test ideas and learn crucial information, because that is the way he asks Reynaldo to investigate his own son (2.1.19–68), "By indirections [the indirections of fiction] find directions out" (2.1.66). Narrative possibilities now instigate dramatic ones. We discuss in class what may cause Polonius's attraction to the power of fiction, the uses of narrative, and we return to earlier class examples, such as the five I have listed, to examine how these fictions too function, not only to make sense but also to prompt action and force (possibly inaccurate) judgments. Each of Hamlet's soliloquies can be unwound into a narrative, implied, coiled, and waiting to be released. (Some or all of these can be class discussions, class reports, paper assignments, or examination questions.)

How do characters in the play respond to such stories? We know that despite Hamlet's instantaneous pact with the Ghost, he comes to question the

Ghost's advice and perhaps even his authority (it might be the devil in the disguise of King Hamlet). Hamlet seems always to question the need to fear the enmity of Fortinbras, for in his dying voice he gives Denmark over to the sworn enemy of his father. So, too, the reports and tales of others might disguise unspoken motivation. Some, to elicit a particular response or prompt an occasion, may be wholly made up, as are Polonius's suggested fictions about Laertes in Paris. Did Hamlet never love Ophelia, as he says? She does not think so (3.1.120). Having just left Claudius supposedly at prayer, does Hamlet really believe he later killed him behind the arras ("I took thee for thy better" [3.4.33]), or is the king-killing narrative blinding him? And what of the pirate ship and the sudden return to Denmark? We have only Hamlet's account for that; it has even been argued that Hamlet formed a conspiracy with the pirates. When we see that such motivated narratives are what give rise to dramatic expectation and action, we can readdress the play itself.

We are, for instance, more keenly aware that King Claudius's tale to Laertes about his father's death is at least shaded if not downright fictitious, in order to promote revenge; but it is of course deliberately parallel to King Hamlet's tale to Prince Hamlet, and now one allows us to reexamine both, in conjunction. That is one reading I introduce, even for students who know the play well. Act 4, scene 7, is another example, a scene of stories usually taken for granted. It ends with Gertrude's account of Ophelia's death and is taken at face value, just as King Hamlet's tale was. But how sensible is it that the queen, witnessing Ophelia's sudden fall into the river, did not shout for help and try to rescue her? Why, in fact, does she wax *poetic* in her tale-telling? Why does she linger on such macabre details, given their context? When we examine this story and its unspoken motivations, we come up with a good many in class. Often one motivation is that Gertrude is projecting her own fate on Ophelia; another is that she is using this story as she fumbles toward understanding her own remorse or guilt. But it is, finally, a story and not altogether reliable testimony. This story is put in this scene following Ophelia's two "mad" appearances. In one (4.5), her songs are obscene ("if they come to't, / By Cock, they are to blame" [60–61]); in the second, she mourns her dead father (188–97). These mad songs enfold stories about courtship and death, but just as the opening line of the last song ("And will 'a not come again?" [188]) can initially suggest either Hamlet or Polonius (for it resembles her farewell to Hamlet in the nunnery scene), so it conflates the story of courtship with the story of death (an Elizabethan commonplace, after all) and conflates Polonius's needless death with Hamlet's (forthcoming)—needless?—death. Her madness obscures the stories she tells herself, but, we discuss, no more than Gertrude's does for Gertrude.

Such class discussions are, of course, preparatory to the final question, which the drama leaves unanswered but which is narrative: What story about Hamlet will Horatio tell? One story follows: the embedded story of Fortinbras, that had Hamlet lived, he would have made a fine soldier. Of course he wouldn't have. Is Fortinbras struggling to find a way to pay sincere tribute to a prince he does not even know? Is he attempting to make his adversary, now his predecessor, his equal? Or in framing a story about Hamlet, is his use of his own perspective finally a fiction, even a lie, about Hamlet, a way to appropriate Hamlet to help claim authority in Denmark? That this follows Hamlet's dying command is unsettling; what would Horatio, the philosopher from Wittenberg, conceive as a proper narrative if he can—or cannot—fathom court politics? *Hamlet* functions as a play by insisting that the narratives it embodies and advances are only as potent and significant as the narratives we, in and out of the classroom, make of it for ourselves.

NOTE

Hamlet quotations are from Hubler.

From Story to Action:
A Graduated Exercise to Teach *Hamlet*

Nina daVinci Nichols

Undergraduates with slight experience of literature and none of drama find it difficult to understand a play as a series of actions occurring in the present. Play, to them, is story. Even when curious about *Hamlet*, the cultural icon, they lack the skills needed to distinguish between their subjective and objective responses to act, theme, and characterization. The following three-stage assignment, extending over several weeks, addresses these handicaps without driving new Shakespeareans to rely either on guides and notes or on sophisticated critical interpretations beyond their grasp.

After some preliminary reading and informal discussion of the play's central events and its continuing popularity, students write a one-page "Story of *Hamlet*." They must include the events already identified as major, thus honing their skill at subordinating and summarizing material; and they must write only in the past tense, in order to understand that story by definition takes place in the past. Beyond those two constraints, they may order events as creatively as they wish and even include some interpretation tangentially. One such story might begin: "Once upon a sad time in Denmark, the perfect prince Hamlet died in a rigged fencing match with the king's favorite courtier, Laertes." Often enough, some students begin with family: "Once upon a time, the son in a dysfunctional family discovered . . ."

A sampling of results is read aloud in class and evaluated, each story for its fidelity to one, authoritative *Hamlet* story. As none exists, even when students agree on which events must be included, and as students must defend their own versions, they rapidly discover the subjective nature of their stories and why referring to any story inevitably leads them far from the text before them. They then lay aside their stories and proceed to the next, more difficult, task of distinguishing between story and action, stage 2 of the assignment. While the class reads the play aloud, when possible scene by scene, each student works independently on a "Sentence Outline of Major Actions" in the order of their unfolding. They must subordinate ancillary to central actions and must use only the present tense: for example, "Hamlet meets his father's spirit, which reveals King Hamlet's murder by Claudius." For each major action listed, students must refer parenthetically to the passage of text providing the information.

Thereafter, in the course of continuing class discussion of scenes in sequence, students keep modifying their outlines, always with an eye to highlighting or subordinating detail. The task is painstaking, sometimes frustrating, as they must forsake their first, easy impressions of a whole play in the process of analytically identifying its parts. They respond at once, for example, to the general idea of a hero struggling for certainty and integrity, or to the plight of a heroine unhappy in love. But as they must tie generalizations to particular lines, they instead begin to see how themes (say, of revenge, injustice, male competition, love and sexuality, appearance versus reality, etc.) emerge out of action plus language—and begin to catch a glimpse of Shakespeare's foggy Elsinore. This stage of study nevertheless involves little attention to language or poetry as such.

For most students, the great challenge of constructing an outline lies in deciding whether and when a soliloquy showing Hamlet's inaction amounts technically to dramatic action onstage. Indeed, it is a problem for experienced readers. As a rough rule of thumb, students must accept that even solitary speech causes something, be it a physical act, a character's discovery, or, more subtly, an alteration in the audience's perceptions. In order to test the premise, students quite happily act out key speeches or scenes: the Ghost's appearances, the "Mousetrap," the nunnery scene, the closet scene with Gertrude, and so on. Since they also, simultaneously, are correcting their outlines at home, the most attentive students begin in a rudimentary way to notice differing kinds and levels of action, from introspective to domestic to ceremonial, from low to high intensity, as these have been pointed out in class. Ideally, it is at this stage, also, that students can begin to see the play's structure along parallels and contrasts in character as well as action.

Finally, study of the play culminates in a short, directed essay intended to move students toward still greater objectivity. They write about five pages on the play's "Modulations of One Theme" (say, the generation gap, fathers and sons, or revenge and justice), referring to their own corrected "Sentence Outline of Major Action" for supporting evidence. This self-reflexiveness at once helps them feel comfortable with the difficult business of writing an essay, while preventing them from simply returning to their initial points of departure when discussing story. Both their story and outline, moreover, must be attached to the essay as two extended endnotes. No formal criticism is required for the essay, but of course any sources must be documented.

Let me add that students find it nearly impossible to plagiarize any part of this assignment. Many have reported that the exercises, against all their gloomiest expectations of unrewarded labor, taught them how to begin appreciating the play as a complex organism. While the three-stage procedure sketched out here differs from that in graduate classes, the implications of each stage remain valid. Experienced students often distinguish readily between subjective and objective responses, yet they just as often need to strengthen their understanding of kinds of action and its patterning before turning to an appreciation of rhetoric and poetry.

A World of Questions:
An Approach Indebted to Maynard Mack

Robert H. Ray

The core of teaching *Hamlet* for me has always been Maynard Mack's essay titled "The World of *Hamlet*," a study that I regard as the best short commentary on the play. Originally published in the *Yale Review*, it has been reprinted in various collections of criticism. I begin the first session on the play by referring to Mack's essay and telling the students that I regard it as the most illuminating treatment of *Hamlet*. Although I do not assign the essay to be read, I inform the students that we will be covering many of its salient points as a way to approach the play. (A few of the most interested students inquire further about the essay when we conclude our discussion of the play, and I direct them to the essay itself.) I first summarize Mack's basic argument: that the world of the play is an interrogative one, deliberately created by Shakespeare to engulf us with questions, riddles, mysteries, and puzzles. I emphasize that Mack takes pains to argue that the confusion is not in Shakespeare himself or in a play hopelessly muddled and contradictory, as some earlier critics in the twentieth century seemed to feel (Mack specifically mentions T. S. Eliot's comment that the play is "undoubtedly a failure"). Rather, the world of the play reflects the confusion, uncertainty, and mystery not only in human nature and humanity—in us and, thus, in our chief representative in the play, Hamlet himself—but also in all reality.

The questions arise in regard to things seemingly trivial at the beginning of the play but rapidly expand into the largest possible metaphysical matters. At this point in the class I raise the questions of whether Mack's argument about the interrogative world of the play can be supported early in the play and, if so, how. If I am lucky, some astute student will point out that the first line of the play ("Who's there?") is a question. If a student does not do so, I hasten to note it. We read the first thirty-two lines of the play. In doing so, we find five more questions. I mention that up to this point there have been uncertainties raised about the identity of people and about the appearance of a ghost ("this thing" [21]). Then I ask the students where and when the scene is occurring. The response should be rapid: on a guard platform of the castle at night (in fact, midnight [7]). Now I can ask what the significances of this setting and time are. With some prodding or outright telling, the students are easily enough led to the implications of night—that is, darkness associated with ignorance, which in turn relates to the confusion and uncertainty in the interrogative world of the play. So Shakespeare uses imagery and symbolism to enforce the idea and feeling of uncertainty from the very first scene. A harder question: Is there any importance in the knowledge that the scene occurs on a guard platform, other than the literal fact that these are, after all, guards carrying out their duty? One might ask the students to visualize the place as elevated or suspended above normal ground level. And one can ask if there might be some connection between the elevation and Hamlet's later question, "What should such fellows as I do crawling between earth and heaven?" (3.1.126–28). Is not that the very position in which we see these men of the first scene? Between earth and heaven and also between the physical world and the spiritual world (as the impinging of the Ghost upon this physical world implies)? Is Shakespeare commenting on the middle state of humankind, on the precarious and uncertain position of the human between animal and angel? Here the teacher can refer to Mack's statement that the opening scene evokes not only Hamlet's world but also our own: "Man in his aspect of bafflement, moving in darkness on a rampart between two worlds [. . .]" ("World" 507). It indeed symbolizes the uncertain and interrogative state of Hamlet and of all humanity. To drive home the idea that the first scene "creates a world where uncertainties are of the essence" (507), the teacher might have the class look at lines 157–65, near the end of the scene. Marcellus's "Some say" and "they say" and Horatio's "do in part believe it" convey effectively the interrogative mood, the uncertainty of the world.

At this juncture I propose to the students that the overriding question in the play that Hamlet is trying to answer is nothing less than the nature of human beings. I argue that the Hamlet *before* the world of the play is implied to have been, in essence, a man exemplifying the ideals of Renaissance humanism, one who saw the human as rational, angelic, noble, godlike, and powerful. These implications are gleaned from several comments in the play that I point out in the course of our study, but especially we see this vision of the earlier Hamlet in Ophelia's remarks about Hamlet's noble mind and about his being a courtier, soldier, and scholar (3.1.150–61). But this nature in Hamlet has been shattered, and in the second scene of the play we see a confused, disillusioned Hamlet whose earlier idealistic conceptions of humanity have been destroyed. In his first soliloquy (1.2.129–59) he is in deep despair over the disillusionment resulting from seeing his mother as worse than an animal in her behavior. He sees the world as an "unweeded garden" (135), as the Garden of Eden taken over by weeds (i.e., sins). If his mother is so sinful, all in the world must be. He even feels that his own flesh now is "sallied" (sullied; 129). This utter contradiction to his earlier visions of human nature call forth his questionings about humanity in general, about specific people he encounters, and about himself. By such questioning through the rest of the play he tries to solve the bafflement and confusion of his world. The basic problem is exemplified by his remarks to Rosencrantz and Guildenstern in 2.2.292–310. It is to this passage that I next direct the students' attention. Hamlet says, "What a piece of work is a man, how noble in reason, how infinite in faculties, in form and moving, how express and admirable in action, how like an angel in apprehension, how like a god! the beauty of the world; the paragon of animals." All this precisely embodies the Renaissance humanistic vision that the students have already been alerted to in the earlier Hamlet. But with the mention of "animals," Hamlet makes a crucial turn to say, "and yet to me what is this quintessence of dust? Man delights not me [. . .]." Here he reflects precisely the older medieval Christian view of the human being as dust, weak, corrupt, sinful, and animalistic. He must reject the simplistic and idealistic view that he earlier held, however painful it might be to do so. He must reconcile himself to the confusing complexity of human nature that he now perceives. The evidence of human corruption has become too overwhelming to avoid: the adultery of Gertrude and Claudius, Claudius's murder of Hamlet's father, and the deceptiveness of Rosencrantz and Guildenstern, to name a few of the mounting discoveries.

I tell the students to notice that from here on some of Hamlet's soliloquies are attempts to solve the question of human nature and of his own nature by looking at and assessing other men. The students should also notice how in each of these soliloquies the question What is a man? is either asked overtly or implied. The first example we look at is 2.2.550–605, the soliloquy following Hamlet's conversation with the players. He berates himself for his inaction regarding Claudius by comparing himself unfavorably to the player who can be more emotional and driven in a role on stage than Hamlet is in real life, although Hamlet has a motive that the player does not. We then proceed to examine 4.4.32–66. This soliloquy comes after Hamlet sees Fortinbras leading an army to fight for his and his country's honor. In his ruminations here Hamlet asks the major question directly: "What is a man, / If his chief good and market of his time / Be but to sleep and feed? A beast, no more" (33–35). He berates himself as being no more than an animal in comparison to Fortinbras, who is a man of brave action for the sake of honor. Hamlet also says that God gave us "godlike reason" that should not "fust in us unus'd" (36–39). He sees Fortinbras's action as a criticism of his own inaction, especially since Hamlet has much more reason to act, on behalf of his murdered father and dishonored mother. So now Hamlet regards brave action as a mark of the true man, an ideal virtue that he sees himself as not possessing.

In some conversations with other people in the play, Hamlet also either directly broaches or implies the question of what the ideal person is. One example for the class to examine is a portion of the scene in which he talks to and criticizes his mother (3.4). Having her contrast portraits of his father and uncle, he remarks that his father had the grace and characteristics of Hyperion, Jove, Mars, and Mercury. He concludes, "A combination and a form indeed, / Where every god did seem to set his seal / To give the world assurance of a man" (60–62). His father's godlike attributes mark his father as a true man. But even more important is an earlier scene with Horatio, for it contains the seed of what Hamlet himself eventually becomes. It points the clearest way for him to answer the question of the ideal nature for human beings and for himself. In essence, Hamlet sees Horatio as the ideal man in 3.2.54–74. Hamlet tells him, "Horatio, thou art e'en as just a man / As e'er my conversation cop'd withal" (54–55). He bluntly says, then, that Horatio is as close as possible to the ideal. In the next several lines he elaborates: Horatio is stoic and accepting of any suffering or of whatever fortune brings, his emotion and reason ("blood and judgment") are perfectly mixed, and he is not a slave to emotion (65–74). These are characteristics that Hamlet lacks, and he realizes it. This fact is most evident when he blindly kills Polonius, mistaking him for Claudius, and when he contributes to the madness of Ophelia. He recognizes the fallen nature of all humanity in himself. How to reconcile himself to the fallen world and fallen humanity and how to live as an ideal person who can contend with the corruption inherent in the world, humanity, and life itself then loom as the large questions remaining for Hamlet to answer.

The turning point that leads to answers is his voyage at sea: here the old Hamlet dies, and a new Hamlet is born. Mack says, "In the last act of the play [...] Hamlet accepts his world and we discover a different man" ("World" 520). In the first scene of the last act we see Hamlet perceive the fact of the fallen world in its results—death, dirt, skulls, and bones. The Garden of Eden indeed has become a graveyard as a result of Adam's sin. As one of the gravediggers says, he is one of those who "hold up Adam's profession" (5.1.312). Adam was the first gardener, and he introduced death and the digging of graves by his fall into sin. Sin infects all humanity and inevitably leads to death. Hamlet now faces and accepts that answer to the question of what life and humanity are in the post-Edenic world, the "unweeded garden" of his first soliloquy.

In the next scene, we witness Hamlet's telling Horatio what happened on the sea voyage. A providential force, "a divinity that shapes our ends" (5.2.10), presented to Hamlet the proper actions to take to escape, live, and return to Denmark. He attributes to this same providential force the provision of his father's signet, which allowed him to use the official seal on the letter ("even in that was heaven ordinant" [48]). One notes that when Hamlet refers to the existence of "a divinity that shapes our ends," Horatio says, "That is most certain" (11). So, Horatio already was living by this philosophy, and he is the one Hamlet admired as ideal. Now Hamlet has achieved the same Christian philosophy of God's providential direction above the corruption and confusion of the world, life, and humanity. The climactic evidence of Hamlet's philosophical solution of submitting himself to the direction of this same providence in answering and contending with the questions of existence is his statement "There is special providence in the fall of a sparrow" (5.2.219–20). He will proceed with the fencing match and accept whatever comes, even if it be death itself. His own stoic nature now equals what he admired in Horatio. The allusion to Matthew 10.29 clearly implies that, rather than play God and try to direct and change the world and humanity, he will now submit himself to providential guidance and be like the sparrow. After penetrating the darkness of the world and human nature, Hamlet not only answered all the questions about them but also found a way to reconcile himself to their real nature and to live as an ideal human being.

NOTES

Hamlet quotations are from Evans et al.

I wish to acknowledge a debt to Clifford J. Ronan, who many years ago graciously allowed me to sit in on his lectures on Shakespeare at the University of Texas, Austin. His insights into *Hamlet* are especially memorable and, combined with Maynard Mack's, have served to open the essence and logic of the play for me.

"That Monster Custom":
Highlighting the Theme of Obedience in *Hamlet*

Joan Hutton Landis

Hamlet is the play I most love to teach. Whether in an introductory class or an advanced Shakespeare course, I am always intent on infecting students with my passion, as it were, and on making the play personal in as many ways as possible. I teach at the Curtis Institute of Music, a conservatory, where students vary in language skills and interest in literature. I have been on a continuous search for pedagogical strategies that are democratic, dramatic, and, above all, productive. Classes are usually heterogeneous, ranging from brilliant readers and writers to those who still struggle with English. When we turn to *Hamlet*, there might be students covertly reading it in Korean, Chinese, Japanese, Russian.

My own favorite tactic for approaching this play is to highlight the theme of obedience. Obviously, every student has experienced the frictions, abuses, and occasional consolations of expected compliance that are inherent in childhood or adolescence. Obedience to one's parents, teachers, and superiors is part of every life. Before entering the play itself, we discuss the ways in which obedience functions in a particular culture or a given child's upbringing. I may ask for a written description of an experience in which being obedient or rebellious has been memorable. The results are often electrifying. One learns, for example, how often young musicians have been trained by threat, coercion, and punishment. Concomitantly, many have chosen their field in the face of parental disapproval or suspicion. I explain that the exercise is preparatory not only for questioning the tropes, customs, and inherited traditions that we all live by but also for seeing how central this subject is to *Hamlet*. My approach lends everyone, but especially the Asian students, a certain bravery, if not bravado, in their navigation through this dark, mysterious, Danish society.

Each teacher will decide whether to read the whole play for plot and general understanding first and then return to retrace a special image or theme or to include such a ploy in discussion from the beginning. I usually do the latter. Before we read 1.2, I ask students to look up the word *obedience*. They discover that it stems from the old French and Latin, *ob-audire* "to listen to or toward, or to give ear to." Often, they will recognize that this act, to obey, is connected to the ear, the organ that is the drinker up of poisons of all sorts in *Hamlet*.

Two more requests: I ask my class to find synonyms for the noun *obedience* and the verb *to obey*. I urge them to consult *Roget's Thesaurus*, a first for many of them. More to the point, I ask them to underline every gesture, phrase, action, or speech that could be linked to the idea of obedience, duty, compliance, authority, command. Writing in their books is, I try to convince them, essential; here, it creates a traceable path of the theme in question. We also recognize that obedience can be an affirmative act, that our critical assessment is necessary at each encounter. Horatio will be a case in point, although some students find his responses to Hamlet overly dutiful in the long run.

I usually underline the easily overlooked responses of Cornelius and Voltimand (1.2.39) to the king's "Farewell, and let your haste commend your duty." They say together, "In that and all things, we will show our duty" (40). There might be bowing and kneeling on stage to underline their fealty. If we haven't done so before, we look at the hierarchical structure of early modern society. (Tillyard's *The Elizabethan World Picture* can still be useful as a schematic simplification.) Of course the king commands and the courtiers obey; that seems too obvious to warrant scrutiny. Yet, as I try to insist in the face of student disbelief, if obedience is one of Shakespeare's real concerns, it will be presented in every available register, even those that are so customary as to be unnoticed. We go on to try to isolate such tropes in our own society or school, so ingrained as to be invisible. I quote Victor Shklovsky's lines that so aptly describe this phenomenon: "Habitualization devours objects, clothes, furniture, one's wife, the fear of war" (qtd. in Scholes 83).

Act 1, scene 2, is rich in examples of verbal repetition as well as acts of obedience. Laertes has his father's leave to return to France, and Hamlet will obey his mother's request to remain in Elsinore. The word "duty" abounds, and the enactment of filial obligation is dramatized in diverse ways. A pattern is, I suggest, now visible.

Act 1, scene 3, is, of course, a *locus classicus* for the observation of obedience in its most familiar form. Ophelia is bidden to obey the orders of both brother and father in an act of renunciation that not only is retrograde to her desire but also marks the beginning of her mental breakdown. Like Gertrude later, her heart will be "cleft [. . .] in twain" (3.4.157). Students will often attack Ophelia for her compliance in this order but will come to see that both males have other reasons for wishing to safeguard Ophelia's "treasure" (1.3.31); they distrust Hamlet not only by virtue of his royal station but also because, like them, he is a male, and, to them, sexual exploitation is customary.

My students usually want to know if Laertes will follow the recipe for correct behavior doled out by his foolish father. The speech itself is an example of reiterated wisdom that can be deconstructed by the wilier readers. We study 2.1 as an answer. Polonius distrusts his son, too, and his directions to Reynaldo are both explicit and disgusting. We have witnessed, then, female submission to male authority and the lengths to which this counselor will go to know if his advice is being followed, to remain in control. Reynaldo may be loath to follow such orders, but he is a servant and is being paid to do so. Thus, he takes his part as another character who is obeying demands that are morally reprehensible. The act of spying is itself part of an emerging pattern, of what will later be referred to as the hidden "imposthume" (4.4.27).

This introductory tracing will alert most students to the fact that Hamlet's swearing to revenge his father's murder is yet another variation, and a central one, on the theme of obedience. Does the fact that revenge was supposedly an accepted mode of action make it unquestionably right for Hamlet? Does he have alternatives? These are questions that we keep foregrounded.

Rosencrantz and Guildenstern present perfect emblems of skewed obedience, as students see without prompting. The clash between obedience to royal power and to friendship is clear and familiar. I ask students both to note the repetition of such clashes and to compare Rosencrantz and Guildenstern with a character such as Osric in 5.2, who is a complier of the first order. His style of witless compliance matches that of Polonius earlier in the play, thus making him here a double of all who act without thought or integrity.

Act 3, scene 4, is a scene on which we spend a full class, reading it aloud and placing it in the context of our theme. Hamlet holds a mirror up to his mother with advice designed to show her why she must shift allegiance and obey her son rather than her husband. What, one can ask, is the paradox at the heart of this scene? I suggest that students underline the verbs in Hamlet's speech at 151–86. These suggest a recipe for revising the moral self. The paradox consists of Hamlet's ability to see his mother's plight clearly while remaining blind to the alternatives for him that his own good advice offers. Do these verbs actually schematize a realistic mode of change, or do they provide a way out of his dilemma at this point? "That monster, custom," is invoked, and students can be asked if and how such custom is connected to the theme of obedience. One answer is, of course, that certain kinds of obedience are themselves such an ingrained custom that, when unquestioned or unexamined, they do become the central monster. In this light, we often revisit Gertrude's motives in marrying Claudius and see her need to base her identity on remaining a wife and a queen: another customary perspective.

Act 4, scene 4, most vividly demonstrates how obedience operates in the world. It can be called a microcosm of the play. I often assign a short paper on this scene, asking students to discuss it first in its context in the act, then to show how it is linked to the larger issues of the play. Again, Hamlet sees the soldier's willingness to "go to their graves like beds" (62) for no good reason other than that they were ordered to fight, and he cannot understand why he, with great cause, still delays to kill his uncle. The tension between true greatness and what a man can do when honor is involved makes a fine riddle for students to try to solve. *Honor* is an ambiguous term and one that students find hard to critique. I argue that Shakespeare found the concept to be one source of tragedy. We read those papers aloud in class, which usually leads to a lively discussion and the chance to compare a dramatic treatment of the effects of obedience with other texts that they may know or want to know. I might describe the thesis of Erich Fromm's *Escape from Freedom.* Recent examples from the class have been Ursula Hegi's *Tearing the Silence* and Kazuo Ishiguro's *The Remains of the Day.* Both are concerned with freeing the self from societal customs and with learning to be a responsible questioner and actor.

One strategy that offers students an inviting riddle is to ask what Polonius's name signifies and why Shakespeare may have chosen it instead of the name

Corambis in the First Quarto. It simply means "the Polish one." Is there a link between that name and the many references to Poland itself? Students will remember that old King Hamlet "smote the sledded Polacks on the ice" (1.1.63). If they connect that geography and that act of anger with Fortinbras's need to go against Poland merely for the lust and love of battle, it becomes clear that Poland represents the repeated violence motivated by quick anger, by appetite for heroism, and by a skewed understanding of duty. Unconsidered action is again visible in Hamlet's enraged and mistaken murder of Polonius.

These tracings are, of course, designed not only to highlight the way the play is constructed and patterned but also to help students get a better purchase on the character of Hamlet and on the rivalries and conflicted obedience that are the causes of his inner war. As we work through act 5, I ask students to list Hamlet's conflicts of loyalty. A volunteer is asked to report on the prince's background, education, age, as these can be gleaned from the text. Hamlet's humanistic and religious training is one clear reason for his delay in killing his uncle. The Old Testament "eye for an eye" ethos is pitted against the New Testament urging toward charity and forgiveness. To goad himself to carry out an act that he abhors, Hamlet takes on roles that validate vengeance. He calls himself "heaven's scourge and minister" (3.4.176), and then, in 5.2, when he defies the message of his heart and quotes the passage about "special providence," he sees himself as a passive actor in a God-directed script. Is Shakespeare suggesting that to place such power in God is one way of denying free will? Has Hamlet accepted this authority as an easement from the terrible difficulties of personal responsibility? This will be a very vexing question, and answers to it depend, usually, on the religious orientation not only of the student but of the teacher as well.

From the ending, one can ask if total allegiance to a father is justified and review the information we have about King Hamlet. This review will give at least some complexity to a question that seems simple to most students, particularly those for whom respect of elders is a given.

Questions that we come back to are: Did Hamlet have alternatives to murder? If so, what were they? Who are Hamlet's doubles in the play, both presented characters and literary or mythic figures? None will be perfectly matched, but a study of doubling in relation to actions prescribed by the custom of obedience to authority will reveal some surprising mirrorings as well as the ambiguity structured so carefully into the play. (For a fuller analysis of doubling, see my essay "Shakespeare's Poland.") Why does Hamlet nominate Fortinbras to succeed him? Is this choice a sign of the force of custom, of obedience to traditional ways? Or is it a sign that Hamlet, for all his moral superiority, has entered into that sphere of political realism and expediency that so marks the actions of other royalty in *Hamlet*?

One conclusion students usually reach during this exploration is that without communication, without the art and awareness of asking difficult moral questions, the tragedies enacted in *Hamlet* will repeat themselves endlessly.

More specifically, students will understand what David Leverenz meant when he wrote, "Hamlet's tragedy is the forced triumph of filial duty over sensitivity to his own heart" (111). This wisdom seems to me not only just but a fine invitation to retrace the path of Hamlet's tragedy retrospectively in play time, to the duel fought on the day Hamlet was born. Violence, revenge, and imposed tradition are not only the stuff of tragedy, they represent tragedy itself and its customary recrudescence throughout time.

NOTE

Hamlet quotations are from Farnham.

Teaching *Hamlet* as a Play about Family

Bruce W. Young

Two words students sometimes use as we discuss *Hamlet* are "long" and "intimidating." Among the strategies I've found effective for making *Hamlet* more accessible is teaching it as a play about family. Despite differences in custom and outlook between *Hamlet*'s world and my students'—and these need to be acknowledged—I find family issues raised by the play to be among those students can most strongly identify with.

An emphasis on family produces several benefits. For one thing, students always raise family issues during the brainstorming with which we begin discussion of the play, and so to focus on family is to spend time on issues they already care about. The last time I taught *Hamlet*, our brainstorming—during which I invite students to raise any questions or issues that concern them—lasted over half an hour, with almost every student contributing and with my role confined mainly to transcribing what they said to the chalkboard. The activity produced over sixty questions, and, of these, almost a third related to family.

Another benefit of focusing on family is that we avoid undue stress on Hamlet as an isolated consciousness. Certainly much in the play invites an emphasis on Hamlet and his psyche. And such an emphasis leads to important questions about individual identity and action. But much is lost if Hamlet becomes the sole focus of discussion. I have found students' experience with the play—and my own—immensely enriched when we think of the world of Hamlet not as a set of isolated egos (with Hamlet's so large as to crowd out almost all the others) but instead as a network of relationships. By viewing the play in this way, we acknowledge its psychic landscape to be intersubjective, and we come to see the identity of individual characters as arising mainly from their roles and their relationships with one another.

As we discuss the questions raised in brainstorming, I encourage students to connect the play with their own experiences. But I also want to help them grow in historical awareness, and so I supplement these personal connections with information about Renaissance family life in order to help students discover both similarities and differences between families in Shakespeare's time and in ours. Much of what my students learn surprises them.

Various kinds of family bonds are important in *Hamlet* and hence in our discussion of the play. In this essay I emphasize the husband-wife bond, but I also touch briefly on parent-child and sibling relationships, which are likewise crucially important in the play. The husband-wife relationships include those of Priam and Hecuba, the Player King and Player Queen, old Hamlet and Gertrude, Claudius and Gertrude—and perhaps the anticipated marriage of Hamlet and Ophelia. As we look at the marriages, we notice that in every case the marriage partners either express mutual love or experience intense grief at the loss of a spouse. Hecuba, described as moving even the gods to passion when her husband is killed, becomes a symbol of authentic grief (2.2.505–18). The Player Queen declares her love for the Player King, fears losing him, and vows never to remarry. The Player King recounts the thirty happy years they have spent "Since love our hearts and Hymen did our hands / Unite comutual in most sacred bands" (3.2.159–60). Old Hamlet (according to his son) was a devoted husband—"so loving to my mother / That he might not beteem the winds of heaven / Visit her face too roughly"—and Gertrude was apparently an affectionate wife who would "hang on [her husband] / As if increase of appetite had grown / By what it fed on" and who grieved passionately at his death (1.2.140–42, 143–45, 148–55). Young Hamlet expresses extravagant grief and love when he learns of Ophelia's death ("Forty thousand brothers / Could not with all their quantity of love / Make up my sum" [5.1.269–71]), despite the rough treatment and apparent rejection he dealt her earlier.

Of course, the play complicates and problematizes these expressions of love. Hamlet remembers his mother's grief only to question its durability and gen-uineness, and he interrupts the "Mousetrap" with biting comments that cast doubt on women's love generally. But I encourage my students to suspend judgment about whether Hamlet is right about his mother and, further, to imagine the story from Gertrude's point of view and consider whether her grief, though not long-lasting, may have been as genuine as any human grief, certainly as genuine as Hamlet's over Ophelia.

I often supplement the play's evidence with quotations from Shakespeare's contemporaries, most of whom imagined marriage to be the most intimate and loving of human relationships: marriage is "the nearest conjunction and the most excellent and perfect society which is in this world" (Perkins 482); "unlesse there be a joyning of hearts and a knitting of affections together, it is not Marriage indeed, but in shew and name" (H. Smith 44); "Marriage is a merri-age, and this worlds Paradise, where there is mutuall love" (Speght 106); conjugal love "must be the most deare, intimate, precious and entire, that hart can have toward a creature" (Wing 44); "Husband and Wife are neerer than Friends, and Brethren; or than Parents and Children" (Gataker 5). I also tell my students of evidence from letters, diaries, and other sources indicating that many husbands and wives actually experienced something approaching the ideal of conjugal love expressed in these quotations.

I emphasize what may seem obvious—that marriage was viewed as a loving, intimate companionship—because many students come with stereotypes about the lovelessness of marriages in the past, and, if they don't begin with such stereotypes, they often encounter them in criticism and other sources. The long outdated account G. M. Trevelyan gives of the Renaissance family, including his pronouncement that "Marriage was not an affair of personal affection but of family avarice" (261; qtd. in Woolf 42), still survives in Virginia Woolf's *A Room of One's Own*; and Lawrence Stone's gloomy assessment of family life in the period continues to be influential, especially in Shakespearean criticism and in student papers that depend on this criticism. At some point, I tell students that, despite its ground-breaking contributions, many historians consider *The Family, Sex, and Marriage in England, 1500–1800* Stone's most flawed book[1] and that other books give a much different and, in my view, more accurate picture of family life in the period. In particular, I refer students to books by Ralph Houlbrooke (*The English Family* and *English Family Life*) and Linda Pollock (*A Lasting Relationship*), which contain excerpts from letters, diaries, and other documents.

But before entering into the historical debate, I want students first to experience the play as observantly and intensively as they can. What they generally find is the clear expectation that marriage should involve mutual love. If that was not the expectation, it would be hard to explain why Hamlet is so deeply disillusioned by what he sees as his mother's failure to live up to the ideal. Even Claudius, though murder taints his marriage, gives evidence for the idealistic view. Far from merely using Gertrude as a stepping stone to the throne, he confesses, "She is so conjunctive to [his] life and soul, / That, as the star moves not but in his sphere," so he cannot "but by her" (4.7.14–16). Part of what makes the closing scene so horrifying for Claudius is that, even before his own fate is decided, Gertrude's drinking from the poisoned cup has already defeated him, draining his life of much of its meaning.

Claudius and Gertrude thus illustrate as well as any of the characters the Renaissance commonplace that "Man and Wife are [. . .] the one ingraffed into the other, and so fastned together, that they cannot againe be sundred" (Gataker 5). But, of course, this commonplace also helps explain Hamlet's view that his mother's second marriage is incestuous. After reviewing the text for references to incest, I ask my students why they think Hamlet and the Ghost make the charge and why the two characters find this kind of incest so abhorrent. Some notice how Gertrude's second marriage has confused the structure of family relations, especially for Hamlet, who refers to his stepfather and mother as his "uncle-father and aunt-mother" (2.2.376). For most, it is obvious that Hamlet's and the Ghost's intimate connection with Gertrude heightens their sense of the horrors of incest. But many are baffled as to why marriage with a brother-in-law would be considered incest in the first place.

At this point I tell my students about "the forbidden degrees of marriage," and I sometimes recount the story of Henry VIII and the contemporary debate about whether his marriage to his brother's widow was incestuous. But the best aid I have found for helping students understand the issue is in *Hamlet* itself. When Hamlet explains his odd insistence on calling Claudius "mother" by saying "father and mother is man and wife, man and wife is one flesh" (4.3.49–52), he is expressing the standard view, derived from the Bible, on which much in "the forbidden degrees" is based: that by marrying, a man and woman become so united as to be virtually indistinguishable (see Gen. 2.24; Matt. 19.5–6). Those to whom a husband and wife are related by affinity—their in-laws—may therefore be considered virtual blood relations. Gertrude is not merely Claudius's sister-in-law but his virtual sister, since she has become one flesh with his brother. Marriage with her is therefore as incestuous for him as marriage with his own sister would be.

As we turn from marriage to other family relationships, I find that combining careful, sympathetic reading with historical awareness again enhances students' engagement with the play. Many students can identify with the feelings of displacement and bitterness exhibited by characters—including Hamlet, Ophelia, Laertes, and Fortinbras—who lose fathers. Historical information deepens our understanding of such feelings by revealing that, while writers of the period advised moderation in grief (advice echoed by Claudius and Gertrude), many of Shakespeare's contemporaries, even with the aid of religious and rational consolation, experienced grief as intense and prolonged as Hamlet's.

Besides noticing the passionate love and attachment characters display for their fathers, most students recognize that, though the father figures have serious flaws, their expressions of affection and desires for their children's welfare are apparently sincere. Here again, historical information is helpful. The play refers twice to parents blessing their children (1.3.52–82; 3.4.171–72), a practice that Shakespeare's contemporaries clearly understood as expressing genuine affection and concern (see B. Young). Debora Shuger demonstrates that, in Renaissance England, fatherhood was associated with kindness, nurturing, and generous self-giving and concludes that it does not "seem plausible that humanists and preachers would appeal so confidently to parental tenderness if such emotions were culturally unavailable" (*Habits* 234–35). Historical evidence thus joins with *Hamlet* in undermining modern stereotypes about the supposed distance in earlier generations between brutal fathers and their brutalized children, stereotypes again promoted by Trevelyan, who writes of children's being "locked up, beaten and flung about the room, without any shock being inflicted on public opinion" (260–61; qtd. in Woolf 42).

This does not mean, of course, that the fathers in *Hamlet* are uniformly kind and generous. Polonius in particular mixes good intentions with demeaning and manipulative treatment of his children. But students are profited by knowing that these fathers' departures from kindness and generosity are departures from a strongly held Renaissance ideal. In fact, it is precisely because they violate the ideal that such departures have distressing and even tragic results.

Historical awareness suggests that, among the play's less than ideal fathers, we must count the Ghost. Hamlet's fervent response to the Ghost's request for revenge is understandable and even, to a degree, admirable. But though filial loyalty is an important value in the play, as it was in Renaissance England, it is not the only value. A persuasive case can be made that *Hamlet* is a play against revenge (see England; Girard; Landis), and that case is strengthened when we consider what Renaissance moralists commonly wrote about parental authority, namely, that parents should not command that which is not virtuous and that the commandment to honor one's parents applies "so long as they pass not their bounds" (Pritchard 31; Bradford 162). My aim in making students aware of such facts is not to force them into taking sides on the revenge question but to sensitize them to details in the play that complicate the issue. I want them to feel the emotional intensity of Hamlet's identification with his father and his desire to honor and vindicate him while, at the same time, they notice the play's association of revenge with hell and damnation and feel the horror involved in that association. If students approach the play openly, they generally discover that the moral bias against revenge is built into the play as firmly as the emotional bias in its favor.

Another familial bond—that between siblings—also has a bearing on revenge, suggesting both why Claudius's murder of his brother is so horrible and why the younger characters' desire for revenge is destructive as well. Claudius feels profound guilt for "A brother's murther," an act that, because it repeats Cain's slaying of Abel, bears "the primal eldest curse" (3.3.36–38). Students understand the enormity of fratricide better when they know that brothers were viewed as having a common physical origin and therefore a shared physical identity. Though this perception applies most potently to literal brothers, the play uses the term "brother" figuratively as well, thereby establishing the fraternal bond as a pattern for all ethical relations. For Hamlet to call Laertes "brother," as he does shortly before they kill each other (5.2.243–44, 253), adds pathos and moral weight to their mutually inflicted deaths, making even more pointed what Laertes says just before wounding Hamlet: "And yet it is almost against my conscience" (5.2.296). The violent deaths of these two quasi brothers thus extend and reinforce the pattern begun by Claudius when he killed old Hamlet.

Ultimately, my students and I grapple with the questions of what, if anything, *Hamlet* means, why it affects us as it does, and why it has acquired such cultural importance. Here again, focusing on family helps us discover answers. In the course of class discussion, it becomes clear that the intensity of family feeling makes for much of the play's intensity and moves to the foreground many of the play's most interesting issues. Both Gertrude's supposed incest and Hamlet's supposed duty to revenge hinge on the question of how heavily marital and familial duties ought to weigh, as opposed, say, to purely personal or political concerns. The play asks what debt we owe to family members, including those who have died. It raises questions about the hazards and benefits of entering into relationships as intense and intimate as those that make up family life. We are led to consider how parents can care for children without suffocating them and how children can respect parental authority without losing a sense of personal autonomy. We consider similarly challenging questions concerning the bond between siblings and between husband and wife. All these questions finally have something to do with self and other—with personal identity and how it is shaped by, perhaps how it arises from, relationships with others.

Inevitably, teaching *Hamlet* as a play about family influences the issues we emphasize. Yet I have found that teaching the play in this way promotes rather than discourages a vigorous and authentic exchange of differing opinions. Students soon learn that, like all teachers, I have my biases. But they also find that the combination of careful attention to the text, historical awareness, and use of personal experience I encourage leaves them plenty of room to disagree with me and argue their own views. The emphasis on family opens the way to making personal connections, connections that render scholarship and criticism on the play more accessible and engaging to students by relating it to issues they care about. But the connections also have a value of their own, enabling students to make of their encounter with *Hamlet* a way of learning more about themselves.

NOTES

Hamlet references are to Evans et al.

[1] For assessments of Stone's book, see Cressy 128 (it is Stone's "most dangerous and controversial" book); Houlbrooke, *English Family* 15 ("Much evidence of love, affection and the bitterness of loss dating from the first half of Stone's period"—i.e., the period most relevant to Shakespeare—"has simply been ignored"); Macfarlane 123, 113 (Stone's book is a "compendium of distortions" that "ignores or dismisses contrary evidence, misinterprets ambiguous evidence, fails to use relevant evidence, imports evidence from other countries to fill gaps, and jumbles up the chronology"); and Thompson 500 (in some respects, the book is a "disaster").

Ten Questions Basic to Interpreting *Hamlet*, with Special Focus on the Ghost

Roy Battenhouse

Andrew M. McLean, University of Wisconsin, Parkside, writes: "Roy Batten-house sent me his 'Ten Questions on Hamlet,' and realizing its value to teach-ers, I asked him to answer the questions himself. I thought he might provide, in so doing, a model for other teachers. In his class, one or another of the ques-tions was used as a springboard for examining the significance of various pas-sages in the play. He usually began with the question about the Ghost, since around this the play opens; but discussion frequently branched out to many of the adjacent questions suggested by the progress of the play's scenes. Roy felt that these ten questions could help the student locate the moral and metaphys-ical factors that interlock and condition a revenge action in its progressive development. And even if the questions didn't get answered in class, they could challenge a student's curiosity or prompt a term paper. In this essay Professor Battenhouse comments on the questions primarily as a resource for the teacher, to be drawn on to whatever extent is useful in treating the questions. He wrote this shortly before his death." I include here the ten questions and Batten-house's full response to his first question. The questions are valuable for stu-dents whichever side of the issues instructors might find themselves, and, though Battenhouse seems to have had one Hamlet and one Ghost in mind, stu-dents can test the answers by comparing several Hamlets, several Ghosts.

—BWK

Synoptic List of Questions

1. The most important question is the one Hamlet poses on meeting the Ghost: "Be thy intents wicked, or charitable [. . .]?" (1.4.42). But since Hamlet never pursues and thus never answers this question, the play chal-lenges us to decide it from evidence given by the Ghost's behavior and speech and the resulting effect on Hamlet. Try tabulating pieces of evi-dence.

2. What defects do you see in the quality of Hamlet's love? What kind of ideal influences his attitude toward his father, his mother, and Ophelia?

3. Is Claudius as bestial as Hamlet supposes? And are Rosencrantz and Guildenstern "adders fang'd" who deserve to be blown to the moon (3.4.203, 209)?

4. Is Hamlet's "Mousetrap" a success or a failure? Does it cause Claudius to rush squealing from the room, as a critic such as Dover Wilson supposes (*What Happens* 196)? Or, on the contrary, does Claudius exit with a peremptory dignity to give notice of royal disapproval of Hamlet's mis-chievous use of drama? Whose guilt, actually, is unkenneled?

5. Is Hamlet's madness real or feigned? Is his "antic disposition" (1.5.172) a mere mask resorted to (as in Saxo Grammaticus's version of the story) for hiding a political purpose until Hamlet can find opportunity to make himself king by destroying a usurper?

6. How satisfactory do you find Hamlet's "repentance" after killing Polonius? Or his apology to Laertes in act 5?

7. Why does Hamlet delay in carrying out the Ghost's command? Is he hampered by external circumstances?

8. Can Ophelia's tragedy be traced in part to family advice? How does her later madness differ from Hamlet's?

9. When Horatio asks "flights of angels" to sing Hamlet to his rest (5.2.360), can we infer that the dying prince will go to heaven a saved soul? Producers of the play have sometimes suggested this by ending the drama with Horatio's "flights of angels" speech.

10. How do the three sons—Hamlet, Laertes, and Fortinbras—resemble or differ from one another as avengers?

Question 1 concerns the moral quality of the Ghost's intent. Signals of a lack of charity are many. Entering armed and frowning, the Ghost arouses dread as it "usurps't" the night (1.1.46). Horatio is reminded of the ghosts that appeared to portend disasters to the Roman state in the times of Julius Caesar. Is it not ominous that when Horatio charges this ghost to speak, "By Heaven" and "If there be any good thing to be done," it shifts away? Later, very significantly, it vanishes at the crowing of the cock, a bird that has Christian associations with the light of God, wholesome nights, and "our Savior's birth" (49, 130, 133, 157–64). To many modern readers (e.g., Battenhouse "Ghost"; Prosser; and Guilfoyle) such signals indicate a framework of traditional lore against which Shakespeare is placing the defective morality of the Ghost. (Guilfoyle, for example, shows the ways in which the play's opening scene is in antithesis to the Christian Advent story.) Horatio sees indications of a "guilty thing," an "extravagant and erring spirit" (1.1.148, 154).

On the other hand, the editor of the Arden edition of *Hamlet*, Harold Jenkins, tends to dismiss the Christian lore reported by Marcellus; his judgment is that "extravagant and erring" carry no suggestion that the erring spirit is an evil one. But Jenkins does not explain on what moral grounds we can exempt from evil such matters as guilt, extravagance, and error. Let us grant that here they seem less than villainous. Yet is it logical to deny that they indicate a taint of evil, hence not a spirit of health, in the Ghost?

The reason Jenkins takes the stand he does is evident when he affirms A. C. Bradley's view that the premise of Shakespeare's play is that "a son should avenge a father's murder" (153). On this assumption, Romantic interpretation in general based its reading of the play. Ignored by this approach, however, is a Bible text well known to most writers of revenge plays, Romans 12.19, "Dearly beloved, avenge not yourselves [. . .]." The standard view of Elizabethan moralists (as Prosser summarizes) was that *private* revenge was "illegal, blasphemous, immoral, irrational, unnatural, and unhealthy" (10). Should we suppose that Shakespeare is disregarding this premise? Such is unlikely in view of the "gracious" alternative to which the lore of Marcellus points us. And further, if we recall from *Measure for Measure* the lament of Angelo that "when once our grace we have forgot, / Nothing goes right" (4.4.33–34), a neglect of divine grace seems to have been for Shakespeare a basic explanation of human tragedy. Shakespeare was no doubt aware, nevertheless, that revenge is a motive that appeals to man's unregenerate or corrupt nature, tempting human beings to their destruction. Indeed, a central purpose of the tragic genre may be to lead readers to experience this temptation vicariously in order that afterward they may confess in retrospect, "There but for the grace of God go I." The arousing of pity and fear belongs to the therapeutic method and goal of the genre of tragedy. In *Othello*, for instance, we see a hero embrace revenge to his own destruction when blinded in regard to his real duty, thus prompting in us a wiser pity and fear.

Besides the signals so far mentioned there is also in the opening scene a report of King Hamlet's duel with King Fortinbras, in which he waged "all those his lands / Which he stood seiz'd of" (1.1.88–89), ignoring the welfare of citizens dwelling in those lands, and the result of which now is that Denmark's armament factories must be kept busy night and day, even on Sunday, to protect the gain achieved by King Hamlet's combat for the sake of personal glory. King Fortinbras, we are told, was pricked on by "emulate pride" (83); but can we not infer that this same motive was that of King Hamlet, whose ghost has now returned to prick on his son? Do these background circumstances allow us to suppose a spirit of health in the Ghost?

When we turn to Prince Hamlet's first encounter with the Ghost in scene 4, we hear Hamlet cry out, "Angels and ministers of grace defend us!" (1.4.39), indicating thus an awareness that not all ghosts are spirits of health. Yet Hamlet, in his eagerness to confront the apparition "though hell itself should gape" (1.2.244), tears himself from Horatio and Marcellus, threatening to kill them when they (like ministering angels) try to protect him against a ghost that he has described as "making night hideous" and that they see making him "desperate with imagination." His excuse for following temptation is that "My fate cries out" (1.4.54, 87, 81). Is he not choosing fatalism rather than good sense? Jenkins offers the explanation, "A man who embraces his human lot must consent to be a sinner" (157). This is scarcely a recommendation of the Ghost's moral quality, and it ignores the alternative that Hamlet has, of listening to his friends rather than yielding to a daredevil passion. Is sin the *only* "human lot" a man has available to him? It can be made so if one is determined to override Christian and Stoic warnings against rash passion. But are those critics wrong (e.g., Grebanier) who name rashness Hamlet's tragic flaw?

In examining scene 5, students should be alert to signals of a kind of falsehood moralists commonly ascribed to a demonic telling of the truth. When

Banquo in *Macbeth* remarks that "instruments of darkness" oftentimes tell us truths "to betray's in deepest consequence" (1.3.124–26), he was warning against the deceptive truth presented by hideous hags. But lesser versions of hideous truth were also suspect in the judgment of Elizabethan moralists. They prescribed various tests of wholesomeness, none of which the *Hamlet* Ghost can be said to pass, such as that a trustworthy ghost must offer comfort, not revenge, as his message.

It is sometimes alleged by modern critics that the *Hamlet* Ghost comes from a Christian purgatory because he speaks of undergoing fires to purge his crimes. Against this interpretation, however, is the fact that none of his talk fits with the repentant humility of a Christian spirit in purgatory, and no critic has been able to cite from literature any example of a spirit from purgatory who returns to ask revenge. We may recall that the ghosts in *Richard III,* who presumably come from a Christian purgatory, preach comfort and angel's help for Richmond and despair to an inveterate sinner such as Richard; they hope for their country's restoration, but not through any counsel of revenge (5.3). Thomas Nashe's Cutwolfe, as Prosser points out, declares, "revenge in our tragedies is continually raised from hell" (40). Hamlet's father may be coming not from purgatory but from a Hades that pagan reasoning *imagined* as a purging place.

The *Hamlet* Ghost focuses his story around affronts to his personal dignity. "Remember *me*" is his plea. Claudius is referred to as "garbage" in comparison to King Hamlet's "celestial" worth, and Gertrude is associated with Lust personified (1.5.91, 57, 56, 55)—although as John W. Draper noted, Gertrude does not act like a slave of lust when we see her elsewhere in the play. Evidently this ghost is motivated by a contempt for any human being who has degraded *him*; he seems to identify his "natural gifts" (1.5.51) with heaven's standards, unaware that this emphasis ignores the warning of Matthew 5.22 against contempt for neighbor, the sign of a heart that violates heaven's injunction against murder. In this respect the Ghost's whole outlook is tainted, unrepentant of his own sins while demanding revenge against Claudius and a no-rescue stance toward a Gertrude viewed as falling off "From *me*." Can so self-centered a morality be that of a spirit of health? Is not his likening of himself to a "radiant angel" a false insinuation (48, 55)?

The effect on Hamlet (whom the Ghost has commended for a haste to "sweep" to revenge) is an impetuous readiness to "couple hell" with heaven and earth in a mind now so "distracted" by thoughts of villainy that only the Ghost's command is declared worthy of remembrance. All "saws of books" (all traditional wisdom) he swears to wipe away, a response that is obviously unhealthy (31, 93, 97, 100). It is accompanied by what his arriving friends call "wild and whirling" words. Then, demanding that his friends take an oath of secrecy regarding what they have seen, he engages in a conjuring with the "old mole" in the cellarage (133, 144, 162), who from this under-stage location (conventionally that of hellmouth) cooperates with a sepulchral demand that they swear to this compact. It is possible for any critic to suppose that "airs from heaven" characterize the Ghost in this scene (1.4.41)?

The ill effects of the Ghost's message of course do not end with act 1. Among the later signals of a malign influence are Hamlet's appearance to Ophelia "[a]s if he had been loosed out of hell" (2.1.80); his desire to hear declaimed the speech about "hellish Pyrrhus" (2.2.463); and his staging of a play that leads to his soliloquy of delight in the witching time of night when churchyards yawn (3.2.388; recall his first impression of the Ghost in 1.4) and "Hell itself breathes out Contagion" (3.2.389–90), as it evidently did in 1.5. Then, soon after, we hear him reasoning that his revenge requires the killing of Claudius only when he can also send his soul to hell, since that is where he suspects his father is. Many readers (such as Samuel Johnson) have been shocked by this soliloquy; it is not only contrary to charity but also to any concern for Denmark's welfare. But cannot Hamlet's desire to damn Claudius be considered a logical development from what was latent in the Ghost's initial message?

In reading Hamlet's explicit statement, however, we need not dismiss altogether the suggestion (e.g., made by Bradley) that there is a subconscious reason, unrecognized by Hamlet, for his not slaying Claudius. A man on his knees at prayer presents an obstacle to a killer's natural conscience, which Hamlet has suppressed by his initial vow to remember only revenge. (Aquinas held that a conscience implanted by man's Creator can be overlaid with sin but not rooted out entirely [967–68].) We should consider Shakespeare's contextual evidence that Hamlet retains occasional glimmers of natural conscience: his remarking to Polonius that "who shall scape whipping?" if every man is used according to his "desert" (2.2.530–31) and his telling Laertes, "Thou pray'st not well," when this avenger cries, "The devil take thy soul" (5.1.259). Would Hamlet have been able to slay Polonius if he had looked behind the curtain and seen a defenseless man? Would he have been able to order death for Rosencrantz and Guildenstern if he had looked them in the eye instead of only imagining them behind a "play" of letters?

NOTE

Shakespeare quotations are from Evans et al.

The "Encrusted" *Hamlet*:
Resetting the "Mousetrap"

Graham Bradshaw

Three-Way Collisions

First, the scene, or setting. I am currently reading *Hamlet* with fourteen students in my postgraduate Shakespeare class at Chuo University, in Tokyo. I taught *Hamlet* a few years ago, in a Kyoto University postgraduate class; the chief difference now is probably that I rely more on handouts, to map out what we're discussing and to ask the students to think about some questions in advance. Our *Hamlet* class meets weekly, through the academic year, and each class is ninety minutes. That may sound like a lot of teaching time, in Western terms, but we often feel hurried. Although we move through *Hamlet* scene by scene, one major problem in planning this course is that of deciding when and how to accommodate issues that are historically complicated, critically controversial, and culturally alien. For example, one needs some kind of excursus on Elizabethan attitudes to ghosts when discussing the first scene, while Hamlet's first soliloquy calls for some more extended discussion of incest and the so-called Oedipus complex.

The uncertainty of the Ghost's provenance needs to be discussed very carefully, because there is no parallel in traditional Japanese drama or in the Shinto and Buddhist religions, where the concept of purgatory is also alien. The early Japanese translators who listed the Ghost in the dramatis personae as "the Ghost of Hamlet's Father" clearly weren't troubled by Hamlet's own intermittent but intense doubts about whether the Ghost was a devil; since the play had been assimilated to the strong Japanese tradition of *katakiuchi* ("blood revenge") drama, the crucial bond was that between father and son. Of course I directed the students to John Dover Wilson's *What Happens in* Hamlet (1935) as the critical and historical landmark in twentieth-century thinking about the "questionable" Ghost. In planning the course it was obvious that this basic issue had to addressed, but what then? We might have tried to call a temporary halt, moving on to the second scene. However, I had already told my students that I didn't even think it possible to study *Hamlet* without considering the overlay of later critical and theatrical assumptions. So we pressed on to consider how Wilson's compelling arguments about the Ghost's provenance affect earlier and later readings.

Going backward in the criticism means confronting one daunting example of the way in which *Hamlet* is, perhaps more than any other work of art, encrusted with unhelpful and contradictory assumptions. English critics in the period from Samuel Coleridge through A. C. Bradley hardly ever discussed Hamlet without discussing his real or alleged delay. Since they disregarded the good reasons Hamlet has for thinking that the Ghost may be a devil, they didn't consider how these were also good reasons for not sweeping to revenge. A long, rich tradition of commentary and speculation was misconceived and misdirected. This tradition is all the more dismaying because, even though the doubts about the Ghost's provenance make those earlier arguments about Hamlet's delay as implausible as Bradley's account of the Ghost as a majestic "messenger of divine justice" (174), the imaginative power of Coleridge's or Bradley's readings has entered and become part of Western thinking about Hamlet in other, more dispersed, and less palpably specific ways.

Going forward in criticism can also involve facing (or failing to see) more recent encrustations. For example, John Dover Wilson and later scholars like Roland Mushat Frye maintained—correctly, I think—that even when the play ends, our doubts about the Ghost have not been resolved. Yet Wilson and Frye were both curiously untroubled by the way in which, after the "Mousetrap" scene, Hamlet himself never again worries about whether the Ghost may be a devil. Perhaps because my Japanese students were having to consider unfamiliar cultural notions about ghosts and purgatory (a Roman Catholic invention, which Protestantism rejected), they were more troubled than Western critics by one alarmingly pressing connection: if the Ghost really is Hamlet's father, so that its references to purgatory are not a devilish (or papist) lie, Protestants were in deep trouble—in Shakespeare's England as well as Hamlet's Denmark. Hence Hamlet's grim joke, and the accompanying reference to the patron saint of purgatory, when he replies to Horatio's "There's no offence, my lord": "Yes, by Saint Patrick, but there is, Horatio, / And much offence too" (1.5.136–37).

Peculiar difficulties arise when a word—like *ghost* or *incest*—is linguistically translatable but the concept is culturally and historically different. Since marrying a dead husband's brother is not prohibited in Japan and has often been encouraged, Japanese readers and audiences won't feel the "abhorrence" that both Wilson (65) and Ernest Jones (61) insisted has a controlling significance in

Shakespeare's play. In Wilson's or Jones's terms this cultural difference would be critically disabling, but it also exposes their own interpretive intransigence, since incest figures less prominently in the play than in their respective accounts of the play. Mentioned only by Hamlet and the "questionable" Ghost, it doesn't disturb (say) Horatio or Ophelia and is altogether forgotten by Claudius when he is dejectedly contemplating his sins in the prayer scene.

I don't want to suggest to my students that they try to build into their responses some revulsion that they don't feel and very few modern westerners feel. Instead, I suggest that the theme of incest may be yet another case where we need to question or guard against the tendency to view *Hamlet* through Prince Hamlet's eyes and also need to distinguish among different kinds of credibility. "No one can doubt for one moment"—Wilson insists, all too insistently—that Shakespeare "expected his audience to look upon it with as much abhorrence as the Athenians felt" for Oedipus's "crime" (65). Well, maybe, but maybe not. The argument's historical credibility depends on whether we can be sure that Shakespeare's audience (not the ecclesiastical statutes) differed so absolutely from modern Japanese and Western audiences, in attaching little or no importance to the distinction between blood relationships and relationships by affinity. Since Wilson's historical argument about what Shakespeare "expected" turns the play into a museum piece, its critical credibility depends upon our finding other, better ways of explaining why Shakespeare is the world's most performed dramatist and why his most popular play has continued to enthrall audiences in different periods and different cultures. We should be wary of any "historical" explanation that diminishes the play without explaining its extraordinary afterlife.

Jones also insisted—no less insistently than Wilson but for very different reasons—on the profound difference in Hamlet's attitude to incest and murder: for Jones, "there can be no question as to which arouses in [Hamlet] the deeper loathing"—that is, incest (68). Although the theory of the so-called Oedipus complex has been so influential in modern Western responses to *Hamlet*, its influence in Japan was far more limited through most of the twentieth century. Just why its influence was limited, and just when and how the earlier Freudian and later Lacanian versions began to be taken seriously, might be the subject of a fascinating cultural study. Trying to explain the theory to students who haven't already in some sense accepted it is a peculiarly sobering exercise. I quoted (while knowing that I couldn't for long take shelter behind) A. D. Nuttall's recent, admirably laconic summary:

> All male children pass through a phase in which they wish to murder their fathers and have sexual intercourse with their mothers. We have grown accustomed to Freud's famous theory of the Oedipus Complex. The simple sentence in which the theory is stated no longer shocks. Does this mean that we have learned to accept the proposition as true? If we have indeed reached a stage of belief—as distinct from mere numb habitua-

tion—then, I suggest, we ought not to have done so. There might indeed
be something salutary in using our imagination to recover the original
shock effect. The shock arose not only from the sexual content of the sentence but also from sheer implausibility. If ever a statement needed to
earn acceptance by vigorous demonstration, it was this.   (123)

Nuttall himself wryly recalls how "the philosopher Sidney Hook asked one psychoanalyst after another what would count as evidence that a child had not got
an Oedipus Complex and never obtained an answer" (128). When students
asked, point-blank, whether I believed in the existence and universality of the
complex, I admitted that I certainly didn't believe it had the demonstrable,
clinical reality of, say, multi-infarct dementia—the grave disease that was
afflicting Lacan when he produced all that work on topological models of psy-
chosis that is still taken seriously by some literary theorists with no medical
training. In other words, the oedipal version of *Hamlet* is another encrustation,
which should be opposed not dogmatically but antidogmatically.

   These preliminary examples should show why it is misleading to suppose
that teaching Shakespeare in a quite different culture produces some quasi-
colonial situation in which the authority explains to the uninformed what
Shakespeare really means. To teach Shakespeare in Oxford or Berkeley is
already to teach Shakespeare in a quite different culture and in what is more
likely to be a two-way situation. There may then be far less resistance from
the natives if the teacher sweeps past those complicated issues I have mentioned and prefers to concentrate on currently privileged Western issues, like
the unholy trinity of race, class, and gender. Similarly, because the words and
concepts seem familiar, Western students are less likely to notice when new
historicist and cultural materialist discussions of concepts of the self, or what
Hamlet calls "that within" (1.2.85), are historically anachronistic: I ask my
Japanese students to stay close to the *OED* when they are reading such critics and to remember that when *Hamlet* was written, words like *individual*,
identity, *personality*, *inward*, *introspection*, *consciousness*, or *character*
either didn't exist or didn't then include the sense or meaning in question. In
Japan, the conditions of the cross-cultural encounter produce fascinating,
excitingly unpredictable three-way collisions, by exposing gaps between modern Western beliefs and assumptions and those at work in Renaissance culture or in *Hamlet*.

Staging the "Mousetrap" Scene

When I can see such three-way collisions coming, I try to engineer them or
stage them effectively. Our approach to the "Mousetrap" scene is also staged
in the other sense: that is, it's deliberately structured—not least because, in my
earlier course at Kyoto University, this scene was one point where our discussions became excited but alarmingly disordered, so that it wasn't always clear

what was at issue. Some readers may think that my structuring of the Chuo classes on the "Mousetrap" is too deliberate, or coercive.

First, I give the students a preliminary handout that asks them to think about certain issues before our next class. Then, in the class, we begin by comparing Laurence Olivier's 1944 film version with the 1980 BBC production. I give the students another handout, which includes extracts from Anthony Dawson's and Bernice Kliman's commentaries on the BBC production (Hamlet), as well as some extracts from W. W. Greg's comments on the "Mousetrap" in his famous or notorious 1917 essay. After inviting different responses to the Olivier and BBC stagings, I set out what I call the basic problem in staging this scene. We then see how this problem reappears in the film versions by Franco Zeffirelli and Kenneth Branagh. Then, and only at this relatively and deliberately late stage in our discussions, I ask the students to return to, and formally review, the issues raised in the preliminary handout— which reads as follows:

Preliminary Handout

1. If you still haven't read Shiga Naoya's 1912 story "Kurôdiasu no Nikki" ("Claudius's Diary" [*Shiga*, vol. 7]), be sure to read it before our next class. Shiga was the first writer to maintain, both through the story and in his later essay "On Claudius's Diary—To Funaki Shigeo" (*Shiga*, vol. 8), that the "Mousetrap" fails to establish Claudius's guilt. Unfortunately, Shiga's view of *Hamlet* was easy to dismiss, since he also maintained that Claudius really was innocent, despite Claudius's later, unequivocal admission that he is guilty of "[a] brother's murder" (3.3.38). But of course we only hear Claudius say this in the scene that follows the "Mousetrap," and Hamlet doesn't hear it at all. What is the force of Shiga's position if we confine ourselves to asking what becomes clear in the "Mousetrap" scene?
2. Peter Hall's famous 1965 Royal Shakespeare Company production seems to have been the first to stage the "Mousetrap" as a test that fails. Read this extract from Anthony Dawson's account of what happened in this staging very carefully, and try to determine where it becomes apparent that Dawson didn't actually see the production in question.

> During the dumb-show, drinks were served, and general chatter covered the dangerous bits. There was an empty chair on the rostrum beside the King and Queen, but Hamlet preferred to remain below. He applauded loudly after the Player Queen's exit and Ophelia followed suit, but the rest of the court pointedly did not; then he moved to his empty chair to pose the question: "Madam, how like you this play?" and the court chatter subsided. The sense was that Hamlet was being gratuitously offensive, and the court watched carefully for the royal cue. It came a few moments later when the King called for lights. Far from being a sponta-

neous manifestation of guilt, the interruption became, in Brewster Mason's hands, a mark of "offended dignity"; he was publicly rebuking Hamlet for an impertinent "social gaffe" [. . .], i.e., for daring to enact a nephew's murderous inclination toward his uncle. But there was also a flicker of fear in his eye, noticeable to Hamlet, if not to the rest of the court. This led to an electric moment when the two met "eye to eye," with Claudius "silently accept[ing] the challenge of a duel to the death" [. . .]. Here perhaps was Hamlet's strongest moment before the finale, but the King had clearly won nevertheless, by turning his nephew's theatrical test into a public relations victory [. . .].   (141–42)

3. John Dover Wilson's very different account of what happens when the King "rises" reads like a vivid stage direction or extract from the scenario for the film Olivier had not yet made:

> Terrified by the thought that "Hamlet knows it all!," [Claudius] pulls himself to his feet, and, squealing for light, he totters as fast as his trembling knees will take him from the terrible, the threatening room. King Mouse has become a shambling, blinking paddock.   (195)

In his vastly influential *Shakespearean Tragedy* (1904), Bradley had similarly assumed that "Hamlet's device proves a triumph far more complete than he had dared to expect":

> He had thought that the King might "blench," but he [Claudius] does much more. When only six of the "dozen or sixteen lines" have been spoken he starts to his feet and rushes from the hall, followed by the whole dismayed Court.   (104)

The idea that Claudius is unable to control himself resurfaces in the new Norton edition of Shakespeare, when Stephen Greenblatt writes, "After the King has stormed out in a rage [. . .]" (1662). Bradley, Wilson, and Greenblatt are all inventing stage directions that they then treat as part of Shakespeare's text or script.

My preliminary handout deliberately stops short of asking what seems to me the most important question, since I hope the students will ask it, independently, before we start comparing the Olivier film and the BBC version. The question is: If we choose to follow Hamlet in supposing that Claudius betrays his guilt in some unequivocal way, *how* does Claudius reveal it, and *to whom?*

That question directs us to what I take to be the basic problem in any staging of the "Mousetrap" scene. If Claudius behaves like Wilson's "blinking, shambling paddock" or the weak bloat king in Olivier's film version, how can we then make sense of the prayer scene, in which Claudius speaks as if nobody but God knows of his "offence"? Wilson's Claudius is "terrified by the thought that 'Hamlet knows it all!,'" but Shakespeare's Claudius isn't. Far from speaking like a man who has just betrayed his guilt, he expresses no fear that anything in "this world" might make it difficult or impossible to "retain" those "effects for which I did the murder, / My crown, mine own ambition, and my queen" (3.3.54–55).

This basic problem multiplies like a cancer when we consider other characters' responses. How, for example, should we make sense of Horatio's apparently doubtful "Half a share" (3.2.267), which is often cut in performance? Would Polonius have the effrontery to tell the queen that Hamlet's "pranks have been too broad to bear with" (3.4.2) and would Rosencrantz and Guildenstern dare speak at such length to Claudius himself about the "cess of majesty" and their "Most holy and religious fear" (3.3.8, 15) if they thought Claudius had killed King Hamlet? Zeffirelli's film shows Ian Holm's thunderstruck Polonius guessing what Claudius must have done, but then it becomes difficult to explain why this Polonius speaks as he does when he is next alone with Claudius in 3.3. Some directors, like Grigori Kozintsev and Ingmar Bergman, stave off such difficulties by making the whole court corrupt, but what should we then make of Gertrude's response to whatever she sees while sitting next to Claudius? Just how wicked, or stupid, do we think Gertrude is? In Peter Wirth's 1960 production, the disturbed Claudius removed his hand from Gertrude's when Lucianus came on, and Gertrude looked at Claudius "in shock and dismay" as she "finally [began] to suspect what her doting husband may have done to win her" (Kliman, Hamlet 149). Such locally thrilling theatrical moments have dramatic consequences. If Gertrude thinks that Claudius murdered her first husband, she will need to be even more brazenly, chillingly self-possessed than Lady Macbeth when she tells her son, "Hamlet, thou hast thy father much offended" (3.4.9) or when she asks her seemingly shocked question, "As kill a king?" (3.4.31).

In the BBC staging these multiplying difficulties disappeared—because Patrick Stewart's Claudius didn't lose control, wobble his knees and his goblet, and "rush" away in panic or "rage." Indeed, there was a pointed reversal of the business with the torch in Olivier's film. After receiving the "lights," this Claudius walked across to Hamlet and held up the torch to examine his nephew's face. When Jacobi's Hamlet laughed nervously and covered his face with his hands, Claudius shook his head, then walked away, as if reluctantly but finally giving up on this hopeless case. In *The Masks of* Hamlet, Marvin Rosenberg objects to "the inadequacy of this non-response" (598), without considering its most striking advantage: this staging makes dramatic sense of what the *other* characters do and say, since they never speak as though they have just seen the king betray his guilt in public. Like Claudius himself in the next scene, they all speak as though they have been watching Hamlet turn the entertainment into an ever more excruciating scandal, which begins when he grossly insults the queen and Ophelia and ends—or is terminated—when he threatens the king.

A Question of Visibility

After offering this account of the basic problem, I restate it more aggressively: There is no way of staging the "Mousetrap" so that Claudius's guilt can be unequivocally revealed to Hamlet without that guilt also becoming apparent to the onstage audience.

This stronger assertion exposes a different difficulty. If the basic problem is so basic, or simple, why hasn't it been generally recognized, and why is the opposed, traditional view still served up in, say, Zeffirelli's opulent fast-food version of *Hamlet*? When I put this question in Kyoto, I remember some students nodding as though they took it as a sudden confirmation that there must, after all, have been something eccentric or wrong in my account of the problem. In Chuo I put the same question, but then suggested that we try to answer it by looking closely at those issues raised in the preliminary handout.

Although the first part of the extract from Dawson's account of the Hall production makes me wish I saw it, the last part reveals that Dawson didn't see it either and shows the trustingly repetitive character of so much performance criticism. How could Dawson know that the audience could and did notice, and correctly interpret, some "flicker of fear" in Claudius's eye that was "noticeable to Hamlet, if not to the rest of the court"? The sheer implausibility of this account prompts a different explanation. Hall's production was challenging the traditional assumption that Claudius must lose control and betray his guilt because the "Mousetrap" must be the success Hamlet takes it to be. That assumption is then surreptitiously reasserted in Dawson's account of a momentary but momentous "flicker of fear," which somehow confirms that Claudius was guilty after all.

Indeed, there is a startling omission in Dawson's account at the point where he writes, "The sense was that Hamlet was being gratuitously offensive, and the court watched carefully for the royal cue. It came a few moments later when the King called for lights." The actor John Bell, who is now director of the remarkable Bell Shakespeare Company in Australia but earlier worked in the Royal Shakespeare Company for several years and acted in the Hall *Hamlet,* tells me that when Hamlet asked Gertrude how she liked the play, Gertrude lost all patience and slapped Hamlet, hard. Enough was clearly enough, and at this point Claudius rose and called for lights—"speaking very quietly," Bell recalled, "but in complete control."

Dawson himself records that the only two earlier attempts to present a more impressive Claudius—in Birmingham (1925) and Stratford (1948)—"disturbed many reviewers and playgoers, who wanted their villains clearly marked"; the *Times* reviewer "objected" that Anthony Quayle's Claudius was "almost sympathetic" (126). This objection in itself shows how much resistance there was to any idea that Claudius can be more impressive than Hamlet says he is. But then, in patiently assembling reviewers' comments on Hall's still more provocative production and in this way providing his own admirably detailed description, Dawson takes over and adds his own authority to the reviewers' accounts of the effect of Hall's staging.

My later handout includes Dawson's comments on the BBC version, which he has seen and clearly knows well. He draws a significant contrast with Hall's production, observing that, although that had "treated the end of the play in a similar way," the earlier Claudius's "cool rebuke was politically astute but morally bankrupt," whereas the rebuke from Stewart's Claudius actually seemed "the *right* response" (221). But Dawson then objects to the "unbalancing produced by the moral as well the political strength of [Stewart's] Claudius" (221), as though the most important consideration was whether Jacobi's Hamlet seemed less impressive than Stewart's unnervingly mighty opposite. Dawson doesn't consider or even mention what I take to be the more important point, which is that the BBC staging made better sense of what the other characters do and say.

In the earlier classes at Chuo we had already discussed other examples of the way in which the struggle to see *Hamlet* through Hamlet's eyes became part of this play's performance history. For example, although audiences are used to seeing Claudius totter around with a goblet, the idea that he drinks excessively is another encrustation for which there is no textual support. True, Hamlet grumbles about how foreigners despise Danes for their heavy drinking, but the newly crowned king can hardly be blamed for that. If pressed for their logical content rather than their disapproving intent, Hamlet's remarks would reflect, rather, on his father, explaining those afternoon naps. The countless productions in which Rosencrantz and Guildenstern appear to be treacherous timeservers similarly strain against the textual evidence in order to be obediently loyal to Hamlet's later idea that they deserve to die. It then becomes difficult to believe that the unfortunate pair could ever have been what Gertrude says they were and what Hamlet himself says they are when he greets them—"My excellent good friends!" Yet the "good lads" don't betray Hamlet (2.2.223, 224), and the play provides no support for Hamlet's assumption that they knew the contents of Claudius's letter to the king of England. The traditional stagings of the "Mousetrap" assume that it must be a success for the same reason that Claudius must be an unimpressive bloat king, that Rosencrantz and Guildenstern must be treacherous, and that Polonius must be a tedious old fool: Hamlet says so.

Shiga was the first writer to protest that the "Mousetrap" fails as a test. In his public letter to Funaki, he recalls how this protest took shape when he was watching the 1911 Imperial Theatre production and felt that he would have responded just like Claudius, even if he were innocent of his brother's murder. Later, after consulting Shoyo Tsubouchi's translation, Shiga became ever more convinced that there is "not a single piece of objective evidence to prove that Claudius murdered his brother" (Kaori Ashizu's unpublished trans.). So far as the "Mousetrap" scene is concerned, Shiga was right, and his intuitive, protesting response to the Tokyo production is all the more interesting because Shiga was unfamiliar with Shakespeare and had gone along to see what all the fuss was about. We too often refuse to allow for such responses when talking about what works in performance, just as our ideas about what Shakespeare's audience might or might not have seen too often exclude responses from spectators of the caliber of Ben Jonson or John Donne. Unfortunately, Shiga went on to maintain that Claudius really was innocent, which made it easy to disregard his more original and challengingly perceptive insights. (Since no promptbook exists, it's not clear whether or not this Claudius confesses in 3.1 and 3.3.)

The second handout includes extracts from Greg's 1917 essay, which show how Greg saw that terminating an offensive performance is no proof of guilt and that when Claudius is praying he never supposes that he has betrayed his guilt. Unfortunately, Greg also shackled and subordinated his best insights to a perverse argument, by maintaining that the Ghost is "Hamlet's hallucination" and not only Hamlet's: Greg even thought we should regard the fact that the Ghost is seen eleven times by four different people as "a freak of collective suggestion, and explain it away as we should any other spook" (401). When Wilson exploded that argument quite conclusively, the English happily supposed he had dealt with Greg in an inclusive way. But Wilson's argument against Greg's view of the "Mousetrap" invents further stage directions and might be politely described as teleological: the king doesn't betray his guilt during the dumb show because he isn't watching it, and we know that he isn't watching it because he doesn't betray his guilt. So far as I can tell, this line of argument began in 1824, with Tieck's suggestion that Claudius doesn't respond to the dumb show because he is talking to Gertrude (Furness 2: 284). But it excludes the very possibility that the "Mousetrap" was meant to allow for and test: Claudius might be innocent. Moreover, the stranglehold of the Hamlet-centered tradition reappears in that unreflecting concentration on what we know rather than on what Hamlet knows. The main object of the "Mousetrap" is to provide Hamlet himself with conclusive proof that Claudius is guilty and that the Ghost is not a devil. And yet, after being morally and logically scrupulous in seeing the need for such a test, Hamlet loses control, spoils the test, and then insists that it was a complete success.

We concluded this part of the course by considering our present confusion about, or indifference to, what is at issue in dramatic and critical terms. Although what I have called the basic problem was already visible by 1917, people chose not to see it. In effect, it went underground for decades. Much later, Greg's worries resurfaced in the work of a few eccentric, dissident critics, like W. W. Robson, A. L. French, and me (*Scepticism* 115–17). But then, doubtless as a result of Hall's production and the still more influential BBC version, the idea that the "Mousetrap" fails began to seem less startling. Michael Pennington takes it for granted in his admirable Hamlet: *A User's Guide*. So why wasn't there an explosion of laughter, or protest, at the absurd fudging in Branagh's film? When Lucianus poisons the king in the spoken play, a close-up of Claudius's face is followed by a flashback in which we see the agonized face of King Hamlet and then see Jacobi's Claudius watching his brother die. In this case we can't even speak of a staging, since what happens is theatrically impossible: we see what Claudius remembers, which is of course not apparent to the onstage audience—including Hamlet! There could be no more facile and infuriating way of staging—or rather, not staging—the "Mousetrap." Some of my students did laugh, bless them.

Let me finish with Jean Martin Charcot's wonderful description of the tyranny of assumptions, which Richard Webster quotes in his devastating *Why Freud Was Wrong*:

> Why do we perceive things so late, so poorly and with such difficulty? Why do we have to go over the same set of symptoms twenty times before we understand it? Why does the first statement of what seems a new fact always leave us cold?
>
> Because our minds have to take in something that deranges our original set of ideas, but we are all of us like that in this miserable world.
>
> (569)

Hence, I take it, our peculiar reluctance to see what has long been visible in this Shakespearean instance: the traditional view of the "Mousetrap" is yet another encrustation.

NOTE

Hamlet quotations are from Hibbard.

Teaching *Hamlet* in a Global Literature Survey: Linking Elizabethan England and Ming China

Paula S. Berggren

Over the past couple of decades, a great deal of energy has been devoted to expanding the literary curriculum to include non-Western texts. But only in the past five years have inclusive, chronologically organized anthologies intended for core courses devoted to literary masterworks become available (see Davis et al.). In these broad surveys, teachers need to find ways to relate wildly disparate texts to one another. *Hamlet* has traditionally been the Shakespearean text of choice for these courses, and when the play is taught within the Western tradition, students who have become familiar with excerpts from Genesis, Sophocles, and Vergil are prepared to understand how Shakespeare responded to tragic themes in writing *Hamlet*. Using these new anthologies, the challenge is to teach *Hamlet* in the light of the great Asian books as well—or, given the time constraints that usually govern these courses, instead. One effective combination is to link Shakespeare's play to the extraordinary Ming novel, *Journey to the West* (Yu; best known to readers in English in Arthur Waley's witty abridgement, *Monkey*), for the intellectual concerns of Ming China and Early Modern Europe mirror each other in remarkable ways.

The Ming dynasty, in marked contrast to the European Renaissance, was until recently seen as a low period in its country's intellectual development. William Theodore de Bary has challenged that view, mentioning, for example, the heroic Ming effort to assimilate the vast achievements of earlier thinkers thrust before them in "the massive Yung-lo Encyclopedia" (9). As in the contemporaneous West, artists and thinkers of the fifteenth and sixteenth centuries were obsessed with reclaiming and revising the burden of tradition and probing the role of the mind and the place of the individual in society.

Consider these words of the philosopher Ch'en Hsien-chang (1428–1500), to whom de Bary attributes the following sayings: "Standing between Heaven-and-earth, what dignity this body of mine possesses"; "This body of mine, small though it is, is nevertheless bound up with ethical principles. The pivot is in the mind" (14–15). The similarity to Hamlet's famous expostulation, "What should such fellows as I do crawling between heaven and earth!" (3.1.124–25), fortuitously leads to a rewarding juxtaposition of Renaissance and Ming thought. Whether standing or crawling between heaven and earth, in both periods human beings seek to assert themselves and their capacities. Both Renaissance playwrights and Ming novelists test their characters' ability to find in a complex intellectual inheritance a balance of mind and body that will give the individual the security to act effectively within society.

Sizable excerpts of *Monkey* can now be found in the expanded edition of *The Norton Anthology of World Masterpieces* (Mack et al. [1995]; I am citing from the text of *Hamlet* printed there) and in *Western Literature in a World*

Context (Davis et al.). Devoting three days to *Hamlet* and two to *Monkey* (generally as much time as one can spare in these surveys) allows one first to introduce students to the unique world of each text. Both anthologies include an episode set in the Kingdom of Crow-cock (chapters 19–20 of Waley's *Monkey*, or 37–39 in the complete novel) that makes for an effective sixth class meeting in which to compare the two texts.

Published in the form we know in 1592, *Journey to the West* interweaves Buddhist, Taoist, and Confucian lore (Plaks, *Four Masterworks* 20), promoting a syncretic wisdom that eludes the grasp of the Christian humanist. The leading character, Monkey (as widely known in the East as Hamlet is in the West), begins by hubristically calling himself, through mischievous punning, the Great Sage Equal to Heaven. Gaining access to Taoist alchemical secrets, showing reverence for Confucian values, and ultimately sublimating his ego to achieve Buddhist nirvana, he combines animal energy and human intuition. Identified in the full-scale novel with a Buddhist allegorical figure, the Monkey of the Mind (Yu 1: 59–62), this lovable protagonist comically achieves the serious goal of self-cultivation assiduously sought by the Ming philosophers of mind in his ultimate subjugation to the pilgrim monk Hsuan Tsang (known as Tripitaka), whose journey from T'ang China to India in quest of Buddhist scriptures gives the full-scale novel its title.

To enable Tripitaka to control the potentially obstreperous monkey, Kuan-yin, the Bodhisattva of Compassion, has taught the monk a secret spell that tightens a metal fillet encircling the monkey's head, binding his too-fertile mind. To escape pain, Monkey must obey his master, and so he is gradually tamed. The novel thus teaches that the individualistic Monkey of the Mind— the solipsistic intellect that goes beyond boundaries—can be harnessed for a greater social good. At least part of Hamlet's personal tragedy lies in the impossibility of his channeling his intellect to the service of the state. He lacks advancement; Denmark's a prison. After a week and a half of study, students are in a position to make this observation and ready to tackle some of the hard truths that turned Renaissance optimism to despair.

Laurence Olivier's *Hamlet* was originally shown in China "excellently dubbed with two attractive titles: *The Ghost Travels West* (part 1) and *The Revenge of the Prince* (part 2)" (Zhang 197). As it happens, these categories underscore the resemblance between the plot of *Hamlet* and what Andrew Plaks casually refers to as the "Hamlet-like usurpation of a conjugal bed and a kingdom" (*Journey* 276) in the realm of Crow-cock. A more extended examination of the connections between two different ghosts and two princes' revenge becomes the fulcrum for studying these two texts together in the global literature classroom.

The Crow-cock episode in *Monkey* begins with Tripitaka meditating in a monastery on a moonlit night, a scene that holds the promise of serene Buddhist enlightenment. Unlike Bernardo and Marcellus nervously waiting for the appearance of the "thing" that has troubled their watch (1.1.21), Tripitaka falls into a sleep. Out of his dream emerges the ghost of a king whose realm has been afflicted by a disastrous drought. The ghost tells Tripitaka that a magician who came to save the Kingdom of Crow-cock stayed on for years as the king's guest, until he murdered the king in his garden, married his queen, and, under the pretense of furthering the boy's studies, sequestered the king's son from his mother. Alerted by a regional spirit to the presence of Tripitaka and his monkey companion (the monkey is famed in spirit circles for his powers of exorcism), the ghost appears both to Tripitaka and to his queen. The challenges to be met resemble those confronting Hamlet: Is the ghost reliable? Can human beings distinguish between seeming and being? (The usurping magician has transformed himself into the king's double, so no one knows that the true king lies at the bottom of the garden well, into which he was pushed three years earlier.) A complicated narrative ensues, culminating in the resurrection of the dead king, the unmasking of the magician, the reunification of the family, and the clarification of the circumstances underlying this foul murder.

At least three points of resemblance between this story and *Hamlet* cast light on themes shared by Ming and Renaissance literature that make for lively classroom debate. A "common denominator" of the Ming novel, according to Plaks, is "an emphasis on the breakdown of order or failure of the will [. . .] whether that is conceived at the level of the external social and political context, or the internal equilibrium of the self" (*Four Masterworks* 504–05).

Could this comment not serve as well as a summary of concerns common to Shakespeare's tragedies? In both forms, the restoration of order depends upon the protagonists' ability to use their minds to discriminate the false from the true, to reconcile external and internal worlds. In the Ming novel, the mind is equal to this task. The syncretizing of Confucian, Buddhist, and Taoist thought seems to support a view of external reality that affirms the value of action in the world, even if that world is a delusion. The intermingling of Christian and classical thought, however, destabilizes the Renaissance tragic world.

Can we trust ghosts, emanations from the past, embodiments of that which we inherit? Even though Hamlet confidently informs Horatio that his father's is an "honest ghost" (1.5.138), what Hamlet has learned from it is "[t]hat one may smile, and smile, and be a villain" (108). And no one has successfully resolved the question that audiences must always confront: Can a bloodthirsty Senecan ghost serve a Christian mission? When the Ghost makes its second appearance in Gertrude's closet, it has changed garments and is not seen by anyone but Hamlet. If Gertrude seems at last capable of distinguishing between the old king and the new when her son forces her to look at the two portraits, she cannot see the Ghost: "Yet all that is [she] see[s]" (3.4.132). The world of seeming and the world of being never come into equilibrium in Shakespeare's play. By contrast, when Tripitaka needs to be convinced of the reliability of the ghost of Crow-cock's ruler (whom he has seen only in a dream), he finds a palpable proof—a jade tablet belonging to the king.

Can family life be sustained? What did Gertrude know and when did she know it? Where *Hamlet* leaves the audience, not to mention the prince, uncertain about Gertrude's complicity in and understanding of her adulterous marriage, *Monkey* provides a perfectly transparent encounter between the long-estranged prince of Crow-cock and his mother. What did the queen of Crow-cock know about her husband's fate and when did she realize she knew it? Monkey counsels the young prince to inquire about the status of his mother's marital relations with her husband. When asked, she reveals how different the couch of Crow-cock is from the incestuous bed occupied by the royal pair of Denmark. Moving from prose to verse, as frequently happens in both Chinese fiction and Renaissance drama, the sobbing mother reveals a deeply held secret:

> What three years ago was warm and bland,
> These last three years has been cold as ice.
> When at the pillow's side I questioned him,
> He told me age had impaired his strength
>   and that things did not work.   (Waley 182)

The impostor in Crow-cock is as impotent as bedridden Norway (and perhaps as old Hamlet), but to an obedient wife this disjuncture between seeming and being did not necessarily indicate that one husband had been superseded by another. Once the fact of imposture is revealed, however, the secret becomes a part of a coherent pattern, and a Confucian family is on the way to complete restoration. Analyzing this brief and underplayed moment in the Ming novel, students may be encouraged to compare different cultures' attitudes toward sexuality. In the one, esoteric Taoist sexual practices bring mind and body into harmony; in the other, Christian guilt and male anxiety virtually guarantee the irreparable rupture of body from mind.

Can the hero destroy his adversary without compromising his own integrity? In both texts, violence produces a bravura conclusion, but only in the Ming novel are the facts satisfactorily laid out and understood. Horatio hopes at the end of *Hamlet* to explain all "[e]ven while men's minds are wild" (5.2.367). If, as is often said, Horatio must repeat for the inhabitants of Elsinore the details of the play that the theater audience has just watched, we know how little clarity that will yield. Seeming and being have not been clearly distinguished. Cogitation yields nothing: "Since no man has aught of what he leaves, what is't to leave betimes?" (196–97).

At the end of the Crow-cock episode, Monkey and Tripitaka validate a heroic view of mind, bringing neo-Confucian politics, Taoist alchemy, and Buddhist spirituality into alignment. Caught in his lie, the counterfeit king eludes capture by shifting his shape one more time. To frustrate the vengeful Monkey, the magician transforms himself into Tripitaka's double. Whom is Monkey to strike with his all-powerful cudgel? The solution lies in the struggling mortal mind: the two Tripitakas are to recite the fillet-tightening spell. The false master does not know the words. To prove his identity, the true master inflicts mental torture on his disciple. And here mental suffering pays: the evidence of his senses correctly shows Monkey which image of his master to attack, and he acts accordingly.

The divine providence that knows the fate of the sparrow does not extend itself to save Hamlet or explain events; the benign Buddha, however, clarifies all. Staying Monkey's hand, the Bodhisattva of Justice, the compassionate Kuan-yin's counterpart, Manjusri, reveals the true nature of the scheming wizard. Instead of a Machiavellian, Cain-like Claudius, the false husband and usurping king is a big pussycat, the gelded lion on whom Manjusri rides, pressed into service to teach the now revived king of Crow-cock a needed lesson. The pathetic ghost is not a saintly martyr but an erring ruler who mistreated Manjusri three years earlier when Manjusri came to him disguised as a priest asking for alms.

Monkey uses conventions that sufficiently resemble comic formulas beloved by students to facilitate free classroom discussion of the serious issues these two radically different masterpieces share. Hamlet's journey to the West ends in death; Monkey's, in enlightenment. Understanding how those final destinations are predetermined by complex cultural conceptions of mind and action shines a new light on *Hamlet*. Rather than feel the loss of Sophoclean and Vergilian antecedents as we read *Hamlet*, comparing it to *Monkey*, we gain a global perspective that illuminates the way literature reflects problems that matter to us all.

Hamlet in a Western Civilization Course: Connections to Montaigne's *Essays* and Cervantes's *Don Quixote*

Ann W. Engar

The sixteenth century, a time of great turbulence and destabilization, saw the exploration of America with its powerful empires and cultures wholly outside the European realm; the Protestant Reformation with its attack on one universal belief in favor of individual priesthood; and the establishment of the Copernican system of the universe, which removed human centrality and destroyed the poetic view of a universe composed of harmonic crystalline spheres. All these changes brought war—imperialistic, religious, and intellectual. No wonder many intellectuals and writers of the late sixteenth and early seventeenth centuries turned to skepticism and nihilism, or alternately to stoicism, with its emphasis on control of the only thing under one's control: oneself. How great a change in the writings of the early and late Renaissance, from the bravado of Pico della Mirandola's "Oration on the Dignity of Man" to Hamlet's despairing "quintessence of dust" (2.2.289)! Many of the later works express deep feeling of loss, loss of surety, of innocence, of idealism, and of poetry. Three great masterworks of European literature—Michel de Montaigne's *Essays*, Miguel de Cervantes's *Don Quixote*, and William Shakespeare's *Hamlet*—emerge from this period of time and reveal its complexity, its self-reflection and its movement toward the modern world.

I teach a course in Western intellectual history to honors students who read primary texts over a three-semester series of classes. The middle-semester course covers the Middle Ages and Renaissance, beginning with Augustine's *Confessions* and ending with Montaigne, Cervantes, and Shakespeare. Of the many possible approaches to these three authors' works, we look at them as products of the late Renaissance. Given the limitations of a survey course, students read only *Hamlet* in its entirety. Of Montaigne they read two essays and selections from a third. In *Don Quixote* they read the early episodes, including the encounter with the windmill; the first few chapters of part 2; the adventure with the Knight of the Mirrors (vol. 2, chs. 12–17); and the ending. The texts are in volume 1 of *The Norton Anthology of World Masterpieces* (Mack), and we spend roughly two and a half weeks on the three writers.

Though many scholars have traced the influence of Montaigne's essays on *Hamlet*, my class's concern is with both Montaigne's and Shakespeare's responding to immense change. Like earlier works of the Renaissance, Montaigne's *Essays* demonstrate individualism but an individualism tinged with uncertainty and awareness of limitations. In "Of Cannibals" Montaigne recognizes the mental and cultural filters through which humans make their judgments, judgments that call the recently discovered Brazilians "cannibals" who nevertheless display great valor in battle and great regard for their wives, but also judgments that blind Europeans to their own "treachery, disloyalty, tyranny and cruelty which are [their] ordinary vices" (156). Yet such remarks do not end in complete relativism for Montaigne: there is a strong sense of the moral achievement of the cannibals. In the essay, he also comments on the instability of what we call knowledge: "I don't know if I can guarantee that some other such discovery [like that of America] will not be made in the future, so many personages greater than ourselves having been mistaken about this one" (150).

Three passages in particular prepare for *Hamlet*. In "Of the Inconsistency of Our Actions," Montaigne begins by insisting on human irresolution and inconsistency rather than holding the earlier Renaissance view of the unity of human behavior. He concludes by discussing the difference between appearance and reality, between action and motivation, and the difficulty in probing beneath the one to find the other. But the most important passage is from "Apology for Raymond Sebond," in which Montaigne praises the awesome perfection of the universe and chastises puny man for audaciously claiming himself master and commander of the universe. Though in *Essays* he attacks earlier conceptions of human nobility and dignity, Montaigne does not slip into complete skepticism or stoicism: he accepts the variety of experience with good humor, delights in the subtlety of his thought, and strives for balance rather than rejection of pleasure.

In addition to the previously named sources of instability in the sixteenth century, the Spanish had the defeat of their invincible Armada and the weakening of their empire. *Don Quixote* reflects these feelings of loss and longings for beauty and stability. Don Quixote may assert, like Montaigne, "I know who I am, and who I may be, if I choose" (Cervantes 1843). The reader is far less sure. Don Quixote is noble in his idealism; and the novel is filled with nostalgia for a world of chivalry, romance, and the clear values of courage, integrity, and ideal love. But Don Quixote is also ridiculous and the butt of pranks, and his actions sometimes lead to violence and destruction. Through the novel's themes of idealism versus realism, reality versus illusion, sanity versus madness and the slippery boundaries between each pair, the reader is left with multiple emotions, multiple perspectives, and no complete resolution of meaning or values.

Hamlet contains many similar reflections and emotions in a world "out of joint" (1.5.189). "Something is rotten in the state of Denmark" (1.4.90), which is now an "unweeded garden" with a snake in it. Hamlet longs for a simpler time, when his father was king, his mother a loyal wife, and values of honor and allegiance seemed clear. He claims, "There's nothing good or bad but thinking makes it so" (2.2.238–39), though he does not accept this relativism: his father's murder was wrong, as was his mother's "o'erhasty marriage" (2.2.57). He cries, "Give me that man / That is not passion's slave" in longing to be a stoic like Horatio, but a stoic cannot be an avenger: he needs passion to carry through with justice (3.2.61–62). Similarly, Hamlet longs to be a Fortinbras with "bloody thoughts" (4.4.66) yet judges Fortinbras's activities to be the "imposthume of much wealth and peace, / That inward breaks" (27–28). Except for Horatio,

Hamlet is surrounded by illusion—by sycophants and spies, people who are empty of honor and dangerous, concerned more with seeming than being. Like Don Quixote, Hamlet is both mad and not mad; and to be mad in a court of bloody ambition, deceitful words, and pompous show may be the only healthy condition. The best he can do, along with Montaigne, is accept the course of life: "If it be now, 'tis not to come; if it be not to come, it will be now; if it be not now, yet it will come; the readiness is all" (5.2.194–95).

Thus Montaigne's *Essays, Don Quixote*, and *Hamlet* all display a new world in which the old sureties and values have been lost and a past world for which one feels nostalgia and melancholy. The new world is a world of multiple cultures and perspectives; a world where it is difficult to know what is real with knowledge shifting so dramatically; a world of human limitations, smallness, and corruption. Yet, as each work searches for meaning, it finds some, especially in friendship and loyalty (Sancho and Horatio), in self-knowledge and responsibility, and in the acceptance of change and uncertainty.

I engage students in various activities to move them to recognize these issues and eventually write a final paper on the subject. I also want them to see the overall richness of the play. At least one class session (or sometimes an evening class party) is devoted to watching a film of the play (I have variously used the BBC, Olivier, Zeffirelli, and Branagh versions). Other class sessions involve discussion, either for the whole class or in small groups, of the following questions (among others):

1. What is the atmosphere of the play? What specific techniques does Shakespeare use in act 1 to create this atmosphere? What other famous play that we have read begins with an unsettled night watch and a theme of kingly murder and a son seeking revenge? (Aeschylus's *Oresteia* is in Mack 1: 548–652.) What broader implications might this setting have, especially to the Europe of Shakespeare's time?

2. Hamlet is a young university student. With what specific issues are young people at this time of life concerned? (Student answers are establishment of careers, relationships with parents, love and sexuality, etc.) On what basis do young people make their moral decisions? How much do their parents' beliefs influence them? How certain are they of the rightness of their actions? How much do they recognize evil? How typical, in other words, are Hamlet's moral confusion, anger at hypocrisy, and inability to act? Does he really believe in a relative, subjective morality? Many scholars have asserted that Montaigne strongly influenced Shakespeare. What evidence do you see to support that assertion?

3. Shakespeare presents several young men besides Hamlet in the play: Fortinbras, Laertes, Horatio, Rosencrantz, and Guildenstern. What is each like? What are his values, his strengths, and his limitations? What characteristics in Hamlet do they highlight or contrast with? Why is each, ultimately, not the hero that Hamlet is?

4. Renaissance artists (such as Albrecht Dürer) and thinkers were intensely interested in psychology. Examine Shakespeare's presentation of madness in *Hamlet*. Is Hamlet truly mad? Or is he merely putting on an "antic disposition" (1.5.170)? How does his madness compare or contrast with Ophelia's? With Don Quixote's? What are the causes of madness? Why do you think late Renaissance writers showed such interest in the operations of the human mind (Montaigne in tracing the succession and source of ideas, Cervantes and Shakespeare in depicting madness)?

With activities such as these I try to stimulate discussion about and understanding of the late Renaissance and *Hamlet*'s important place in the history of ideas.

NOTE

Hamlet quotations are from Mack.

The Pyrrhus Speech:
Querying the Uses of the Troy Story

Lisa Hopkins

One passage that I find particularly rich when teaching *Hamlet* is the Pyrrhus speech. Although it constitutes only a very short part of the play, many over-arching issues are touched on in it, and I find that it provides a nice balance between prompting me to offer information to students (much of which will, I hope, be new, interesting, and relevant to them) and allowing them to produce ideas and insights of their own.

We start with a clip from Kenneth Branagh's film of *Hamlet*, in which the Pyrrhus speech is given unusual emphasis. As Charlton Heston speaks it, we cut to a re-creation of the actual sack of Troy, with Judi Dench as Hecuba and John Gielgud as Priam. The film is noted for its use of stars in vignettes—elsewhere Gerard Depardieu appears briefly as Reynaldo, and Jack Lemmon as Marcel-lus—but even so the concentration of stars in this scene is striking, as is the magnitude of their celebrity: Heston, Dench, and Gielgud are indeed names to conjure with. Gielgud, in particular, is famous for his own performance of Ham-let, and although in Branagh's film he is by no means the only distinguished pre-vious performer of the role—Derek Jacobi, here playing Claudius, is another obvious example—he does indeed seem to loom as a figure embodying an orig-inary authority, a father not only literally but also metaphorically.

I point out to the students that though Shakespeare's original audience did not have the benefit of Gielgud to make this point about Priam's status, they would nevertheless have been acutely aware of it. Priam was king of Troy, and Troy was the city from which Britons themselves were supposed to derive. Aeneas, fleeing from the burning city, carried its cultural and imperial author-ity with him to his new home in Italy, and it was transmitted thence to England by his grandson Brutus, after whom Britain was said to be named. Trojan iden-tity, therefore, lies at the heart of British identity, and Priam is, in this play of fathers, in a sense the ultimate father. Moreover, though we may see Gielgud in the role, Shakespeare's original audience would have possessed an added imaginative stimulus that we now miss, for they would assuredly have heard echoes of Marlowe. Though there is not an exact parallel between the words of the Pyrrhus speech and that of any speech in Marlowe's *Dido, Queen of Carthage*, the general similarity of mood, plot, and diction is unmistakable and has been much commented on by critics (see, e.g., Bradbrook, "Inheritance"; Hattaway, "Marlowe"; and Charney, "Voice," though Charney finds the note of *Tamburlaine* rather than of *Dido, Queen of Carthage* in the speech). I there-fore invite students to compare the Pyrrhus speech with the roughly equivalent section of *Dido* and ask them to consider whether—and, if so, why—they think Shakespeare might be alluding to Marlowe here. If they have not made the connection themselves, I would in particular draw their attention to the depiction of Marlowe as an overwhelming early influence on Shakespeare in two other Shakespearean films, Richard Loncraine's *Richard III*, in which the first words spoken are actually Marlowe's, as "Come live with me and be my love" is sung at the victory ball, and *Shakespeare in Love,* in which all but one of those who audition for *Romeo and Ethel, the Pirate's Daughter* choose a Marlowe speech to deliver.

I would myself suggest that Marlowe loomed before the early Shakespeare much as classical culture does before moderns, so reference to a Marlovian play with a classical setting is doubly appropriate. Thus whether, as now, we see Gielgud, or whether, as then, we hear Marlowe, the inevitable conclusion of our experience of the Pyrrhus speech will be the same: a powerfully developed sense of being overshadowed, of despair that we can ever equal the achievements or the status of a gigantic forerunner. Moreover, this is of course exactly the effect that the speech produces on Hamlet himself, who, just as he fears that he is an unworthy successor to his idolized father, feels that his own displays of emotion are grossly inadequate beside those of the Player. "What's Hecuba to him, or he to her, / That he should weep for her?" he furiously demands (2.2.553–54); and the answer that the original audience would be able silently to supply would of course be "His famous ancestor," an epitome both of the Trojan culture that originates and authorizes the British one and of all those earlier retellings of the story of Troy—of which Marlowe's was perhaps uppermost in Shakespeare's mind but by no means the only instance—against which Shakespeare's work must be matched.

There is, however, also an elision taking place here, to which it may well be worth paying attention. Hamlet, interestingly enough, assumes that the Player is weeping specifically for Hecuba; but this is not in fact entirely clear. What the Player actually says is:

> But if the gods themselves did see her then,
> When she saw Pyrrhus make malicious sport
> In mincing with his sword her husband's limbs,
> The instant burst of clamour that she made,
> Unless things mortal move them not at all,
> Would have made milch the burning eyes of heaven
> And passion in the gods.   (2.2.508–14)

But are none of those tears for Priam? I ask the students this, and point out that both in Hamlet's life and in the speech it is a father who has died and a mother who (in however distressed a condition) survives. Moreover, Hamlet knows only too well from experience that a wife's tears for her husband, however loud at the time, need not express any very deeply felt sorrow. Why, therefore, does he assume that it is the plight of Hecuba rather than that of Priam that moves the Player to tears, and why is there imagery of milk surrounding Priam's head and the gods' eyes? I would link this image to the Player Queen's later reference to "treason in my breast" (3.2.173), followed by Hamlet's to "wormwood" (176), which, as Juliet's nurse reminds us (*Rom.* 1.3.27–33), was applied to the nipple for weaning purposes and could thus be seen as representing the first and most traumatic of all "treasons in the breast." I would also suggest that in the Renaissance mind, the ultimate location for bad practices associated with both milk giving and mothering was Ireland. Hamlet swears by Saint Patrick, and in his final speech it is possible to trace echoes of the Irish writer Richard Stanyhurst, who contributed the description of Ireland to Holinshed's chronicles, while Essex, with whose fall *Hamlet* has often been connected, had served in Ireland, as we are reminded in *Henry V*. I would want to link the possibility of an Irish connection to the debate the play seems to stage between Protestantism and Catholicism (visible in such areas as the representation of repentance and the spirit world and the teasing reference to the Diet of Worms) and ask what might be added to that debate by the introduction of classical gods as well.

In addition to some unusual gendering (including the fact that Hamlet himself, starting the speech, actually quotes Dido's words rather than those of Aeneas), one might also argue for references to race in the speech. The first thing we hear about Pyrrhus may well surprise an audience familiar with the Troy story: he has "sable arms, / Black as his purpose" (2.2.448–49). The Arden note informs us that these words refer to his armor's being black, but immediately it adds that the image is without precedent in the Vergilian source; and if that is so, why do we then go on to read almost immediately of his "black complexion" (451)? Students may have experience of other imagings of blackness in Renaissance literature that would be relevant here; I always recommend Kim Hall's *Things of Darkness* when, in the previous semester, we look at Petrarchan poetry. I would suggest that the blackness of Pyrrhus serves at least two purposes: it makes for a particularly striking contrast between him and his "milky" victim, Priam, and it aligns him with Hamlet, who is also dressed in black. This similarity encourages us to compare their behavior. I would therefore conclude by asking whether there were any other points of identification to be found between Pyrrhus and Hamlet, and if so, what they might tell us about both Hamlet and *Hamlet* as a whole.

NOTE

Hamlet quotations are from Jenkins.

From Elsinore to Mangalore and Back:
Hamlet between Worlds

Ralph Nazareth

Producing *Hamlet* in its entirety may take around five hours of stage time, which is, with or without an intermission, well beyond the tolerance level of contemporary spectators, including, I daresay, diehard fans at a baseball doubleheader at Yankee Stadium.

Except, perhaps, for Indians! Nursed from infancy on our interminable epics, we revel in long performances, often held under the stars, extending deep into the night and sometimes until "the glowworm shows the matin to be near" (1.5.89). We like to linger at plays well past the curfew set for the ghost of Hamlet's father. We might actually wish that the play not be summarily snipped by the fast and furious actions that pile up in dire haste at the end of act 5, that it stretch a while longer.

What lies behind *Hamlet*'s prodigious length? Is it partly that, as Northrop Frye notes (*Northrop Frye* 83), just about everyone in the play talks too much? As an Indian, I'd say to the garrulous crowd in Elsinore, "Welcome to India," and especially to my hometown, Mangalore, where the tongues are a mile long and words in perpetual inflation! We are a loquacious people. When we are not talking to others, we talk to ourselves. Harangue, dialogue, or soliloquy, whatever your pleasure, it's yours for the choosing.

No, you think, the play's inordinate length is caused not by long-windedness but by the famous "delay." Now, I ask you, have you met an Indian who was ever in a hurry to do anything?! *Mañana* and Mangalore, I'd say, are identical twins. Timeless India, and all that . . .

But you want to get serious and suggest with Nietzsche (51) that Hamlet's no mere procrastinator. He is loath to act because he has looked deeply into the true nature of life. He realizes that no action of his can bring about a change in the eternal condition of things. Again, isn't this precisely the habit of mind, born of exactly such a philosophical understanding of reality, that one ascribes to the Indian?

Having faced the practical issues involved in the production of a long play like *Hamlet*, my teacher, the noted Polish critic and director Jan Kott, used to say that you can perform only one of several *Hamlet*s potentially existing in the archplay (58). And as you cut and paste the original to suit your predilections and view it through your cultural lens, you end up producing a *Hamlet* that mirrors your world, be it Irish, Nigerian, Chinese, Brazilian, or, in my case, Indian and Mangalorean.

An Indian approach to *Hamlet* requires that my students first understand "India" as such—an India that is different from its historically dated and naive as well as self-serving distortions in Orientalist representations. And as for the

stereotypes about India I have so far played with, my students are quick to realize that they are applicable to humans everywhere. After all, for every timeless,
cyclically disposed, laid-back Indian, can't we find Western counterparts? Or,
for that matter, for every talkative Indian isn't there some American match in
the likes of Jimmy Swaggert, Henry Hyde, Dr. Ruth, or the proverbial local
teenager? Indians, because of their uniquely philosophical disposition, are supposed to get lost in the thicket of infinite possibilities and speculation, rendering them indecisive, inactive, and ineffective. By this definition, shouldn't
Jimmy Carter and his ilk be declared supremely Indian?! By now my students
are apt to wonder if India is indeed fundamentally different from the world
they are familiar with. Their questions and challenges are very much to the
point, especially now with the emergence of a global culture that is flattening
out, if not erasing, diversity. Yet, I impress upon them the need to recognize difference, to see how it holds—at the historical as well as the philosophical level.

Presenting India's otherness is a unique challenge because, of all the major
global cultures, India is possibly the only one whose present identity is actively
and inextricably woven with its past. India's past is a living present. Postmodern, postcolonial India is still propelled, in simple and complex ways, by many
of the assumptions and visions of classical and ancient India. The texts, beliefs,
and practices that dominated life and imagination for a thousand years before
the common era still hold sway, vivifying, and occasionally vitiating, Indian
society today. It's a complex unity of diverse elements. My students need to
understand this.

I explain to them that among the many elements that set Indian culture
apart from the West is the nearly total absence in India, at the deepest levels of
consciousness, of the tragic, as the West has defined it. Of course, we are not
talking here about disasters and calamitous happenings, of which India has its
doleful share. What we have in mind is its attitude of detachment toward those
dire happenings, and in general toward life and history. This attitude is based
on a time curve that suggests the cyclical, and is shaped by a temperament
essentially comic, in that it doesn't admit of radical, world-shattering endings
with an unimaginable waste of life and spirit. India goes on, in a manner of
speaking, or the Indian believes that self, life, and death are mere illusions in
the *lila* or play of God's continuing creation. The downturns in life, and analo-
gously within a play, are not tragic, and their pathos doesn't result in some profound, revolutionary perception or the creation of a new order. Emotion does
accrue to them, and they rivet one's attention, but all in all they are seen from
a perspective on being and time within which self, identity, and suffering figure
in the scheme of things differently from the way they do within the Western
conception of life and history. The Indian self is not individualistic and prone
to loneliness and despair as its Western counterpart is, and death, which is a
mere aspect of the general transience of life and reality, does not have a comparable sting. Certainly, these are complex and potentially confusing assertions
about essential cultural differences, but presented with care and patience, they

form the nucleus of an approach that invites my students to be attuned to the Indian other.

Having laid this groundwork, I point out to them that as an Indian I have a distinctive relation to English texts, especially those that address issues of power and conquest, of agency and victimhood. *Hamlet* was entered in the Stationers' Register by James Roberts on 26 July 1602, a mere two years after Elizabeth signed the charter of the East India Company, setting in motion one of the bloodiest colonizations of a land and a people and as heinously murderous as the one to which the play symbolically bears witness. Although not as explicitly and pointedly focused on issues of power and control as Shakespeare's histories, *Hamlet* is, all the same, embroiled in them. The play leaps into special significance when Indians, given the burden of their history, approach it with ever troubling questions about the horrors of usurpation; the syndrome of the strumpet-wife selling out from within; the lethal madness of power; the related pathologies of servility, hypocrisy, and opportunism; and, above all, the paralysis of action within a condition of internal exile.

I find it necessary to explain to my students that this postcolonial perspective, while questioning the designs of empire, also reinterprets India's own classics as they inform contemporary realities. For instance, the great epics *Mahabharata* and *Ramayana*, structured on divinely ordained kingship and a hierarchically ordered society, are constantly reread and critiqued in the light of our present-day democratic and anticaste ideals. Sita and Savitri, epic embodiments of the devoted wife and feminine virtue, are seen differently by readers today, for whom the struggle for the equality of women throws a revisionist light on the chauvinist models—no matter how benign—of a patriarchal society.

With this background, my students are now poised to read *Hamlet* between worlds. The field is wide open at this point. I can have them look at contemporary appropriations of *Hamlet* in India from Marxist or postcolonial points of view, for instance. Or have the weighty quandaries in the play illuminate, and be illuminated by, the comparable dilemmas faced by profoundly reflective leaders of the Independence struggle such as Gandhi and Nehru. We can examine the revenge theme that powers the play and see how Indians, at all levels, from rulers to peasants, connect with it. These are all rich options. But I choose to go back to the epic, the *Mahabharata*, which along with the other great epic, the *Ramayana*, still occupies center stage in the Indian literary and political imagination. I ask my students to think about *Hamlet* alongside what they have heard from me of the great struggles at the heart of the *Mahabharata*. The very same tensions at the heart of the play swell to epic proportions in this ancient Indian dynastic saga of desire and death, illusion and salvation. Yet we know better than to see them both simply as repeating the same old human story.

Hatred and revenge anchor the action in both play and epic. Age-old animosities run rampant between familial sheets, poisoning filial and public affairs. At the climactic moment, Arjuna, chosen to lead the Pandavas to victory, broods on the edge of the cosmic battlefield of action, conscience-stricken. Not unlike Hamlet. Whether it is the instruction of Lord Krishna, Arjuna's chario- teer, that ushers the hero out of his swoon or, as in Hamlet's case, it is the pas- sage of time and the wild wisdom of the graveyard that push him to act, detached from the original project of revenge and now open to providential design—we begin to see the stories, set side by side, animating each other. The seeming detachment that marks Hamlet's action toward the end of the play is something Indians talk about endlessly. The notion of detachment is in fact the problematic and crucial center of the *Bhagavad Gita*, one of the central Hindu texts. That it is, more often than not, observed in the breach in India—not unlike the lip service that the distinctive notion of *caritas*, for example, obtains among us here—becomes part of classroom discussion of the putative differ- ences in Western and Indian attitudes toward action, insight, and salvation. Arjuna and Hamlet appear to be confronted with similar predicaments and solutions. Yet is there not a world of difference between them?

Karna, among the more tragic of the characters in the epic, provides yet another foil for Hamlet. He is the ultimate image of the displaced and disaf- fected—a man with a hidden identity, humiliated by circumstances not of his own making, a man of fierce loyalties and passions, doomed by crucial flaws, large enough to be able to see the darkness at the heart of things. He serves as a poignant entry point into the theme of exile that looms over the entire action of the epic. Fathered by the sun god and born of Kunti, Karna shares the same mother with the Pandavas. Abandoned by his mother soon after birth, he is raised by a chariot driver and grows up as an outcast. Hidden and invisible, he enters the conflict between the Pandavas and Kauravas incognito, an exile. Karna and Hamlet, both exiles though native here, help us understand the absence that pervades their respective worlds. Exile, the crux of tragedy, is at the center of their experiences. Hamlet says he is "too much i'th'sun" (1.2.67). The pun that shadows the whole play is stunningly present in the *Mahabharata* as well. Karna, an offspring of the Sun, is eclipsed by a mother's betrayal. Kunti and Gertrude are tied in knots the unraveling of which is achieved at great cost. My students are riveted by the parallels and excited to note the universality of tragic irony.

When one thinks of exile in the *Mahabharata*, one normally thinks of the Pandavas, who are literally condemned to a life of exile. However, the princi- pal but invisible Pandava is Karna, condemned to an exile far more painful and hopeless than that of his five younger brothers. The eldest, forced into the position of the leading warrior of the enemy, provides for us an example of self- division and exile unsurpassed in literature, illustrating the perennial tragic problem of being destined to sleep with the enemy, who is, paradoxically, none other than the self. Karna's exilic identity throws a light on the exile of the Pan- davas and ultimately on the human condition, a condition that Vyasa and India seem to want to take us beyond by alerting us to its ultimately illusory nature. Indeed, there are significant differences in the way these issues are resolved in the climactic scenes of these two masterpieces, but in noting the similarities, my students get a better appreciation of the distinctive resolutions that mark these great Eastern and Western portrayals of human experience.

Revenge, exile, and detachment are important themes in both *Hamlet* and the *Mahabharata*. But my students cannot be completely satisfied with a comparative exercise. They have been invited to enter the complexities of comparing disparate worlds—ultimately human, no doubt, but moved by subtle and sometimes fundamentally different ideas of time, self, action, and death.

I try to communicate to my students my feeling that there is more to a multicultural approach than a study of analogues. Ideally, it should involve a genuine exposure to the other, perhaps even a vulnerability to the other, including the possibility of being seriously interrogated as well as rendered whole by the world of the other. I call it radical reciprocity, a veritable interanimation of souls.

Vyasa, the mythic composer-narrator of the *Mahabharata*, accompanies Yudhistira, the eldest brother of the Pandavas, king and lone survivor of the great war, on his last journey through heaven and hell. He finds his enemies, the Kauravas, the evil ones, rewarded in heaven while his own brothers and wife, the virtuous ones, are consigned to the darkness of the underworld. He is confused and distraught, until Vyasa tells him that this is indeed the last illusion. Time and death are but mere elements in the creative artifice of eternity.

Can the entrance of Fortinbras be seen in these overarching terms, a seemingly all-healing perspective at the end of *Hamlet* as he institutes a new order, time, and world? Does the pathos of Hamlet lend itself to being so summarily dissolved as that of the Pandavas, who have also lost all? Does the Indian scheme of things invite us to consider the possibility that Shakespeare's tragedy is finally a comedy, in that time is set right once again? Or should we question, if not reject, the seemingly facile resolution at the end of the *Mahabharata* and infuse it with a sense of the finality of tragic dissolution that unravels human reality in *Hamlet*? The disparate texts and contexts seed each other, as I affirmed earlier. But, we notice, this process results in a state of suspended animation, in which questions hang in the air like swords, like fruit, depending . . .

NOTE

Hamlet quotations are from Kittredge (1967).

The Gertrude Barometer: Teaching Shakespeare with Freud, Eliot, and Lacan

Julia Reinhard Lupton

Hamlet's first soliloquy, delivered before the Ghost has revealed the parameters of the play's primal crime, shows the hero already burdened by the emotions and behavior that distinguish him from those of other tragic heroes of his time and before. Above all, Hamlet is incapacitated by an overwhelming sense of fractured paternity, his sense of father divided between Hyperion and the satyr, between an Olympian ideal kingship and its adulteration in the figure of the usurper. Moreover, this fracture in the image of the father has been revisited on the psyche of the son: in Hamlet's devastating ratio, Claudius is "no more like my father / Than I to Hercules," an equation that implicitly identifies Hamlet with the moral failings of the satyr-king (1.2.152–53). This crippling concern with the father-son relation is continually interrupted by Hamlet's rising disgust at the actions of his mother, who has "post[ed] / With such dexterity to incestuous sheets" (156–57). Finally, Hamlet's view of human nature as an "unweeded garden / That grows to seed" (135–36) universalizes his sense of guilty inadequacy, itself the result of his split identifications between two fathers, while its image of rank growth echoes the wanton desires he attributes to his overripe mother.

The psychic scenario established by the first soliloquy lends itself beautifully to psychoanalytic interpretation, whether the class be a Shakespeare survey, an introduction to literature, or a course on theory and criticism. Sigmund Freud's comments on the drama of paternity in *Hamlet* and their consequences for the psychic mechanisms of guilt and suicidal melancholia remain cogent and fresh, especially when deployed in the direction of symbolic and social structures rather than brute character analysis. Jacques Lacan, the French psychoanalyst who reread Freud's work in the context of semiotics, mathematics, and modern philosophy, put new emphasis on the disturbing role of the mother's desire in this scenario. As such, Lacan rendered in psychoanalytic terms some of the key concerns raised by T. S. Eliot's 1919 essay "*Hamlet* and His Problems." Though the essay is by no means a work of feminist criticism, Eliot's focus on the problem of Gertrude's guilt recenters the play's drama of paternity around the question of the mother's desire. The essay can be used to introduce undergraduates to psychoanalytic methods via a foundational work of modern criticism, allowing students to see literature, criticism, and theory in productive interplay with one another.

I always begin with Freud's own comments on *Hamlet* in *The Interpretation of Dreams*, published in 1900, at the very beginning of the psychoanalytic adventure. Freud introduces Shakespeare's play in conjunction with *Oedipus Rex*:

> Another of the great creations of tragic poetry, Shakespeare's *Hamlet*, has its roots in the same soil as *Oedipus Rex*. But the changed treatment of the same material reveals the whole difference in the mental life of these two widely separated epochs of civilization: the secular advance of repression in the life of mankind. In the *Oedipus* the child's wishful fantasy that underlies it is brought into the open and realized as it would be in a dream. In *Hamlet* it remains repressed; and—just as in the case of a neurosis—we only learn of its existence from its inhibiting consequences. (298)

In a basic Shakespeare or literature course, the above passage reproduced on a handout is often enough to introduce students to the basic features of Freud's reading of *Hamlet* and to some fruitful aspects of psychoanalytic reading more generally. First and most obviously, Freud gives an oedipal reading of Hamlet; he will go on to suggest that the hero delays in revenging his father's death because Claudius has executed in reality what Hamlet desired in fantasy, namely, to marry Gertrude and kill King Hamlet. In Freud's words, "Hamlet is able to do anything—except take vengeance on the man who did away with his father and took that father's place with his mother, the man who shows him the repressed wishes of his own childhood realized" (299).

Remaining at this basic level, you can explore with students the benefits and limits of such a reading. It taps, for example, Hamlet's penchant for self-reproach, already in full flower in the first soliloquy. Even when Hamlet begins to direct his animosity toward an increasingly repugnant Claudius, he continues to berate himself and indeed all humanity for its rotten state. In a favorite line of Freud's, Hamlet says, "Use every man after his deserts, and who shall scape whipping?" (2.2.524–25). Even King Hamlet is included within the ban of general guiltiness: "A took my father grossly, full of bread, / With all his crimes broad blown, as flush as May" (3.3.81–82). Hamlet's relation to his father is one of both adoration and ambivalence, a split visualized in the play's two fathers, King Hamlet and Claudius, and brought to bear on Hamlet's own fractured psyche in the form of guilt, self-doubt, and suicidal longing.

All this, of course, keeps us at the level of character analysis. Yet another dimension animates Freud's comments as well, what we could call the dimension of interpretation as such, of a method of reading that moves between literal and symbolic, conscious and unconscious meanings. In this scheme, Oedipus is the hidden meaning of Hamlet, and Claudius's crime figures forth the hidden substratum of Hamlet's desire. These levels can be graphed on the board.

manifest	Hamlet	Claudius's crime
latent	Oedipus	Hamlet's desire

Freud's method of reading also implies a historical dynamic; when he suggests that *Hamlet* demonstrates the "difference in the mental life of these two widely separated epochs of civilization," Freud is making an argument about the temporal processes that distinguish modern from ancient drama. Part of *Hamlet*'s modernity, students can come to see through their encounter with Freud, lies in the hero's internalization of dramatic conflicts and the consequent distention and delay of the dramatic action. In classical literary terms, Sophocles's play emphasizes plot (mythos), while Shakespeare's play emphasizes character (ethos). But Shakespeare's brilliant characterization comes about not because of a greater realism but as a result of the repression and internalization of key narrative types from previous periods of literary history.

modern tragedy	ethos	characterization
ancient tragedy	mythos	plot

Freud's interpretive initiatives, then, can lead students to appreciate not only Hamlet as a character but also *Hamlet* as a stratified work composed of symbols, allusions, and identifications that imply major shifts in the nature of tragedy over time. Indeed, it is these very shifts in the genre of tragedy that promote the psychological focus on character; the generic and structural changes by which modern tragedy supplants ancient tragedy are the means by which character can come into focus as a legitimate category of analysis in the first place.

If Hamlet's love-hate of his father is explained by the Oedipus complex, his relation to Gertrude is less easily accommodated by the plot of the ancient play, since Hamlet's attitude toward her is characterized more by sexual revulsion than by sustained attraction. In this regard it is useful to supplement the classic oedipal reading of the play with a focus on the mother both within and beyond the oedipal frame. Here, Lacan's insights on the play prove useful; he explains that the mother, as the first bearer of nourishment, the first agent of loss and separation, and the original locus of language, represents the initial field in which the child's desire is alienated—takes shape, comes into being, but never as its own desire, never as an expression of its own psychic autonomy (Lacan, "Desire" 12–13; Lupton and Reinhard 74–82). The child experiences its desires as coming from outside, coming from the mother, in the form of her demands (on the child) and of her own desires—for people or activities that are not the same as the child itself. In the process, the child discovers that it cannot be the mother's everything, that she has needs and interests that the child cannot fulfill.

Yet I rarely teach Lacan directly, except in the most focused and advanced courses. Eliot's not dissimilar emphasis on the mother's desire in "*Hamlet* and His Problems" offers a useful historical and conceptual counterpoint to Freud's oedipal reading. Eliot puts forth his theory of the "objective correlative," with *Hamlet* as his counterexample. He argues that the emotions called forth in characters should be correlated to objective features in their situation; otherwise, the work of literature is not convincing emotionally or satisfying aesthetically. Hamlet's responses to his mother, Eliot suggests, are insufficiently explained by Gertrude's behavior: "Hamlet is up against the difficulty that his disgust is occasioned by his mother, but that his mother is not an adequate equivalent for it; his disgust envelops and exceeds her" (25). Gertrude, as Eliot puts it, is "negative and insignificant"; nothing in her staged behavior or language would seem to elicit the kind of intense reaction that washes over Hamlet when he is confronted with the fact of her remarriage. Eliot points to a disparity between Hamlet's emotions (sexual disgust) and their cause (the largely blank and indeterminate character of Gertrude, the object of those emotions). He finds in this disparity the problem of the play: what makes it less than satisfying as a work of drama, but also what generates its interest and action, what makes it tick.

The rather different analyses of Eliot (Gertrude is negative, is lacking) and Lacan (Gertrude wants, desires) converge on this basic point. The scandal of the mother's desire, a desire in excess of both the son and the dead father, takes shape in the play as her marriage to Claudius. In Hamlet's obsessively revolted language, it is an obscene and lascivious desire, the ultimate rank flower in the unweeded garden of the wayward world. Yet, as Eliot points out, it is not clear that Gertrude's behavior warrants this response; the play leaves a troubling gap between affect and cause. Gertrude's desire for Claudius, I suggest to students, surely also operates at the level of law and language, through the civil contract of marriage and the requirements of political self-interest. She may have married Claudius because it was expedient, sensible, and convenient for her to do so, a way of resolving her dangerously single state during a period of transition from one monarch to another. I teach this as the difference between the wet mother of primal fantasies of nursing and sexual enjoyment and the dry mother whose function is more symbolic than biological and who uses language and the institutions of society to adapt to a changing social order. Where do we locate Gertrude on the barometer of maternal desire? How do we measure the intensity, direction, and moisture content of that desire as it manifests itself in Hamlet's language (almost always drenched with the son's salacious dread of his mother's torrid sexuality) and in other, more subtle weather indicators that might indicate some drying trends, blowing north-north-west (2.2.374), against the current of Hamlet's shaping fantasies?

The scandal of remarriage in the play triggers in Hamlet fantasies of the wet mother. Fleshy, corporeal, undisciplined, the Gertrude of Hamlet's invectives lives "in the rank sweat of an enseamed bed, / Stew'd in corruption, honeying and making love / Over the nasty sty" (3.4.92–94). Yet Gertrude's circumspect and restrained behavior has a certain dryness to it, a matter-of-fact, unromantic legality that may end up being more an affront to the son's sensibilities than the wet fantasies that flood him. She remarries, I suggest to students, not only out of attraction to Claudius but also because it is the logical and legal thing to do, for herself and for the state. This act of rational self-interest rather than erotic abandonment gives the desire of the mother its painful edge in the play, since it is a desire at odds with motherhood itself in its deepest infantile constructions. In *Hamlet,* remarriage is the ultimate sign of the mother's desire, since it signals her refusal to be completed by her son and her dead husband, yet, unlike adultery it locates her in the intrinsically legal, sociosymbolic world of a civil institution conceived largely apart from the wetness of weepy romanticism, loving lactation, or lustful climax.

It is this dryness of the maternal function in the play that Hamlet calls up in his flippant farewell to Claudius as "dear mother":

> HAMLET.   Farewell, dear mother.
> KING.   Thy loving father, Hamlet.
> HAMLET.   My mother. Father and mother is man and wife, man and wife
> is one flesh; so my mother.   (4.4.52–55)

By referring to the legal and sacramental definition of the marriage ceremony as the joining of man and woman into one corporate body, Hamlet acknowledges despite himself the civil foundations of the union between Claudius and Gertrude. They are not adulterers locked in the passionate embrace of a forbidden liaison but a lawful couple married with pomp and circumstance in a sequence of state occasions, "funeral baked meats [. . .] furnish[ing] forth the marriage tables" (1.2.180–81).

Claudius and Gertrude are contracted to each other, they exist as a legitimate unit in civil society, but because their union occurs as a *second* marriage, the "one flesh" celebrated by the marriage ceremony degrades into the prurient and putrefying flesh of Hamlet's sexual revulsion. What is the mechanism of this decline from the beauty of sacramental union to the slimy sublime of second marriage? Whereas marriage as a singular and initiatory occurrence binds together love and law, passion and discipline, in the ideal of a coupling that meets the desires of both parties within a socially legitimate form, the repetition effected by remarriage tears apart these two aspects of the sacramental union, refusing to allow them to meld into a perfect harmony. Whereas marriage is temperate—a tempering of sexual passion by the forms of law—remarriage is tempestuous, running alternately hot and cold, wet and dry.

Remarriage, that is, holds in dangerous tension the two climates of maternal desire without allowing them to moderate each other: sexual enjoyment in all its wetness and the legal status of marriage in all its dryness. Remarriage is a suturing or stapling rather than a melding and blending of these desires. On the one hand, remarriage is too sexual, indicating a continuing appetite for satisfaction beyond the requirements of reproduction and the romantic bounds of first love. On the other hand, remarriage is too legal, lacks heart, signaling the replacement of selfless dedication by politic liaisons. In the words of Hamlet to Gertrude, "such a deed / As from the body of contraction plucks / The very soul" (3.4.45–47).

The "body of contraction" refers once more to the union ("contraction") of man and wife in the contract of marriage. Whereas a first marriage achieves the perfect coupling of man and woman, head and body, spirit and matter, remarriage "plucks the soul" from that body, leaving a purely legal husk, dry as the letter of the law, sitting in an infernal pool of seamy sweat. The act of remarriage desiccates the marital dream of sacramental joining, triggering Hamlet's wet dreams of the enseamed bed. Legalism and lust are two ends of the same barometer.

The overwrought positivity of Hamlet's affect is caused, as Eliot suggests, by the "negative and insignificant" nature of Gertrude's guilt, its denouement within a purely legal, civil realm. Its soul has been plucked because remarriage is conducted at the level of pure contract, of letter without spirit. Eliot, it seems, would be more satisfied with the play if Gertrude's actions were less legal, if she rose to the criminal heights of Lady Macbeth or Clytemnestra, becoming the agent of a clear moral and legal breach that would inspire the corresponding horror of her son. Yet Eliot holds back from rewriting Shakespeare's play, instead concluding that this vagueness in Gertrude's characterization in fact explains the poisoned and dilatory emotions of her son:

> To have heightened the criminality of Gertrude would have been to provide the formula for a very different emotion in Hamlet: it is just *because* her character is so negative and insignificant that she arouses in Hamlet the feeling which she is incapable of representing. (25)

Put otherwise, the lack of an objective correlative—of a clear and definitive moral and sexual failure on Gertrude's part—itself becomes the objective correlative in Hamlet's case, the adequate external explanation for his distinctive behavior. Hamlet's problem—what makes the play flawed in Eliot's estimation—is also ultimately the play's problematic, its central generative question, and hence the mark of its modernity.

Eliot, like Freud, sees *Hamlet* as a stratified text, though he conceives of this layering more narrowly, as a function of its local literary history, its imperfect incorporation of various competing *Hamlet* plays, rather than as the result of a historical dynamic by which the secular advance of repression transforms the plots of antiquity into the characters of modern tragedy. Yet Eliot's concern with the text's stratification reminds us to consider the question of Gertrude's desire in relation to literary history as well as pure psychology. If in ancient tragedy, the mother's desire is manifested in clear transgressions against both family and social order—adultery, husband killing, infanticide—in Hamlet's modern tragedy contract has replaced crime.

Hamlet	contract	reaction (ethos)
Orestes	crime	action (mythos)

The legality of Gertrude's contracted relationship with Claudius removes a clear objective cause for definitive filial action and produces instead the vagaries of Hamlet's emotional responsiveness. When contract replaces crime for the mother, psychological reaction replaces dramatic action for the son. The soulless legality of Gertrude's behavior provides a stage for Hamlet's acting out, including his revolted fantasies of her obscene enjoyment.

In sum, if we teach *Hamlet* with Freud, Lacan, and Eliot, we learn that the problem with Gertrude is not her criminality but her legalism, her willingness to pursue her desire within civilly sanctioned forms. In this, she resembles not Clytemnestra but rather—returning to Freud's original reading—Jocasta, whose only crime, like Gertrude's, was the civil act of remarriage in the public theater of state.

NOTE

Hamlet quotations are from Jenkins.

"She Chanted Snatches of Old Tunes": Ophelia's Songs in a Polyphonic *Hamlet*

Nona Paula Fienberg

Of all Shakespeare's plays, *Hamlet* seems peculiarly susceptible to quick judgment by undergraduate students like those I teach at Keene State College. Some students have always already been taught everything they need to know about *Hamlet*. Perhaps the play's thematics of the difficulty of knowing tantalizes students to feel not only that they know but also that they can judge. It seems particularly tempting to dismiss the women in the play: "They have so few words; they aren't really important. Ophelia is just a ditz. She is weak-minded and weak-willed." Without deliberate strategies to foreground the play's questions, particularly the questions the play raises about its two female characters, students who have once studied or seen a *Hamlet* may be as tempted as Rosencrantz and Guildenstern to feel that they have plucked out the heart of the play's mysteries. So teaching *Hamlet* is best served by strategies to destabilize any one approach. If students collaborate in small groups to study a variety of ways of knowing the play, group reports will present alternative contexts for understanding.

Early in the semester, students sign up for a group project, where each group concentrates on its choice from an array of interdisciplinary materials that it will present to the class. In a class of about thirty-five, we have about nine possible sets of supplementary materials through the semester in an upper-level undergraduate course entitled Shakespeare's Tragedies and Romances. For our three weeks on *Hamlet*, about twelve students have formed collaborative groups to teach the rest of the class the materials they have studied. Although everyone in the class does not read or view everything, everyone assumes responsibility for a particular perspective and is challenged to interrogate *Hamlet* in different ways.

One group reports on Queen Elizabeth's parliamentary addresses. It often elects to stage Elizabeth's negotiations with her parliament regarding the execution of Mary, Queen of Scots. Elizabeth's own words bring issues of gender, power, and rhetoric in the Renaissance vividly to life as she engages the horrifying prospect of killing a monarch and a kinswoman. Beyond the *Hamlet* films and *Rosencrantz and Guildenstern Are Dead*, we have viewed *Shakespeare Wallah*, the Merchant Ivory film of the late 1960s, which situates Shakespeare and *Hamlet* in postcolonial India. Students have staged excerpts from contemporary transformations of Shakespeare, like Heiner Muller's *Hamletmachine*, Paul Rudnick's *I Hate Hamlet*, or Richard Curtis's outrageous *The Skinhead Hamlet*. Since many of my students are preparing to become elementary and secondary school teachers, groups compete to present their material in an exciting way. We get everything from sock puppets to slide shows to guitars and lutes. Some of the texts we explore are unsettling. All of them interrogate what students thought they knew about *Hamlet*. Those who have not signed up for a

Hamlet group will, later in the semester, prepare their presentation on materials that supplement our later tragedies or romances: viewing Akira Kurosawa's *Ran* or *Throne of Blood*, reading a critical essay on *Macbeth*, presenting scenes from Aimé Césaire's *A Tempest* or Paula Vogel's *Desdemona*. In one class period, a single group presentation may take half an hour, while my comments and discussion will take about fifty minutes. On occasion, when there may be two group presentations in one day, my role is to facilitate as needed. On group-work days throughout the semester, my critical approach and teaching style are decentered, while students assume leadership responsibility in the class.

Since my scholarly and pedagogical interests are dedicated to feminist approaches, this essay focuses on the group that challenges the rest of the class to reevaluate Ophelia by working on Ophelia's mad songs with the use of Renaissance and contemporary music. A focus on the culture of songs makes it more difficult to label the female characters as without a voice, the easiest and least interesting appropriation of feminism. Many good collections of Shakespeare songs and other Renaissance songs are easily accessible and inexpensive. When Hamlet and Ophelia communicated their private feelings, they did so through song; Laertes warns Ophelia of the danger she faces "[i]f with too credent ear you list his songs" (1.3.30). Polonius, casting aspersions on Hamlet's talent as a poet, cites the trimeter rhymes that Hamlet sent and doubtless sang to Ophelia:

> Doubt thou the stars are fire,
> Doubt that the sun doth move,
> Doubt truth to be a liar,
>   But never doubt I love.   (2.2.116–19)

And when Ophelia laments the overthrow of Hamlet's noble mind, she fondly remembers his "music vows" (3.1.159). As students shift their attention from Shakespeare's heroic line to the slender trimeter or tetrameter of the play's songs, the rhythm of the class also shifts. Students enter an early modern world where, as in their own world, songs were pervasive and where the songs of one generation often served as a marker distinguishing it from others, especially distinguishing young people from their elders. Students pause to attend to a language that they share, as they explore another crucial way to experience Shakespeare's world historically, a world richly interwoven with the songs of their time.

From their initial shock at how bawdy some of the songs are, both those Ophelia sings and other Renaissance songs now recorded extensively, I guide students, through the study questions I provide for each set of supplementary materials, to the insight that the lyrics test and subvert social taboos. Most important, students slow us down through 4.5 so that they can listen to and hear Ophelia's voice. When they attend to Ophelia's songs, to their lyrics, they are amazed. In 4.5 she intervenes strongly in the play, although Claudius sees only her madness and not the method in it. Her songs introduce the voice of oppressed women in society, protesting the cruelty and injustice of the double standard:

> By Gis, and by Saint Charity,
> Alack, and fie for shame!
> Young men will do't if they come to't,
> By Cock, they are to blame,
> Quoth she "Before you tumbled me,
> You promised me to wed."
> So would I 'a' done, by yonder sun,
> An thou hadst not come to my bed.   (57–64)

The ballad at once communicates her frustrations with the social order and veils the dimensions of her rebellion against the values of the court. Her audience has been one of women, real and imagined, "Come, my coach! Good night, ladies, good night, sweet ladies, good night, good night" (69–70).

The music helps bring Ophelia from the margins to the center of discussion and classroom performance. In 4.5, when an importunate Ophelia intervenes, "Where is the beauteous majesty of Denmark?" (21), she seizes center stage to hold the mirror up to the court. She reveals their nature. It is as if she has been inspired by the vagabond players whose performance so shocked Claudius. Since we last saw her as an audience at the "Mousetrap," she has, like the players, become a wandering minstrel, subject to the searching gaze and interpretive pleasure of others. When she returns to the court, she echoes the rebellious message Laertes openly espouses. Where she earlier protested her own and women's oppression, she now confronts the court's failure to mourn appropriately. In her ballad lament,

> They bore him barefaced on the bier,
> Hey non nony, nony, hey nony,
> And on his grave rained many a tear   (4.5.163–65)

she corrects that failure to honor either life or death rightly in time, ritual, and ceremony. She dares assign Claudius and Laertes parts in the funeral song, "You must sing 'Down, a-down', and you, 'Call him a down-a'" (169–70). Her rebellious performance demands the taking up of parts in a song, in contrast to Laertes's taking up of arms in a battle or taking up a sword in a fencing match.

Although Ophelia's audience does not see itself in the snatches of old tunes, Ophelia expresses her allegiance with Gertrude, who understands. From the start of Ophelia's intervention in 4.5 it is Gertrude who recognizes the different power she wields: "'Twere good she were spoken with, for she may strew / Dangerous conjectures in ill-breeding minds. / Let her come in" (4.5.14–16). Later, when Gertrude reports the death of Ophelia, she intrudes, as Ophelia did, upon the male plotting to insist that life and death be honored in appropriate rites. Gertrude's elegy provides an allegorical interpretation of Ophelia's career and her voice:

> Her clothes spread wide,
> And mermaid-like a while they bore her up;

> Which time she chanted snatches of old tunes,
> As one incapable of her own distress,
> Or like a creature native and endued
> Unto that element. But long it could not be
> Till that her garments, heavy with their drink,
> Pulled the poor wretch from her melodious lay
> To muddy death.   (4.7.146–54)

In the description of Ophelia's death, Gertrude recalls the last moments of her court life, as the "mermaid-like" singing, like her mad songs, sustains her after political disappointment and fall. While both Gertrude and Ophelia die "heavy with their drink," only Ophelia is granted the "melodious lay" that tells her story.

In much the same way as Gertrude, students may come to a more subtle appreciation of the different languages Ophelia speaks through her songs and flowers. One group member has composed her own melodies for Ophelia's lyrics, while the others in her group relate these songs of rebellion to cuts they play for us of Tori Amos, or Sara McLachlan, or Jewel. Students play and trace Natalie Merchant's retelling of Ophelia's story, "a tempest, cyclone, a goddamned hurricane."

The music approach works importantly in *Othello* too, with Desdemona's willow song: "an old thing 'twas, but it expressed her fortune" (4.3.28). In both plays, if students focus the class on the voice of the women, they will themselves put into question (rather than judge) Shakespeare's representation of women. Undergraduates discover a feminist critique encoded in Ophelia's and Desdemona's songs from the ballad culture of Renaissance England, a critique that they may have thought belonged exclusively to their world. Through music, feminist perspectives enter the classroom.

To bring music into a Shakespeare classroom is useful in many ways, most obviously because music played so significant a role in Shakespeare's world and in his plays. In addition, for those students who are connected to the cultural semiotics of music from a life of MTV, music provides a connecting strategy. But to use it as part of a polyphonic Shakespeare classroom, where, metaphorically, different voices sing different melodies, serves larger goals. The polyphonic approach invites students to destabilize their understanding of *Hamlet*, to reconsider their assumptions about Ophelia, and to attend carefully to the different discourses through which early modern women shaped their lives.

NOTE

Hamlet and Othello quotations are from Greenblatt et al.

Decentering *Hamlet*: Questions and Perspectives Concerning Evidence and Proof

Terry Reilly

Much like critics who describe *Hamlet* as a "poetic puzzle [. . .] a dramatic sphinx [. . .] and the Mona Lisa of literature" (H. Levin 4), I see the play as both a variation on the rather rigid genre of revenge tragedy and a series of interlocking puzzles made up of forensic exchanges that interrogate and critique concepts of evidence and proof. During the past few years, I have shifted my focus when teaching *Hamlet*; instead of trying to "discover" or "explain" the maddeningly complicated multilayered issues that make up the text, my students and I try to formulate questions that address those issues. Such an approach is loosely based on the idea that an answer to a riddle makes sense only if one knows and has some understanding of the question or questions the riddle poses. A discussion of such questions—in effect, questioning such questions—helps both decenter and deconstruct *Hamlet*. By this I mean that such an approach almost immediately reconfigures the focus of Shakespeare studies in the classroom—from one of finding a meaning to one that is a dialogue about ways that texts produce meanings. Moreover, such an approach considers knowledge as pluralistic rather than hierarchical, an attitude I consider sound in a multicultural, multivalent society. Here, I would like to outline some of the strategies I have found useful in teaching this type of approach to *Hamlet*.

Two years ago, one of the students in my senior level undergraduate Shakespeare class suggested that instead of spending a week and a half on each of eight plays (four to five one-hour classes per play, or approximately one class per act), we should do one play in depth at the beginning of the semester. A "thorough" knowledge of one play early in the semester, he argued, would help students learn the ensuing plays "more quickly." Despite this strange logic, I decided to try his idea and chose *Hamlet* for our in-depth play. The following semester we spent more than three full weeks (ten one-hour classes) on the play, reading and rereading the text, watching various film productions, and discussing the text in class. This approach worked so well that I have continued it in subsequent classes.

The assignment I have found most interesting and most successful when teaching *Hamlet* is the list of questions appended. I distribute the questions before we start *Hamlet* and ask students to support their answers, when possible, with direct quotations (appropriately cited, of course) from the text. This process helps students learn basic research skills, citation formats, and so on. The exercise also helps them see the play as a series of interlocking and perhaps unsolvable puzzles, what Stephen Greenblatt, quoting Stephen Booth, refers to in the new Norton Shakespeare as "the tragedy of an audience that cannot make up its mind" (1649).

The questionnaire I distribute initially makes some students uncomfortable, since they are accustomed to finding facts or conclusive evidence that will prove a point. Eventually, however, many learn to relish the joy of arguing a point that they know they cannot conclusively prove or of arguing a point or number of points from various perspectives. Such a process duplicates the practice of *argumentum in utramque partem*—argument on all sides of a question—that informed pleadings in English common law and that Joel Altman considers the foundation of an early modern legal education. Such a process, then, gives students insight not only into how a portion of Shakespeare's contemporary audience would have viewed and interpreted the play but also into how that information can be used to produce concepts of knowledge.

When students begin to realize that there is no single answer to most of the assigned questions concerning *Hamlet*, they look for alternative solutions. Such a process leads to what educators have termed divergent rather than convergent thinking, a broad learning strategy long used in "gifted" elementary school classrooms, an approach that in itself is tremendously useful for developing more complex thought processes. *Hamlet* encourages students to look for new evidence and to write their own versions of the play. In turn, they learn that this writing is, in effect, what they do when they read any text. The most difficult aspect of the approach is setting the limits of the decentralization of *Hamlet*. How far can we go with this form of interpretation before the whole play just collapses into a pile of fragments? How can you make a sustained argument about any feature of *Hamlet* when the evidence you must use to support that argument is inherently suspect?

In order to begin discussing ways that shifts in dramatic perspective produce questions in *Hamlet*, I show the students overheads or slides of several works by M. C. Escher and Salvador Dalí, several of which I discuss here. I compare the early Ghost scenes to Escher's *Waterfall*. We discuss the possibility of our being confronted with something "real" yet counterintuitive, something that we know rationally cannot exist yet is plainly manifest at least in a visual context. I then compare the play within the play to one of Escher's metamorphosis drawings, for example, *Day and Night*. This comparison emphasizes the inability of the eye to focus on more than one thing at a time: in Escher's drawing we see either the white birds or the black birds, just as in *Hamlet* we see either Hamlet or Claudius or Gertrude or Ophelia or the play within the play. Finally, I show Escher's *Hand with Reflecting Globe* and discuss concepts of inversion and distortion as they relate to vision, hearing, and other forms of perception. We then use these approaches as a basis to discuss issues such as Hamlet's solipsism in his "Alas, poor Yorick" speech and distortions in the "maimed rights" of Ophelia's funeral procession (5.1.219). By using such comparisons and conflating visual and verbal analogies, students learn how the tendency to privilege one perspective influences their interpretation of the play, while at the same time they learn to develop and appreciate the validity of alternative views.

Using overheads or slides of several of Dalí's trompe l'oeil paintings (I like *Slave Market with the Disappearing Bust of Voltaire* and *Old Age, Adolescence, Infancy [The Three Ages]* in particular), we discuss how exaggerated or unnaturally arranged concepts of physical and cognitive distance change concepts of perception and understanding. In Dalí's paintings, the "surface" image is often radically at odds with other images represented either within or in front of it. The image of Voltaire, an antislavery advocate, both "appears" among and takes shape from smaller figures who are bidding for slaves. In similar ways, many of the traditional cruxes of *Hamlet* take shape from literary analogues for such shifting forms and distances. Most students understand that the dumb show and the play within the play reenact the murder of Old Hamlet by Claudius. Yet close reading of one line from this scene, Hamlet's comment that the murderer "is one Lucianus, nephew to the king" (3.2.244), radically reconfigures our understanding of the play; a king killed by his nephew may refer to Hamlet's killing Claudius. Similarly, when we first look at Gertrude's description of Ophelia's death (4.7.137–54), most students, even at the graduate level, initially are quite certain that Ophelia's death is a suicide, because they fail to realize that the form of Gertrude's speech is that of an eyewitness account. Once they do, however, the questions proliferate: Was Gertrude there? If someone told Gertrude the story, who was it? And, perhaps most important, why didn't this eyewitness try to save Ophelia? Such questions inform the hundreds of paintings of Ophelia's death, as artists invariably assume the perspective and gaze of an eyewitness. Moreover, such a focus on relations between form and content sets up the gravedigger scene and makes it not simply an interlude but an integral, comprehensible, interactive, and dynamic part of the play.

Finally, after discussing the speech concerning Ophelia's death, we return to consider Hamlet's "To be or not to be" speech. I ask students to consider the speech three ways—first as a conventional soliloquy in which Hamlet, alone, reveals to the audience his innermost thoughts. Second, I ask them to consider that Hamlet knows that Claudius and Polonius are within earshot (the BBC production with Derek Jacobi is staged this way) and that therefore the speech is a pseudosoliloquy meant to be overheard by the two father figures. Finally, I ask them to see how modulation of voice—loud in some places, soft in others (Ralph Fiennes does this in his *Hamlet*)—can influence our understanding not only of the speech as perhaps an unorthodox form of soliloquy but also of the play as a whole.

Other points I stress when teaching *Hamlet* are that perceptions of truth can be relative rather than absolute and that the epistemology of truth in the play often works against the prevailing legal and scientific ideologies of the time (as espoused in the works of Bacon, Coke, and others). Relativism is particularly important in the type of multicultural classroom I encounter here at the University of Alaska, since many of my students are either from indigenous Indian or Eskimo groups or from foreign (mostly Pacific Rim) countries. Many of these students have had limited exposure to some of the underlying philosophical tenets of Western culture, and both learning and emphasizing that there are different ways of perceiving different truths (emphasis on the plural here) are extremely important to concepts of intercultural exchange and negotiation.

Questions for Class Discussion

1. What is the length of time between Old Hamlet's death and Gertrude's marriage to Claudius?
2. What time is it at the beginning of 1.4?
3. What is the title of the play within the play?
4. What is the plot of the play within the play?
5. How does Old Hamlet die?
6. How does Ophelia die?
7. Who sees the Ghost? Who hears the Ghost? Who both sees and hears the Ghost?
8. Who handles the letters that Hamlet sends Claudius in 4.6 and 4.7? Does Claudius read the letters in their entirety aloud? What messages or meanings do they convey?
9. Does Ophelia receive a Christian burial?
10. Is Hamlet's "To be or not to be" soliloquy (perhaps the most famous speech in English literature) actually a soliloquy?
11. Does Gertrude know that the wine is poisoned before she drinks it?
12. Who is the "rightful" king of Denmark at the end of the play?
13. What is the "primal eldest curse" mentioned in 3.3.37?
14. Why does Horatio remain in Denmark after Hamlet has been sent to England?

NOTE

Hamlet quotations are from Evans et al.

More than Child's Play:
Approaching *Hamlet* through Comic Books

Marion D. Perret

Formerly the bane of English teachers, comic books—and their audience—
have matured. So has the attitude of many teachers toward what they once
scorned as a substitute for real reading and a deterrent to thinking. These
teachers have discovered that an intriguing panel can capture students' wandering attention: it can also stimulate imaginative, focused freewriting and
spark thoughtful discussion from good readers. For students not well prepared
to deal with Shakespeare's text, particularly those without adequate English or
reading skills, a sophisticated graphic narrative version, though no substitute for
the play, can be an attractive entry to *Hamlet*. High school and college students
more accustomed to watching television than to reading often find Elizabethan
English dauntingly obscure, but comic books speak visually. A well-chosen
graphic version can, with the teacher's help, assist eye-oriented students not
only in understanding the plot but also in becoming more sensitive to words,
nuances of character, and patterns of dramatic structure.

Comic books encourage this sensitivity, because the text illuminates the
graphics as much as the reverse. First the pictured action draws attention; then
the reader turns to the words for deeper understanding. Since the visual representation influences response to the verbal text, the teacher will find that
some comic books are of more use than others. For instance, the original
(1952) Classics Illustrated version of *Hamlet* clumps the entire "To be or not to
be" soliloquy (3.1.57–89) into the upper right quadrant of a full-page panel.
Dense lettering, which makes the speech difficult to follow, drives the eye away
to visual details that provide information, create mood, and remind us of the
framing action: Claudius and Polonius spying on Hamlet as he encounters
Ophelia. In contrast, the new (1990) Classics Illustrated version directs our
attention to the solitary man, boxed in between sea and castle walls, visually
trapped behind bars (the shadows cast by columns of the gallery where he
paces), and blocked in by the last four speech balloons, which are linked across
the bottom of the inset panel. Because each of the sixteen staggered balloons
contains a logical unit of Hamlet's soliloquy, the reader can easily follow the
argument Hamlet develops within himself. In this version the page, the prince,
and the reader all focus upon Hamlet's thoughts.

Full of graphic interest and activity, the new Classics Illustrated *Hamlet*,
available from comics dealers on the Internet, is consistently thought-provoking and complete enough for serious use as an entry into Shakespeare's text. All
Hamlet's soliloquies are included in some form. The adapter, Steven Grant,
cuts increasingly more from the scenes in the fourth and fifth acts; as a result,
the plot, like its hero, sweeps to the act of revenge. Grant's selective editing
often bares Shakespeare's dramatic structure. Because in this graphic version
Old Hamlet charges his son to "[r]evenge his foul and most unnatural murder"

but not to "[r]emember me" (1.5.25, 92), it is striking that after the Ghost has left, Hamlet vows remembrance rather than revenge. This condensing helps the teacher by emphasizing a motif of the play's second act: Hamlet turns a call to action ("Revenge!") into a call to thought ("Remember!").

The artist, Tom Mandrake, extends the text's resonance. In the closet scene, he gives us ever tighter closeups as Hamlet, half hidden behind his mother, speaks daggers to her. The last panel (3.4.99–108) cuts in to a very tight closeup of their right eyes. Her eye is closed, its gaze turned in upon her very soul, and tears are on her cheek. His eye is opened wide, and its pupil contains the image of a skull. Seeing this, we may think of the uncle Hamlet calls "a murderer and a villain"; of the fact that Hamlet, too, is now a murderer; of the death he plans for Claudius; or of the Ghost, who suddenly appears in the next panel. The richness of possible interpretations challenges the student to become cocreator of the panel's meaning.

What makes such skillfully conceived graphics especially useful to the teacher is that they both clarify and complicate response. The three-page sequence from "O what a rogue and peasant slave am I!" (2.2.550–606) to "To be or not to be" (3.1.57–89) sets up conflicting dimensions of the characters and keeps the reader's mind busy. The first page shows three images of Hamlet, surrounded by whirling words, like a player trying on various roles to find one that feels right. The second page shows two aspects of Hamlet's "mighty opposite." On the left, we get an overhead shot of Claudius striding down a hall, already acting on his decision; on the right, Polonius instructing Ophelia, and the king, arrested by painful introspection. No sooner do we realize that Claudius has a conscience that troubles him than we get an overhead shot of the prince, who is quietly pacing down a gallery, contemplating death and thinking about how such contemplation destroys the ability to act. The graphic compression of this three-page sequence highlights the playwright's artistry in moving the reader from emotional identification with Hamlet to critical detachment, from objective consideration of Claudius to some sympathy for him.

Mandrake's drawings create a kind of commentary, suggesting what the characters feel but do not say. In the largest of the five panels that make up the first soliloquy, we see Hamlet in the foreground, unleashing his frustration by kicking over a bench. To remind us that because he is a prince, his personal tragedy always has a political dimension, a vortex of shaded lines circles Hamlet and the empty thrones behind him. Expressionistic graphics give rise to an unsettling sense that things are out of control. In the last panel of the "'Tis now the very witching time of night" soliloquy (3.2.387–98), only the prince is perpendicular. The setting tilts to the right; the arch Hamlet walks through is off-center and skewed. It appears that the further Hamlet moves toward revenge, the more his world is out of joint. That Mandrake draws for the mind's eye is a boon for the teacher.

Similarly, the panel of the royal audience settling down to watch the "Mousetrap" illustrates how the artist's manipulation of perspective provokes useful questions. Where is the stage? At first glance we cannot tell whether the steps lead up to a stage in the background or down from the stage in the foreground. Our eye is initially drawn to Hamlet, at the focal point of the panel, apparently on a raised area flanked by walls and topped by a swag of curtain, with the court audience around this platform. As we look again, we notice in the foreground a pattern of boards suggesting a stage other than the one where the family drama is playing out. On this stage are three dark shadows, silhouettes of prop trees, which call to mind the points on a crown and remind us that we watch from the perspective of a god—or the Ghost: we look from above and behind the scene toward the facing "stage." This panel is a picture puzzle reminding us that "all the world's a stage, / And the men and women in it merely players" (*AYL* 2.7.138–39).

Considering the graphic presentation apart from the words can help make students more aware of the theatrical dimension of the play. In the new Classics Illustrated *Hamlet* the prayer scene is particularly interesting, because in this version only Claudius's soliloquy (3.3.36-72) is voiced. Mandrake's visual equivalent of the prince's "Now might I do it pat" soliloquy (3.3.73–96) shows that Hamlet has the opportunity to kill Claudius but does not take it. Each of three bottom panels on this page shows Claudius kneeling before a cross and, behind him, Hamlet standing, sword in hand. In the first panel we look past the king to a dark shadow with a raised sword. In the next panel we get a closer view of the king's anguished face and a glimpse of the prince's face, coldly illuminated by the light glancing off the blade. In the third panel we look over the shoulder of the kneeling man toward the departing white-shirted figure. Interplay between the figure of Hamlet and the words of Claudius creates the irony of "My words fly up, my thoughts remain below. / Words without thoughts never to heaven go" (3.3.97–98).

If we had the same panels without the words of either man, we would see Claudius as repenting and Hamlet as rejecting a crime, and we would wrongly imagine both to be virtuous. As it is, a reader unfamiliar with the play is likely to deduce that this prince finds he cannot stab a praying man in the back—after all, he has just shown his morality by resolving not to harm the mother who deeply hurt him. Our apparently noble Hamlet, with no desire to damn the king's soul, is more sympathetic than the playwright's Hamlet at this point in the play.

To help students in thinking about the complexity of Shakespeare's scene, the teacher can divide the class into two groups, giving one group only the prayer scene page from the comic book and the other this page and a handout of the omitted "Now might I do it pat." Both groups are to consider the same questions: Who gets your sympathy? Why? What could be Hamlet's motivation for leaving? How do you feel about Hamlet at this point in the action? about Claudius? The resulting discussion, which takes about twenty minutes, tends to become lively as the students realize how little admirable their hero really is at this moment.

Simplified yet not simplistic, the 1990 Classics Illustrated *Hamlet* is both respectful and intelligent in its adaptation. By eliciting student responses to its evocative graphics and by augmenting its condensed presentation with handouts of omitted material, teachers can make this *Hamlet* an exciting and thought-provoking introduction to Shakespeare's text.

NOTE

Quotations not from the comic book are from Bevington, *Complete Works*.

Hamlet and Sylvia, Shakespeare and Bambara: Reading *Hamlet* as Context

Mary S. Comfort

Because it includes *Hamlet* (Meyer 1383–480) and Toni Cade Bambara's "The Lesson" (179–85), *The Bedford Introduction to Literature* can be used to introduce students to the practice of "Signifyin(g)" (Gates, *Signifying Monkey* 46). According to Henry Louis Gates Jr., black writers use figurative language to recall and revise, or signify upon, other texts. To become more fully engaged with African American literature, therefore, and to appreciate the interrelatedness of canonical texts, it is necessary to read both the literal meaning and the figurative meaning of a word or phrase. "For a critic of black literature to be unaware of the black tradition of figuration and its bearing upon a discrete black text is as serious a flaw as for that critic to be unaware of the texts in the Western tradition which the black text echoes, revises and extends" (6). Though I do not explore in detail the theoretical grounding with my students, I consider my use of signifying to deconstruct Bambara's story a postmodern move: it dismantles boundaries between genres and between fiction and criticism. Whether or not they accept that figuration as deliberate and purposeful, students can use Gates's guidelines profitably to compare seemingly dissimilar texts (see Andreas, "Signifyin'"). For example, their comparisons of Bambara's best-known story and Shakespeare's most famous play shed light on both.

In preparation for this comparing, my students write papers about *Hamlet* and participate in a class discussion about "The Lesson." When they write about the play by itself, many seem awed by the task, and they attempt to find right answers, to analyze characters as Shakespeare must have intended them to be understood. When they write about both texts, they seem more willing to take risks. Approaching these extraordinary literary playthings, they dare to compare the story and the play and to claim that they understand characters in *Hamlet*. Encouraged to read closely, figuratively, and playfully, students appreciate its richness and relevance, and they experience their role as readers with unique perceptions, valuable insights, and active imaginations.

"The Lesson" recounts a field trip to the F. A. O. Schwartz toy store, an excursion arranged by Miss Moore and recounted by Sylvia, Miss Moore's most reticent charge. Sylvia begins her narrative by describing the circumstances in her neighborhood when Miss Moore arrives: "Back in the days when everyone was old and stupid or young and foolish and me and Sugar were the only ones just right, this lady moved on our block with nappy hair and proper speech and no makeup" (179). The children take two cabs to Fifth Avenue, where, as they point to objects like a microscope and a paperweight, the college-educated Miss Moore improvises lectures. They enter the store briefly, then ride home on the subway. After the field trip, Sylvia makes a resolution: "[A]in't nobody gonna beat me at nuthin" (184).

I explain signifying and propose that students read this story figuratively. I also demonstrate, by suggesting comparisons to which students relate easily, how figuration can be allusive. In the first sentence, I suggest, there may be an echo from "Goldilocks and the Three Bears." In a population where everyone else is either foolish or stupid, Sylvia is just right—for learning, perhaps, or for critical thinking, or for leadership. Furthermore, if she is like a lukewarm porridge or a soft-enough chair, she may be both attractive and vulnerable to outsiders. If Miss Moore is genuinely interested in the children, she may hope to identify and empower potential leaders, children who are "just right" for this role. If she is like the educators who made the others stupid and foolish, she may intend to consume or break those deemed "just right." It may be that Sylvia is wrong, that she must learn to value others before she can help anyone. Students can often come up with more similarities to "Goldilocks": Miss Moore snoops around in the children's houses, for example. Students can ponder other implications of the comparison.

Another possible comparison is found in the story's final sentence. Strictly informed by the story's context, Sylvia's comment about not being beaten may be a response to Sugar's invitation to race her to a nearby bakery for refreshments. It may be a triumphant boast, indicating Sylvia's belief that she has successfully resisted Miss Moore's efforts to educate her. It may signal her plan to overcome her poverty. If the comment is read with *Narrative of the Life of Frederick Douglass*, it becomes even more suggestive. Douglass divides his experience into two parts, the first recounting the abuses he endured at the hands of a slave breaker, the second tracing his escape from slavery and his development as a writer. The climactic turn between these sections is marked by his declaration that he will never allow anyone to beat him again. If Sylvia's comment is compared to Douglass's, it could indicate that she is a retrospective narrator. The field trip was the experience that showed her she has been beaten economically; her retrospective narrative would then be evidence that she has found a way to share that information with others—by telling the story to others without using Miss Moore's alienating proper speech.

Throughout the story, there are images and echoes that could be contextualized with, and become a context for, *Hamlet*. For example, the setting, considered literally, is similar to an attitudinal setting in *Hamlet*. Just as the children are shown toys they cannot afford, the characters in the play are tempted by figurative toys, experiences they dare not risk. Using searchable hypertext, students can find these references easily. Laertes advises Ophelia to dismiss Hamlet's affection as "a toy in blood"; Horatio cautions Hamlet against pursuing "toys of desperation"; and Queen Gertrude fears that "[e]ach toy seems prologue to some great amiss" (1.3.6, 1.4.75, 4.5.18). Like these characters, the children consider toys to be attractive but not worth saving for. By contrast, Miss Moore insists that an expensive toy microscope can make living things visible and that a gem-laden paperweight can keep paper weighed down on a desk. Literally, Miss Moore may be recommending that the children struggle against their poverty in order to purchase such items. If her lesson is considered figuratively, it could hint that the children should take the time and effort to study Fifth Avenue literature—like *Hamlet*, another text that could make some characters more familiar, more visible, a play that could give greater weight to Sylvia's narrative.

If we then return to the play and consider the implications of using the image of toys to describe certain experiences, the imagery indicates a shared thematic concern. Like Miss Moore, Hamlet values toys. Despite Horatio's warnings, he follows the Ghost. While others fear the unknown and carefully avoid risk, Hamlet goes with his father's ghost, willing to take any consequence to discover the truth. In the story, doubts about the value of toys are expressed by children; in the play, adults fear toys. Comparing story and play suggests that, in addition to political concerns in his assessment of Denmark, Marcellus may sense some rottenness that paralyzes the imagination (1.4.90).

A comparative reading can increase awareness of characters' concerns. Sylvia describes her teacher as "black as hell, cept for her feet, which were fish-white and spooky" (179). Her description recalls two characters from *Hamlet*. To the extent that she is black as hell, Miss Moore may be like Claudius who, when he is at prayer, has a soul that is "black / As hell" (3.4.94–95). Perhaps Miss Moore is also a villain. Perhaps her proper speech—her failure to use Black English—is proof that she has been influenced by her college experience, that she plans to encourage the children to compete with one another to accumulate material wealth, thus destroying their own community in pursuit of a goal that remains, for many African Americans, illusory. At the same time, Miss Moore has those white feet that are "spooky." Since Hamlet's father's ghost is, by definition, spooky, Miss Moore may bring important information from college; she may be a wise elder bringing liberating knowledge to Sylvia's oppressed neighborhood. Again, the story increases interest in the play, amplifying Hamlet's concern about a ghost that may be either a manifestation of the devil or a sincere guide.

Piled into a cab, Sylvia and the other black children are "putting lipstick on each other," presumably readying themselves to attract boys (89). Their behavior might reveal the children's immaturity, but it also recalls Hamlet's description of the sack of Troy, of Pyrrhus who "lay couched in the ominous horse," with "this dread and black complexion smeared [. . .] With blood" (2.2.474–79). In this context, Sylvia's friends may be seen as progressing toward Fifth Avenue as part of an invasion—into the upper-class economy, perhaps, or, figuratively, into anthologies traditionally reserved for literature by white male authors. Reexamined in the light of the story, Hamlet's reference to the Trojan horse reveals his state of mind, his feeling that he, too, is entering the castle in disguise, intending to use trickery to incriminate and kill Claudius.

Hamlet can be a context for Sylvia's last exchange with Miss Moore. When Sylvia asks a question, Miss Moore answers with another: "Are you mad about something?" (183). Literally, Miss Moore expresses interest in the cause of

Sylvia's anger, but if her question is read figuratively, or euphemistically, it could liken Sylvia to Hamlet: perhaps both are putting on an antic disposition (1.5.172). Then, describing Miss Moore's appearance, Sylvia says her teacher was "lookin very closely at me like maybe she planning to do my portrait from memory" (183). This statement is very like Ophelia's report that Hamlet fell "to such perusal of my face / As 'a would draw it" (2.1.89–90). Like Ophelia, Sylvia may be uncertain about whether this gaze signals insanity or affection. Like the "Goldilocks" echo and the reference to Miss Moore's blackness, then, when it is read in a Shakespearean context, this statement more clearly emphasizes Sylvia's confusion about Miss Moore's intentions. The comparison also suggests that, despite her initial concerns, Sylvia suspects that Miss Moore's scrutiny is symptomatic of love. As Polonius says in response to Ophelia's description, "This is the very ecstasy of love" (2.1.101). Apart from *Hamlet,* Sylvia's simile is a vivid but undeveloped image. Read with the play, it can inform the dynamic relationship between a teacher and her student. For students, this comparison is helpful in comprehending Ophelia's character. Like Sylvia, she is confused and concerned, not knowing whether Hamlet's scrutiny of her face results from madness or from genuine love for her.

When students compare the two texts, some challenge or expand upon the ideas I provide. I suggest, for example, that since it is a kind of soliloquy, Sylvia's meditation on the subway ride home might be compared to Hamlet's most famous soliloquy. It can even be broken into lines of roughly ten syllables, and it contains the same number of lines. Checking my math, one student discards this connection but offers that the children, when they hesitate about entering the toy store, are all deciding, albeit figuratively, whether or not to be citizens in America. Another student, more interested in the subway-soliloquy connection, elaborates on it to show that, despite superficial differences in race, gender, and class, Hamlet and Sylvia are remarkably alike when attempting to make (or postpone) a difficult decision. Sylvia seems interested only in whether or not to ask for a toy, but, read with *Hamlet,* her concern seems more important, almost a matter of the life and death of her self-esteem. And, since the option of forgoing the toy is attributed by Sylvia to her mother, the comparison enriches our understanding of Hamlet's choices: although he does not attribute to Queen Gertrude either being or not being, Hamlet's choice between fighting against wrongs or tolerating them is likely to be influenced by his feelings toward his mother.

Another student compares Hamlet's relationship with Ophelia to Sylvia's friendship with Sugar, noting that Hamlet and Sylvia use severity to protect their loved ones from inevitable disappointment. When Sugar caresses an expensive toy sailboat, Sylvia considers punching her; likewise, says Rebecca, a student, Hamlet sends Ophelia away to "protect Ophelia from the imminent results of his perceived, and actual, madness."

Another student focuses on references to entitlement and birthright. Recalling Laertes's observation to Ophelia that Hamlet is "subject to his birth" (1.3.18), she notes a parallel to the children's insistence, upon first seeing the items displayed, that they are "born for" these toys (Bambara 181). Read in isolation, she explains, the children's exclamation "means that the kids really want the toys," but, read with "the play as [. . .] reference," the same line becomes ironic. "I understand it as being sarcasm from the children," she continues. "The meaning changes to reflect their poverty" and their awareness that their race and economic status will deprive them of their birthright.

Johnson, a transfer student, inventories "The Lesson" for symbolic references to slavery, then reads *Hamlet*, as she supposes African Americans might perceive it, for Shakespeare's view of slavery. She notes that Hamlet's foul, down-gyved stockings resemble shackles (2.1.79), that Polonius's advice to Laertes is like the rules one might use to instruct a slave. Johnson compares Claudius's description of the "corrupted currents of this world" (3.3.57) with Sugar's comment that "This is not much of a democracy if you ask me" (184).

A returning student compares *Hamlet*'s Danes and Sylvia's family, who moved to New York then "spread out gradual to breathe" (179). The Danes also spread out, attempting to conquer other lands. She also notes that, in his statesmanlike demeanor and his criminal behavior, Claudius is like the much-ridiculed, self-deceived junkman in "The Lesson." Carefully quoting story and play to point out similarities between Polonius and Sylvia's Aunt Gretchen, she characterizes both as compliant "gofers."

While students in an introductory course are engaged by the comparison itself, graduate students may want to consider the signifier's identity and purpose. According to Claudia Mitchell-Kernan, signifying requires both indirection and intention: "A precondition for the application of 'signifying' to some speech act is the assumption that the meaning decoded was consciously and purposely formulated at the encoding stage. In reference to function the same condition must hold" (318). Perhaps Bambara signifies to challenge or to support Hamlet's claim that his blackness is more than just an inky cloak. Perhaps Sylvia signifies to signal that her understanding is out of joint in Harlem and that she was born to set it right: refusing ever to be beaten again, she is just right for revolution. This approach liberates readers from traditional boundaries to the study of Shakespeare. As trickster readers, students can imitate Polonius, indulging their teacher's antic disposition by agreeing that the story looks very like the play. In turn, when instructors encourage students to turn repeatedly from story to play, they trick them into performing "a fine revolution" (5.1.77). Thus, literary criticism becomes a performance, and the playing with literature is the thing wherein we catch the interest of the students.

NOTE

Hamlet quotations are from Meyer.

Act 1, Scene 3: An Introduction to *Hamlet*

Michael J. Collins

As I begin teaching *Hamlet* (ordinarily in an upper-level elective course for both majors and nonmajors), I propose that whenever we read, write about, perform, or teach the play, we inevitably complete a script we find somehow incomplete; we create or imagine characters, relationships, motivations, and actions that are, in relation to the script, at best plausible but never compelling. In other words, we tell a story that answers the questions the script of *Hamlet* leaves unanswered, a story that to some degree makes certain what the script leaves uncertain.

Perhaps because they see it as one of the greatest plays of our culture, perhaps because they have learned to expect firm readings in the classroom, or perhaps because, like the world at large, they crave definite answers to complex questions, some students are inevitably uneasy with the proposal that *Hamlet* tells not just one compelling story but many plausible stories, that the same script will to some degree tell a different story each time it is read, interpreted, taught, or performed.

To help them understand my initial proposal and finally recognize the inherent uncertainty of *Hamlet*, I ask students to analyze, rehearse, and then act out (or at least walk through) act 1, scene 3, playing Ophelia, Laertes, and Polonius. I choose this scene because its substance (the dialogue of a brother and sister, a father and son, and a father and daughter around the son's departure and the daughter's romance) inevitably encourages them, as they analyze and rehearse the scene, to draw on their own experience with siblings, parents, romances, and departures. I divide the class into groups of four (three actors and a director) and provide each group a list of questions (to define at least some of the choices the scene offers actors) and sometimes an edited script that cuts lines from the long speeches of Laertes and Polonius in the last part of the scene. The edited script is a mixed blessing. Since the speeches of Laertes and Polonius are long and linguistically complex, an edited script gives students who have no training as actors a greater opportunity actually to act the lines rather than simply struggle to get them said. But it does to some degree obscure important values of the scene—the linguistic parallel of Laertes and Polonius and the relative silence of the woman in relation to the two men.

With a class of forty, the exercise usually takes two seventy-five-minute classes. Students first rehearse the scene for about thirty or forty minutes and then act it out toward the end of the first class and over most of the second. As the students prepare, I move from group to group, answering questions and occasionally suggesting some possibilities. To narrow the field for comments, questions, and comparisons, I ordinarily break each performance into two parts: all the groups act the first part (up to the departure of Laertes) one after the other and then move on to the second part (the exchange between Ophelia and Polonius).

My immediate goal here is to help students see that since the script is reticent about such issues, anyone who reads, directs, interprets, or acts the scene must imagine the characters, their motivations, their relationships and responses to one another, and, in the case of actors, articulate what they have imagined on the stage through action and tones of voice. Once the students have completed staging the scene themselves, they watch (in the first half of a third class) several versions of it on film in order to see acted both their choices and those they may have either rejected or never imagined. The easily available films (with Laurence Olivier, Nicol Williamson, Derek Jacobi, Mel Gibson, and Kenneth Branagh as Hamlet) differ sufficiently from one another to make clear the varied possibilities of the scene: Olivier's version shows an Ophelia who teases Laertes during their father's "few precepts" (58); Williamson's anticipates the closet scene by suggesting incestuous feelings between Laertes and Ophelia; Derek Jacobi's Polonius is a gentle, loving father; and Mel Gibson's Ophelia, with considerable annoyance, resists both her brother's and her father's admonitions.

I have found this acting exercise a particularly useful introduction to *Hamlet*. While students seem always to enjoy the opportunity to analyze, rehearse, and finally stage the scene, they not only experience for themselves its uncertainty—its openness to a range of interpretations—they also recognize that the uncertainty they have experienced is to some degree suppressed or made certain once they have decided how to act the scene. At the same time, the exercise increases their facility with the language of the plays: the process of defining thoughts, feelings, relationships, and motivations and then choosing the actions and tones of voice to articulate them demands that they read the text carefully and turn Shakespeare's verse into (their own) living speech. Then, by inviting them to draw on their experiences to act the scene, the exercise also offers students the concomitant opportunity to replicate and thus better understand the way actors work. Finally, students come to recognize another significant point about *Hamlet* (and indeed about all plays): the theatrical questions of how to perform the script soon become human questions about men and women, their motivations, their relationships, their values.

As students next turn their attention to other parts of *Hamlet*, they often see more readily how the scene they have acted connects to other moments in the play, for example, to Ophelia's inordinate grief after her father's death, and thus they begin to recognize *Hamlet*'s complex design. More important, the acting exercise leaves them more sensitive to other uncertainties in the play, to its openness to a variety of readings. As a result, they become more willing, perhaps, to believe that what our culture really values in *Hamlet* is not the meanings we find in it or make from it but our experience of it, our experience of a profoundly complex, richly patterned structure of vibrant words brought to engaging life by our own wit and imagination.

Questions for Act 1, Scene 3

1. How are Laertes and Ophelia positioned on the stage and in relation to each other as they speak? Do they ever move, do they change positions, or do they remain fixed in one place?
2. How does Laertes speak to Ophelia? What is/are his tone(s) of voice?
3. How does Ophelia respond to Laertes? What is/are her tone(s) of voice in "No more but so" (10) and particularly in the lines beginning "but, good my brother" (46)?
4. How does Polonius enter? What, if anything, does he do when he says to Laertes, "There, my blessing with thee" (57)?
5. How does Polonius say the famous speech beginning "And these few precepts in thy memory / Look thou character" (58–59)? What is/are his tone(s) of voice?
6. Where is Polonius positioned as he gives the speech? What is his attitude toward Laertes? Why does he give the speech?
7. Where is Laertes positioned during Polonius's speech? Where is Ophelia? How (if at all) does she respond as Polonius speaks to Laertes? Does Polonius give her any attention?
8. How does Polonius say the last line of his speech, "Farewell. My blessing season this in thee" (81)? What, if anything, does he do?
9. How, if at all, does Laertes respond to the speech? How does he respond, if at all, to Polonius?
10. How does Laertes speak to Ophelia as he leaves? How does she reply? What are their tones of voice?
11. How does Laertes take his leave? What, if anything, does he do with Polonius? with Ophelia? How does he exit the stage?
12. In what tone of voice does Polonius ask Ophelia, "What is't, Ophelia, that he hath said to you" (88)?

13. How does Polonius speak to Ophelia in the lines that follow? What is/are his tone(s) of voice? Is he angry, stern, gentle?

14. How are Polonius and Ophelia positioned on the stage and in relation to one another in the lines that follow? Do they ever move, do they change positions, or do they remain fixed in one place?

15. How strongly does Ophelia resist Polonius between lines 110 and 114? What is/are her tone(s) of voice?

16. How does Polonius say his last long speech in the scene? What is/are his tone(s) of voice?

17. Do the actors do anything toward the end of Polonius's last speech? Does his tone of voice change?

18. Do the actors do anything at the end of the speech (i.e., between "with the Lord Hamlet" and "look to 't, I charge you"; between "look to 't, I charge you" and "Come your ways"; and between "Come your ways" and "I shall obey, my lord")? What is/are Polonius's tone(s) of voice (134, 135, 136)?

19. How does Ophelia say, "I shall obey, my lord" (136)?

20. How do they exit? Do they go off together, separately, or one behind the other? Or does one remain on stage while the other exits?

NOTE

Hamlet quotations are from Barnet, *Shakespeare*.

Act 2, Scene 1, 75–120:
Psychoanalytic Approaches

H. R. Coursen

In teaching *Hamlet*, some reference to Sigmund Freud and the psychological approach would seem inevitable. The approach via twentieth-century psychology is easily dismissed as anachronistic and nonhistorical. To disregard it, however, is to ignore the pervasiveness of what Terence Hawkes calls A. C. Bradley's "commitment to the almost palpable existence of single unitary individuals and the developing relations between them as the core of each play's interest," which may reflect "deep [. . .] dimensions of Western ideology" (Introduction 5).

In what sense are Shakespeare's characters real? Is it true, as Harold Bloom asserts, that Shakespeare invented our contemporary sense of what a person is (*Invention*)? Can psychological approaches be applied successfully to Shakespeare's characters, particularly theories invented long after the plays were written? Are such approaches valid in responding to performance, making us "more alert to the ways in which we are involved in the plays" (Wheale 131–32)? These are huge questions, of course.

This essay looks at a small segment of script—act 2, scene 1—in the light of major modern psychological approaches. It should serve as a staging area for a student's further exploration of the theories themselves, the scene itself, and other scenes in *Hamlet*. The scene raises many specific questions. One question of long standing is, Has the visit of Hamlet that Ophelia reports to Polonius in fact occurred? In what ways do father-daughter relationships differ in different productions? Some of the differences, of course, result from editing, but most are the product of different actors in the roles and of different emphases in the productions. How is madness defined in the play and by various psychological theories? (See, in addition to Freud and to Jung, Horney; Fromm). A focus on forty-five lines from this vast script will show a student how much the play contains for analysis. It is an antidote to superficial responses. I offer only the barest outline for further student delving into psychological theory and its application to plays as performed. The approach via Ophelia has the advantage of decentering Hamlet and insisting that he not be our moral interpreter of the play that bears his name.

Pedagogically, I would not lecture on the psychological material but have students read excerpts from key texts in the field. I might even ask a student to be an "expert" on one psychological approach. Then I would ask, How would a Freudian, a Jungian, a Lacanian deal with the scene? This question would lead to discussion, would remove the teacher from the need to argue a preference, and would show students that theory is there to be applied to text and not merely to be spun out as a primary and independent entity.

Into a scene from which Polonius sends Reynoldo to spy on Laertes's life in Paris bursts his daughter, with the story of her life in Elsinore. The Laurence

Olivier film shows her alone in her room, sewing. She becomes aware of Hamlet's approaching behind her. While we see what she describes to Polonius, the scene ends with her going back to her sewing. In contrast to, for example, Lalla Ward's Ophelia in the BBC-TV production (1980) and Kate Winslet's Ophelia in the Kenneth Branagh version (1996), Jean Simmons's Ophelia does not report to Polonius.

The physicality of the scene in the Olivier film reinforces Ophelia's report to the smallest detail. Or does it? Since the scene begins and ends with a close-up of Ophelia and is separated from the rest of the film by dissolves, could Hamlet's visit be the product of "intense imagination at work in a framework of boredom" (Pennington 61n2)? The film invites that possibility. Bernice W. Kliman argues that the scene's beginning and ending with a full light on Ophelia's face frames the narrative as "Ophelia's mental, subjective recollection of Hamlet's visit" (*Hamlet* 28).

The psychological approach often attempts to show that what people accept as reality is really symbolic. Let us assume, with James Kirsch, that "we must accept Ophelia's report as a product of her imagination and not as fact" (60). If Hamlet did *not* appear, we are witnessing the first scene of her madness—a made-up adventure that she can report to the only person in her world who may believe her. One irony, of course, is that it is Ophelia who is originating the story of Hamlet's madness. Certainly that is the emphasis in the script:

> POLONIUS. Mad for thy love?
> OPHELIA. My lord, I do not know,
>   But truly, I do fear it.   (85–86)

Perhaps the only way she can get her father to see her as a woman and not as "a green girl" or "a baby" (1.3.101–05) is to create a prince in whom love has curdled into a madness to be feared. It may be that because she wants "the opposition [to her relationship with Hamlet] lifted, [she] tries to establish [Hamlet's] loving concern for her [and thus presents] a prevaricating story" (Marks 51–52).

Freud's great contribution to the *Hamlet* debate is, of course, the note that Ernest Jones developed into *Hamlet and Oedipus*. We are warned, however, that "no subject confused Freud so much as feminine psychology and female development" (Lidz 217). Freud might argue that Ophelia comes to her father with her story because he has delivered a shattering blow to her self-esteem. The power of the blow, says Freud, derives from its having been delivered by "some person whom the patient loves, has loved, or ought to love" (*Standard Edition* 20: 158). The motherless and now brotherless Ophelia needs no Electra complex (a woman's unconscious incestuous love for her father) to make her completely dependent on Polonius. He has sneered at her recently while simultaneously blocking her from Hamlet. She has something to prove and may, by the time she delivers her report, believe that it represents a real event.

Ophelia is trapped in "the conflict between the father and the lover, a recurrent theme in myth" (Lidz 113). Polonius, however unwittingly, has blocked Ophelia from the "essential transition from daughter to wife and mother" (217). Freud would attribute Ophelia's report to her hysteria, a syndrome that will develop into schizophrenia and by this declension to suicide—if a madwoman can commit suicide.[1]

Freud argues, "To begin with we knew only sexual objects" (*Standard Edition* 12: 105). C. G. Jung says that "Freud's incest theory describes certain fantasies that accompany the regression of libido and are especially characteristic of [. . .] hysterical patients" (*Symbols* 419). What might be happening, then, is that Ophelia's psychic energy (libido) is moving back (regressing) to that time when she knew only sexual objects. Psychic energy shifts toward Thanatos, the destructive tug of the death instinct. In the simplest terms, to repress sexual energy is to give that energy the power to burst forth at some later, inappropriate moment: in Ophelia's case, in madness.

Carol Thomas Neely differentiates Ophelia's authentic madness from Hamlet's feigned lunacy by suggesting that hers is a "quoted discourse": "formulas [. . .] which ritualize passages of transformation" (81 [Garner and Sprengnether]). While Ophelia's description of Hamlet's visit to her closet is more coherent than her later mad scenes, it tends toward quotation in its description of the stereotypic male lover and toward ritual ("thrice his head thus waving up and down" [93]). The links with madness are underlined by the eerie echoing of the appearance of the Ghost ("pale [. . .] As if he had been loosed out of hell / To speak of horrors" [84–85]). In a sense, this is Ophelia's ghost—the numen of lost love, the return of something dead from the burial place of her psyche. Harold Goddard compares Hamlet's appearance, possibly during "a doze for a few seconds over her needle" (465), to the later appearance of the ghost of King Hamlet in Gertrude's closet. Bernard McElroy shrewdly second-guesses Hamlet's "perusal of [Ophelia's] face" (21): "Scrutinizing her closely, he sees something, or, more likely *fails* to see something he wants to" (68). This fictional Hamlet sees through her fantasy. Weston Babcock suggests that Hamlet believes that Ophelia has taken a new lover (61–67). Uncannily, her invented Hamlet pierces through to her own inauthenticity, as if exposing the lie of her story even as she creates it. She who claims to look at Hamlet is, in a sense, not there either. His look mirrors her own gaze at something that isn't there—Hamlet or madness. Her report to Polonius captures both "female hysteria and feigned male melancholy," as Neely says (81), and her own invention of a man who wasn't there, a ghost rising from the prison house of her repression. The Hamlet who visits her may be, as Philip Armstrong's Lacanian approach suggests, "a fascinated absorption with [her] own reflection" (221).

Frances Barber, who played Ophelia in 1984 opposite Roger Rees's Hamlet and Kenneth Branagh's Laertes, provides a neat Jungian analysis of Ophelia: "She actually presents the female counterpart and counterpoint" to Hamlet

(139). Were Ophelia to take a Myers-Briggs test, she might be an "extroverted feeling" type. (Hamlet would be an "introverted thinking" type: see Coursen, *Compensatory Psyche* 63–99). Her psychic energy goes outward toward objects. She evaluates those objects according to how she feels about them— they lose value "when givers prove unkind" (3.1.102). Visible things—letters, remembrances, clothes, flowers—hold an intangible value for her. That Ophelia is "freighted with emblematic significance" (Showalter 80 [Parker and Hartman]) is partly of her own making. It could be argued that, with only needle and thread for company in 2.1, she invents the intense physicality she describes. She wants harmony, needs to be appreciated, is hurt by indifference, and needs people around her. She may idealize relationships. She avoids disagreeable facts and also wants control over her world. Add to this agenda of persona that she is young, motherless, and that her brother has just left for France. Her report to Polonius shows, if false, that she has begun to avoid disagreeable facts by making them up, thus giving herself control over her world. For Jung, though, regression can be positive. For Jung "at its deepest level neurosis was a positive attempt to construct the meaning of life" (Homans 95). Ophelia's flight to her father is an effort to get at her animus—the male archetype in woman—that must finally be internalized. In attempting to prove Hamlet's madness, which may be feigned, Polonius seems to promote real madness in his daughter. Her animus emerges through the destructive sexuality of which she sings in her madness. It is ironic that, in her madness, she achieves political power, as Horatio makes clear: "she may strew / Dangerous conjectures in ill-breeding minds" (4.5.14–15).

The Elizabethan could easily ascribe Ophelia's madness to erotomania: women "willingly run into everlasting paines of hell fire, by cruelly murthering them selves that they may thereby escape [. . .] the boyling brendes of *Cupide*" (qtd. in C. Camden 254). This diagnosis overlooks the damage wrought by a society wherein women are "objects of exchange within [a] system of sexuality" (McLuskie 97). For Ophelia the oppression is greater than that of even a "normal" patriarchal society, which "projected all outward power on men, while it imposed a narrow idealized role on women" (C. Douglas 55), resulting in the "shrinking [. . .] even stunting" of the woman's growth (Neuman 83), particularly the upper-class woman's growth (see L. Brown). In Ophelia's case, "her father and her former lover have prepared her for madness by demanding that she be virginal while treating her like a whore, and by discouraging her from thinking for herself, in which case she might perceive the incongruity of their demands" (Nardo 193–94). Whether the scene with Hamlet occurs or not, it is a bridge to madness, for what happens to Ophelia.

R. D. Laing says, "In her madness there is no one there. [. . .] There is now only a vacuum where there was once a person" (195n). No, the sensual young woman who might have been "Hamlet's wife" (as Gertrude says in her eulogy [5.1.234]) is there, however distorted the emergence of what has not been channeled positively. Ophelia's songs are "one sanctioned form of self-assertion as a woman" (Showalter 81). They come as they do because her progress to womanhood has been thwarted, not sanctioned.

Marjorie Garber, working from the theories of Lacan, argues that the Ghost's description of his poisoning is a "fantasy-nightmare of his own castration" (*Ghost Writers* 136). Regardless of that dubious substitution of the diaphanous for what seems irrefutable—the death by poison of King Hamlet—for Ophelia the nightmare is reality. According to Lacan, Ophelia is "O-phallus" ("Desire" 11). So, Lacan mockingly suggests, is her name derived. Lacking male potency—a political fact, at least—she goes to the only male to whom she can appeal, with a fantasy nightmare of her own castration—that is, the removal of the male organ for which she wishes, Hamlet's. Her narrative is a displacement for what she does not have, a story exploding out of what Freud called penis envy. To Hamlet, she is, says Lacan,

> a vision of life ready to bloom, of life bearing on all other lives, and it is as such that Hamlet positions her in order to reject her—"wouldst thou be a breeder of sinners?" This image of vital fecundity demonstrates for us more clearly than anything else the equation I have already established: Girl = Phallus.   (35)

It follows, perhaps, that Ophelia rejects that specificity in her description of Hamlet's visit and censors it through the narrative of conventional lover, distraught and unkempt. That interpretation is far-fetched, of course, and a committed Lacanian could do much better. Lacan "treat[s] the unconscious *as* a language," thus adding "a crucial third term [. . .] language" to the discourse (Murfin 248). I find the approach via the language of castration so far removed from dramatic context as to be irrelevant (see Vickers, *Appropriating* 272–324, and, more positively, Murfin; Holland; Wheale; Wofford).

Elaine Showalter cites Charlotte Yonge to show that Lacan's etymology is wrong (91n1). Yonge suggests the name comes from *ophis*, meaning "serpent." One of Ophelia's modes is to bring wisdom. Her songs are subversive, as Neely argues (93 [Garner and Sprengnether]). In fact, if we read back from her burial in Yorick's grave, we can see Ophelia as fool—a wise if slantwise commentator and singer of songs that undercut the pretensions of power. She takes the role Hamlet abandoned on his sea voyage—the role of Yorick (see Coursen, *Shakespeare* 205–08).

Do voyages into the zodiac of psychology have anything to do with performance? Can Jung, whose work has been labeled "garbage" (Bate 192) say anything to production? Anything said about the plays that does not relate to the plays as plays is irrelevant. As Barber shows, however, a consideration of the psychology of the character in relationship to other characters—and Jung's psychological types can be useful here (see Coursen, *Compensatory Psyche*, 189–92)—is often a prelude to playing a role on stage. If speculation into the psyche of characters—even if a fallacy, even if an anachronism ("Not historical!"

we hear at the end of the accusing index finger)—helps an actor project a role to an audience, then it should be included within the other approaches to Shakespeare as more relevant than many. An actor playing Ophelia must decide when her character shows the first signs of the madness that will engulf her later. Her description of Hamlet's visit may be that place.

In a play with so many corrupted rituals, Ophelia's death can only be a reverse baptism, a sinking into mud (as in Ragnar Lyth's film) and possible damnation, as opposed to a cleansed rising into potential salvation. Her psychic journey to that stream must be charted by the actor, who knows where her character is going, even if Ophelia does not. The process must be carefully observed and experienced by the spectator. Students who have introduced themselves to the psychological approach to the plays are very likely to experience them more richly in production than students who have not explored that area. The former can begin to understand how their psychology of perception is involved in responding to the play and to the actors who depict its characters.

NOTES

Hamlet quotations are from Hibbard.

[1]Freud's interest in hysteria is signaled by his publication of *Studien über Hysterie* in 1895, five years before his landmark *Die Traumdeutung* (*The Interpretation of Dreams*).

The Closet-Scene Access

Maurice Charney

The closet scene, coming almost in the exact middle of the play, is an excellent place to discuss important issues with students. Using it as an access, we can plunge into its possibilities as a means to consider the entire play. Psychologically oriented critics have noted how the play is skewed to Hamlet's relation to his mother rather than to the obvious central conflict of the play between Hamlet and his father-uncle Claudius, the "mighty opposites" of the action (5.2.62). Gertrude is the most important mother in Shakespeare's tragedies, more important than Volumnia in *Coriolanus* or Lady Capulet in *Romeo and Juliet*. Lady Macbeth says, "I have given suck," but she plays an antimaternal role, especially in her unsexing.

The context of the closet scene is extremely significant. At the end of the play scene (3.2), Hamlet has a soliloquy in which he tries to convince himself not to murder his mother. Immediately after his homicidal declaration, "Now could I drink hot blood" (398), he resolves to go to his mother, but he has to strengthen his resolution not to act like the matricidal Emperor Nero: "Let me be cruel, not unnatural; / I will speak daggers to her, but use none" (403–04). In the scene that follows (3.3), Hamlet almost kills Claudius but decides to wait for a more damnable occasion than when the king is praying: "When he is drunk asleep, or in his rage, / Or in th' incestuous pleasure of his bed [. . .]"(89–90). This murderous mood carries into the closet scene, which follows at once.

It is a question well worth discussing whether Hamlet means to kill his mother. He certainly thinks that she is complicit in the murder of his father, as reported in all its gruesome details by the Ghost. After he stabs through the arras and kills Polonius, Hamlet directly accuses Gertrude: "A bloody deed— almost as bad, good Mother, / As kill a king, and marry with his brother" (3.4.29– 30). The queen responds with astonishment: "As kill a king?" (31), and that is the end of the matter. The actor has a lot to do to make this sound totally convincing—Hamlet never refers to Gertrude again as a murderer.

From the very beginning of the scene, it certainly looks as if Hamlet, despite his resolution in the soliloquy that ends act 3, scene 2, is ready to kill his mother. His first words before he even comes on stage are the hysterical exclamations "Mother, Mother, Mother!" (6). He begins his moral exhortation against Gertrude almost immediately—"Mother, you have my father much offended" (11)—but the stage action is crucial in scaring Gertrude. In his wildly elevated mood, Hamlet forces his mother to sit down: "Come, come, and sit you down. You shall not budge" (19). It is at this point that the frightened queen cries out for help: "What wilt thou do? Thou wilt not murder me? / Help, ho!" (22–23). Polonius answers from behind the arras, seeming to call to servants for further aid—"What, ho! Help!" (24)—and Hamlet runs him through immediately and without further reflection or identification: "How now? A rat? Dead for a ducat, dead!" (25). Hamlet here acts the part of a swaggering swordsman, like Pyrrhus in the Dido and Aeneas play. He even uses a gambler's oath: "Dead for a ducat, dead!" In other words, "I bet a ducat that he is surely dead."

One way of emphasizing the gravity of this scene is by eliciting feelings of the students about matricide as a fantasy or dream theme. There is no doubt in the playing of the scene that Gertrude doesn't relish being forced into a chair by her son and held there by his overwrought strength. Hamlet displays a frantic energy. He gradually discloses why he is so angry, but it is an anger mixed with powerful but frustrated love for his mother. There are strong infantile and oedipal reactions in this scene that are later more fully developed by Shakespeare in the relations of Coriolanus with his mother, Volumnia. Behind Hamlet's intense misogyny throughout the play lies a child's desire to be loved perfectly by his mother and, by extension, by Ophelia too.

Another point worth discussing about the closet scene is Hamlet's inflamed sexual imagination. On the one hand, he believes that his mother is menopausal and too old for physical love, as he says so scornfully: "You cannot call it love, for at your age / The heyday in the blood is tame, it's humble, / And waits upon the judgment [. . .]" (69–71). All this may be true physiologically, but Hamlet's feverish and adolescent thoughts conjure up images of disgusting and animal-like lovemaking between Gertrude and her new husband-lover. It is clearly a projection of primal scene fantasies.

Even when Gertrude explicitly declares her contrition, Hamlet presses on with sexual images: "Nay, but to live / In the rank sweat of an enseamed bed, / Stewed in corruption, honeying and making love / Over the nasty sty" (92–95). "Seam" is fat or grease, the kind used to lard meat for roasting, and it is part of Hamlet's exceedingly graphic pornographic imagination. Toward the end of the scene, Hamlet cannot let go of his obsessive and voyeuristic thoughts. He cannot give up the exciting release of "speaking daggers" (3.2.404) to his mother, this time in relation to Claudius, the irresistible superstud:

> Let the bloat King tempt you again to bed,
> Pinch wanton on your cheek, call you his mouse,
> And let him, for a pair of reechy kisses,
> Or paddling in your neck with his damned fingers,
> Make you to ravel all this matter out [. . .]   (3.4.183–87).

Presumably, Gertrude cannot resist these disgusting, amorous caresses, at least in Hamlet's eyes.

If we turn our perspective around and try to conceive the closet scene from Gertrude's point of view rather than from Hamlet's, everything changes. First of all, no bed is needed on stage to enforce the sexual points that are already explicit in the dialogue, although the scene is usually played with a bed on the modern stage—if not actually *in* the marriage bed itself. This is histrionic overkill. In the Elizabethan household, a closet was a private, withdrawing room, whereas a chamber was a room with a bed in which one slept. The distinction is important as a way of conceptualizing the relation of Hamlet to his mother.

At the beginning of the scene, Gertrude is astounded by her son's ferocity. She was put up to this interview by the king, and the king's agent, Polonius, is concealed behind the arras, or drapery hanging, at the back of the room. Gertrude probably expects this to be a passionate, heart-to-heart talk between a mother and her loving but errant son. She doesn't anticipate that Hamlet will make her sit down by brute force, and she fears reasonably that her son intends to murder her. I think Gertrude's surprise is an important discussion point for students; it reveals much about the nature of this scene as a piece of acting. Once Polonius has been rather offhandedly slain by Hamlet, Gertrude is even more terrified when her son accuses her of participating in the murder of her husband: "As kill a king?" But his accusation is deflected with unexpected ease.

Hamlet's long sermonistic discourse on the pictures in miniature of his father and Claudius changes the mood completely, and Gertrude is now remorseful: "O Hamlet, speak no more. / Thou turn'st mine eyes into my very soul, / And there I see such black and grainèd spots / As will not leave their tinct" (89–92). But Hamlet cannot stop his exhortation, and Gertrude again pleads for compassion: "O, speak to me no more. / These words like daggers enter in my ears. / No more, sweet Hamlet" (95–97). Hamlet is deaf to any entreaties, and he speaks passionately and quickly, as if wound up. Gertrude's last "No more" (102) immediately precedes the entrance of the Ghost, as if he is coming to enforce his earlier command to his son: "Leave her to heaven / And to those thorns that in her bosom lodge / To prick and sting her" (1.5.86–88). This is exactly what Hamlet is not doing.

The entrance of the Ghost provides a completely new movement in the scene. Hamlet is preoccupied with the frightening image of his father, but Gertrude cannot see the Ghost at all and thinks her son mad. Remember that Lady Macbeth could not see the ghost of Banquo. Gertrude feels genuine sorrow for her son's breakdown and tries to comfort him: "Forth at your eyes your spirits wildly peep, / And as the sleeping soldiers in th' alarm / Your bedded hair like life in excrements / Start up and stand an end" (120–23). Garrick actually used a fright wig in the eighteenth century to mechanically make his hair stand on end.

Hamlet is disappointed that his mother is incapable of seeing the Ghost, and he thinks it is because of her deteriorated spiritual condition. He takes her incapacity as an excuse for further moral exhortation, so that Gertrude says with some finality: "O Hamlet, thou hast cleft my heart in twain" (157). But this complaint only spurs her son on to make one of the worst puns in the play: "O, throw away the worser part of it, / And live the purer with the other half" (158–59). The dramatic point is that Hamlet seems incapable of bringing his moral discourse to an end. His rhetoric is so wildly excessive that there is no way for him to respond to his mother's strong feelings of remorse and spiritual dejection: "What shall I do?" (181). Again, Hamlet launches into an inflamed speech about revolting lovemaking: "Let the bloat King tempt you again to bed" (183). That seems to be the last thing that Gertrude is thinking about at this moment.

How might a student conceive the closet scene? There is an acute disparity between what Hamlet is feeling about his mother and what Gertrude feels about him. Hamlet is accusatory and moralistic, but Gertrude not only fears for her life at the beginning of the scene but also fears Hamlet's hysterical and punishing madness, which seems to alienate him completely from her. It is not the sexual and oedipal disturbances of the closet scene that matter most. What is especially memorable about the scene is the strange lack of understanding between mother and son, their jarring and incompatible discourses. But there is a deep and unspoken tenderness, too, right before Claudius ships Hamlet to what is intended to be his instant death in England. Act 3, scene 4, represents a moment of pause and passionate argument. Hamlet and Gertrude both turn out in the end to be victims equally of Claudius's homicidal rage.

NOTE

Hamlet quotations are from Hubler.

Language, Structure, and Ideology: Act 4, Scene 5

John Drakakis

The substance of what follows is a lecture that I give in a course on Shakespeare's tragedies to a class of students who have had some minimal familiarity with the study of Shakespeare but who have not thus far asked questions about the details of dramatic structure, the practice of reading, or the business of imagining the ways in which a text becomes performance. This lecture would come early in a discussion of Hamlet, *possibly the second in a series, in which the first dealt with the different early texts of the play, the dating of performance, and the question of genre.*

In *What Happens in* Hamlet (1935), John Dover Wilson observes that the return of Laertes in act 4, scene 5, offers a direct parallel to the case of Hamlet: "There is, for example, the still more exact parallel with Laertes, a man of Hamlet's age, and with family troubles and a problem to solve almost identical with his own" (263). More recently the Arden editor, Harold Jenkins, suggests that in this scene Laertes "is all the situation asks for. He appears indeed to have been conceived to exhibit, even to the verge of caricature, all that Hamlet as revenger might have been" (142). The purpose of my analysis of this pivotal scene in the play is, first, to examine its structure and the meanings that we might generate from it; second, to consider carefully the question of whether or not Laertes is in fact a figure exactly parallel to Hamlet; and third, to show how this scene opens up for analysis the political investments that ideology makes in language (representation).

Let us first of all examine the structure of the scene as we have it in the quarto of 1605 and the folio of 1623. The scene opens with the queen, Horatio, and an unnamed gentleman, who provide a prologue for the entry of the mad Ophelia. The deranged Ophelia enters and is followed by Claudius. She exits followed by Horatio, which provides an opportunity for Claudius to comment on the death of Polonius and Ophelia's state of mind: "poor Ophelia / Divided from herself and her fair judgement, / Without the which we are pictures or mere beasts" (4.5.84–86). This brief definition of madness incorporates into it an element of mimesis, a process of imitating or picturing that is directed outward to Ophelia but also points inward to Claudius himself, who is throughout the picture, but not the substance, of a king. A messenger enters, heralding Laertes's arrival, and in the process offers another definition, that of rebellion and popular protest, which brings into alignment the cognate spheres of the political and the linguistic: "Antiquity forgot, custom not known— / The ratifiers and props of every word" (4.5.104–05). At issue here is the grounding of representations in a history that provides them with stability. Deprived of a past and of those social rituals that receive their validity through repetition over time, words become empty signifiers, counters that serve the desire of the speaker without limit or restraint. It is precisely this context that is created for the arrival of Laertes, who immediately confronts Claudius. This meeting is then punctuated by the reentry of the mad Ophelia. The sight of his mad sister serves to intensify Laertes's desire for revenge, which Claudius will later work upon, but it also aligns the concept of madness as a form of radical derangement with the category of the feminine. The scene ends as Claudius, a political revisionist of immense skill, promises Laertes some retribution for the death of his father.

Exercise 1

1. Compare and contrast the formal structure of 4.5 with that of 1.2, paying particular attention to language as a process of signification. How are meanings generated in both scenes, and how might those meanings be contested?
2. Think carefully about the staging of either scene. How would you organize the scene to emphasize the meanings that your reading of the text has produced?

Madness

Let us isolate the issue of madness, since this is crucial to our reading of the play. The structure of the scene as a whole brings together madness and revenge in a tendentious alliance, and the result is a redistribution of these categories in the play in such a way as to clarify the central dramatic conflict. The question of "madness" resonates throughout the play, but it is not until this scene that the range of its meanings becomes clear. Earlier in the play, at 1.5, after he has communed with the Ghost, Hamlet refers to the theatrical stir that its appearance has generated and also hints at an inner turmoil that is close to madness: "Remember thee? / Ay, thou poor ghost, whiles memory holds a seat / In this distracted globe" (1.5.95–97). Hamlet is "distracted" (as indeed may be the theater audience), but it is memory, the repository of a temporally based legitimacy, that stabilizes the troubled psyche. Claudius's regicide has effectively expunged the past while at the same time pretending that there is a seamless continuity between past and present. It is that continuity, articulated in its most superficial of forms by Claudius himself, that we shall see later in act 4, scene 5, associated with language itself, and that receives its validity and authority from custom. We recall also that in Claudius's Denmark custom "is more honoured in the breach than the observance" (1.4.15–16). We may project this concern into the realm of theatrical genre; it is as though the genres themselves, life-affirming comedy (marriage) and death-preoccupied tragedy (funeral), have become party to this confusion. Examples of this kind of confusion are everywhere in the play. What we perceive as a form of social dislocation is given a particular focus in the comments of Polonius, charged as he is with finding out what is wrong with Hamlet. He concludes, in a somewhat Derridean manner, with the view that

Hamlet is mad, but that madness itself is indefinable: "Your noble son is mad. / Mad call I it, for to define true madness / What is't but to be nothing else but mad?" (2.2.92–94). Later, when Hamlet confronts Gertrude in the closet scene (3.4) and after the Ghost appears to him to remind him of his purpose, he refers to his own madness negatively, in that he seeks to prevent his mother from using it as an excuse for her behavior: "Mother, for love of grace, / Lay not that flattering unction to your soul, / That not your trespass but my madness speaks" (3.4.146–48). Even before the Ghost's appearance Hamlet wants to wring his mother's heart, "If it be made of penetrable stuff, / If damned custom have not braz'd it so" (36–37), and he associates her behavior a little later in the exchange with the kind of mutiny associated with "[r]ebellious hell" (82).

Exercise 2

1. Consider the connections between madness, sexual license, femininity, political rebellion, custom, and language as they develop in the play up to the point of 4.5.
2. What kinds of infection do you see in the play, and what are the metaphors used to describe it? Look particularly at Claudius's aside at 3.4.149–53. Why is there a link established between the prostitute's makeup and the operations of language?

At the beginning of act 4, scene 5, there is an uncanny repetition of Hamlet's own situation as the anonymous gentleman announces the arrival of Ophelia. The cause of her derangement is the death of her father, killed in mistake by Hamlet; the manifestation of her madness as described by the gentleman is her seemingly involuntary dislocation of language from thought:

> Her speech is nothing,
> Yet the unshaped use of it doth move
> The hearers to collection. They aim at it,
> And botch the words up to fit their own thoughts,
> Which as her winks and nods and gestures yield them,
> Indeed would make one think there might be thought,
> Though nothing sure, yet much unhappily.   (4.5.7–13)

It is one facet of a more general process to which Hamlet himself has been particularly sensitive as he wrestles throughout with the problem of trying to reintegrate the inner world of thought with the external world of utterance and action.

The very event that produced Hamlet's own madness is now displaced onto the female figure of Ophelia. Hers is an uncanny repetition that serves to open up the question of derangement and its causes in the play. Her madness is part of a detailed definition of chaos, a form of social disintegration prevented only by the operations of a language that concentrates in the act of representation all those crucial functions of cementing identity and role together in such a way as to guarantee the efficient operation of the historically grounded human subject. To this extent conscience, something of which we catch a brief glimpse in Claudius's private recognition of the dislocated world he inhabits (3.3), functions as a normative regulating force that governs the behavior of the human subject. Ophelia becomes, in a sense, Hamlet's mimetic double; she is the picture of his madness in terms of both its effects and its cause.

Gertrude's aside at 4.5.17–20 intensifies, through the communication of its sense of dislocation, the impact of Ophelia's entry. Hamlet himself stimulated Gertrude's conscience into activity in the closet scene (3.4). It is as though the figure of Hamlet is bifurcated at the beginning of this scene, with the madness separated from it and allocated to the female figure of Ophelia and the potential for a certain kind of revenge displaced onto the figure of Laertes. For Ophelia the madness is directed toward her inner psychological turmoil and is a mark of her weakness under extraordinary pressure, but it also offers us a glimpse by analogy of Hamlet's mental and emotional turmoil. This is madness defined at the level of the human subject, the victim of external pressures. Moreover, the displacement of madness in this scene onto Ophelia and its subsequent resulting in her suicide represent a path that the tragic hero is prohibited from following in the play. Madness entails here both a loss of control and a loss of authority, neither of which is permissible for Hamlet, who is encouraged by the ghost of his father to perceive himself as both a "scourge" and a "minister" to Denmark (3.4.177).

Following on from the episode involving Ophelia, the imminent arrival of Laertes threatens to destroy even the picture of political order and monarchical rule that Claudius represents. It is no accident that brother and sister are linked in juxtaposition at this moment: together they articulate the problems that beset the very public responsibility that Hamlet must sooner or later discharge.

Revenge

The pattern of Ophelia's entry is mirrored in her brother's. Again an anonymous messenger fulfills the function of yet another prologue, whose image of the sea eating up the land is as analytically tendentious as anything we have encountered so far:

> The ocean, over-peering of his list,
> Eats not the flats with more impetuous haste
> Than young Laertes, in a riotous head,
> O'erbears your officers. The rabble call him lord,
> And, as the world were now but to begin,
> Antiquity forgot, custom not known—
> The ratifiers and props of every word—
> They cry, "Choose we! Laertes shall be king."   (4.5.98–105)

Laertes, it is asserted, is a popular king who is elected by the people ("the rabble"). Here the prospect of a truly elected monarch presents itself, but it does so as a return to a more primitive stage of social order, a stage before language. Laertes is a rebel whose actions represent an attack on political institutions and upon the very language in and through which they are represented and sustained. Revenge is here characterized by the sheer lack of restraint. When Laertes bursts in, he rejects Gertrude's invocation to be calm with a justification for his anger that calls to mind the very foundations of the social order:

> That drop of blood that's calm proclaims me bastard,
> Cries cuckold to my father, brands the harlot
> Even here between the chaste unsmirched brow
> Of my true mother.   (117–20)

Is there a faint suggestion here that Hamlet's reluctance to embark on a revenge of this kind implies a challenge both to his mother's moral probity and to his dead father's integrity? If Laertes is correct here, then failure to act, no matter what the consequences may be, signals a questioning of one's own parentage and, more especially, suggests the promiscuity of one's mother. In a brilliant moment that recalls to mind Hamlet's earlier encounters with his mother, it is Gertrude who initially confronts Laertes and who seeks to blunt the purpose of his revenge.

It is, however, Claudius, a player-king of consummate skill, who has engineered the sequence of cause and effect that is the action of *Hamlet*, who talks of causes: "What is the cause, Laertes, / That thy rebellion looks so giant-like?" (120–21). This is a disingenuous question, since the interrogator knows exactly what has caused this rebellion, as his earlier speech before Laertes's entry makes clear. But consummate actor that he is, Claudius then proceeds to play the role of the legitimate king:

> Do not fear our person.
> There's such divinity doth hedge a king
> That treason can but peep to what it would,
> Acts little of his will.   (122–25)

The effect of this disclosure is remarkable. The player-king, himself a rebel who has overturned the state and usurped power, confronts the rebel intent on revenging the death of his father. And what does the usurper do? He audaciously avails himself of the rhetoric of divine right and claims that the position of the king is protected by God. Of course, had this been true, then there would have been no way Claudius could possibly have been allowed to commit an act of regicide. At the same time as the play exposes the mimetic fraud that the player-king perpetrates upon an unsuspecting audience, it reveals a fundamental contradiction that it is the function of the ideology of divine right to smoothe over or occlude. There seems to be no question but that the play resists any temptation to challenge the ideology of divine right, a position that the ending powerfully reinforces, but there is here a momentary sense that a literal belief in the efficacy of divine right may no longer be valid. In *Hamlet* it is the villain who demystifies ideology, thereby weakening to some extent the full impact of the exposure of contradiction. Nevertheless, a contradiction is exposed here that does not reflect on the practices of Old Hamlet so much as reinforce the sense that revolutionary power emanates from an evil source. It is the play's way of ameliorating the threat to the dominant ideology that Claudius's regicide inadvertently poses.

Exercise 3

1. What do you understand by the term *ideology*? In what ways does Claudius's invocation of the divine right of kings expose a contradiction in its efficient operation?
2. Does it make a difference that the justification for the divine right of kings is placed in the mouth of the villain of the play?

Let us turn now to Laertes's responses, because they return us to the question of Hamlet's purpose and behavior, as it were by the route of a series of parallels and contrasts. Much has been made of the similarities between the position that Laertes finds himself in and that of Hamlet, and both Q2 and the folio text do little to dispel this. However, in Q1 at the beginning of 5.2 Hamlet regrets his having forgotten himself in his encounter with Laertes over the grave of Ophelia but he does so in such a way as to reinforce the distinction between his cause and that of Laertes:

> Beleeue mee, it greeues mee much Horatio,
> That to Laertes I forgot my selfe:
> For by my selfe me thinkes I feele his griefe,
> Though there's a difference in each others wrong.   (I2r)

That "difference" is crucial, nowhere more so than in the scene with which we are presently concerned. We need only observe what it is that Laertes is prepared to renounce in pursuit of his revenge to realize that this is clearly not a route that Hamlet could ever have taken:

> To hell, allegiance! Vows to the blackest devil!
> Conscience and grace, to the profoundest pit!
> I dare damnation. To this point I stand,
> That both the worlds I give to negligence,
> Let come what comes, only I'll be revenged
> Most throughly for my father.   (4.5.131–36)

"Vows," "conscience," "grace," the very things that Hamlet strives throughout the play to uphold, are here thrown aside in the interests of a single pursuit, that of a thoroughly individualized revenge. Confronted with the task of
pursuing revenge for the death of his father, Laertes rejects out of hand the
obligations to which he is bound as a political subject, in favor of a more private domestic marker of identity, entailed in his membership of a family. It is
for these reasons that the public figure of Hamlet, about whose interiority we
know much more than we do Laertes's, cannot pursue the kind of revenge that
his ostensible counterpart is prepared to undertake. In short, it is the difference between the two figures that this scene labors to articulate, allowing us to
be drawn into the emotional turmoil that Laertes represents, before caution-
ing us of the dangers of pursuing this line of action.

Laertes's wild justice contrasts in this scene with Hamlet's much more hes-
itant and deliberative approach. Laertes's actions risk collapsing all sense of difference into an inchoate mass. Meanwhile, and when confronted with this
radical threat, Claudius labors to reestablish, in the manner of a picture, the
very order that his own archetypal regicide has threatened. With a subtle irony
that we should not miss, Claudius questions whether Laertes's revenge should
involve the decline into confusion: "[I]s't writ in your revenge / That swoop-
stake, you will draw both friend and foe, / Winner and loser?" (141–43). Here
is the player-king gambling with his crown in the face of a threat that could easily unseat him from his rotten state. It is only after he has calmed Laertes that
Ophelia enters. She is, Laertes says, "A document in madness" (176), something to be read and interpreted, much in the way that Rosencrantz and
Guildenstern attempt, and fail, earlier in the play to read and interpret Hamlet's madness (3.2.345–63). This entry also allows Claudius to reassert control.

In act 4, scene 5, of *Hamlet* the juxtaposition of political contradiction and
the dismantling of the psychic structure of the subject of power, along with the
potentially disruptive impulse to revenge, serves to clarify for us the action of
the play. Moreover, the tripartite structure of the scene itself permits the complex unfolding of these interconnected issues while at the same time reinforcing their deep structural connections.

Exercise 4

1. Consider carefully the metaphors of dissolution that the messenger uses. How
   do they compare with those used to describe Ophelia's madness?
2. To what extent does the juxtaposition of the entries of Ophelia and Laertes
   suggest that the personal is the political in this play?
3. How typical is 4.5 of the structure of particular scenes in *Hamlet*?

NOTE

Hamlet quotations are from Jenkins.

The Fencing Scene

Laurie E. Maguire

I teach *Hamlet* in a first-year introduction to drama, where it features in a unit on tragedy that covers *Oedipus, Hamlet,* and *Death of a Salesman*. I also teach it in a second-year Shakespeare survey. In both courses the students come to the play with ennui or prejudice, having already studied it in high school, and my challenge is to recontextualize and defamiliarize the (over)familiar.

We talk, of course, about revenge tragedy (using Northrop Frye's helpfully schematic analysis of *Hamlet* in *Northrop Frye on Shakespeare*) and about the structure of the play (using Harold Jenkins's superb identification in his Arden introduction of patterns and patterning—the brother kings, the sons, the second revenge, the dual role). We talk about the domestic and political dimensions (using Tony Church's essay on playing Polonius in *Players of Shakespeare*). We examine the prominence of theatrical motifs (using Anne Righter's *Shakespeare and the Idea of the Play*). We spend much time with pictures of memento mori symbols, discussing Elizabeth Maslen's excellent but undercited article, which extends the arguments of Roland Mushat Frye ("Ladies") and Marjorie Garber ("Remember Me") and which brings together our earlier discussions of Northrop Frye on revenge and Jenkins on mortality.

I could, I think, leave *Hamlet* at this point, as we have covered the major bases. However, I choose to spend two more classes on the play. I introduce the students to textual variants with one class on the Q1, Q2, and F1 *Hamlets*, in which we look at stage directions, soliloquies, and the reduction of act 4, scene 4; and I do a practical theater class on staging the fencing match. If, as sometimes happens, I choose not to get the students up on their feet for the match, the class works equally well as a discussion of practical dramaturgy. The students bring their skills in deductive logic, observing the way in which the fencing match is cued and choreographed by the dialogue, and they are alert to the differences in stage directions in Q1, Q2, and F1, having already been exposed to textual variants. Often one or more students have fenced; many of them have sporting interests; and all of them have had exposure to a *Hamlet* film available on video (I put seven on reserve: BBC, Olivier, Zeffirelli, Branagh, Richardson, Orlova). I usually pass around facsimiles from *Three Elizabethan Fencing Manuals*: Giacomo di Grassi, *His True Arte of Defence* (1594); Vincentio Saviolo, *His Practice* (1595); George Silver, *Paradoxes of Defence* (1599). Thus, we have much material to juggle: early printed texts, film interpretations, fencing books, edited dialogue (we use the *Riverside* [Evans et al.]), and our own practical sense. The class is a dramaturgical exercise with a textual foundation; sometimes I offer a thematic, interpretive coda. The textual and interpretive points are not original to me. The textual are cued by (and modified from) John Dover Wilson's introduction to Silver's *Paradoxes of Defence* (Shakespeare Assn. facsim., 1933), and the interpretive come from

George Walton Williams's essay, "With a Little Shuffling." Adapted to the classroom, these two scholars' insights combine very well.

What are the weapons used in the fencing match? We begin with Osric's conversation with Hamlet in 5.2, which answers our query:

> HAMLET. What's his weapon?
> OSRIC. Rapier and dagger.
> HAMLET. That's two of his weapons—but well.   (144–46)

We briefly consider fencing techniques—the short dagger (or poniard) for coming in close, the long rapier (or foil) for thrusting (Saviolo devotes several chapters to this subject and has helpful illustrations), and I touch on the development in fencing fashions. By 1603, when Q1 was printed, the rapier and dagger had replaced the sword and buckler, and by 1623, when the Shakespeare folio was printed, the dagger had itself fallen from fashion to be replaced by the gauntlet (a change reflected, the students later observe, in the folio stage direction at TLN [through line numbers] 3674–76). At this point students usually recall fencing references from the first tragedy we have read: Mercutio's satire on Tybalt's Italian fencing style in *Romeo and Juliet* (3.1.74–85).

Having clarified the weapons to be used in the fencing match, we now need to understand what is at stake. Osric, continuing in the same speech, explains the nature of Claudius's bet—six Barbary horses against Laertes's six French swords (5.2.147–50). He then offers further information:

> The King, sir, hath laid, sir, that in a dozen passes between yourself and
> him, he shall not exceed you three hits; he hath laid on twelve for nine.
>   (5.2.165–67)

This information is crucial to our understanding of the fencing scene. The first part of the sentence is straightforward: "passes" means bouts, and the students are clear that the winner has to be three up. The phrasing about the score is, in fact, more specific than this. The winner is not simply to be three up at the end of a dozen passes; at no time can the difference be more than three. Thus, the players need not complete twelve bouts for the match to be over.

The second half of the sentence is more difficult to grasp: "he hath laid on twelve for nine." To whom does the pronoun "he" refer, we wonder—the king or Laertes? The answer to this depends, symbiotically, on what the phrase means. The students are eager to offer suggestions, and their suggestions run the gamut of those surveyed by Jenkins in his Arden long note to this "insoluble problem" (561–65). "Laid" has betting overtones, but we usually conclude that these overtones are a red herring, and that "laid" means laid down—in other words, some "he" has stipulated twelve passes instead of nine to increase the chances of Laertes's winning. (Wilson identifies "he" as Laertes, but since both Laertes and Claudius have a vested interest in Laertes's winning the match, we conclude that "he" may refer to either.)

What was the usual number of passes in a fencing match? None of the fencing manuals answer this question. I offer the students a quotation from Silver, who hints at nine. He invents a mock challenge that proposes three bouts of three: "Three bouts apeece with three of the best English Maisters of Defence, & three bouts apeece with three vnskilful valiant men, and three bouts apeece with three resolute men half drunke" (501, sig. B2r). As Wilson points out (Introduction xiii), this satiric challenge would only make sense if nine was the usual number of bouts.

Hamlet wins the first two bouts, and the third is a draw: "Nothing, neither way" (5.2.301). In all the films we watch, Laertes's assurance to Claudius ("My lord, I'll hit him now") is met by the king with clenched-teeth dismissal: "I do not think't" (5.2.295). Hamlet is presumably the better player—he has assured Horatio that he has been in continual practice during Laertes's absence in France—and after just three bouts Laertes is in a parlous condition. We engage in some diverting mathematical calculations, which help us understand Laertes's desperate attack on Hamlet after the third bout, working out how many matches he must win and lose (or win, lose, and draw) to lead by three. At the moment, things look good for Hamlet, who need win only two more bouts to win the match. As I stressed above, it seems to be the difference of three rather than the completion of twelve passes that determines the winner.

We know from act 4, scene 7, that the rapier that is to kill Hamlet is to be unbated and envenomed. Poison is invisible, but what does an unbated rapier look like? As we consider this question, our video viewing proves helpful. The Laurence Olivier *Hamlet* lingers on the two foil points in close-up, Hamlet's buttoned, Laertes's clearly not. The Kenneth Branagh film provides a close-up of the two foils, both at this stage unbuttoned. Later, while Gertrude is mopping Hamlet's brow, a lord (the messenger from Osric, who introduced the fencing match at 5.2.195–99) wipes the tip of Laertes's foil with a handkerchief, a gesture that covers his surreptitious removal of the button.

Our consideration of the foils introduces the important question of an accomplice to Laertes's-Claudius's treachery. Even if an unbuttoned foil is invisible from afar, its introduction cannot be accomplished without assistance. That this assistance is provided by Osric is clear from the text, from fencing convention, and in all the video films. Who is responsible for overseeing fencing foils? The judge(s). Who judges the fencing match? Osric. Here 5.2 repays close study, for Shakespeare's control of blocking and staging is carefully written into the text.

The stage direction at line 225 provides for the introduction of foils and daggers (the *Riverside* stage direction is based on Q2):

> *A table prepar'd, [and flagons of wine on it. Enter] Trumpets, Drums, and Officers with cushions, foils, daggers;* KING, QUEEN, LAERTES, [OSRIC,] *and all the State.*

The plural "foils" refer to many more than two. Just as professional tennis players today enter the court with armfuls of rackets of different weights and tension, so fencers were given a selection of weapons. In the Branagh film Osric wheels in a cart filled with foils; the Tony Richardson–Nicol Williamson film shows a rack of six foils. In two of the three films that staged the fight with swords, Richard Burton's *Hamlet* and Natalia Orlova's animated *Hamlet*, Burton's showed Osric with his arms full of swords and Orlova's showed a rack of swords. The sword-foil selection must at this stage include the lethal weapon, and it is crucial that Hamlet be prevented from choosing it.

The two fencers shake hands and offer each other long speeches of apology, after which Hamlet requests the foils and Laertes echoes his request. The requests are obviously not complied with, for four lines later the king repeats the instruction: "Give them the foils, young Osric" (259). Osric acts on this instruction, which is clearly a prearranged cue. Look you now what follows: Claudius immediately waylays Hamlet in conversation ("Cousin Hamlet, / You know the wager?" [259–60]). In one of the class's walk-throughs of the scene, Claudius put his arm around Hamlet's shoulder and steered him downstage—a casual action beautifully consonant with the studied leisure of Claudius's speech. Laertes must take a foil at this point and engage in trial thrusts, although no editor provides a stage direction to this effect. Claudius's conversational diversion is clearly strategic, enabling Laertes to engage in trial parries, for Laertes declares himself dissatisfied with his foil and requests another—the poisoned weapon. (At this point in the Olivier film, Osric nods at the king, indicating the successful completion of the transaction.) My students and I presume that it is too dangerous for the unbated weapon to be selected by Laertes at the start of this sequence, as his first choice, lest Claudius fail in his attempt at conversational diversion and Hamlet choose the "treacherous instrument" (316). The weapon is available but not yet prepared; or it is available but not to Hamlet.

At this stage the thoughtful and creative video variants in preparing and introducing the lethal instrument are recalled with surprising accuracy by the students. In the BBC version, Osric wears a belt with two foils; Laertes reaches over to withdraw the prepared foil (the other is used by Osric as a starting signal for the match). In the Branagh film, the removal of the foil button after two bouts have been played prompts Laertes's line "I'll hit him now" (295)—an intention he can now state with purpose, because he is in possession of the prepared point. The Franco Zeffirelli film reorders the dialogue, making Laertes change swords (the film's substitute for foils) after the third bout. His straightforward remark that his sword is too heavy comes after a sequence in which Hamlet has been clowning, collapsing in exaggerated mock pretense at the weight of his sword, winking at the queen, jogging around the playing platform—and frustrating Laertes into a request for the prepared sword. In the Richardson-Williamson film, the lethal foil is in the rack from the start. The fencers choose their foils before the conversation between Claudius and Hamlet occurs, and Laertes then changes his foil after Hamlet has made his selection. How can Laertes avoid the possibility of Hamlet's having already chosen Laertes's second choice? Simply by having Laertes's hand hover over it: the camera close-up shows Hamlet's hand moving toward, but prevented from grasping, the lethal foil.

All the films make clear what the text implies: that an accomplice is necessary, and that that accomplice is Osric (albeit at one remove, as in the Branagh film, which uses Osric's messenger). Certainly there seems to be a complicity between Osric and Laertes. Laertes addresses his dying words to Osric, not confession or explanation to a stranger so much as acknowledgment and acceptance, a laconic shorthand to one already in the know: "as a woodcock to mine own springe, Osric; I am justly killed with mine own treachery" (306). The question of accomplice was nicely underlined in the Olivier *Hamlet*, where Horatio was Hamlet's fencing support as Osric was Laertes's, chatting between bouts and checking together the tip of the foil that wounds Hamlet. Osric's haste to attend the fallen Laertes—"How is't Laertes?" (305) parallels Horatio's attendance on Hamlet—"How is't my lord?" (304). Osric is to Laertes as Horatio is to Hamlet.

We now watch the fencing match again in two or three of the films, observing a part of the scene I have deliberately ignored in discussion, since the text leaves it to the actors' discretion: how Laertes wounds Hamlet and how the actors "scuffle" and "change rapiers" (302). Fight scenes are always fun to watch, and here the BBC, Olivier, and Zeffirelli films make for particularly interesting contrasts.

I mentioned a thematic coda. Sometimes, if time permits, I relate the fencing scene and its need for an accomplice to Williams's fascinating argument that Polonius helped Claudius gain the throne of Denmark. Our link between these topics is the word "shuffling." When Claudius persuades Laertes to participate in the rigged fencing match, he assures him that the treachery may be accomplished with "a little shuffling" (4.7.317). Earlier, when Claudius contemplated heaven, he ruefully acknowledged, "*[T]here* is no shuffling" (3.3.61; emphasis added). We realize the nature of the shuffling in the fencing match; but what is Claudius's earlier shuffling?

In the first court scene (1.2), Claudius tells Laertes that he is grateful to Polonius for the throne of Denmark. In this same scene, he reminds the courtiers that their "better wisdoms [. . .] have *freely* gone / With this affair [his election] along" (15–16; emphasis added). Williams argues that in unctuously thanking the courtiers, Claudius doth protest too much.

Williams points out that just as Old King Hamlet has his ear poisoned physically "with juice of cursed Hebanon" (1.5.62), so do the people of Denmark metaphorically, by false report, which presents the murder as an accident. When we see Polonius later in 2.1, he is engaged in poisoning the public's ear by a "forged process" (1.5.37)—slandering Laertes—and Williams wonders if he behaved similarly before the election, acting as Claudius's PR agent and spreading favorable propaganda. Certainly Denmark is a state "founded on rumor and forged process, poisoned words from mouth to ear" (Williams 157), as we observe when Laertes returns from France and "wants not buzzers to infect his ear / With pestilent speeches of his father's death" (4.5.91–92). Laertes acts as the king's agent in the fencing scene in act 5. Did Polonius also act as the king's agent? Williams asks. Like son, like father?

The question is a tantalizing one, and I raise it because it brings us back to some of the issues with which we began (fathers/sons, Polonius as political animal / domestic animal, patterns, structure) and shows that a consideration of practical dramaturgy has more than just localized value.

NOTE

Hamlet quotations are from Evans et al.

Shaping Our Ends: A Workshop on the Last Scene

Arthur Kincaid

As actors with Oxford Chamber Theatre touring Shakespeare in various countries, my partner Deirdre Barber and I have often been called upon to lead workshops in schools and colleges. When a whole class is to be actively involved, we sometimes work through *Hamlet* 5.2, from the court's entrance to Hamlet's death. Moving a play always necessitates consciousness of relationships and motivations. This scene is particularly fruitful in implied stage directions and crucial production choices. Active, with clear foci of attention, it involves the emotions of student participants so they forget to be embarrassed. With a class too numerous for all to appear on the stage, many can remain in the body of the room, designated as members of the court. Individuals may be assigned to provide sound effects. Entrances through the audience draw in nonspeaking participants, making good use of space when the workshop occurs in a classroom. Everyone is equally involved in the play and equally free to offer opinions when questions arise. These are some of the questions:

Setting the stage   What furniture: thrones; a table (or would it get in the way? This introduces the question of modifying the script); anything else? Do you want to start the scene (over 200 lines earlier) with these onstage or have attendants bring them on?

Entrance of the court   Who needs to be in the scene aside from the named characters? What props need to be brought on—cup(s), table, foils—and how many people are needed to bring them? How would having lady attendants affect the atmosphere? Who is already onstage, and what do they do as the rest of the court comes on? Note that what characters are actually feeling may be different from what they show. What is—and what seems to be—Claudius's mood? And Gertrude's? Is she still aligned with Claudius, or does she feel estranged? On what side of him does she sit, and where in relation to Hamlet? Who else has to be there? At what point (at the same time or not?) do the king and queen sit?

"*Come, Hamlet [. . .] take this hand from me.*" *(221)*   What does this line tell us about (1) the positions of Claudius, Hamlet, and Laertes relative to one another and (2) the action?

"*Give me your pardon [. . .] brother.*" *(222–40)*   Does Hamlet think this is true, at least in some sense? If he is lying, why?

"*I am satisfied [. . .] will not wrong it.*" *(240–48)*   Is this true? Does Hamlet believe it? Why?

"*Give us the foils [. . .] one for me.*" *(250–51)*   What happens here? Do they get the foils?

"*You mock me, sir.*" *(254)*   Is Hamlet mocking? Why should Laertes think he is? Notice how touchy a situation this is, Hamlet having killed Laertes's father, Laertes about to kill Hamlet—and they were once on good terms.

"*. . . young Osric.*" *(256)*   Where is Osric in relation to Claudius? to Laertes? to Hamlet? Is he holding the foils, or are they in a stand? How many are there? Is Osric in on the plot? If so, how does he show it?

"*Cousin Hamlet [. . .] weaker side.*" *(256–58)*   Why does Claudius start this conversation just at the point of selecting foils? What actions occur while he and Hamlet talk?

"*Set me the stoups of wine [. . .]*" *(264)*   Do you want one cup or more? Where is it / are they before this direction? Where one of them goes from now on is very important. Claudius's speech here suggests sound effects, but now or later? Is he announcing what will happen if Hamlet wins an early bout, or is he giving an advance demonstration, drinking to Hamlet and having the guns shot off now?

"*[. . .] you, the judges*" *(276)*   Who are they? Is Osric the sole judge or conveying the consensus of several?

"*They play.*" *(278)*   This should not be tried in a workshop. It needs noting that the fight has to be convincing and that a decision must be taken whether to use foil and dagger or just foil, citing pros and cons of each (e.g., choreographers for foil are easier to find, but the script mentions both).

"*[. . .] this pearl*" *(284)*   Is this the poison? If so, can Claudius show the audience it is? When does he drink, and when does he put it in the cup? Where do we want the sound effects to come (consult Claudius's speech for their order)?

"*He's fat*" *(290)*   must mean sweaty, but a modern audience will not grasp this. Should you change it?

"*Here, Hamlet*" *(291)*   Does she get up and go to him? Where is the cup now and how does she get it?

"*Gertrude, do not drink.*" *(294)*   Where are Claudius and Gertrude positioned now in relation to each other? Is he close enough to whisper to her, or must he risk court suspicion by speaking loud enough for everyone to hear? Is he caught off guard? Why doesn't he stop her physically or dash the cup out of her hand? Has she already drunk, or does he have to stay still and watch her drink? Try this several ways. (Alternatives: he fears she has begun to "rumble" him and needs to get rid of her; she has "rumbled" him and drinks to save Hamlet or commit suicide. Would it be possible to show either of these?)

"*[. . .] it is too late.*" *(296)*   Does Claudius speak to himself or to Laertes, who will soon be close enough to converse with him privately? Try it both ways. When you have made the intervening decisions, replay it from "Another hit" to "'gainst my conscience," since this needs to go very fast with a lot happening at once.

"*Nothing, neither way.*" *(305)*   Why does the bout end here? Is it timed, or do the contestants think there has been another hit?

"*Have at you now.*" *(306)*   If this is where Hamlet is wounded, how is it done? Is it during a bout, or does Laertes lunge before the match has resumed? How does Hamlet react?

"*They exchange rapiers.*" *(306)*   How? Does Hamlet engineer this (disarming Laertes and offering his weapon in exchange), or does it just happen?

Do the contestants know it has happened? How would Laertes react, know-ing—Hamlet does not—that the foil is poisoned?

"Part them [. . .]" (307)   Does anyone try?

"[. . .] come again." (308)   How long before Hamlet wounds Laertes? Laertes dies first, so is his a worse wound? Is Hamlet trying to kill him or so carried away that he doesn't care (remember his killing Polonius)?

"Look to the Queen" (309)   Where is Osric that he sees this first? Does this stop the match, or has Hamlet's wounding Laertes stopped it?

"How is't Laertes?" (311)   Does Osric ask because he is nearest, or does this question suggest friendship (or complicity)?

"Let the door be lock'd." (317)   Why does he ask this? Does anyone move? Osric has an entrance about thirty lines later but is given no exit in any early text. You could send him off here, unless you prefer him to stay near Laertes. But would anyone respond? Hamlet is not king.

"Treason!" (328)   Does this suggest everyone is outraged at the king's being struck, or is it a confused response because of Laertes's accusation and Ham-let's popularity?

"O yet defend me [. . .]" (329)   Does anyone try? Why or why not? If they try, why do they stop?

"Drink off this potion." (331)   Where is the cup now, and how does Ham-let get it? Where does he put it?

"Heaven make thee free of it [. . .]" (337)   Do Hamlet and Laertes take hands here? How are mood and attitude to Laertes affected if they do?

"I am dead, Horatio." (338)   What is Hamlet's attitude to this? Can we let it be funny to the audience? Is Hamlet moving or still during this speech? Try it both ways. Remember that from now until his death he is effectively the king. Does he show awareness of this responsibility? Do the breaks in his speech sug-gest the effect of poison or just that events are too complex to summarize?

"[. . .] mutes or audience" (340)   Who? The court? Theater audience? Both?

"Let go [. . .]" (348)   Where was the cup when Horatio got it? This final struggle keeps Hamlet on his feet. Does the urgency to make Horatio under-stand keep him there, or does he collapse? Will it be more effective to have Hamlet on his feet until death, or does he ever sit? Where (in the script and on the stage)? Try several ways. Notice how this quick, active segment is both prefaced and followed by slower and calmer ones.

"Young Fortinbras [. . .] warlike volley" (355–57)   Would you rather keep Osric on throughout and make this response be an educated guess or have someone else enter and whisper to him? In what mood or tone does he speak (bear in mind what he was like earlier)?

"The potent poison [. . .]" (358)   How does the poison affect Hamlet? How much is he struggling against it? Perhaps the need to clarify guilt and inno-cence and see to the succession keeps him conscious.

"Dies." (363)   How does he show it? What does Horatio do?

If there is time, it would be valuable to run the scene again without stopping, noting the many fluctuations in tempo and intensity.

Students feel that the workshop makes the play clearer, and their involvement helps them identify with all the characters, not just the ones they played. The effect of staging on interpretation is often a revelation: many students have never before considered that where an actor stands in a scene can change the whole meaning of the play. This workshop seems to achieve its purpose of opening up alternatives and provoking discussion.

NOTE

Hamlet quotations are from Jenkins.

The Prince of Punk in the Festive Classroom

James R. Andreas Sr.

Hamlet is an exciting play to teach young people, because of the contagious enthusiasm of its festive protagonist—an enthusiasm that never seems to lag despite the tyrannical odds lined up against it—and because of the festive energy the play generates in an audience that can be gathered anywhere and anyplace by teachers who want to develop a minifestival in the classroom devoted to it. In a session called "Shakespeare and Rock and Roll" at the 1998 meeting of the Shakespeare Association of America—convened appropriately in Cleveland, the home of the Rock and Roll Hall of Fame—Hamlet was characterized as the prince of punk. Why not? He is at once contemptuous of hypocritical parents, the target of spying authorities, and the "hectic" raging in the king's blood (4.3.66), while he remains one of the bawdiest characters in the Shakespeare pantheon, friend of the players but snide with onstage audiences, and ambiguously intimate with the audience for his own play. To convey the nostalgic and feisty festivity of this most complicated of literary characters, teachers have to pull out all the pedagogical stops in their classrooms. It won't do simply to pore over the text—focusing simply on "words, words, words," as Hamlet himself says with book in hand (2.2.192)—but as always, that's the place to start. From there this character and play must spin off like Hamlet's own special energy—centrifugally, as Mikhail Bakhtin would say—to film versions, e-mail arguments, multimedia and virtual reality demonstrations, Internet Web sites, and finally to that alpha and omega for drama, the living stage, the playful arena that can never be displaced by any medium that would transform it, including the literary text.

There is a good deal of transtextual help for teaching the festive *Hamlet*. The first way to lift the text off the page is to draw, of course, on the plethora of film versions of this play that provide students with a history both of film and of Shakespeare's chameleonlike reputation throughout the twentieth century. I show students six different film *Hamlet*s in my teaching of the play: the productions of Asta Nielsen (1920), Laurence Olivier (1948), Nicol Williamson (1969), Derek Jacobi (1980), Mel Gibson (1990), the animated *Hamlet* (1992), and Kenneth Branagh (1997). I compare presentations of given scenes; discuss cuts of scenes and lines made in the various productions; contrast different interpretations of characters and incidents in the play; and analyze costuming, choreography, and props. I try to draw distinctions among the various media represented in these films: film per se, televised versions, filmed productions, and animated renditions. Briefly, Nielsen inverts the gender of the hero, drawing on the occasionally effeminate mannerisms of Hamlet that Olivier underscores as well. Her portrayal decenters the play, pulling the gender props from underneath the student audience in fine festive fashion. Olivier's effete reading of Hamlet and insolent Freudian behavior in his mother's chamber with the incestuous kiss always interest and even scandalize students. Williamson offers a normative performance as an older, doughty Hamlet against which to measure the aberrations that follow. The interesting performance in the Tony Richardson production is Anthony Hopkins as an angst-ridden Claudius, displaying nervous tics throughout the film. The animated *Hamlet* offers yet another traditional rendition of Hamlet, just considerably younger—melancholy, romantic, persecuted, and passive. The punk *Hamlet* begins to take shape with Jacobi's performance in one of the only truly courageous productions in the entire BBC series. Jacobi gives the students personal access to a sensitive, shrinking hero who vents his disgust through manic episodes of play and explosive outbreaks in front of confused parents (Patrick Stewart as Claudius and Claire Bloom as a fragile, terrified Gertrude). His counterpoint with an exasperated, sweating Claudius in the "guts of a beggar" exchange (4.3.31) is priceless and culminates in the contemptuous address of his uncle-stepfather as "mother" (49). Students need no introduction to Gibson, whom they admire as the edgy cop in the Lethal Weapon series (whose wife, like Hamlet's father, has been villainously murdered) and as the Scottish hero of *Braveheart*, a film about William Wallace's rebellion against the British that students tend to identify as Shakespearean. Gibson is the punk Hamlet personified, explosive in his encounters with the turncoat Rosencrantz and Guildenstern, saucy with a placid Claudius, unpredictably brazen with a near-crazed Helena Bonham Carter as Ophelia, and playfully intimate with Glenn Close as his mother. Branagh, schooled by Jacobi, who plays an understandably baffled and petrified Claudius in the production, converts the play into a political intrigue with which this post–Viet Nam, -Iran, and -Monica generation can identify.

Like many teachers, I have discovered that e-mail dialogue via a class electronic mailing list re-creates in cyberspace the festive conditions of verbal and dramatic exchange that energize the play. The students write entries that, like conversation, are instantly available to other students to share, extend, controvert, and hoot off the server. As the teacher, I stay off the line, although I'm allowed to eavesdrop like Prospero on Caliban and company. Students eventually assemble a portfolio of their contributions to the debate that includes their responses to topics and exchanges with other students. I grade these portfolios as their reading, viewing, and listening journals for the course. The topics I initiate, like tossing a basketball for the jump, quickly generate—or degenerate—into issues the students themselves want to discuss about the play: Hamlet's "mole of nature" (1.4.24), Hamlet as tragic hero or brutal murderer, Denmark as police state, what Gertrude really knows, how madness operates in the play, Ophelia as victim or daddy's girl, the "absolute" comedy of the gravedigger (5.1.137), Hamlet's idea of "providence" (5.2.220), and so on.

Cyberspace is the new festive zone for the classroom, and in many ways that extend beyond the electronic mailing list. I offer students the chance to do multimedia, virtual reality, and Web site projects in lieu of the traditional research paper. A past student at Clemson, Karl Herbst, has constructed the Globe Theatre in virtual reality for us. Subsequent students have contributed film clips that compare and contrast this virtual space with more traditional theatrical venues on campus, including a black box theater that seats a hundred and fifty, a Globe-like theater reconstructed from a basketball court (seats 800), and the traditional proscenium theater (seats 1,000), all of which house the productions of the Clemson Shakespeare Festival, which I discuss shortly. Yet another student has provided a narrative and stills of historical theaters to establish Shakespeare's virtual Globe as the perfect acoustic space for festive dramatic presentation. Although there is a *Hamlet* CD-ROM available from Films for the Humanities, featuring Stanley Wells, it is limited in scope and consists mostly of scholarly voice-overs. I encourage students to do their own multimedia projects on *Authorware* or *Hyperstudio* that include clips from films versions; stills; narrative; oral interviews with fellow students; and clips from productions, lectures, and workshops featured in the Clemson Shakespeare Festival archives. Finally, in each of my Shakespeare classes one student is designated class ethnographer and another Web impresario. These two compose the class Web page, which assembles the course syllabi; daily lesson plans; topics for discussion; bibliography on the subject of the course; appropriate stills; excerpts from the class electronic mailing list discussions; and pertinent clips from film versions of the play, in-class performances, and the Clemson Shakespeare Festival. Much of this material has been assembled on a comprehensive Clemson Shakespeare Web site that can be reviewed at www.clemson.edu/ shakespeare.

Shakespeare has been at the cutting edge of all the new technologies of production and presentation that have characterized the emergence of the early modern period: the stage, the book, aural recording, the screen, and the computer. But the stage represents the beginning and the end of the dramatic reproduction of a text. We have featured two Hamlets in the past ten festivals at Clemson University: Thadd McQuade as a quintessentially angry, punk

Hamlet in a Shenandoah Shakespeare Express production of 1995 and Trevor Anthony as a wistful Hamlet in a 1996 production of the Warehouse Theatre Company, an Equity troupe based in Greenville, South Carolina. Both McQuade and Anthony played upon the zany Hamlet established by Gibson in the Zeffirelli film of the play. These were productions designed to appeal to students of the so-called generation X.

McQuade's performance was riveting to students because of his shaved head, his piercings, and his manic energy. Drawing liberally from Shenandoah's famous interactive, dialogic style, McQuade leaped around the stage, dashed off into the many exits of the Globe-like space of Tillman Hall, stood from time to time on the banisters along the entrances glaring at patrons, buttonholed individuals to deliver lines to—especially the soliloquies—and even chased down an unfortunate student who tried to leave the auditorium early. The students were enchanted with this type of stage management or domination, having associated it with the menacing presence of some rock and roll bands they had grown up with.

After generations of forty-plus *Hamlets*, the Warehouse director Jack Young was looking for a youthful Hamlet, Hamlet as a college student, in his production. Anthony brought out the nerd in Hamlet, the quality that would have motivated him to study German metaphysics at Wittenberg. In the stateroom scene Anthony swept the emotional string from wisecracks about Claudius to the audience ("a little more than kin, and less than kind"), to a cool respect for his mother ("I shall in all my best obey you, madam"), to the maniacally explosive first soliloquy ("O that this too too sallied flesh would melt" [1.2.64–65, 120, 129]), culminating in his response to the revelation of Horatio that he has seen the ghost of Hamlet's father on the battlements. Hamlet's famous soliloquies were never private voice-overs but rather dialogic exchanges with the audience or other actors on stage behind a curtain or hiding in a closet. In Anthony's mercurial portrayal of the melancholy Dane, moods modulated unexpectedly and spontaneously. Anthony's Hamlet was young, unformed, emotionally battered from his father's death and mother's "o'er-hasty marriage" (2.2.57), and he did not keep his grief to himself. He constantly stepped from what Robert Weimann ("*Platea*") calls the *locus* (the castle and its courtly confines) to the *platea* (the apron of the stage), that bully pulpit of the people where he can speak in his own voice—as opposed to the polite speech of the court—directly to an audience he assumed would champion him, as the people ultimately do when he is banished to England. Anthony introduced dialogically deviant stage behavior: he slithered down the stone steps of the castle when he dispatched Polonius as an old graybeard with "eyes purging thick amber and plumtree gum" (2.2.98). He made grotesque faces at Claudius behind his back while describing how a king can make "a progress through the guts of a beggar" (4.3.31). He kicked at Ophelia's backside when he would send her packing to the nunnery and frantically mimicked his mother when she played the stooge to her manipulative husband. Anthony's was the thoroughly irreverent, wisecracking, disrespectful Hamlet of generation X who might justify his insolence by asking, "Well, what exactly does Hamlet have to respect?"

Students discuss performances among themselves on the class electronic mailing list, comparing and contrasting the production techniques of the various companies, relating productions to film versions of the plays they have seen, and discussing the relations of the performances to the model of the play derived from lectures and class debate. They know that the informal reviews of the productions they critique might well be e-mailed to the actors and directors of the productions themselves, so they take this process very seriously.

I have tried to show how centrifugal the energies of *Hamlet* are and how festive the classroom where it is taught can become. Teachers and their students can re-create their *Hamlet* and remodel their Denmark, no matter how rotten the circumstances for such entertainment may appear to them in their respective institutions. They can gather actors in minifestivals, just as Hamlet gathers the players around him; they can mount a film festival on the play for a song; and they can sponsor a lecture series on the play, even if the scholars are from their own institution or classroom. And finally, such festive energy can be extended to the latest technological frontier, as Shakespearean energies always have been, in the preparation of Web pages and sites that will provide "the abstract and brief chronicles" (2.2.524–25) of the play and their generation's appropriation of it.

NOTE

Hamlet quotations are from Evans et al. [1974].

An Interdisciplinary Approach to *Hamlet* in a Distance-Learning Classroom

Anthony DiMatteo

> That state is truly fortunate which has justice for a
> boundary line.
>
> —Pompey the Great

Hamlet is the first play I teach in my Shakespeare course broadcast live before a student audience in Old Westbury, New York, to my college's two other campuses, in Manhattan and Central Islip. The class thus spans the New York metropolitan area with its diverse populations usually well reflected among students. Teleconferencing allows our three groups to speak to one another and see themselves in real time on large monitors. Since some members meet only as televised identities, I give explicit notice in my course syllabus to the ambiguous role that appearances tend to play in human communication, to wit, "the schematism by which our understanding deals with the phenomenal world" (Kant, qtd. in Gombrich 63). Analogous to virtual encounters over TV is the one-way contact made with the characters of plays, those speaking pictures who have only ghostlike existence in dramatic texts and performances, unlike, presumably, class members standing outside the TV camera. Beyond such blunt categorical differences, however, the relations of things and signs, *res et verba*, are always more complicated than one can think. I accordingly ask students to join me in pondering throughout the semester how images on screens or in plays are always loaded, always dangerous, both in our distance-learning "postmodern mode of information" (Poster 123) and the any-age way of taking the illusory for the substantive. Teleconferencing chronically requires an awareness of the Magritte-like seductiveness of images. *Hamlet* in my teleconferenced Shakespeare course especially bogged us down in consciousness-raising of imagery's power, consuming us for six weeks though I had planned on only three in a fifteen-week semester. We indulged the classroom's video technology to explore iconographic material from the sixteenth century heavily charged with the legal, ethical, and political valences of governing the "body living," as Sir Thomas Elyot calls the common weal, that public entity partly phantom, partly flesh (1). Within the very real struggle for dominion and right rule fought between and in the nations of sixteenth-century Europe, the political or civil body is distinguishable from what I encourage students to call the body natural and its law of natural kinds (*jus naturale*), a main conceptual focus of the course.

Shakespeare shows this struggle operating across international borders in the three families represented in the play, those of Polonius, Hamlet, and Fortinbras. The conflict of civil and natural bodies, of the mixed allegiances they bring and demand, is especially expressed in the tragic love of Hamlet and Ophelia, whose natural bodies are thwarted by their civil ones, to overstate the case a bit. The dilemma of *Hamlet* falls along a fault line between sets of laws, one serving God and nature, the other Caesar. Does Hamlet heed natural laws of allegiance to a father and his natural right to retaliation (lex talionis) or positive, civil law, with its long history of tending to grant even tyrants, especially in time of war, the extralegal status of an absolute body unbound by laws (*princeps solutus legibus*)? In *Henry IV, Parts 1 and 2*, which follow *Hamlet* in my syllabus, Shakespeare again dramatizes the relatedness and conflict of civil and natural law, with Prince Hal and Falstaff standing in for the two at the living political border that the two sets of law shape. In this way, the plays reflect a crucial conflict of the late Renaissance and early modern period among various theories and practices of political justice and governance, a struggle that stems from the differences between a nation as a natural or native people and a nation as a state. This dynamic of the period Francis Bacon, for example, tried to stabilize for the English Crown by his term "Great Britain," expressive of his hope for the "perfect union of bodies, political as well as natural" (qtd. in Kantorowicz 24). When we go on to read *Measure for Measure*, *Macbeth*, and *The Tempest*, my students have a vocabulary of legal bodies most useful in articulating some striking concerns of the plays.

I especially want students to become conversant with terminology related to "the dominion of things."[1] As Anthony Pagden explains (*Spanish Imperialism* 16–24) and Heinrich Rommen summarizes (62–66), *dominium rerum* was a dense legal phrase describing the relations among persons, things, and actions and applying to what liberty that men and, to a lesser degree, women and children lawfully had over their bodies, goods, and actions. Any civil or positive law that infringed on this unwritten natural law and duty was at least questionable. J. W. Allen summarizes key legal boundaries in sixteenth-century battles over dominion and its determining or sovereign powers that directly apply to *Hamlet*: "A conception of the power of the Crown, or of any possible sovereign, as necessarily limited by something described as natural law was, it must be noted, very general, even among lawyers" (287). Hamlet, whose conscience the play pivots upon, has been justly called "the Natural Law hero par excellence" (White xi).

To translate what was at stake in this contest for dominion between natural and positive (civil and imperial) bodies of laws and practices, I ask an odd question: "To whom do our bodies belong?" Students usually respond, "We own ourselves, professor." The idea of identity constituted by multiple bodies, by something other than an ego or personal self, seems unimaginable to them. They need assistance in conceptualizing natural, civil, and divine components of identity, the multiple frameworks of law and philosophy in which people thought of themselves in Old World Europe when they thought of themselves at all. Our class by implication has to deal with non-Romantic views of art and poetry. Art not personally expressive of an author's feelings seems strange or at least shallow to many students. Isn't Shakespeare exposing his heart in his sonnets, for example?

Helping students understand identity in multiple legal frameworks are Elizabethan maps depicting England in the figure of Queen Elizabeth, such as Michael Drayton's frontispiece to *Poly-Olbion* (Helgerson 336). In *Hamlet* too, the fate of kings is written into the fabric of things. No character or place can be understood in isolation from the concept of sovereignty. A conflict of traditional laws holds sway over who Hamlet thinks he is and what it is just for him to do. Claudius, however, heeds only his sovereign self-interest. His actions are describable in terms of the Roman jurist Ulpian's famous maxim regarding royal power: "Whatever pleases the ruler has the force of law" ("*Quod principi placuit, legis habet vigorem*" [qtd. in Kantorowicz 150–51]). Arguably seen in Claudius, moreover, is a new style of entrepreneurial sovereignty fully identified by Machiavelli and contrasting with the ancient style of kingship also seen in the play. Where natural and divine laws constrained monarchs of old, as in Hamlet Senior's ordeal-related oath to Fortinbras, new-style kingship had no apparent natural-law borders requiring that one keep one's word. Rulers like Cesare Borgia and Claudius disconnect the sword of civil power from the holy word as expressed in both the book of nature and the book of God. In contrast, the ideal monarch or hero links or heeds all three frames of meaning, as the tragic Hamlet arguably attempts to do.

Usefully illustrating the ideal unity of natural and civil dominion are Renaissance portraits of kings and explorers typically crediting them with the twin powers of natural truth speaking and civil coercion. Symbolizing a just dominion over things is what the figures stand on or next to or hold or touch with left and right hand, as in the coronation painting of Elizabeth, who holds the civil scepter in her right hand and rests her left upon an orb of the world crowned by a cross (C. Levin 27), or in an engraving of Columbus, who holds at his right side a staff flagged with a crucifix above and, in his left hand resting on his sword's hilt, scrolls of maps (Grafton 64). Even the natural hero Hercules, often alluded to by Hamlet, was capable of mediating the powers of Apollonian right speaking and martial force, as Achille Bocchi's emblem depicts him, a branch of golden apples in his left hand, a club in his right (98). Claudius's hands proffer poison at the plot's beginning and end, and in its middle, "Offence's gilded hand" (3.3.58) cannot direct his prayers to God. His crippled admission of guilt in this prayer scene (3.3) echoes the passage from Ecclesiasticus 34 that prompted Bartolomé de Las Casas to convert from slave-owning *encomendero* to crusader for the Indians: "Tainted his gifts who offers in sacrifice ill-gotten goods" (Las Casas 87). In class, I ask students to explore why Claudius retains civil dominion while Las Casas divests himself of his.

Such contrasting perspectives on dominion situate the play in the sixteenth century. Who justly wields the sword was a burning issue of the period. Could even a patently unjust king be resisted? Claudius is an unjust king *ex defectu tituli* and thus, as even the political moderate Jean Bodin in his *Six Books of a Commonweal* maintains, represents one of the few cases in which sovereignty could be overthrown (Skinner 2: 286). The play, however, ending with a foreign sovereign on the throne of Denmark, represents the tragedy that results rather indifferently from the just or unjust killing of kings. On the one hand, the play seems conservative in upholding natural law, Hamlet heeding the law of talion in response to a supernatural command to do so. On the other hand, kings in *Hamlet* are not *legibus soluti* or freed from laws, as Roman imperial law phrased it. Divine sanction of tyrannicide seems given to Hamlet's slaying of Claudius. Also, Hamlet Senior answers to the beyond in his night walking. "Let the fate of kings be left to God and his agents," the play implies, but how does one determine who these agents are? As in the political thought of Shakespeare's time, the issue of what to do about unjust sovereigns remains ambiguously posed by the play. A broader question also seems left unanswered: "Whose property is the body of the king?" (Hadfield 54). At play's end, three legal domains lay symbolic claim to Prince Hamlet's body: Horatio speaks of divine escort ("flights of angels" [5.2.365]), Fortinbras of natural devouring ("proud Death" feasting on princes [369–70]), while the "four captains" who carry off the princely corse enact a new sovereign's civil command.

We spend a lot of time on these legal implications of the play when many students expect Freudian analysis of Hamlet's melancholy. Helping underscore these implications are two crucial passages from the Bible that we discuss many times: Genesis 1–11 and Paul's Epistle to the Romans 13, the first for its indication of the moral and cosmic parameters of Judeo-Christian life, the second for its crucial political stricture regarding how Christians are subject to the civil powers. Claudius's killing of his brother Hamlet in a garden resonates with overtones of the first murder, the Cain and Abel story, which is thrice referred to in the play (1.2.105, 3.3.38, 5.1.76). The chapter from Paul, one of the most contested biblical passages in the sixteenth century, relates because the play's story line, involving both the killing of just king (Hamlet Senior) and unjust king (Claudius), revolves around the complex political and moral issue of who ultimately wields the right of the sword, sovereign or subjects. This specific issue is discussed again and again in commentary on Paul's Epistle. Furthermore, fathers' treatments of sons and daughters as well as rulers' treatment of their subjects relate together as different aspects of the rights and duties of just dominion. Any just lordship must be gauged in terms of the triple worlds of nature, humanity, and divinity. Any authority figure that does not heed this cosmic perspective is an obviously flawed *dominus*. Claudius, Henry IV, Hotspur, Egeus, Angelo, and *The Tempest*'s Antonio are obvious candidates. From this triune perspective upon just dominion, Hamlet comes closest to perfecting the role of the hero. At the same time, the tragedy, especially in the aborted natural love of Ophelia and Hamlet, as I argue elsewhere, exposes the mythical aspects of harmonizing the three sets of standards by which human beings were legally and morally described (DiMatteo, "*Hamlet*").

Helping students connect with these old but not outdated concepts is our class's online forum. Students log on to an electronic caucus in which I have included a student chat room, rooms dedicated to exchange of comments about specific aspects of the plays, and an "ask the professor" room. In my last class, Hamlet and Ophelia became a cross-room focus as class members weighed if their love was true. I asked students to consider Venus's curse upon love in *Venus and Adonis*: "They that love best their loves shall not enjoy" (line 1164). In view of her archetypal curse, can true love exist in an unjust world? This naive question prompted focus on numerous conflicts in the plays where love and justice seem providential modes of each other, beyond human dominion. As students felt more and more comfortable with the broader implications of this terminology and as they wrote in our forum more to one another rather than "for the professor," they began probing rather than repeating the legal concepts I was summarizing in class lectures and discussions. The most striking use of the concept of dominion were the many comments of Diomaris Padilla, a physics major. Ophelia and the French princess Katherine of *Henry V* were treated as if they were "spoils"in a war for civil dominion over native and foreign soil. Yet, like endlessly contested lands, women were in some sense "beyond dominion," she wrote, even though "male sovereignty" strove for some permanent determining of their fate. Shakespeare thus seems to stage both the beliefs of his time and their inadequacy to account for "the realities and potentials of his characters" (Padilla).

NOTES

Hamlet quotations are from Jenkins.

[1]J. W. Allen 434–44; Figgis 74–76; Keller, Lissitzyn, and Mann 3–22, 45–50; Oakley 66–92; Skinner 2: 127–34; Tuck 38, 70; Green and Dickason 241–49; R. Williams 218–21; Hadfield 52–54; Pagden, *Lords* 29–62.

E-Mail to Facilitate Discussion

Eric Sterling

I teach *Hamlet* at a campus in which many of the students are nontraditional (often in their thirties, forties, and fifties), and, because of the quarter system, the class meets for a few long periods rather than frequent short periods. Most of my students work full-time, and many have spouses and children; they are very grateful that Auburn University, Montgomery, offers some classes that meet in four-hour segments once per week (often on weekends) so that they can juggle a college education with their jobs and familial obligations. Because my typical weekend course meets only seven times during the quarter and covers Western literature from the ancient period through the Renaissance, I can devote only one class to *Hamlet* (14% of the course).

I have found that e-mail discussion groups during the week facilitate and supplement class discussion, which is especially important because class time is so limited. Every student must participate, and I teach those students who have never used e-mail how to access and send messages. Auburn University, Montgomery, provides free e-mail accounts for all students and allows them to access their accounts on university computers; therefore, those people who do not own computers can send and read e-mail messages on campus or at their jobs. Even my students who have never used e-mail before discover that this tool can help them interact with other classmates. For instance, my students and I have enjoyed long e-mail discussions about Hamlet's murder of Polonius—whether Hamlet confuses Polonius for Claudius or whether Hamlet realizes that he is slaying Polonius. I provide some direction by handing out a list of possible discussion topics during the previous class meeting, but I do not restrict what the students can write their messages about; I encourage them to ask questions and test theories through e-mail. Furthermore, I request that the message writers cite passages that they refer to so that other students can easily find the lines. I construct a master list of e-mail addresses, so whenever students have a question or want to make a comment or ask a question during the week, they simply send the message, which I then distribute to everyone in class.

I find that the participation on e-mail is excellent, perhaps because some students, especially the shy ones, feel more comfortable when interacting electronically than in class discussion, partly because they can edit and revise their comments before sending them and can even pause to decide whether in fact they wish to circulate their ideas. They also possess the advantage, denied them in a typical classroom situation, of seeing what their comments look like in writing before sending them. Because many students consider these e-mail message boards to be nonthreatening, they feel less inhibited about contributing to class discussion. This point is especially important in a core-requirement literature class in which most of the students are nonmajors, have been out of school for several years, and feel nervous about reading a sophisticated author such as Shakespeare.

Below I list samples of e-mail exchanges from the week before our class meeting on *Hamlet*:

Question: I don't see the role that Fortinbras plays in the story. What's his role?

Answer: Fortinbras is a prince like Hamlet. They are mirrors to each other. I guess the reader is supposed to compare them. How Fortinbras acts and is aggressive while Hamlet just stands around and does zilch.

Answer: I agree. I read the play in high school and we talked about how Hamlet procrastinates all the time while Fortinbras is a man of action.

Professor: Does Hamlet procrastinate? Perhaps he does. But before you concur, ask yourself when he has an appropriate chance to take revenge on Claudius. He must first test whether the ghost is telling him the truth or misleading him (hence the play within a play), and he cannot kill Claudius when he believes that his uncle is praying, because then Claudius would go to heaven, thus defeating the purpose of his revenge: "O, this is hire and salary, not revenge" (3.3.80). He wants Claudius, as in the case of King Hamlet, to have no chance to repent for his sins before dying.

Question: If we're supposed to compare Hamlet with Fortinbras, can we also compare Hamlet to Laertes? They're both angry that their fathers are murdered and both want revenge.

Answer: Yes, both Fortinbras and Laertes are contrasted with Hamlet. I think they are called foils. We learn more about Hamlet by juxtaposing him with these other two characters. Both have lost their fathers and want vengeance. They are determined. Hamlet takes his time. Laertes can't wait, so Claudius has a hard time ruffling his feathers when he returns from France.

Question: Is Polonius supposed to be a wise man or a foolish man? I can't tell if he's supposed to be taken seriously.

Answer: I think he is a fool. Hamlet is always making fun of him. Like, "What do you read, my lord?" "Words, words, words." "What is the matter, my lord?" "Between who?" "I mean, the matter that you read, my lord" (2.2.188–92).

Answer: I think that Polonius is supposed to be an intelligent man. After all, he is the king's right-hand man. Claudius wouldn't have picked him if he was dumb.

Answer: I rented the video [the Kenneth Branagh version]. Lots of the characters are played by comedians (Robin Williams, Billy Crystal, Jack Lemmon). I get the idea that some of the characters (maybe Polonius) are supposed to be funny. Even though it's a tragedy.

Answer: Maybe Polonius is supposed to be a villain. He's always listening in and spying on people. He goes against Hamlet and even spies on his own son. I didn't feel bad when he was killed.

Professor: I see Polonius as a somewhat comical figure, partly because of the trite advice he gives to Laertes before the son departs for France and partly because he is so long-winded. He might also be a comical figure because he is the object of Hamlet's mockery; for instance, see the passage about the clouds (3.2.340–47) in which Hamlet teases the adviser for being a sycophant. As to the comment about Polonius's being wise because he is Claudius's adviser, please bear in mind that Denmark was an elective monarchy. The throne was not automatically handed down from father to son; instead, the nobles (but not the common citizens) elected the king. Perhaps Polonius helped Claudius to the throne and, in turn, accepted the reward of becoming Claudius's main adviser. I'll elaborate more on that on Sunday.

During the subsequent class meeting, I integrated the e-mail conversation into our class discussion. We discussed the relationships among Hamlet and other characters, such as Fortinbras and Laertes, to come to an understanding regarding the protagonist's actions and inactions. For instance, we contrasted Laertes's impetuous and instinctive comportment with Hamlet's cautious and circumspect behavior. The comments concerning Hamlet's procrastination, such as his decision not to kill Claudius when Claudius attempts to pray, promoted a discussion of the revenge tragedy and the religious aspects of Shakespeare's play. And our e-mail question regarding Polonius as a comic character facilitated a discussion about the role of comedy in a tragedy.

NOTE

Hamlet quotations are from Mack et al.

Hamlet Refracted through Three
Definitions of Tragedy

"The best actors in the world [. . .] for tragedy," says Polonius (2.2.396). To begin the study of *Hamlet*, I ask students what range of meanings "tragedy" might have had, beyond what can be inferred from Polonius. Three brief definitions, of varying antiquity and availability, suggest some possibilities. These statements—by Evanthius, Chaucer, and Aristotle—link to individual passages in the play and open consideration of how they might and might not help us understand Shakespeare's characters, plots, and themes.

Evanthius's formulation (AD c. 350) was regularly reprinted in school editions of Terence during Shakespeare's time (Doran 106–07, 415; Lerner 299–300). Chaucer's Monk (MkT 7.1971–98) illustrates the medieval tradition deriving from Boethius. Widely available now, Aristotle's *Poetics* was much less regarded in Shakespeare's time. Useful bits of these definitions fit on a one- or two-page handout and often apply in class discussion, essay topics, and test questions.

All three describe tragic characters in social terms, characters of great estate or high degree and who are likely to be historical figures. All analyze tragic plots; Aristotle's analysis, with its concern for completeness and complexity, is the most sophisticated. They vary in their statements about language. Evanthius says nothing about language. The Monk considers tragedy a narrative genre, in verse or prose, rather than dramatic. They differ more in their views of tragic action and theme. For Evanthius, tragedy simply affirms that human life should be rejected. The Monk considers that tragic falls come from the workings of Fortune, and therefore no one should "truste on blynd prosperitee" (MkT 7.2000). Aristotle prefers "a man who is not pre-eminently virtuous and just, and yet falls into misfortune [. . .] through some flaw" (47 [*Poetics* 13.5]). For "flaw" Aristotle uses the word *hamartia* ("mistake").

ENL 303: Questions and Topics on Tragedy and *Hamlet*

1. Give three examples that suggest that things are peaceful at the beginning (before the Ghost's dialogue with Hamlet). Give three examples that suggest upset at the beginning.
2. Give three examples that suggest that things are upset at the end (after the

death of Claudius). Give three examples that suggest things are peaceful at the end.

3. Give three passages in the play that express the view that human life should be rejected.

4. Give three exceptions the play suggests to the view that human life should be rejected.

5. Relate the Monk's view of tragedy to the joking about Fortune in 2.2.228–41.

6. Relate the Monk's view of tragedy to the First Player's speech (2.2.493–511).

7. Relate the Monk's view of tragedy to Hamlet's statement about Horatio (3.2.56–74).

8. Relate the Monk's view of tragedy to Hamlet's statements about "a divinity" and "special providence" (5.2.10, 219–20).

9. Give reasons for and against the view that *Hamlet* has a beginning as defined by Aristotle.

10. Select an episode in the middle of the play and give reasons why it does and does not follow necessarily or probably from something earlier.

11. Give reasons for and against the view that *Hamlet* has an end as defined by Aristotle.

12. Select an episode that might be considered an Aristotelian reversal and give your reasons for this choice.

13. Select an episode that might be considered an Aristotelian recognition and give your reasons for this choice.

14. Relate Hamlet's comment about "some vicious mole of nature" (1.4.24) to Aristotle's tragic flaw-mistake.

15. Relate Hamlet's comment about "thinking too precisely on th'event" (4.4.41) to Aristotle's tragic flaw-mistake.

16. Aristotle prefers a tragic character who is neither preeminent in virtue and justice nor vicious. Give reasons for and against regarding Hamlet as an example of such a character.

17. Aristotle does not prefer a character who is vicious and evil. Give reasons for and against regarding Claudius as an example of such a character.

18. Use Aristotle's criteria (question 16) to evaluate the other characters whose deaths are staged or described in the play: King Hamlet, Gertrude, Polonius, Laertes, Ophelia, Rosencrantz and Guildenstern, Priam, Julius Caesar, Gonzago.

NOTE

Hamlet quotations are from Evans et al.

David G. Hale

Francis Bacon's "Of Revenge"

Francis Bacon's brief (500-word) essay "Of Revenge" is an abstract of issues crucial to *Hamlet*: the relation between law and revenge, the dilemma posed by a wrong perpetrated by the source of law and order (the king), the distinction between private and public revenge, the psychology of a person obsessed with revenge. Prior exposure to the situations of private revenge in *Romeo and Juliet* or public revenge in *Julius Caesar* helps students appreciate how minutely Shakespeare has defined Hamlet's problem. Contemporary discussions of capital punishment will also serve to give students some sense of the careful distinctions Bacon makes.

"Of Revenge" might have emerged out of a commonplace book, a notebook where someone records quotations and thoughts worth remembering. Hamlet refers to such a book: "My tables—meet it is I set it down [. . .]" (1.5.107). Students can imagine Bacon's extracting all the observations about revenge from his commonplace book and organizing them into this essay.

The text of the essay in the Penguin paperback, edited by John Pitcher, is briefly and helpfully annotated. Reading and discussing the essay can occupy a class profitably for all or part of a fifty-minute period even before students begin or have finished reading *Hamlet*. The essay is also useful to shape discussion near the end of a unit on the play. And it can be revealing to ask students what quotations or observations they would take from *Hamlet* and class discussion of *Hamlet* to write on various topics (e.g., madness, death, guilt, love) in their own (even if imaginary) commonplace books.

NOTE

The *Hamlet* quotation is from Evans et al.

Margaret Maurer

Introducing Students to Effective Refutation

Our department has elected to use *The Riverside Shakespeare*, second edition, for all sections of graduate and undergraduate Shakespeare classes. One of the more effective assignments I use for teaching *Hamlet* is to make the middle section of Frank Kermode's introduction to *Hamlet* a class exercise in "refutation" (1185, beginning with "*Hamlet* is a multiple play" and continuing for four paragraphs). The task is to present reasonable counterarguments to Kermode's position that Shakespeare deliberately overwrote the play. This exercise forces close attention to why some of the more obscure and tangential parts of *Ham-*

let are necessary to the full action, and I think it results in deeper appreciation of the richness of the play.

Kermode's analysis introduces students to a probing claim of interpretation, one more sophisticated than the traditional acceptance of Hamlet's delay as the character trait that results in tragedy. In order to present the counterarguments to Kermode—that Polonius's instructing Laertes *does not unnecessarily* delay Hamlet's meeting with the Ghost, that the players' connection to the main plot is *not* simply delayed by a "long lecture on acting," that "hundreds of melancholic lines on death" *do not* dilute the import of Ophelia's fate, and that "over a hundred affected lines" between Hamlet and Osric are *not* mere "postpone[ment of . . .] the imminent catastrophe" (Kermode 1185–86)—students need to examine carefully not only the targeted excessive writing but also the larger fabric of the play in the light of Kermode's listed instances of the play's deliberate "delays and doubts." Refuting any part of his reasoning makes a fruitful exercise. For instance, we could refute his single claim that "even Hamlet's soliloquies seem slightly misplaced" (1186) or that Fortinbras is only present in order to provide the "occasion" for Hamlet to complain about his inaction (1185) through a close tracking of each of Hamlet's soliloquies. The challenge for students is then to prove that Hamlet's swings between emotion and decision to act arise out of the circumstances at hand, or that the final entrance of Fortinbras permits a more effective catharsis.

Sometimes the format of the exercise consists of group projects and reporting; at other times I may require a formal essay that measures reasoning skills. After we consider the best logical counterarguments, I can invite students not only to debate whether Kermode's ultimate purpose is to admire *Hamlet* for how it alters the typical revenge tragedy but also to examine how the expansive plot of *Hamlet* compares with that of other plays. I can also ask students to find essays appropriate for further refutation exercises. Previously, the semester course on Shakespeare's early plays considered the multiple-plot device in some of the comedies (*Shrew*, *Dream*, *Twelfth Night*), looked at *Richard III* as a play that seems overwritten and yet also makes a forceful condensation of historical narrative, and studied *Othello* in the context of Shakespeare's effective transformation of a crude tale in Cinthio into a work that contains Aristotelian notions of tragedy. Graduate students by this time have encountered more probing and comprehensive strategies of refutation in Brian Vickers's *Appropriating Shakespeare* and are eager to pursue their own dismantling of critical theories with newly honed powers of close reading and textual analysis.

Joanne E. Gates

Believing and Doubting Ideas about *Hamlet*

The believing and doubting game is a valuable and many-layered technique for students to use both in reading published work and in shaping their own essays. Peter Elbow described the game in *Writing without Teachers* (157–91) to help students develop and refine their essays, but it is also applicable to literary criticism. An instructor's lecture might also be the site of the believing-and-doubting game. Believing a critical text encourages a reader to enter into the writer's point of view and fully understand the argument. Doubting a text forces the reader to enter into a dialectical relation with the writer's ideas. Both approaches compel the reader to go back to the original work of literature to find evidence for the various positions or to check the validity of the critic's examples. All this engagement requires careful reading and rereading of the primary work.

A simple way to introduce students to the technique is to ask them, individually, to mark three or more points in a critical essay that they believe and an equal number that they doubt and to say why (with specific reference to the primary work). In class, they can pair or group up to discuss one another's choices and try to reach some consensus on the most convincing and unconvincing points made by the author. These groups can then present the results to the class and respond to the almost inevitable counterassertions by other groups.

A more advanced task would be for students to construct a fuller outline of the critic's argument and believe and doubt the major points. For example, they could respond to Kay Stanton's "*Hamlet*'s Whores,' a provocative article that focuses on the prostitution imagery in the play and raises issues of sexuality, motivation, revenge, and playacting. Stanton sees almost every character as a whore or as using another as a whore. She suggests that Hamlet, in accusing Polonius of being a whoremonger for his daughter, cannot see that the Ghost has made Hamlet a whore to the father's revenge—for which Hamlet has to give up study and love. Stanton invites readers to see that Hamlet was on another path and is forced into the violence required by revenge. Readers might believe Stanton's assertion, citing Hamlet's reluctance to perform the act of revenge. Or they might doubt this interpretation, because they see the necessity of personal revenge in a lawless state.

As a bridge to writing about the play, the class can generate some topics of their own and believe and doubt them. Moving back and forth between believing and doubting enables students to experience *Hamlet*'s complexity. They can apply the process to their essays on *Hamlet* as they are developing them. The final phase of the process is for students to believe and doubt one another's completed essays in the same way they did with the published article.

Meta Plotnik

Students as Characters, Speaking in Character

A short time after we have begun working together on *Hamlet*, I ask the class to prepare for an exercise with which we'll begin the next session. The assignment is for students to imagine themselves as any character in the play, with the exception of Hamlet, and to come to class prepared to speak in the voice of that character. I suggest that they imagine that the play, the life of which they are now a part, has arrived at about act 3, so that most of the characters are on the scene. We begin the next session by going around the class (we generally sit in a large circle) and having the participants, each in turn, describe what is happening from their perspective. All participants speak in the first person. This exercise offers students a glimpse of the process that actors use as they prepare a role: they have the opportunity to imagine the motivation and perceptions of everyone from Bernardo to Gertrude, from Guildenstern to Ophelia. Over the years that I have used this exercise, students have taken on almost every role in the play. The discussion continues in character after all members of the class have offered their individual perspectives. (And, yes, I as the instructor take on a role as well.)

Christine Mack Gordon

Two Ways to Use Film for Student Writing

Of the two ways I suggest to use film for student writing, the first is to read (and fill in) between the lines with Tom Stoppard's *Rosencrantz and Guildenstern Are Dead*.

Stoppard's film is a decentered view of *Hamlet* in which Stoppard reaches beyond the footlights and gives Rosencrantz and Guildenstern their own story. He fills in the blanks of these two minor characters and, in doing so, comments on the universe of *Hamlet*. The idea he presents adds another dimension of dramatic possibilities to Shakespeare, and this dimension can be explored in assignments that encourage students to fill in the blanks of a character or characters of their choice. They might write added scenes between characters, or they might compose diary entries for a given character.

For instance, a student in my discussion section of Shakespeare wrote a journal for Ophelia. In this clever work, the student imagined the feelings and reactions Ophelia would have in her scenes: when she is admonished by her father and brother, when she encounters the prince in his madness, when she is placed between her father and Hamlet, when she goes mad, and so on. Such an assignment could provide a basis for discussion involving recent feminist readings of Ophelia's muted role within the Danish court.

Other characters could be similarly expanded on. For example, students could compose bedroom scenes between Claudius and Gertrude in order to shed light on some of the debated aspects of their relationship. Did Gertrude fall into Claudius's arms after the king's death, or were they lovers before? Does she make comparisons between the two—as Prince Hamlet does? What is the nature of their marriage? Is she truly (as her son suggests) too old to be overtaken by lust? And how did she allow someone other than her son, the rightful heir, to ascend to the throne?

The second way, making the student a director, is to compare Franco Zeffirelli's *Hamlet* (1990) and Todd Louiso's *The Fifteen-Minute Hamlet* (1993).

Many students might be familiar with Zeffirelli's *Hamlet* (as the "Mel Gibson *Hamlet*") but unfamiliar with Louiso's twenty-two-minute film short, which portrays Shakespeare as a filmmaker who has been provided with only one fifteen-minute roll of film with which to shoot his screen tragedy of *Hamlet*. Initially, students may view these two as opposites: Zeffirelli's play being the serious one and Louiso's the spoof—and of course they would be right, to an extent. Yet a closer reading of both films can draw the students' attention to issues that their directors must have considered, such as casting and editorial decisions.

In Louiso's film (itself an adaptation of a Stoppard screenplay), Shakespeare presents the fifteen-minute film to his king-patron. The film is received poorly by his royal audience, and Shakespeare is sent back to the editing room. He cuts and pastes (with scissors and thread!) and returns with a five-minute version, which—of course—becomes a big hit.

After studying Louiso's film, students may then consider Zeffirelli's *Hamlet*. There is no interaction between Hamlet and the Players, nor do we get to see Hamlet's encountering the forces of Norway—in fact, the Norway-Denmark conflict is entirely absent from the film. Thus, we get no scenes in which Hamlet ponders his inaction for a great cause (revenging his father's murder) versus the action of others for lesser causes (the amusement of an audience, the winning of a worthless plot of land). When Hamlet witnesses Ophelia's burial, he is denied the self-affirmation of "This is I, Hamlet the Dane"; instead, his silent approach is merely witnessed by Laertes, leading to their graveyard scuffle. Later, when Hamlet suddenly soliloquizes on the providence in the "fall of a sparrow" and on "the readiness is all" (Weller 116; 5.2), it has not been prepared for, and the sentiment comes across as merely a self-motivational exercise.

In Louiso's film, Austin Pendleton plays an unlikely Hamlet. He is old, balding, a Prufrockish tragic hero—a great contrast to the Mel Gibson type. Pendleton's Hamlet recites his lines with a delighted self-awareness, and he exaggerates moments of sorrow, anger, and glee, seemingly to compensate for those lines lost from the source play. In the "divinity that shapes our ends" scene, Pendleton is on a moving platform, being transported from an exterior view to a barn interior at his soliloquy's end. The shot is a visual gimmick, but the physical movement implies a thematic movement. By the time Pendleton says, "The readiness is all," he has achieved a touching if tacky transcendence, one that is trite but nevertheless true to the original, source text.

After screening both films, the teacher has a number of points from which to draw essay questions. Here are some examples:

1. Compare Gibson's portrayal of Hamlet with Pendleton's performance. Most people would say Gibson fits more closely the popular image of Hamlet. Do you agree? Are you able to relate with Pendleton's "Prufrockish" Hamlet? [Note: Eliot's poem would be discussed prior to the assignment.] If you had to cast one of your classmates in the role of Hamlet, who would it be? Could Hamlet be portrayed by a female classmate? Explain the reasons for your choice.
2. If you have a Cliff's Notes version of *Hamlet*, consider how much of the five-act play must have been sacrificed when it was reworded to a thirty-page prose summary. What is lost in the translation?
3. It could be said that Louiso's Hamlet learns in fifteen minutes what Zeffirelli's does not in two hours and eighteen minutes. Do you agree?
4. Imagine that you are a director of a new film version of *Hamlet*. The film's producer has told you to trim (or considerably shorten) three scenes from the play. You don't want to, but it is the only way that the film will be produced. Pick which scenes you will shorten or throw out and explain why. Keep in mind that your goal is to remain faithful to the issues and sentiments that you see in the original (uncut) play. Evaluate your textual changes and explain the effects they have on the overall play.

NOTE

Hamlet quotations are from Weller.

Rob Kirkpatrick

Hamlet Is Not Mad

I teach Dramatic Literature in a three-year professional training program for actors, and in that course *Hamlet* is an important text at the end of the first year. Because I help train actors who must learn to handle difficult texts on their own after graduation and because Shakespeare's texts offer excellent examples of both explicit and implied stage direction within the dialogue, *Hamlet* is a crucial text. I have found over the years that students tend to escape from the most difficult textual problems contained in Hamlet's speeches by pleading that since he is mad, what he has to say isn't always supposed to make sense. As a result, lines such as "For if the sun breed maggots in a dead dog, being a go[o]d kissing carrion – Have you a daughter" (2.2.181–82) are written off as mad ravings (intentional or unintentional) rather than seen as revelatory of Hamlet's revulsion with the corporeal world and explanatory of later "ravings" such as "Let her not walk i'th'sun" (184). Therefore, I have taken the position in this class that Hamlet is not *permitted* to be mad; he can tell a "hawk from a handsaw" in all winds. As a result, the students are forced to confront the text without an escape clause.

NOTE

Hamlet quotations are from Jenkins.

D. Buchanan

Defamiliarizing Hamlet:
Hamlet with and without His Soliloquies

I ask students to read *Hamlet*, first skipping each of Hamlet's soliloquies (I provide a list). Then, they reread the play, this time with the soliloquies, and rank each soliloquy in two ways: according to what each contributes to the play (i.e., what narrative information it provides that is not found elsewhere) and according to what each contributes to Hamlet the character (i.e., why he speaks these words at this particular point in the action). Finally, students write a few paragraphs (say, two pages), sketching out what they have discovered from this double reading, both about the play and about the figure called Hamlet. Since Hamlet's soliloquies are the play's most familiar feature and since readers tend to "become" Hamlet and to collapse their subjectivities into his well-known interiority, eliminating that possibility to begin with redirects attention to the play's structure and narrative as well as to the functions of other characters. Students discover that, with few exceptions, the soliloquies provide little information that is not found elsewhere, usually embedded in speeches occurring either just before or after a soliloquy. They also find that the soliloquy they usually rank as most necessary to Hamlet, "To be or not to be," seems least necessary to the play. Useful for prompting class discussion, this assignment also can form the basis for a longer paper.

Barbara Hodgdon

Helping Chinese Students Study *Hamlet*

All Chinese students know *Hamlet*, but their understanding is different. The students of English departments in Chinese universities may take History and Anthology of English Literature, in which Shakespeare has an important place and is given about fifteen class hours. The study of *Hamlet* requires six hours. They already know something about Shakespeare and his life, his plays, and his sonnets.

For my part, the ways to help Chinese students study *Hamlet* are as follows:

Hour 1: Introductory information
In a lecture the teacher provides information regarding the play's source, dramatis personae, style, and plot and the interpretive commentary of both past and present. From the teacher's lecture, the students should get their first impression of the tragedy and know it is the most important of all Shakespeare's plays.

Hours 2 and 3
Chinese students would not be able to read the whole original in a short time. The teacher must select some useful passages for them to study. All these passages are about the hero and his mind, especially the several soliloquies that have a bearing on Hamlet's behavior and psychology ("sullied flesh" [1.2.129–59]; "O what a rogue" [2.2.550–604]; "To be, or not to be" [3.1.55–89]). The teacher annotates all these passages in detail so that the students can prepare before class. They must understand the meaning of each sentence, try to know Hamlet's action as if Hamlet were real today. What he says should have some motive or psychological tendency; the locutionary acts and illocutionary acts should be clear. In general, the teacher should direct students to discover the mental language of Hamlet, the relation among the soliloquies, and the theme of the play—the conflict between his words and deeds, the significance of his weak points, and the relation between his personality and tragedy.

At the end of the lecture, the teacher assigns topics: Hamlet's weak points, the meaning of "To be, or not to be," his Oedipus complex, the Ghost's honesty, Hamlet's inner world, and so on. Students also work on specific lines for linguistic analysis: (1) "Taint not thy mind, nor let thy soul contrive / Against thy mother aught. Leave her to heaven" (1.5.85–86); (2) "The time is out of joint— O cursed spite, / That ever I was born to set it right!" (1.5.188–89); (3) "To be, or not to be: that is the question" (3.1.55); (4) "Now cracks a noble heart. Good night, sweet prince, / And flights of angels sing thee to thy rest!" (5.2.359– 60); (5) "O what a rogue and peasant slave am I!" (2.2.550); "O that this too too sallied flesh would melt, / Thaw, and resolve itself into a dew" (1.2.129–30).

Hours 4 and 5: Class debate
Each student must prepare thoroughly and write an outline for class debate. Students not only express their opinions but also criticize one another.

Hour 6: Summary
The teacher gives a final lecture on *Hamlet* on the basis of the students' discussions. It includes a summary of the topics covered in the first lecture and also a comparison of *Hamlet* and *An Orphan in Zhao's Family*, a classic Chinese drama (Chuanxiang).

NOTE

Hamlet quotations are from Evans et al.

Luo Zhiye

Oral Reports on Criticism

That there exists a more than four-hundred-year-long continuous body of commentary on Shakespeare's work offers both a challenge and an opportunity for teachers and students. I use this exercise at the freshman college level to help students gain some perspective on the play and to reinforce basic researching, citing, and speaking skills.

As we begin reading *Hamlet*, on which we will spend several weeks, I announce that each student is responsible for making a brief oral report, approximately five minutes in length, summarizing what three critics have had to say about one character in the play. The students must identify the critic and the date and place of original publication of the criticism and also identify where they found it if not in the original publication. I give them approximately two weeks. Depending on the size of the class, the reports can take one or more class periods; they can be done one after another until all students have reported, or a few can be done at the beginning or end of several classes, or both can be done: there can be a designated report day and chances for makeup in subsequent class sessions.

In recent years the English department at LaGuardia Community College, City University of New York, has adopted a requirement that students attach photocopies or printouts of all sources that they use in a paper, at least of the pages cited and of the pages that identify the source. For this oral report exercise I now require that students have the photocopies or printouts with them so that if there are any questions about the source, we have the information to provide answers on the spot.

LaGuardia's student body is particularly diverse. At the last count of which I am aware, more than 114 countries were represented; in any one class if there are thirty students, for example, they are likely to be from twenty-five different countries. Many students' prior educational experiences have discouraged them from speaking in class: doing so is not appropriate in their culture. This oral exercise thus is also designed to help provide a structured situation that gives each student practice speaking informally before a group. To make the exercise as nonthreatening as possible, I announce that, while done for credit, it will not be graded. Instead I use a system of checks with pluses and minuses to record the degree of effort each student puts into the project. Although I acknowledge that this is not a public-speaking class and that students will not be graded on their performance, I encourage them to establish eye contact with their audience and to speak loudly and clearly enough to be heard. When the class is hearing the reports, students themselves encourage the reporting student to speak in a way that makes the report as comprehensible as possible.

The course in which I use this exercise is called Writing through Literature and is the upper-level composition course (ENG 102). For most students it is the last writing course they will take; for many it is also the only literature course. In the lower-level composition course (ENG 101), students should have written research papers, but if a long time has elapsed between the two courses, they may have forgotten (or not learned well in the first place) how to do college-level research. This oral-report exercise thus sharpens those skills before students have to write a research paper for the upper-level course. We briefly discuss which sources are and are not appropriate at the college level, an element of this exercise that has become increasingly important with the advent of Internet research.

When we are listening to the reports, I encourage the class to sit in a circle and allow the students to speak from their seats as a way of making the exercise less intimidating. Occasionally a student will prefer to stand at the front of the room.

Since many of LaGuardia's students have family and work responsibilities in addition to their classes, I allow them to use compilations like the Gale *Shakespearean Criticism* and *Shakespeare for Students*. Ahead of time I arrange with the library to move the relevant volumes from the reference shelves to the reference desk so that the needed volume is readily available and not just left out on a table somewhere (to use a book from the reference desk, students must leave their ID card and can use the book for a restricted time period). In each class as we hear the reports, students show a wide range of enterprise, a function of how much time and interest each brings to the assignment. Several will choose the most prominent character, Hamlet, rely just on one volume of *Shakespearean Criticism* for excerpts, and choose the first three critics that they come across, such as Samuel Johnson, William Hazlitt, and Samuel Coleridge. Others will choose a character more difficult to research, such as Horatio or Osric, and travel to other libraries to find articles in little known publications. In a recent class both the riches and dangers of Internet research became apparent when one student found a letter written in 1880 by an actress who had played Ophelia, while another gave us excerpts from what turned out to be a draft paper by a high school student.

Generally I let students choose whatever character they wish, even if some characters are reported on by many students and some are not reported on at all. But one could easily ask students, before they sign up for a character, to state in class which character they wish to report on and then encourage some to choose instead an underselected character.

Even when several students choose the same character and the same critic to summarize, what they say and how they say it is sufficiently distinctive that whatever repetition occurs is not a problem. We usually hear diverse and interesting ideas about the many characters. But perhaps the most valuable aspect of this exercise occurs after we have heard approximately ten student reports, which means we've heard what thirty critics have had to say at various dates, since students must identify the date of each critic's comments. Just from hearing the date of the criticism, the critic's gender, and the character's name, students begin to be able to predict what a critic will say. They thus gain valuable insight into the passing fashions in intellectual history, a lesson that the long time span of Shakespearean commentary facilitates.

An observation that I've not yet made known to students after this exercise is that the character and criticism that they select not only reveal something about the time in which each critic wrote but also suggest insights into the students at that moment in their life.

The broad range of information that we hear greatly enriches everyone's understanding of the characters, of the play, and of the many approaches that have developed historically and continue to develop. Students are often inspired by something another student has uncovered and will pursue that idea in a paper of their own. Thus researchers' being able to mark the trail by providing all necessary citation information so that someone else can retrace their steps becomes a meaningful responsibility. For those few students who have trouble mastering what I call double citation, which reports on both the original location and the location where the criticism was actually found, the repeated class attention to documentation provides the kind of reinforcement that should make double citation clear.

This oral-report exercise offers many advantages to students and teacher alike. As I use it at LaGuardia, this exercise helps students sharpen their researching, citing, and public-speaking skills at the same time that it gives students a broad perspective on the characters, the play, and intellectual fashions.

Edna Zwick Boris

Teaching Text and Performance through Soundscripting

Soundscripting is the addition of sound cues and effects to the dialogue. It follows along the lines of a Foley artist in film or television, who adds or "sweetens" the sound. The long-term process in class involves four steps, including three performances. First, the students, in groups, read their scenes aloud in class, like a sight-reading. Second, they soundscript the text by designating and devising the sound effects. Third, the second performance is the sound effects alone with question and answer between audience and performers. The fourth and final project is a combined performance of text and effects, with any sound-track music from a recording or played live. Selected scenes from *Hamlet* for soundscripters are:

> 1.5 . Establishing the haunted mood and the nature of the Ghost
> 3.2. Performing the Players' play by adding sounds to explain how the court responds
> 5.2 . The furious action of the duels, the deaths, and Fortinbras with army

Soundscripting is flexible enough to be done either at no cost or with the advantages of modern media. The text goes from one dimension to a two-dimensional voice to a three-dimensional performance, then into a fourth dimension of nuance, thunder, and music.

Michael W. Young

More Matter (but Not Necessarily Less Art): Using My Coloring Book to Introduce Seventh Graders to *Hamlet*

Though Hamlet faces a formidable dilemma when he muses, "To be or not to be," as a teacher I too regularly confront a weighty problem: to achieve curricular objectives in a heterogeneous classroom of a small conservative school. Yet, by incorporating students' prior knowledge of pop culture, their understanding of animal imagery in literature, and the anthropomorphic coloring book I had created while studying *Hamlet*, I successfully introduced a taste of Shakespeare into a seventh-grade poetry unit.

Since most students are familiar with parental guidance, we began with Polonius's advice to Laertes (1.3.58–81). First, I instructed students to summarize the movie plot of *The Lion King*, which imitates the story line of *Hamlet*. With piqued curiosity, students next brainstormed similes that included animals, based upon fables and fairy tales, starting with lions and ending with boars. While more able students saw the connection to the homophone *bore*, weaker students needed support to define what *boring* meant. To facilitate comprehension of the text, I had the class work on difficult vocabulary before I distributed the coloring-book pages (fig. 1) and the text. While *thy* and *thine* initially daunted them, a comparison to the grammar of my school's mandated second language, Hebrew, quickly eliminated this problem. After the distribution of the pages, students worked in small groups paraphrasing Polonius's speech to Laertes as I circulated, providing support and encouragement. Follow-up discussion revealed that everyone understood the content. Students recognized the implication that parental advice can be *boring* (and therefore might be ignored).

Fig. 1. Laertes dutifully listens to some *boring* parental advice.

With instructions to memorize appealing lines at home, students then colored the page. The following day, they wrote down their chosen lines, thoughtfully explaining what made them memorable, while I heard enthusiastic inquiries requesting the next installment of *Hamlet*. (For another sample page,

Fig. 2. Rosencrantz and Guildenstern try to *ferret* out information from an uncooperative Hamlet.

see fig. 2, which illustrates Rosencrantz and Guildenstern interrogating Hamlet in 4.2.)

NOTE

Hamlet quotations are from Spencer.

Denise M. Mullins

Priming Questions for the "Mousetrap"

Miniperformance is a good teaching tool—not too demanding and yet able to bring out the action possibilities in the text. I give a volunteer for each character about a week to meet and discuss with the other volunteers what they, as a group, will make of the reading with action of a key scene. One good choice for *Hamlet* is the "Mousetrap" scene. Thinking through the following questions has helped my students with their assignment:

1. Hamlet presents himself as many different characters in this play. In 3.2 how many different Hamlets do we meet? How can actors bring out this multiplicity?
2. Tension begins mounting about line 45. How can an actor believably bring out Hamlet's tension in body language and tones of voice?
3. How might you distribute the characters on stage for the play within the play, taking into consideration the way Hamlet creates tension and rivalry between Ophelia and Gertrude?
4. What happens on the players' stage during the dumb show? What happens in the "audience"?
5. What is Hamlet doing during both the dumb show and the play within? What is Horatio doing?
6. How would you capitalize on the drama of lines 255–64?
7. How would you make the transition from the public Hamlet (with Rosencrantz and Guildenstern, with Polonius) to the Hamlet with Horatio during the aftermath of the play within?

After the student actors talk through and demonstrate what they have decided, spectator students on three sides of the designated stage area pose questions for the actors. Alternatively, when group work seems too formidable for a particular class, I assign scenes to individual students to discuss at the board, answering the same sorts of questions and also responding to the questions of the other students.

NOTE

Hamlet references are to Evans et al.

Bente Videbaek

Puns and Wordplay in *Hamlet*

Understanding figures of speech is essential for appreciating early modern drama and poetry. Puns, for example, whether defined as simple wordplay or more sophisticated rhetorical strategies, saturate *Hamlet*. Most students use puns in daily conversation and have a practical knowledge of how puns work. This experience allows teachers a wonderful vehicle to explore the complex (and not so complex) uses of language in the play. Moreover, emphasizing wordplay and figures of all types grants both the novice and the sophisticated reader of poetry exposure to complex material.

Although editors gloss many puns, one particular pun in *Hamlet* has largely escaped attention. This pun, far from superfluous wordplay or nonsensical evasion, actually captures a central tension apparent throughout the play. In act 1, scene 5, moments after the Ghost leaves Hamlet alone on stage, Horatio and the others rejoin Hamlet. He dismisses them with the following:

> I hold it fit that we should shake hands and part,
> You, as your business and desire shall point you,
> For every man hath business and desire,
> Such as it is, and for my own poor part,
> I will go *pray*.   (1.5.128–32; emphasis mine)

Recognizing the pun between *pray* and *prey* creates several avenues for exploration. Hamlet wants to be a preyer but is unable. Later in 3.3, Claudius, the preyer, wants to utter a repentant prayer but is unable ("pray can I not" [38]). The action of *Hamlet* continues to highlight the pray-prey and prayer-preyer tension.

Recognizing this pun (and a host of others) allows for some interesting connections with other plays and early modern literature. Shakespeare, for example, uses the *pray-prey* pun in *Henry IV, Part 1*; he may even use it in *Othello*. Shakespeare, of course, was not unique in his use of puns. In early Renaissance literature courses, looking for puns works equally well. Other major poets, in fact, used the same *pray-prey* pun. Spenser used it in his *Amoretti* sequence; Marlowe, likewise, employed the pun in *Hero and Leander*. Other commonly used puns (*eye-I* and *sun-son*) provide immediate points of study both within Shakespeare and among various early modern poets and playwrights.

The objective of such an emphasis, it should be noted, is not to find the one pun that crystallizes the entire play but to get students interested in and excited about the playful possibilities of language: finding the pun makes for active reading. Poetic language, especially from the sixteenth and seventeenth centuries, can test the reading faculties of most undergraduate and graduate students. Exploring simple wordplay gives the students confidence and allows them to recognize various thematic forms of wit, irony, and paradox. A close study of wordplay not only enhances appreciation of *Hamlet* but also provides both teachers and students an opportunity to isolate and create puns.

NOTE

Hamlet quotations are from Evans et al.

Paul J. Voss

Leaping into the Text:
Teaching Stage Directions in Act 5, Scene 1

According to Shakespeare, "[a]ction is eloquence" (*Cor.* 3.2.76), and a fifty-minute session devoted to an analysis of the stage directions in Hamlet and Laertes's struggle during Ophelia's "maimed rites" (5.1.250) evinces this eloquence.

Method   With a copy of the indispensable *Three-Text* Hamlet (Bertram and Kliman), I divide the class into small groups of three or four and have each group examine all three renditions of the scene in which Hamlet and Laertes confront each other following Ophelia's death: in Q1, Laertes leaps into the grave, followed by Hamlet; in Q2, no stage directions for dramatic leaps are provided, but an implicit stage direction could suggest Laertes's leap; in F1, Laertes leaps in, with no sign of Hamlet's duplication of the action. The groups analyze each version and in a collaborative discussion decide the staging that would be most effective dramatically. In the second half of the session, all the groups participate in a class discussion on staging the scene. This interaction encourages students to discover the role of stage directions in establishing stage practices. It facilitates, in Michael Goldman's phrase, their "entering the text" (*"Hamlet"*).

Group or Individual Projects   This session engenders a range of questions: How would this scene have been staged for an Elizabethan audience? If a trapdoor is used for the grave, what are the thematic and emblematic implications of using the same trapdoor for Hamlet Senior's ghost and Ophelia's burial? Does the relocation to a naturalized setting, as in cinematic versions, alter one's choice of staging? In a second session, cinematic treatments of the scene can further heighten the role of stage directions in determining the staging of this agon between Laertes and Hamlet.

NOTE

The *Hamlet* quotation is from Evans et al.

Hardin L. Aasand

Groups Debating Issues

A group of five or six students choose a topic and get into the text to see what evidence is available and then single out one question for argument. They work out pro and con cases, taking notes as they go. Then they appoint among them two lawyers, and at the end of the discovery-of-evidence session these argue the two sides. The class is the jury and brings in a verdict based on what it has heard from the two lawyers. The judge (the teacher) can instruct the jury if any evidence is to be ruled irrelevant or improper.

Group A: Ghosts and spirits from beyond the grave

Can a ghost from anywhere but hell ask for a revenge murder?
Do ghosts ever carry messages from God?
Can one person see a ghost and another nearby not?

Group B: Religion

Is Old Hamlet religious? If so, was he a Catholic while alive?
Is Hamlet religious? If so, is he Protestant or Catholic?
Is Claudius religious? If so, is he Catholic or Protestant?
Is Hamlet's mood as he approaches the final duel religious or fatalistic?

Group C: Young love

Are Hamlet and Ophelia engaged?
What is Polonius's reason for breaking them up? Is it an excuse?
Are the couple suited to each other?

Group D: Mature love

Did Gertrude love Old Hamlet, her first husband?
Does she love Claudius?
Did she sleep with Claudius while still married to Old Hamlet?

Group E: Kingship and voting

Should Hamlet automatically have become king when his father died?
Is the kingship of Denmark decided by some group voting on it?
If Hamlet had killed Claudius in his mother's room, would Hamlet have
    become king right away?

Group F: Age and time

Is Hamlet an undergraduate or graduate student at Wittenberg University?
Is Hamlet a late bloomer, maybe thirty?
Is Laertes a student in Paris? If so, what is he studying?
How much time passes between the Ghost's appearance in act 1 and the
duel in act 5, when Hamlet is poisoned? Months? Years?

These six groups can be dropped to five or even four—that is, adjusted to
the size of the class. After all the verdicts are in, students and teacher can discuss how the questions and answers affect their perceptions of the play. The
teacher may wish to set a written assignment requiring the students to find out
how reputable scholars and critics have tackled these questions and whether
any consensus has been reached.

David George

Existential Questions

I like to confront a class with Hamlet's questions. This confronting follows
classes that suggest that *Hamlet* is a work that expresses all the anxiety, intellectual excitement, and uncertainty of an age undergoing massive changes, an
age when seemingly established certainties concerning the nature of God and
creation and the status of humankind within creation were being questioned by
"new philosophy" (yes, we look at Donne's poem [line 205]) and the influence
of such figures as Montaigne, Calvin, Machiavelli, and Galileo. Hamlet faces
these very questions but also has pressing personal issues to contend with. I
divide my class into groups that later report to the class as a whole. Each group
discusses Hamlet's struggle with a selection from the following broad questions: To be or not to be? What is the nature of the universe? just "a foul and
pestilent congregation of vapors"? What is a human being? just a "quintessence
of dust" (2.2.302–03, 308)? Why is the world sick ("Something is rotten in the
state of Denmark" [1.4.90])? What do I know? (Remember Montaigne's "Que
scais-je?" [Emerson 319].) How does one determine the correct solution to any
ethical dilemma when all is in doubt and chaos? Each group is also assigned
some of Hamlet's more personal questions: Why has my mother re-married?
Why has she committed incest? Why am I not king? Is the Ghost really my
father's spirit? Is Ophelia honest? Who are my true friends? Why do I keep
delaying what is supposedly my filial duty ("This thing's to do" [4.4.44])?

NOTE

Hamlet quotations are from Evans et al.

Alan R. Young

Writing to Make Personal Connections

I do a prewriting exercise with my high school seniors to help them make personal connections as we read the play. They answer the following questions in writing, and we discuss them in class:

> Imagine that you are away at college and receive news that your father has died. What is your immediate reaction? What would you do?
>
> On returning home, you discover that your uncle (your dad's brother) and your mom have got married. How do you think you would feel about such a marriage?
>
> After returning home, you begin having dreams in which you converse with your father's ghost, and he tells you that your uncle murdered him. What would you do in such a situation? Do you think you would attempt to avenge his death based on a conversation with a ghost?
>
> In the meantime, your longtime girlfriend all of a sudden breaks up with you and refuses to give any reason. How do you think you would feel? What would you do?
>
> While all this is going on, two friends of yours from high school, who have been away at college, also suddenly appear in town and want to spend a lot of time with you. Would this seem strange to you? Can you think of any reason to be suspicious of them?
>
> Upon your father's death, your uncle has taken over the family business, which was supposed to go to you when you graduated from college. How do you feel about this?

Mike Sirofchuck

EDITOR'S NOTE

The *Hamlet* film directed by Michael Almereyda (2000) can show students how a production answers some of these same questions.

Words, Words, Words:
Comparing, Cutting, Explaining

Marvin Spevack's *Complete and Systematic Concordance to the Works of Shakespeare* can be a valuable resource for students. It helps locate examples of images or other linguistic patterns. Given that Old Hamlet is murdered by poison in the ear, how many times does the word *poison* appear in the play? Where are other references to the ear? Do these data lead to an argument about a recurring aspect of the play? *Concordance* is also of value in comparative assignments. Students can look up the sizes of roles in various plays and then be asked to comment on the implications of their findings. What difference does it make that Hamlet speaks almost 40% of the lines, compared with about 10% for Claudius, whereas Iago speaks 31% and Othello 25% of their play? How do these plays compare with the effect of Falstaff's, Hal's, and Hotspur's each speaking about 20% of the lines in *Henry IV, Part 1*, or with the ensemble nature of comedies like *Twelfth Night* and *Much Ado* (each with several characters speaking around 12% of the lines)? Finally, the data can give a sense of the linguistic texture of a particular character's lines: how often does Hamlet refer to his mother compared with how often other characters refer to her? Numerical data can provide evidence to support speculative or impressionistic observations, making them more convincing.

To help students appreciate how *Hamlet* is put together, I assign a five-to-seven-page paper that asks them to cut the play by 25% (a percentage large enough to require significant cuts). The cuts must eliminate entire characters, scenes, and speeches in order to heighten a general aspect of the play, and the cuts must be supported by an argument for the broad principles behind them, along with counterarguments about what is lost. This is not to be a list of every cut or an account of how each individual cut can be plausibly achieved in the theater. The goal is not to create a performable script but to understand how severe cutting changes the internal balances of the play. An essay cutting Gertrude and Ophelia, for example, on the grounds that notions of what women should be like are to Hamlet more important than the actual women in his world must also explain how the absence of the two women removes their voices as observers of Hamlet, reduces the audience's sense of the emotional cost of vengeance, and so, in effect, reproduces the very depersonalization of women that Hamlet engages in. By stressing the importance of being ruthless and of acknowledging the cost, the assignment results in inventive essays that reveal the depth of a student's thinking about the play.

To help teach the linguistic complexity of *Hamlet*, I assign an hour-exam analysis of a single, unannounced passage of twenty to thirty lines. The exam format requires students to be concise and to focus on only the most important details. What is needed is not a line-by-line paraphrase but an argument organized by the major internal divisions of the speech, an argument that identifies the shifts or extensions in a speaker's thoughts and feelings (which may return to their initial state by the end of the speech) as marked off by prominent linguistic features such as the logical markers *if, but, so*; the interjections and apostrophes *fie* or *O*; and punctuation (dashes, exclamations, question marks). A particularly good passage for students to analyze is Hamlet's soliloquy in 1.5 after the Ghost departs. It is varied enough in its structural elements and shifting thoughts to sustain a detailed analysis and short enough for an analysis to be completed under time constraints.

Nathaniel Strout

Hamlet and Subjectivity

I ask my students if Hamlet, the dropout from Wittenberg who really doesn't want to kill anyone, seems more like us, no matter how diverse a group we are, than the senile Lear, the jealous-mad Othello, or bloodthirsty Macbeth? I use this question to begin a discussion of the issue of subjectivity in *Hamlet*. Hamlet, unlike Everyman, is possessed of a conspicuous interiority, so that thought, directly related in the play to inaction, displaces retribution as the primary matter of revenge tragedy.

Hamlet ponders, philosophizes—"To be or not to be"—in a way that endows him with a recognizably modern psychology. As more than one student has pointed out, Hamlet needs a shrink. That is, *Hamlet* can be seen to represent a watershed in the history of the subject. The play's hero embodies an emerging conception of subjectivity or, in less theoretical parlance, what it means to be human. The term *human* is itself, I point out, a humanist definition of the subject—it implies a certain existential angst, which derives not from external economic, social, or other material conditions but from a kind of neurotically conceived mystery at the core of life itself.

I then segue into what humanism meant in the Renaissance as opposed to the later bourgeois humanism characteristic of full-scale capitalism. We also discuss the exalted image of Renaissance humanity (Michelangelo's *David* is a useful visual analog of the paragon of the animals) versus the Reformation understanding of humanity congenitally depraved (e.g., Calvinist doctrine). Asking the class to consider the contradictions among these various discourses, we assess whether Hamlet was a humanist prince, albeit one incapable of dealing with a singularly Machiavellian moment. The class then discusses the degree to which the term "the subject" converges with or deviates from "the human being" or "the individual." I point out that none of these terminologies is entirely satisfactory: while the human being is conceptualized as a free-floating entity hovering in ether (albeit in a spontaneous and authentic fashion), the subject is understood as being weighted down by the historical determinations (social circumstances, economic conditions) of its production. I put forward the notion that *Hamlet*, whose hero has been seen as the prototypical and paradigmatic subject of the era of modernity (i.e., after the Middle Ages through to the postmodern—when the subject allegedly morphed again into the fractured surfaces of cyberculture and consumerist desire), itself rehearses the issues of what the subject or the human means in a way that challenges all our categories.

My final point about subjectivity relates to gender. It is particularly interesting that all the vacillation and inaction that make Hamlet the tragic hero whose conception of himself seems so close to our own are what have also traditionally been understood to make him feminine (though no less misogynist for all his femininity). I wonder with my students if Hamlet really constitutes the model of being that subsequently would be accorded (by Thomas Paine among others) the rights of man, since he so clearly does not conform with the rigorous masculinity that subject-position requires.

Dympna Callaghan

Cheating Death: The Immortal and Ever-Expanding Universe of *Hamlet*

Maria M. Scott

As he is dying, surrounded by the corpses of half the Danish court, Hamlet begs his friend Horatio to hold off swelling the casualty list by one more in order to tell his—Hamlet's—story. Horatio agrees, and begins to make good on his promise as he prepares Fortinbras to hear

> Of carnal, bloody, and unnatural acts
> Of accidental judgments, casual slaughters
> [. . . . .]
> And in this upshot, purposes mistook
> Fall'n on th' inventors heads.   (5.2.363–67)

Thanks to Horatio, the "true" story of the prince of Denmark is made known to future generations.

You see Horatio, as I tell my students, is not a single person but a tradition. He is anyone who has printed, directed, or acted in *Hamlet*. He is all the teachers and all the students and all the readers who have encountered, absorbed, and passed on *Hamlet*. And he is the individuals and cultures that continue to appropriate and reinvent *Hamlet* from their own perspectives.

Perhaps more than any Shakespearean text, *Hamlet* is embedded in our collective cultural consciousness long before we actually encounter the gloomy Dane in the pages of his play. The question "To be or not to be?" is as overdetermined as the direction to "have a nice day." However, rather as in the game of Post Office, the original text has been reinterpreted and retransmitted so many times that what we receive sometimes only vaguely resembles the original message.

> To go outside, and there perchance to stay,
> Or to remain within: that is the question.
> Whether 'tis better for a cat to suffer
> The cuffs and buffets of inclement weather
> That Nature rains on those who roam abroad,
> Or take a nap upon a scrap of carpet,
> And so by dozing melt the solid hours
> That clog the clock's bright gears with sullen time
> And stall the dinner bell.   (Beard)

This collision of the sublime with the ridiculous is not just in writing; there is a whole decade's worth of students for whom Hamlet is Mad Max in tights. If the dilemma facing Shakespeare scholars today is that there's just not that much more we can say about him, surely that dilemma is doubly pronounced in relation to *Hamlet*. I claim, however, that it is the very profusion of what I call subsequent texts that makes *Hamlet* a thriving industry and an accessible object of study.

Best known for his Horatian effort with *Rosencrantz and Guildenstern Are Dead*, Tom Stoppard has also swollen the *Hamlet* corpus (forgive the pun) with *The Fifteen-Minute Hamlet* and now with the film *Shakespeare in Love*. *Rosencrantz and Guildenstern* presents *Hamlet* from the perspective of those two minor characters, who provide a useful paradigm of textual reading to students. The two are faced with the task of reading and interpreting textual fragments of *Hamlet*, which they ultimately fail to piece together into any coherent totality. At the close of the play, Guildenstern reassures himself, "Well, we'll know better next time" (126). But of course they won't. Rosencrantz and Guildenstern, like all the characters in *Hamlet*, are doomed to repeat the same cycle again and again, just as the Players reenact the *Hamlet* within *Hamlet*. In his 1990 film version, Stoppard further exploits the play-within concept with multiple and concentric performances of the play into which the hapless protagonists have stumbled.

Rosencrantz and Guildenstern allows students to feel empowered, since however difficult a text *Hamlet* may be for them, they can rest assured that they know more about it than Rosencrantz and Guildenstern do. Stoppard's play also gives students an opportunity to encounter *Hamlet* from the perspective of two characters for whom it is an absolute unknown, something not possible for students with the popular assumptions of four hundred years imprinted on their cultural subconscious. *The Fifteen-Minute Hamlet*, in its turn, promotes profitable discussion. In paring down the play to its plot essentials, Stoppard has excised thousands of lines in order to bring a four-hour play into a fifteen-minute parameter. What is lost? What is clarified? What characters are eliminated altogether, and how does that change the play?

Like *Rosencrantz and Guildenstern*, Lee Blessing's *Fortinbras* tells the story of *Hamlet* from the perspective of a minor character. *Fortinbras* is a delightful exposé of political spin doctoring, in which Fortinbras calmly dismisses Horatio's account as politically ineffective. The new king proceeds to construct his own version of the story, involving Polish spies, to justify Norway's annexation of Denmark (creating Denway—or Normark; "It doesn't matter," remarks Fortinbras [21]) and subsequent invasion of Poland. Blessing's title character airily disregards Horatio's appeal to truth with the statement "I'm not here to finish their story. They were all here to begin mine. It's the new perspective. Master it" (17). Unfortunately for Fortinbras, his Norweenish—or Daneweegian ("It doesn't matter," says Fortinbras)—empire spirals out of his control, and the spirits of Hamlet, Ophelia, et alia appear one after the other, lobbying him from the grave to tell their stories properly. The trouble is, they've all got different stories to tell. What began as Hamlet's story sprouts into a series of competing stories as the ghost-characters clamor for attention.

Most interesting of these stories is Ophelia's. Blessing does more to recuperate Ophelia in an accessible manner for college students than twenty-five years of feminist scholarship. To Laertes, who is having some trouble adjusting to no longer being alive, she remarks, "That's what happens when you think you're immortal. You should've been raised as a girl. Then you'd have been ready" (34). Later, she explodes in response to Hamlet's insistent, "The story will be told!"

> OPHELIA: From whose point of view? Yours? Mr. Hamlet-It's-All-about-Me the Dane? Oh sure—your point of view is clearly the most rewarding, the most complex. No wonder it has a special right to exist.
> HAMLET: Ophelia—
> OPHELIA: I will not . . . be . . . marginal! (51)

At the end of the play, Fortinbras is dead and has, along with the rest of the ghosts, dispersed. Only Marcellus, Barnardo, and a couple of Polish maidens are left. They find a tattered book, and one of the girls begins to read, in halting, broken English, "For in . . . For in dat . . . Sleep? Sleep of . . ." (67). And we're off again.

Examples of Hamlet's perpetuation go on and on. Paul Rudnick's *I Hate Hamlet* (1992) is a harmless bit of fluff in which the ghost of the great John Barrymore appears in order to coach a young TV actor taking on—against his better judgment—the part of Hamlet in a production in Central Park (à la Joseph Papp). The latest addition (Feb. 2000) to the *Hamlet* oeuvre comes from no less than John Updike, in his novel *Gertrude and Claudius*. Using the source fragments of the *Hamlet* story, Updike's narrative provides a prequel to the play, tracing a long-sublimated attraction between Geruthe and Fengon (later Claudius) from the earliest days of her marriage to his brother. It also psychologizes the young Hamlet as the sardonic, distant son of a sardonic, distant king whose claim to the throne of Denmark derives primarily from his marriage to Gertrude.

Both Rudnick and Updike, in very different ways, reflect a consciousness of *Hamlet* as a cultural product, something we would do well to stress to students, who often get an unfortunately rigid notion of textuality as it applies to so-called canonical works. Indeed, the more canonical a text, the more a student tends to see it as impermeable. A student reading *Gertrude and Claudius* might say indignantly, "But that doesn't happen in the play!" Another could object to the character of John Barrymore in *I Hate* Hamlet, who radically oversimplifies (even trivializes) Hamlet's pseudomythic status.[1] These kinds of reactions can be useful entrées into discussion of text as commodity, open to appropriation, transformation, and, quite frankly, resale.

Perhaps the most startling present-day manifestation, though, is Richard Curtis's *The Skinhead Hamlet*, which one may access over the Web (be warned, however: it's pretty raw; I usually distribute it to students in a brown paper wrapper). The Internet has transformed Shakespeare studies in recent years by making all sorts and conditions of textual analyses widely available at the click of a mouse, with or without a price tag. Indeed, a search of "hamlet" on the *Excite* search engine turns up 19,158 postings. Even if he is dead in Elsinore, Hamlet still thrives on the World Wide Web. We have the opportunity to learn with our students here, to take advantage of this new technology without letting it take advantage of us. There are valid *Hamlet* sites, and not-so-valid ones. Working with students to distinguish between them, we can foster analytic and critical skills that will serve them long after they leave our classes.

Teachers of *Hamlet* can also benefit enormously by accessing any number of the performance accounts of the play. In addition to the texts described above, performance histories can better help students new to Shakespeare understand not only the text itself but also the way its interpretation is shaped by the context of that interpretation. One might include, for example, excerpts from Laurence Olivier's autobiography concerning the influence on Olivier's production of Ernest Jones's oedipal criticism of the play.[2] More broadly, Anthony Dawson's *Shakespeare in Performance* traces the the long and varied tradition of *Hamlet* performances since the 1600s. These texts provide opportunities for cultural criticism of almost infinite scope. Marvin Rosenberg's *Masks of* Hamlet is even more exhaustive.

Whatever subsequent texts we choose, we have the opportunity to show that *Hamlet* remains relevant as a cultural icon and continues to evolve. Students already recognize *Hamlet* as a known cultural phenomenon; the chance to see how that phenomenon relates to their own culture through various interpretations of the story can make Shakespeare in general more accessible to them. For more seasoned undergraduate or graduate students, subsequent textuality raises important critical questions, some literary, some sociopolitical. If, as some humanists have claimed, Shakespeare's *Hamlet* constitutes a paradigm of human experience, the texts that *Hamlet* itself has generated reflect the multivalent quality of that experience. Thus in order for us to pass on Hamlet's story faithfully, we present-day Horatios should consider the original text of *Hamlet* rather as astronomers think of the big bang and *Hamlet* itself as the ever-expanding universe.

NOTES

The *Hamlet* quotation is from Wofford.

[1]Barrymore, at one point, makes the definitive pronouncement that *Hamlet* is the bulge in his tights.

[2]The autobiography also, though briefly, refers to the 1937 production of the play at Elsinore, which begs the question of how real space and performance space are and are not the same.

NOTES ON CONTRIBUTORS

Hardin L. Aasand is professor of English at Dickinson State University, where he specializes in Shakespeare, Renaissance drama, and the history of the English language. He has published essays on court masques, the Jacobean court, editing *Hamlet*, and Shakespeare. He has written book reviews for *Renaissance Quarterly*, *Seventeenth-Century News*, and *Medievalia et Humanistica*. He is a member of the MLA New Variorum *Hamlet* editing team.

Randall Anderson's scholarship is in textual criticism, theoretical bibliography, and the sociology of texts—specifically paratexts and the nature of anthologies. He is author of "The Merit of a Manuscript Poem," *Print, Manuscript, and Performance* (Ohio State UP, 2000). He also writes about the literature of mountaineering and is beginning a translation of *De alpibus commentarius* (1574).

James R. Andreas Sr. is professor emeritus of English at Clemson University and currently visiting professor of English at Florida International University. He is editor of *The Upstart Crow: A Shakespeare Journal* and has published widely on Shakespeare, Chaucer, and African American literature. He is author of "Signifying on Shakespeare: Gloria Naylor's *Mama Day*," *Shakespeare and Appropriation*, ed. Robert Sawyer and Christy Desmet (Routledge, 1999); "Teaching Shakespeare's Bawdry: Orality, Literacy, and Censorship in *Romeo and Juliet*," *Approaches to Teaching Shakespeare's* Romeo and Juliet," ed. Maurice Hunt (MLA, 2000).

Roy Battenhouse was an ordained priest of the Protestant Episcopal Church and professor of English at Indiana University, Bloomington. He is author of "The Ghost in *Hamlet*: A Catholic 'Linchpin'?" *Studies in Philology* (1951); "Hamlet's Apostrophe on Man: Clue to the Tragedy," *PMLA* (1951); *Shakespearean Tragedy and Its Christian Premises* (Indiana UP, 1969); and editor of *Shakespeare's Christian Dimension: An Anthology of Commentary* (Indiana UP, 1994).

Paula S. Berggren, professor of English at Baruch College, City University of New York, is author of several essays on English Renaissance drama, including "The Woman's Part: Female Sexuality as Power in Shakespeare's Plays," *The Woman's Part: Feminist Criticism of Shakespeare*; *Teaching with The Norton Anthology of World Masterpieces, Expanded Edition* (1995). She has developed *The Experience of Pilgrimage*, instructional software for the teaching of culturally diverse texts.

Edna Zwick Boris, professor of English at LaGuardia Community College, City University of New York, is on the Belle Zeller Scholarship Trust Fund board of trustees, a member of the SHAKSPER advisory board, and associate editor of *Shakespeare and the Classroom*. She has published on Shakespeare, on the teaching of writing, and on legal writing.

Graham Bradshaw is professor of English at Chuo University, Tokyo, and taught at the University of Saint Andrews, Scotland, for more than twenty years. He is author of *Shakespeare's Scepticism* (Cornell UP, 1987); *Misrepresentations: Shakespeare and the Materialists* (Cornell UP, 1993). He has just completed a book on Ted Hughes and is currently writing, with Tetsuo Kishi, a study of Shakespeare in Japan.

D. Buchanan is professor of theater history and dramatic literature at Dawson College, Montreal. He is author of *And One Classical: A Shakespeare Audition Handbook* (Dawson College P, 1989). He is a working technical director and lighting designer and directs a Shakespeare play each year as a graduating-year major production.

Stephen M. Buhler, associate professor of English at the University of Nebraska, Lincoln, has taught Shakespeare for high school students, university undergraduates, graduate students, and teaching professionals. His essays on early modern texts in performance, in pedagogy, and in popular culture have appeared in such journals as *Cahiers Elisabéthains*, *Extrapolation*, *Post Script*, and *Shakespeare Quarterly*. In 1999 he received the Outstanding Teaching and Instructional Creativity Award from the University of Nebraska. He is the author of *Shakespeare in the Cinema: Ocular Proof* (State U of New York P, 2001).

Dympna Callaghan is William P. Tolley Distinguished Teaching Professor in the Humanities at Syracuse University. Her latest book is *Shakespeare without Women: Representing Race and Gender on the Renaissance Stage* (Routledge, 2000).

Maurice Charney is Distinguished Professor of English, Rutgers University, and a former president of the Shakespeare Association of America. He has written several books on *Hamlet*, including *Style in* Hamlet (Princeton UP, 1969); *Hamlet's Fictions* (Routledge, 1988).

Frank Nicholas Clary, professor of English at Saint Michael's College, Vermont, is a member of the MLA New Variorum *Hamlet* editing team. He is researching the 1965–66 Royal Shakespeare Company production of *Hamlet*. He is author of "'The Very Cunning of the Scene': Hamlet's Divination and the King's Occulted Guilt," *Hamlet Studies* (1996); "Hamlet's Mousetrap and the Play-within-the-Anecdote of Plutarch," *Reading Readings: Essays on Shakespeare Editing in the Eighteenth Century*, ed. Joanna Gondris (Associated UP, 1998); "Hamlet and the Mirror up to History: Allegory, Analogue, and Allusion," with Hardin Aasand, *Hamlet Studies* (1999).

Michael J. Collins is dean of the School for Summer and Continuing Education, Georgetown University, where he also teaches in the Department of English. He has edited or coedited several books, including *Text and Teaching: The Search for Human Excellence* (Georgetown UP, 1991); *Shakespeare's Sweet Thunder: Essays on the Early Comedies* (U of Delaware P, 1997). He has published essays in *Shakespeare Bulletin*, *Critical Survey*, *Shakespeare Quarterly*, *Shakespeare Yearbook*.

Mary S. Comfort teaches composition and literature at Moravian College. She is author of "Bambara's 'Sweet Town,'" *Explicator*; "Liberating Figures in Toni Cade Bambara's *Gorilla, My Love*," *Studies in American Humor*; an essay on Paulo Freire and Bambara's "The Lesson" in *Representations of Education in Literature* (Mellen, 2000). Her biographical-critical essays on Mary Delaney, Mary Wortley Montague, Hester Piozzi, Hannah Glasse, and Jane Adams appear in *The Encyclopedia of British Women Writers*.

H. R. Coursen's recent books on Shakespeare include *Shakespearean Performance as Interpretation, Watching Shakespeare on Television, Reading Shakespeare on Stage, Shakespeare in Production: Whose History?, Shakespeare: The Two Traditions*, and Greenwood Guides on *Macbeth* and *The Tempest*. He is coeditor and founder of *Shakespeare and the Classroom*.

Anthony DiMatteo, professor of English at the New York Institute of Technology, has translated Natale Conti's *Mythologies* (Garland, 1994) and written articles on Shakespeare, Spenser, and poststructural approaches to teaching writing. He is writing a book of poetry; a novel; and a study of Orpheus and natural law in More, Camões, Spenser, and Shakespeare.

John Drakakis is professor of English studies at the University of Stirling, where he teaches Shakespeare, Renaissance literature, and critical theory. He has edited *Alternative Shakespeares* (1985), *Shakespearean Tragedy* (1992), the Macmillan New Casebook volume on *Antony and Cleopatra* (1996), and he is general editor of the Routledge English Texts series and the New Critical Idiom series. He is editing *The Merchant of Venice* for the Arden 3 series.

Mary Judith Dunbar is associate professor of English at Santa Clara University. She has published essays in *Shakespeare Quarterly*, *Theater Journal*, and *Shakespeare: Man of the Theatre*. Her book on *Winter's Tale* in performance will be published by Manchester UP.

Ann W. Engar teaches in the Honors Program at the University of Utah. She has contributed to several collections, including volumes of *Dictionary of Literary Biography*, *Britain in the Hanoverian Age, 1714–1837* (Garland, 1997), and *Utah History Encyclopedia*.

Nona Paula Fienberg is professor of English and chair of the English department at Keene State College, New Hampshire. Her work on Shakespeare, teaching Shakespeare, teaching Judith Shakespeare, Sir Philip Sidney, Margery Kempe, and Mary Wroth appears in *PMLA*, *Modern Philology*, *Shakespeare Quarterly*, *SEL*, and collections. She has written on professional issues for the *ADE Bulletin* and *Profession*.

Joanne E. Gates is professor in the English department at Jacksonville State University. She teaches Shakespeare and Renaissance drama and specializes in women's literature and computer-assisted composition. She is author of *Elizabeth Robins, 1862–1952: Actress, Novelist, Feminist* (U of Alabama P, 1994); editor of *Votes for Women*, by Elizabeth Robins, in *Modern Drama by Women, 1890–1920: An International Anthology*, ed. Katherine Kelly (Routledge, 1996); and coeditor with Victoria Joan Moessner of *The Alaska-Klondike Diary of Elizabeth Robins, 1900* (U of Alaska P, 1999).

David George is professor of English at Urbana University. He is editor of *Shakespeare's First Playhouse* (1981) and *Records of Early English Drama: Lancashire* (1991). He is coeditor for the MLA New Variorum edition of *Coriolanus*.

Christine Mack Gordon is an academic adviser and occasional instructor at the University of Minnesota and works with local theater companies as a dramaturge. She has recently worked on productions of *Twelfth Night*, *The Taming of the Shrew*, *Titus Andronicus*, and *The Two Gentlemen of Verona*.

David G. Hale is professor of English at the State University of New York, Brockport. He is author of *The Body Politic* (1971) and articles on medieval and Renaissance literature in *Shakespeare Quarterly*, *Shakespeare and the Classroom*, and *Shakespeare Yearbook*.

Barbara Hodgdon is Ellis and Nelle Levitt Professor Emeritus of English at Drake University. She is author of *The End Crowns All: Closure and Contradiction in Shakespeare's History* (Princeton UP, 1991); *Henry IV, Part 2*, in the Shakespeare in Performance series (Manchester UP, 1996); *The First Part of King Henry the Fourth: Texts and Contexts* (Bedford–St. Martin's, 1997); *The Shakespeare Trade: Performances and Appropriations* (U of Pennsylvania P, 1998). She is editor of the Arden 3 *Taming of the Shrew*.

Lisa Hopkins is senior lecturer in English at Sheffield Hallam University. She is author of *John Ford's Political Theatre* (Manchester UP, 1994), *The Shakespearean Marriage: Merry Wives and Heavy Husbands* (Macmillan, 1998), *Christopher Marlowe: A Literary Life* (Macmillan, 2000), and several notes and essays in *Hamlet Studies*. She is editor of *Early Modern Literary Studies*.

T. H. Howard-Hill, formerly C. Wallace Martin Professor of English at the University of South Carolina but now emeritus, is editor of *Papers of the Bibliographical Society of America*. His Shakespearean publications include the *Oxford Old-Spelling Shakespeare Concordances* (1969–73), book chapters on *Othello* and *Romeo and Juliet*, and articles on the text of *King Lear*.

Arthur Kincaid has taught and directed Shakespeare in universities of England, Germany, Portugal, Canada, the United States, and Estonia, where he is professor of English at the Humanitaarinstituut. A professional actor and director, he spent years performing Shakespeare and giving workshops internationally. He has written on Tudor history writing, Shakespeare in education, and nineteenth-century poetry and theater history. His edition of Sir George Buck's *History of King Richard III* appeared in 1979.

Arthur F. Kinney is Thomas W. Copeland Professor of Literary History; director of the Massachusetts Center for Renaissance Studies at the University of Massachusetts, Amherst; and adjunct professor of English at New York University. He is editor of the Blackwell anthology *Renaissance Drama* (1999) and author of *"Lies like Truth": Shakespeare,* Macbeth, *and the Cultural Moment* (2001).

Rob Kirkpatrick is a doctoral candidate at the State University of New York, Binghamton. His interests include Shakespearean film and twentieth-century American road narratives. He works as a book editor and freelance writer.

Bernice W. Kliman, professor of English emeritus at Nassau Community College, coordinates the group working on the New Variorum *Hamlet* project, funded by the NEH. She led a project to foster active learning across the disciplines at NCC funded by the Fund for the Improvement of Postsecondary Education. Her scholarly work is on Shakespeare in performance, especially film, and on editing and the history of editing.

Joan Hutton Landis is chair of the Department of Liberal Arts and professor of English at the Curtis Institute of Music. She has worked extensively in the theater and published poetry in such journals as *Transatlantic Review* and *Parnassus*. Her criticism and interviews have appeared in *Midway, Salmagundi, Hamlet Studies, Shakespeare Quarterly*, and *Upstart Crow*. She is working on a book of poems.

Julia Reinhard Lupton is associate professor of English and comparative literature at the University of California, Irvine. She is coauthor with Kenneth Reinhard of *After Oedipus: Shakespeare in Psychoanalysis* and author of *Afterlives of the Saints: Hagiography, Typology, and Renaissance Literature*. She is founding director of Humanities Out There, an outreach program between Irvine's School of Humanities and local schools.

Laurie E. Maguire is university lecturer and tutorial fellow at Magdalen College, Oxford. She is author of *Shakespearean Suspect Texts* (Cambridge UP, 1996); coeditor of *Textual Formations and Reformations* (U of Delaware P, 1998); and has written many articles on feminist, textual, and theatrical issues.

Margaret Maurer is professor of English at Colgate University, where she regularly teaches a course in Shakespeare. She has published essays on Shakespeare's plays and on the court poetry of John Donne, Ben Jonson, and others. She has been a resident scholar at the Teaching Institute of the Folger Shakespeare Library.

Denise M. Mullins teaches at the Hebrew Academy of Long Beach. When time allows, she works on the restoration of her century-old farmhouse in Baiting Hollow, volunteers at the Pearl Theatre in New York, or attends classes on topics ranging from Latin to Gaelic.

Ralph Nazareth is associate professor of English at Nassau Community College. He has published his poetry in *Christianity and Literature* and *Connecticut River Review*. He received two NEH Summer Fellowships at Yale in 1991 and 1995 and a grant for poets from the Connecticut Commission on the Arts in 1996. He is the managing editor of Yuganta Press, Stamford, CT.

Nina daVinci Nichols, professor of English and drama at Rutgers University, regularly teaches Shakespeare. She has written literary criticism, novels, plays, and play adaptations; has translated and produced classic twentieth-century drama; and serves as literary adviser and dramaturge to a professional theater company in New York.

Ellen J. O'Brien is resident voice and text consultant for the Shakespeare Theatre of Washington, DC, where she also teaches voice, text, and speech for the Academy for Classical Acting. She has worked on Shakespeare productions for the North Carolina Shakespeare Festival, the People's Light and Theater Company, and Shakespeare Santa Cruz. Her essays on Shakespeare have appeared in *Shakespeare Quarterly* and *Shakespeare Survey*. She is writing a book on Shakespeare's language for actors, directors, and voice coaches.

Marion D. Perret, professor of English at Manhattanville College, teaches Shakespeare and a wide variety of courses. She has published articles in *Review of English Literature, American Literature, SEL, Shakespeare Studies*, and *Shakespeare on Film Newsletter*. She writes poetry and explores Shakespeare on film and in comic books.

Meta Plotnik is professor of English at Nassau Community College. Her main literary interests are women's studies and Victorian literature. She is writing a literary history of conversations between men and women, with special emphasis on Shakespeare and on the English novel.

Robert H. Ray is professor of English at Baylor University. He is editor of *Approaches to Teaching Shakespeare's* King Lear (MLA, 1986) and the author of "Ben Jonson and the Metaphysical Poets: Continuity in a Survey Course," *Approaches to Teaching the Metaphysical Poets*, ed. Sidney Gottlieb (MLA, 1990). He is compiler and editor of *The Herbert Allusion Book*, author of *John Donne Companion, George Herbert Companion*, and *An Andrew Marvell Companion*.

Terry Reilly is associate professor of English specializing in Shakespeare and Renaissance studies at the University of Alaska, Fairbanks. His primary teaching and research interests are interrelations among Shakespeare, Renaissance literature, and English law. He has published articles on Shakespeare, Goethe, Joyce, Pynchon, Doris Lessing, and the literature of the French Revolution.

Edward L. Rocklin, professor of English at California State Polytechnic University, Pomona, has published articles in *Shakespeare Quarterly, Journal of Dramatic Theory and Criticism*, and *College English*. He is author of "Performance Is More Than an 'Approach' to Shakespeare," *Teaching Shakespeare through Performance*, ed. Milla Cozart Riggio (MLA, 1999). He is working on a book entitled "Measured Designs, Redesigned Measures: Exploring the Texts, Promptbooks, and Performance Editions of *Measure for Measure*."

Kenneth S. Rothwell, professor emeritus of English at the University of Vermont, is compiler, with Annabelle H. Melzer, of *Shakespeare on Screen: An International Filmography and Videography* (Neal-Schuman, 1990) and the author of *A History of Shakespeare on Screen: A Century of Film and Television* (Cambridge UP, 1999).

Maria M. Scott is associate professor of English at Randolph-Macon College. Her specialty is Renaissance and dramatic literature, and she has designed a number of classes around Shakespeare and performance. She is working on a study of literary, dramatic, and multimedia representations of "Jane" Shore.

Michael W. Shurgot teaches writing and literature courses at South Puget Sound Community College. He is author of essays on Shakespeare and medieval drama in performance and contributes theater reviews to *Shakespeare Bulletin*. He is author of *Stages of Play: Shakespeare's Theatrical Energies in Elizabethan Performance* (U of Delaware P, 1998).

Mike Sirofchuck is chair of the Kodiak High School Language Arts Department and an adjunct faculty member of Kodiak College. He teaches writing and literature.

Eric Sterling is associate professor of English at Auburn University, Montgomery. He is author of *The Movement towards Subversion: The English History Play from Skelton to Shakespeare* and articles on Shakespeare, Spenser, Jonson, and Martha Moulsworth.

Nathaniel Strout is associate professor of English at Hamilton College, where he chairs the department and teaches courses in Shakespeare and the literature of his contemporaries. He has published articles on Jonson's poems and court masques and on Ford's *'Tis Pity She's a Whore*. His article on *As You Like It* and mutuality will appear in 2001.

Jesús Tronch-Pérez is tenured lecturer at the University of Valencia and member of the Instituto Shakespeare. His main interest has been the texts of *Hamlet*. He has published a book on the First Quarto *Hamlet* and is completing an annotated critical-synoptic edition of the Second Quarto and First Folio versions of the play.

Bente Videbaek was born in Denmark and graduated from the University of Copenhagen and Northwestern University. She teaches at the State University of New York, Stony Brook, and Suffolk Community College. She is author of *The Stage Clown in Shakespeare's Theater* (Greenwood, 1996) and is working on another book about Shakespeare.

Paul J. Voss, associate professor of English at Georgia State University, teaches a wide variety of English Renaissance literature courses. He is the author of *Elizabethan News Pamphlets: Marlowe, Shakespeare, Spenser, and the Birth of Journalism* (Duquesne UP, 2001) and has published on Thomas More, Milton, Elizabethan poetry, and the sixteenth-century book trade.

George T. Wright, Regents Professor of English Emeritus at the University of Minnesota, is author of *Shakespeare's Metrical Art*, "Hendiadys and *Hamlet*," "The Lyric Present: Simple Present Verbs in English Poetry," and other essays on Shakespeare and modern poetry. He is author of *Aimless Life: Poems, 1961–1995*.

Alan R. Young is professor emeritus at Acadia University, where he teaches Internet courses on Shakespeare. He has published articles and reviews in *Emblematica, History Today, Journal of English and Germanic Philology, Renaissance and Reformation, Shakespeare Quarterly, Studies in English Literature, Theatre Notebook,* and *University of Toronto Quarterly*. He is author of *Tudor and Jacobean Tournaments* (1987), *His Majesty's Royal Ship: A Critical Edition of Thomas Heywood's* A True Description (1990), *Emblematic Flag Devices of the English Civil Wars, 1642–1660* (1995), and *Henry Peacham's Manuscript Emblem Books* (1998).

Bruce W. Young, associate professor of English at Brigham Young University, specializes in Shakespeare and English Renaissance literature. His Shakespearean interests are performance (he served as dramaturge for a production of *The Winter's Tale*), early modern social history, and the plays' ethical dimensions. His essays on *King Lear* and *The Winter's Tale* appeared in previous volumes of the MLA series Approaches to Teaching World Literature.

Michael W. Young teaches in the Department of English at La Roche College. He has published articles on teaching Shakespeare, composition, and creative writing. He edited Maynard Mack's *Everybody's Shakespeare* (1992). He is a published poet; short story writer; and critic on American, British, and Canadian literatures.

Luo Zhiye has taught at Jiangxi University, Jiaxin Normal College, Hang Zhou University, and Nanchang University, where he was professor in the Department of American Culture and Linguistics. From 1960 to 1980 he labored in the mountains. He is author of "Again on *Hamlet*," *Journal of Nanchang University* (1996); "Shakespeare on Stage Arts," *Journal of Shanghai Theatre Academy* (1994). He is currently at Pui Ching Commercial College.

SURVEY PARTICIPANTS

The following Shakespeare instructors generously responded to the survey on teaching *Hamlet* that preceded preparation of this volume. Without the invaluable information and insights they provided the book would not have been possible.

Hardin L. Aasand, *Dickinson State University*
Randall Anderson, *Lawrence University*
James R. Andreas Sr., *Clemson University*
Catherine Belling, *State University of New York, Stony Brook*
Arthur Asa Berger, *San Francisco State University*
Paula S. Berggren, *Baruch College, City University of New York*
Edna Zwick Boris, *LaGuardia Community College, NY*
Graham Bradshaw, *Chuo University, Tokyo*
D. Buchanan, *Dawson College*
Stephen M. Buhler, *University of Nebraska, Lincoln*
Maurice Charney, *Rutgers University*
Frank Nicholas Clary, *Saint Michael's College*
Michael J. Collins, *Georgetown University*
Mary S. Comfort, *Moravian College*
H. R. Coursen, *University of Maine, Augusta*
Terry Craig, *West Virginia Northern Community College*
Scott Crozier, *Saint Michael's Grammar School, Melbourne*
Peter Cummings, *Hobart and William Smith Colleges*
Deborah T. Curren-Aquino, *Folger Shakespeare Library*
Anthony DiMatteo, *New York Institute of Technology*
Steven Doloff, *Pratt Institute*
John Drakakis, *Sterling University*
Mary Judith Dunbar, *Santa Clara University*
Ann W. Engar, *University of Utah*
Nona Paula Fienberg, *Keene State College*
Robert F. Fleissner, *Central State University, Ohio*
Donald W. Foster, *Vassar College*
Ruben Friedman, *Westbury High School, NY*
Joanne E. Gates, *Jacksonville State University*
David George, *Urbana University*
Christine Mack Gordon, *University of Minnesota*
Susan Blair Green, *Mary Baldwin College*
David G. Hale, *State University of New York, Brockport*
Jamey Hecht, *Castleton State College*
James Hirsh, *Georgia State University*
Barbara Hodgdon, *Drake University*
Lisa Hopkins, *Sheffield Hallam University*
T. H. Howard-Hill, *University of South Carolina*
Kathy Howlett, *Northeastern University*

David Kastan, *Columbia University*
Yoshiko Kawachi, *Kyorin University, Tokyo*
Arthur Kincaid, *Eesti Humanitaarinstituut, Estonia*
Arthur F. Kinney, *University of Massachusetts, Amherst*
Rob Kirkpatrick, *State University of New York, Binghamton*
Ian Lancashire, *University of Toronto*
Joan Hutton Landis, *Curtis Institute of Music*
Alexander Leggatt, *University of Toronto*
Michael LoMonico, *Farmingdale High School, NY*
Anthony Low, *New York University*
Laurie E. Maguire, *Magdalen College, Oxford University*
Margaret Maurer, *Colgate University*
Jo McMurtry, *University of Richmond*
Michael Mullin, *University of Illinois, Urbana*
Nina daVinci Nichols, *Rutgers University*
Elizabeth Oakes, *Western Kentucky University*
Ellen J. O'Brien, *Shakespeare Theatre, Washington, DC*
Christopher Patterson, *Iona College*
Marion D. Perret, *Manhattanville College*
Eric Rasmussen, *University of Nevada, Reno*
Robert H. Ray, *Baylor University*
Terry Reilly, *University of Alaska, Fairbanks*
Edward L. Rocklin, *California State Polytechnic University, Pomona*
Peter Saccio, *Dartmouth College*
Patricia P. Salomon, *University of Findlay*
Maria M. Scott, *Randolph-Macon College*
Michael W. Shurgot, *South Puget Sound Community College, WA*
Judy Kesig Sieg, *Spartanburg Technical College, SC*
Mike Sirofchuck, *Kodiak High School, AK*
Eric Sterling, *Auburn University*
Nathaniel Strout, *Hamilton College*
Bente Videbaek, *State University of New York, Stony Brook;*
    Suffolk Community College, NY
Paul J. Voss, *Georgia State University*
James Michael Welsh, *Salisbury State University*
Robert F. Willson Jr., *University of Missouri, Kansas City*
Douglas E. Wilson, *Anniston, AL*
Patricia B. Worrall, *Gainesville College*
George T. Wright, *University of Minnesota*
Alan R. Young, *Acadia University*
Bruce W. Young, *Brigham Young University*
Michael W. Young, *Robert Morris College*
Luo Zhiye, *Pui Ching Commercial College, China*

WORKS CITED AND
MATERIALS FOR FURTHER STUDY

Editions

Single-Play Editions

Andrews, John F., ed. *Hamlet*. By William Shakespeare. Everyman. London: Dent, 1993.

Barnet, Sylvan, ed. The Tragedy of Hamlet, Prince of Denmark [by William Shakespeare], *with New and Updated Critical Essays and a Revised Bibliography*. Signet Classic Shakespeare. 3rd ed. New York: Signet, 1998.

Bertram, Paul, and Bernice W. Kliman, eds. *The Three-Text* Hamlet: *Parallel Texts of the First and Second Quartos and First Folio*. New York: AMS, 1991.

Bevington, David, ed. *Hamlet*. By William Shakespeare. New York: Bantam, 1988.

Edwards, Philip, ed. *Hamlet, Prince of Denmark*. By William Shakespeare. New Cambridge Shakespeare. Cambridge: Cambridge UP, 1985.

Farnham, Willard, ed. *Hamlet Prince of Denmark*. By William Shakespeare. 1957. Pelican Shakespeare. Gen. ed. Alfred Harbage. Middlesex: Penguin, 1984.

Furness, Horace Howard, ed. Hamlet: *A New Variorum Edition of Shakespeare*. 2 vols. Philadelphia: Lippincott, 1877.

Greg, W. W., ed. Hamlet: *First Quarto*. By William Shakespeare. Introd. Greg. Shakespeare Quarto Facsims. 7. Oxford: Clarendon, n.d.

——, ed. Hamlet: *Second Quarto*. By William Shakespeare. Introd. Greg. Shakespeare Quarto Facsims. 4. London: Sidgwick, 1940.

Hapgood, Robert, ed. *Hamlet Prince of Denmark*. Shakespeare in Production. Text ed. Philip Edwards. Cambridge: Cambridge UP, 1999.

Hibbard, G. R., ed. *Hamlet*. Oxford Shakespeare. Oxford: Oxford UP, 1987.

Hoy, Cyrus, ed. *William Shakespeare*: Hamlet: *An Authoritative Text, Intellectual Backgrounds, Extracts from the Sources, Essays in Criticism*. Norton Critical Ed. New York: Norton, 1963.

Hubler, Edward, ed. The Tragedy of Hamlet, Prince of Denmark [by William Shakespeare], *with New Dramatic Criticism and an Updated Bibliography*. Signet Classic Shakespeare. 2nd ed. New York: Signet, 1987.

Irace, Kathleen, ed. *The First Quarto of* Hamlet. New York: Cambridge UP, 1998.

Jenkins, Harold, ed. *Hamlet*. By William Shakespeare. Arden Ed. London: Methuen, 1982.

Jennens, Charles, ed. Hamlet, Prince of Denmark. *A Tragedy. By William Shakespeare. Collated with the Old and Modern Editions*. London, 1773.

Kittredge, George Lyman, ed. *The Tragedy of Hamlet Prince of Denmark*. By William Shakespeare. Boston: Ginn, 1939.

——, ed. *The Tragedy of Hamlet Prince of Denmark*. By William Shakespeare. Rev. Irving Ribner. Waltham: Blaisdell, 1967.

Kliman, Bernice W., ed. *The Enfolded* Hamlet. Spec. issue of *Shakespeare Newsletter* Apr. 1996: 1–44. 26 Feb. 2001 <http://www.global-language.com/enfolded.html>.

Kliman, Bernice W., Eric Rasmussen, Frank Nicholas Clary, and Hardin Aasand, eds. Hamlet. *A New Variorum Edition of Shakespeare*. New York: MLA, forthcoming.

Mowat, Barbara A., and Paul Werstine, eds. *Hamlet*. By William Shakespeare. New Folger Lib. New York: Washington Square, 1992.

Spencer, T. J. B., ed. *Hamlet*. By William Shakespeare. Harmondsworth: Penguin, 1980.

Weller, Shane. *Hamlet*. By William Shakespeare. Dover Thrift Eds. Toronto: Dover, 1992.

Wilson, John Dover, ed. *Hamlet*. New Shakespeare. 2nd ed. Cambridge: Cambridge UP, 1936.

Wofford, Susanne L., ed. Hamlet: *Case Studies in Contemporary Criticism*. New York: Bedford–St. Martin's, 1994.

Complete Works

Allen, Michael J. B., and Kenneth Muir, eds. *Shakespeare's Plays in Quarto*. Berkeley: U of California P, 1981.

Barnet, Sylvan, ed. *The Complete Signet Classic Shakespeare*. New York: Harcourt, 1972.

Bevington, David, ed. *The Complete Works of Shakespeare*. Updated 4th ed. New York: Longman, 1997.

Clark, William George, John Glover, and William Aldis Wright, eds. *The Works of Shakespeare*. London: Macmillan, 1863–66.

Evans, G. Blakemore, et al., eds. *The Riverside Shakespeare*. 1974. 2nd ed. Boston: Houghton, 1997.

Greenblatt, Stephen, et al., eds. *The Norton Shakespeare: Based on the Oxford Edition*. New York: Norton, 1997.

Hinman, Charlton, ed. *The Norton Facsimile: The First Folio of Shakespeare*. London: Hamlyn, 1968. 2nd ed. Introd. Peter W. M. Blayney. New York: Norton, 1996.

Kittredge, George Lyman, ed. *The Complete Works of Shakespeare*. Boston: Ginn, 1936.

Kökeritz, Helge, ed. *Mr. William Shakespeares Comedies, Histories, and Tragedies*. New Haven: Yale UP, 1954.

Ribner, Irving, and George Lyman Kittredge, eds. *The Complete Works of Shakespeare*. Lexington: Xerox, 1971.

Wells, Stanley W., and Gary Taylor, eds. *The Complete Oxford Shakespeare*. Oxford: Clarendon; New York: Oxford, 1986.

Anthologies

Bain, Carl E., ed. *Norton Introduction to Literature: Drama*. New York: Norton, 1973.

Barnet, Sylvan, et al., eds. *An Introduction to Literature: Fiction, Poetry, Drama.* 11th ed. New York: Longman, 1997.

Bevington, David, et al., eds. *Four Tragedies:* Hamlet, Othello, King Lear, Macbeth. By William Shakespeare. New York: Bantam, 1988.

Charters, Ann, and Samuel Charters, eds. *Literature and Its Writers: An Introduction to Fiction, Poetry, and Drama.* Boston: Bedford, 1997.

Coldewey, John C., and W. R. Streitberger, eds. *Drama: Classical to Contemporary.* Upper Saddle River: Prentice, 1998.

Davis, Paul, et al., eds. *Western Literature in a World Context.* 2 vols. New York: St. Martin's, 1995.

Guth, Hans P., and Gabriele L. Rico, eds. *Discovering Literature.* Compact ed. Upper Saddle River: Prentice, 2000.

———, eds. *Discovering Literature: Stories, Poems, Plays.* 2nd ed. Upper Saddle River: Prentice, 1997.

Hunt, Douglas, ed. *The Riverside Anthology of Literature.* Boston: Houghton, 1988.

Jacobus, Lee A., ed. *Literature: An Introduction to Critical Reading.* Upper Saddle River: Prentice, 1996.

———, ed. *Literature: An Introduction to Critical Thinking.* Upper Saddle River: Prentice, 1996.

Mack, Maynard, ed. *Norton Anthology of World Masterpieces.* 6th ed. 2 vols. New York: Norton, 1992.

Mack, Maynard, et al., eds. *Norton Anthology of World Masterpieces.* Expanded ed. 6th ed. 2 vols. New York: Norton, 1995.

———, eds. *Norton Anthology of World Masterpieces.* Expanded ed. in 1 vol. New York: Norton, 1997.

Meyer, Michael, ed. *The Bedford Introduction to Literature: Reading, Thinking, Writing.* 5th ed. Boston: St. Martin's, 1999.

Roberts, Edgar V., and Henry E. Jacobs, eds. *Literature: An Introduction to Reading and Writing.* 5th ed. Upper Saddle River: Prentice, 1998.

———, eds. *Literature: An Introduction to Reading and Writing.* Compact ed. Upper Saddle River: Prentice, 1998.

Worthen, W. B., ed. *Harcourt Brace Anthology of Drama.* 3rd ed. Fort Worth: Harcourt, 2000.

References and Guides

Abbott, E[dwin] A. *A Shakespearian Grammar: An Attempt to Illustrate Some of the Differences between Elizabethan and Modern English.* 1870. 2nd ed. New York: Dover, 1966.

Allen, J. W. *A History of Political Thought in the Sixteenth Century.* London: Methuen, 1928.

Andrews, John F., ed. *William Shakespeare: His World, His Work, His Influence.* 3 vols. New York: Scribner's, 1985.

Aquinas, Thomas. *Summa Theologica*. Vol. 1. New York: Benziger, 1947.

Aristotle. *Poetics*. Trans. W. Hamilton Fyfe. Loeb Classical. Lib. Cambridge: Harvard UP, 1927.

Armstrong, Katherine, and Graham Atkin. *Studying Shakespeare: A Practical Guide*. London: Prentice, 1998.

Asimov, Isaac. "Hamlet." *Asimov's Guide to Shakespeare*. Illus. Rafael Palacios. 1970. New York: Avenel, 1978. 77–147.

Bacon, Francis. "Of Revenge." *The Essays*. By Bacon. Ed. John Pitcher. New York: Penguin, 1985. 72–73.

Bakhtin, Mikhail. *Rabelais and His World*. Trans. Helene Iswolsky. Cambridge: MIT P, 1968.

Bentley, Gerald Eades. *The Profession of Dramatist in Shakespeare's Time, 1590–1642*. Princeton: Princeton UP, 1971.

Bergeron, David M., and Geraldo U. De Sousa. *Shakespeare: A Study and Research Guide*. 3rd ed. Lawrence: UP of Kansas, 1995.

Blayney, Peter W. M. Introduction. *The First Folio of Shakespeare*. Washington: Folger Lib., 1991.

Bocchi, Achille. *Symbolicarum Quaestionum de Universo Genere*. Bologna, 1574. New York: Garland, 1979.

Boyce, Charles. *Shakespeare A to Z: The Essential Reference to His Plays, His Poems, His Life and Times, and More*. New York: Facts on File, 1990. Rpt. as *The Wordsworth Dictionary of Shakespeare*. Fwd. Terry Hands. Ware: Wordsworth, 1996.

Bradford, John. *Godly Meditations on the Lord's Prayer, Belief, and Ten Commandments, with Other Exercise*. 1562. *The Writings of John Bradford, M.A.* Vol. 1. Ed. Aubrey Townsend. Cambridge: Cambridge UP, 1848. 113–220. 2 vols.

Breuer, Josef, and Sigmund Freud. *Studies in Hysteria*. Trans. A. A. Brill. New York: Nervous and Mental Disease, 1936.

Bullough, Geoffrey, ed. *Major Tragedies:* Hamlet, Othello, King Lear, Macbeth. London: Routledge, 1973. Vol. 7 of *Narrative and Dramatic Sources* of Shakespeare.

Campbell, Oscar James, and Edward G. Quinn, eds. *The Reader's Encyclopedia of Shakespeare*. New York: Crowell, 1966.

Chambers, E. K. *The Elizabethan Stage*. 4 vols. Oxford: Clarendon, 1923.

Champion, Larry S. *The Essential Shakespeare: An Annotated Bibliography of Major Modern Studies*. New York: Hall; Toronto: Maxwell Macmillan Canada, 1993.

Conklin, Paul S. *A History of* Hamlet *Criticism, 1601–1821*. New York: Humanities, 1957.

Corum, Richard, ed. *Understanding* Hamlet: *A Student Casebook to Issues, Sources, and Historical Documents*. Westport: Greenwood, 1998.

Coye, Dale F. *Pronouncing Shakespeare's Words: A Guide from A to Zounds*. Westport: Greenwood, 1998.

Daniell, David. *Shakespeare: A Bibliographic Guide*. Oxford: Clarendon, 1990.

DiMatteo, Anthony, trans. *Natale Conti's Mythologies: A Select Translation*. New York: Garland, 1994.

Donne, John. *An Anatomy of the World. The First Anniversary*. London, 1611.

Elyot, Thomas. *The Book Named the Governor*. New York: Dutton, 1962.

Emerson, Ralph Waldo. "Montaigne; or, The Skeptic." 1850. *Ralph Waldo Emerson*. Ed. Richard Poirier. Oxford Authors. Oxford: Oxford UP, 1990. 312–28.

Ferguson, Margaret W., Maureen Quilligan, and Nancy J. Vickers, eds. *Rewriting the Renaissance: The Discourses of Sexual Difference in Early Modern Europe*. Chicago: U of Chicago P, 1986.

Figgis, John Neville. *Studies of Political Thought from Gerson to Grotius, 1414–1625*. Cambridge: Cambridge UP, 1931.

Freud, Sigmund. *The Freud Reader*. Ed. Peter Gay. New York: Norton, 1989.

———. *The Interpretation of Dreams*. 1900. Trans. and ed. James Strachey. New York: Avon, 1965.

———. *The Standard Edition of the Complete Psychological Works*. Trans. James Strachey. 24 vols. London: Hogarth, 1953–74.

Fromm, Erich. *Escape from Freedom*. New York: Rinehart, 1941.

———. *Man for Himself*. New York: Rinehart, 1947.

———. *The Sane Society*. New York: Fawcett, 1955.

Gataker, Thomas. *A Good Wife Gods Gift*. 1623.

Gates, Henry Louis, Jr. "Criticism in the Jungle." *Black Literature and Literary Theory*. Ed. Gates. London: Routledge, 1990. 1–24.

———. *The Signifying Monkey: A Theory of Afro-American Literary Criticism*. New York: Oxford UP, 1988.

Goffman, Erving. *Frame Analysis: An Essay on the Organization of Experience*. Cambridge: Harvard UP, 1974.

Golding, Arthur. *Metamorphoses: The Arthur Golding Translation*. 1567. Ed. John Frederick Nims. New York: Macmillan, 1965.

Green, L. C., and Olive Dickason. *The Law of Nations and the New World*. Edmonton: U of Alberta P, 1989.

Hadfield, Andrew. *Literature, Politics and National Identity: Reformation to Renaissance*. Cambridge: Cambridge UP, 1994.

Harbage, Alfred. *Shakespeare and the Rival Traditions*. 1952. New York: Barnes, 1968.

Hoeniger, F. David. *Medicine and Shakespeare in the English Renaissance*. Newark: U of Delaware P, 1992.

Horney, Karen. *Our Inner Conflicts*. New York: Norton, 1945.

Houlbrooke, Ralph A. *The English Family, 1450-1700*. London: Longman, 1984.

———, ed. *English Family Life, 1576–1716: An Anthology from Diaries*. Oxford: Blackwell, 1988.

Hull, Suzanne W. *Chaste, Silent, and Obedient: English Books for Women, 1475–1640*. San Marino: Huntington Lib., 1982.

Jung, C. G. *The Structure and Dynamics of the Psyche*. New York: Bolingen, 1960.

———. *Symbols of Transformation*. New York: Bolingen, 1956.

———. *Two Essays on Analytical Psychology*. New York: Bolingen, 1953.

Kantorowicz, Ernst. *The King's Two Bodies: A Study in Mediaeval Political Theology.* Princeton: Princeton UP, 1957.

Kastan, David Scott, ed. *A Companion to Shakespeare.* Oxford: Blackwell, 1999.

Kernan, Alvin. *Shakespeare, the King's Playwright.* New Haven: Yale UP, 1995.

Kyd, Thomas. *The Spanish Tragedy.* 1594. Ed. J. R. Mulryne. New York: Hill, 1970.

Lacan, Jacques. "Desire and the Interpretation of Desire in *Hamlet.*" *Yale French Studies* 55–56 (1977): 11–52.

———. *Feminine Sexuality: Lacan and the Ecole Freudienne.* Ed. Juliet Mitchell and Jacqueline Rose. Trans. Rose. New York: Norton, 1982.

———. "On *Hamlet.*" *Jacques Lacan.* Ed. Jonathan Scott. Twayne World Authors 817. Boston: Twayne, 1990. 108–22.

Laing, R. D. *The Divided Self.* Harmondsworth: Penguin, 1965.

Las Casas, Bartolomé de. *Bartolomé de Las Casas: A Selection of His Writing.* Ed. and trans. George Sanderlin. New York: Columbia UP, 1938.

Levin, Carole. *The Heart and Stomach of a King: Elizabeth I and the Politics of Sex and Power.* Philadelphia: U of Pennsylvania P, 1994.

Macfarlane, Alan. Rev. of *The Family, Sex, and Marriage in England, 1500–1800.* By Lawrence Stone. *History and Theory* 18 (1979): 103–26.

M[arkham], G[ervase]. *A Second Part to the Mothers Blessing; or, A Cure against Misfortunes. Divided into Certaine Principal Receipts, to Cure the Mind of Man.* 1622.

McDonald, Russ, ed. *The Bedford Companion to Shakespeare: An Introduction with Documents.* New York: Bedford–St. Martin's, 1996.

Mitchell-Kernan, Claudia. "Signifying, Loud-Talking, and Marking." *Rappin' and Stylin' Out: Communication in Urban Black America.* Urbana: U of Illinois P, 1973. 315–35.

Mooney, Michael E., ed. Hamlet: *An Annotated Bibliography of Shakespeare Studies, 1604–1998.* Pegasus Shakespeare Bibliogs. Gen. ed. Richard L. Nochimson. Asheville: Pegasus, 1999.

Morrison, Toni. "Unspeakable Things Unspoken: The Afro-American Presence in American Literature." *Michigan Quarterly Review* 28.1 (1989): 1–34.

Mullaney, Steven. *The Place of the Stage: License, Play, and Power in Renaissance England.* Chicago: U of Chicago P, 1988.

Neuman, E. "The Psychological Stages of Feminine Development." *Spring* 18 (1959): 63–97.

Newman, Karen. *Fashioning Femininity and English Renaissance Drama.* Chicago: U of Chicago P, 1991.

Nietzsche, Friedrich. The Birth of Tragedy *and* The Genealogy of Morals. Trans. Francis Golffing. New York: Doubleday, 1956.

The Oxford English Dictionary. 2nd ed. 1989.

Olivier, Laurence. *Confessions of an Actor: An Autobiography.* New York: Simon, 1982.

Onions, Charles Talbut. *A Shakespeare Glossary.* 1911. Enl. and rev. ed. Robert D. Eagleson. Oxford: Clarendon, 1986.

Orwell, George. "Politics and the English Language." *A Collection of Essays*. New York: Harcourt, 1981. 156–71.

Partridge, Eric. *Shakespeare's Bawdy*. 2nd ed. London: Routledge, 1968.

Perkins, William. *Epieikeia; or, A Treatise of Christian Equity and Moderation*. 1604. *The Works of William Perkins*. Ed. Ian Breward. Appleford, Eng.: Sutton Courtenay, 1970. 477–510.

Pinciss, Gerald M., and Roger Lockyer, eds. *Shakespeare's World: Background Readings in the English Renaissance*. New York: Continuum, 1990.

Pollock, Linda, ed. *A Lasting Relationship: Parents and Children over Three Centuries*. London: Fourth Estate, 1987.

Pritchard, Thomas. *The Schoole of Honest and Vertuous Lyfe*. 1579.

Prosser, Eleanor. *Hamlet and Revenge*. 2nd ed. Stanford: Stanford UP, 1971.

Raven, A. A. *A Hamlet Bibliography and Research Guide, 1877–1935*. Chicago: U of Chicago P, 1936.

Richmond, Hugh. *Shakespeare and the Renaissance Stage to 1616, Shakespearean Stage History, 1616 to 1998: An Annotated Bibliography of Shakespeare Studies, 1576–1998*. Pegasus Shakespeare Bibliogs. Gen. ed. Richard L. Nochimson. Asheville: Pegasus, 1999.

Robinson, Randal F. *Hamlet in the 1950's: An Annotated Bibliography*. New York: Garland, 1984.

Rommen, Heinrich. *The Natural Law: A Study in Legal and Social History and Philosophy*. Indianapolis: Liberty Fund, 1998.

Rubenstein, Frankie. *A Dictionary of Shakespeare's Sexual Puns and Their Significance*. London: Macmillan, 1984.

Sandys, George, trans. *Metamorphoses*. By Ovid. Facs. New York: Garland, 1978.

Schmidt, Alexander. *Shakespeare Lexicon and Quotation Dictionary: A Complete Dictionary of All the English Words, Phrases, and Constructions in the Works of the Poet*. 3rd. ed. Ed. Gregor Sarrazin. New York: Dover, 1971.

Schoenbaum, S. *A Compact Documentary Life*. New York: Oxford UP, 1987.

———. *Shakespeare: The Globe and the World*. New York: Folger Shakespeare Lib., Oxford UP, 1979.

———. *Shakespeare's Lives*. Oxford: Clarendon; New York: Oxford UP, 1991.

Scholes, Robert. *Structuralism in Literature*. New Haven: Yale UP, 1974.

Sewall, Richard. "The Tragic Form." *Essays in Criticism* 4 (1954): 345–58.

Shuger, Debora K. *Habits of Thought in the English Renaissance: Religion, Politics, and the Dominant Culture*. Berkeley: U of California P, 1990.

———. *The Renaissance Bible: Scholarship, Sacrifice, and Subjectivity*. Berkeley: U of California P, 1994.

Silver, George. *Paradoxes of Defence [and] Brief Instructions upon My Paradoxes of Defence*. 1599. Introd. John Dover Wilson. Shakespeare Assn. facsim. Oxford: Oxford UP, 1933.

Skinner, Quentin. *Foundations of Modern Political Thought*. 2 vols. Cambridge: Cambridge UP, 1978.

Smith, Henry. *A Preparative to Mariage*. 1591.

Speght, Rachel. "From *A Mouzell for Melastomus.*" 1617. *The Paradise of Women.* Ed. Betty Travitsky. New York: Columbia UP, 1989. 104–07.

Spevack, Marvin. *A Complete and Systematic Concordance to the Works of Shakespeare.* 8 vols. London: Hildesheim, 1968.

——. *The Harvard Concordance to Shakespeare.* Cambridge: Harvard UP, 1973.

Stone, Lawrence. *The Family, Sex, and Marriage in England, 1500–1800.* New York: Harper, 1977.

Theobald, Lewis. *Shakespeare Restored: Specimen of the Many Errors, as Well Committed, as Unamended, by Mr. Pope in His Late Edition of This Poet. Designed Not Only to Correct the Said Edition, but to Restore the True Reading of Shakespeare in All the Editions Ever Yet Publish'd.* 1726. London: Cass, 1971.

Thompson, E. P. "Happy Families." Rev. of *The Family, Sex, and Marriage in England, 1500–1800.* By Lawrence Stone. *New Society* 8 (1977): 499–501.

Three Elizabethan Fencing Manuals. Introd. James L. Jackson. Delmar: Scholars' Facsims and Rpts., 1972.

Tillyard, E. M. W. *The Elizabethan World Picture: A Study of the Idea of Order in the Age of Shakespeare, Donne, and Milton* London: Chatto, 1943.

Tourneur, Cyril. *The Revenger's Tragedy.* Ed. R. A. Foakes. Revels Plays. 1966. Manchester: Manchester UP, 1980.

Trevelyan, George Macaulay. *History of England.* London: Longman, 1926.

Tuck, Richard. *Natural Rights Theories: Their Origin and Development.* Cambridge: Cambridge UP, 1979.

Wells, Stanley, ed. *Shakespeare: Select Bibliographic Guides.* Oxford: Oxford UP, 1973.

Whitney, Geoffrey. *Whitney's Choice of Emblemes: A Facsimile Reprint.* Ed. Henry Green. London: Reeve, 1866.

Williams, Robert A. *The American Indian in Western Legal Thought: The Discourses of Conquest.* New York: Oxford UP, 1990.

Wilson, John Dover. Introduction. Silver v–xx.

——. *The Manuscript of Shakespeare's* Hamlet *and the Problems of Its Transmission.* 2 vols. Cambridge: Cambridge UP, 1963.

Wing, John. *The Crowne Conjugall.* 1620.

Criticism

Adelman, Janet. "Man and Wife Is One Flesh: *Hamlet* and the Confrontation with the Maternal Body." *Suffocating Mothers: Fantasies of Maternal Origin in Shakespeare's Plays,* Hamlet *to* The Tempest. New York: Routledge, 1992. 11–37.

Alexander, Nigel. *Poison, Play and Duel: A Study in* Hamlet. London: Routledge, 1971.

Alexander, Peter. *Hamlet, Father and Son.* Oxford: Clarendon, 1955.

Altman, Joel. *The Tudor Play of Mind: Rhetorical Inquiry and the Development of Elizabethan Drama.* Berkeley: U of California P, 1978.

Andreas, James R. "The Vulgar and the Polite: Dialogue in *Hamlet.*" *Hamlet Studies* 15 (1993): 8–22.

Armstrong, Philip. "Watching Hamlet Watching: Lacan, Shakespeare and the Mirror/ Stage." Hawkes, *Shakespeares* 216–61.

Ashton, Geoffrey. *The Collector's Shakespeare*. New York: Crescent, 1990.

Babcock, Weston. Hamlet: *A Tragedy of Errors*. Purdue: Purdue U Studies, 1961.

Barber, C. L. *Shakespeare's Festive Comedy: A Study of Dramatic Form and Its Relation to Social Custom*. Cleveland: Meridian, 1963.

Barber, Frances. "Ophelia in *Hamlet*." *Players of Shakespeare 2*. Ed. Russell Jackson and Robert Smallwood. Cambridge: Cambridge UP, 1988. 137–50.

Barker, Deborah, and Ivo Kamps, eds. *Shakespeare and Gender: A History*. London: Verso, 1995.

Barker, Francis. "Which Dead? *Hamlet* and the Ends of History." *Uses of History: Marxism, Postmodernism and the Renaissance*. Ed. Barker, Peter Hulme, and Margaret Iversen. Manchester: Manchester UP, 1991. 47–75.

Bate, Jonathan. *Shakespeare and Ovid*. Oxford: Oxford UP, 1993.

Battenhouse, Roy. "The Ghost in *Hamlet*." *Studies in Philology* 48 (1951): 161–92.

———. "Hamlet's Apostrophe on Man." *PMLA* 66 (1951): 1073–113.

———. *Shakespearean Tragedy: Its Art and Its Christian Premises*. Bloomington: Indiana UP, 1969.

Beckerman, Bernard. *Dynamics of Drama: Theory and Method of Analysis*. New York: Drama Book Specialists, 1979.

———. *Shakespeare at the Globe, 1599–1609*. New York: Macmillan, 1962.

Belsey, Catherine. *Subject of Tragedy: Identity and Difference in Renaissance Drama*. London: Methuen, 1985.

Bertram, Joseph. *Conscience and the King: A Study of* Hamlet. London: Chatto, 1953.

Bevington, David. *Action Is Eloquence: Shakespeare's Language of Gesture*: Cambridge: Harvard UP, 1984.

———, ed. *Twentieth-Century Interpretations of* Hamlet: *A Collection of Critical Essays*. Englewood Cliffs: Prentice, 1968.

Bloom, Harold. *Shakespeare: The Invention of the Human*. New York: Riverhead, 1998.

———, ed. *William Shakespeare's* Hamlet. New York: Chelsea, 1996.

Booth, Stephen. "The Coherence of *Henry IV, Part I* and *Hamlet*." *Shakespeare Set Free*. Ed. Peggy O'Brien et al. New York: Washington Square, 1994. 32–46.

———. "On the Value of *Hamlet*." *Reinterpretations of Elizabethan Drama*. Ed. Norman Rabkin. New York: Columbia UP, 1969. 137–76.

Bradbrook, Muriel. "The Inheritance of Christopher Marlowe." *Theology* 47 (1964): 298–305.

———. *Shakespeare: The Poet in His World*. New York: Columbia UP, 1978.

Bradley, A. C. *Shakespearean Tragedy:* Hamlet, Othello, King Lear, Macbeth. 1904. Cleveland: Meridian, 1963.

Bradshaw, Graham. *Misrepresentations: Shakespeare and the Materialists*. Ithaca: Cornell UP, 1993.

———. *Shakespeare's Scepticism*. Ithaca: Cornell UP, 1987.

——. "State of Play." *International Shakespeare Yearbook*. Ed. W. R. Elton and John Mucciolo. London: Ashgate, 1999. 3–25.

Bradshaw, Graham, and Kaori Ashizu. "Reading *Hamlet* in Japan." *Shakespeare in the Twentieth Century: The Selected Proceedings of the International Shakespeare Association World Congress, Los Angeles, 1996*. Ed. Jonathan Bate, Jill L. Levenson, and Dieter Mehl. Newark: U of Delaware P; London: Assoc. UP, 1998. 350–63.

Bristol, Michael D. *Carnival and Theater: Plebeian Culture and the Structure of Authority in Renaissance England*. New York: Methuen, 1985.

Brower, Reuben Arthur. *Hero and Saint: Shakespeare and the Graeco-Roman Heroic Tradition*. Oxford: Clarendon UP, 1971.

Brown, John Russell. *Free Shakespeare*. London: Heinemann, 1974.

Brown, Lyn Mikel. *Raising Their Voices: The Politics of Girls' Anger*. Cambridge: Harvard UP, 1998.

Burnett, Mark Thornton, and John Manning, eds. *New Essays on* Hamlet. New York: AMS, 1994.

Calderwood, James L. *To Be and Not to Be: Negation and Metadrama in* Hamlet. New York: Columbia UP, 1983.

Camden, Carroll. "On Ophelia's Madness." *Shakespeare Quarterly* 15 (1964): 247–56.

Cantor, Paul A. *Shakespeare*: Hamlet. Landmarks of World Lit. Cambridge: Cambridge UP, 1989.

Cartwright, Kent. "Remembering *Hamlet*." *Shakespearean Tragedy and Its Double: The Rhythms of Audience Response*. University Park: Penn State UP, 1991. 89–137.

Cavell, Stanley. "Hamlet's Burden of Proof." *Disowning Knowledge in Six Plays of Shakespeare*. Cambridge: Cambridge UP, 1987. 179–91.

Charney, Maurice. *Hamlet's Fictions*. New York: Routledge, 1988.

——. *Style in* Hamlet. Princeton: Princeton UP, 1969.

——. "The Voice of Marlowe's *Tamburlaine* in Early Shakespeare." *Comparative Drama* 31.2 (1997): 213–23.

Church, Tony. "Polonius in *Hamlet*." *Players of Shakespeare: Essays in Shakespearean Performance by Twelve Players with the Royal Shakespeare Company*. Ed. Philip Brockbank. Cambridge: Cambridge UP, 1985. 103–14.

Clayton, Thomas, ed. *The* Hamlet *First Published (Q1, 1603): Origins, Form, Intertextualities*. Newark: U of Delaware P, 1992.

Cohan, Michael. Hamlet *in My Mind's Eye*. Athens: U of Georgia P, 1989.

Cohn, Ruby. *Modern Shakespeare Offshoots*. Princeton: Princeton UP, 1976.

Coleridge, Samuel Taylor. *Coleridge's Criticism of Shakespeare*. Ed. R. A. Foakes. Detroit: Wayne State UP, 1989.

Coursen, H. R. *Christian Ritual and the World of Shakespeare's Tragedies*. Lewisburg: Bucknell UP, 1976.

——. *The Compensatory Psyche: A Jungian Approach to Shakespeare*. Washington: UP of Amer., 1986.

——. *Shakespeare in Production: Whose History?* Athens: Ohio UP, 1996.

——. *Shakespearean Performance as Interpretation*. Cranbury: Assoc. UP, 1992.

Coyle, Martin, ed. Hamlet: *William Shakespeare*. New Casebooks. New York: St. Martin's, 1992.

Cressy, David. "Foucault, Stone, Shakespeare, and Social History." *English Literary Renaissance* 21 (1991): 121–33.

Crowl, Samuel. *Shakespeare Observed: Studies in Performance on Stage and Screen.* Athens: Ohio UP, 1992.

Cummings, Peter. "Hearing in *Hamlet*: Poisoned Ears and the Psychopathology of Flawed Audition." *Shakespeare Yearbook* 1 (1990): 81–92.

Dash, Irene. "Conflicting Loyalties: *Hamlet*." *Women's Worlds in Shakespeare's Plays.* Newark: U of Delaware P, 1997. 111–53.

Davison, Peter. Hamlet: *Text and Performance*. London: Macmillan and Humanities Intl., 1983.

Dawson, Anthony. *Shakespeare in Performance:* Hamlet. Manchester: Manchester UP, 1995.

de Grazia, Margreta, Maureen Quilligan, and Peter Stallybrass, eds. *Subject and Object in Renaissance Culture*. Cambridge Studies in Lit. and Culture 8. Cambridge: Cambridge UP, 1996.

Desai, R. W. "Hamlet as 'the Minister of God to Take Vengeance.'" *English Language Notes* 31 (1993): 22–27.

Dessen, Alan. "Imagery and Symbolic Action for the Viewer's Eye." *Elizabethan Drama and the Viewer's Eye*. Chapel Hill: U of North Carolina P, 1977. 71–109.

DiMatteo, Anthony. "*Hamlet* as Fable: Reconstructing a Lost Code of Meaning." *Connotations: An International Journal for Literary Debate* 6.2 (1997): 158–79.

Dollimore, Jonathan. *Radical Tragedy: Religion, Ideology, and Power in the Drama of Shakespeare and His Contemporaries*. Chicago: U of Chicago P; Brighton: Harvester, 1984.

Donaldson, Peter S. "Ghostly Texts and Virtual Performances: Old Hamlet in the New Media." Annual Conf. of the Shakespeare Assn. of Amer. Atlanta. 2 Apr. 1993.

Doran, Madeline. *Endeavors of Art: A Study of Form in Elizabethan Drama.* Madison: U of Wisconsin P, 1954.

Douglas, Claire. *The Woman in the Mirror: Analytical Psychology and the Feminine.* Boston: Sigo, 1990.

Draper, John W. *The* Hamlet *of Shakespeare's Audience.* Durham: Duke UP, 1938.

Dusinberre, Juliet. *Shakespeare and the Nature of Women*. 1975. 2nd ed. New York: St. Martin's, 1996.

Eastman, Arthur M. *A Short History of Shakespearean Criticism*. 1974. Lanham: UP of Amer., 1985.

Eliot, T. S. "Hamlet and His Problems." *Athenaeum* 26 Sept. 1919: 940–41. *Selected Essays*. New York: Harcourt, 1950. 121–26. *Hamlet*. Norton Critical Ed. Ed. Cyrus Hoy. New York: Norton, 1963. 176–80.

Empson, William. "Hamlet." *Essays on Shakespeare*. Ed. David B. Pirie. Cambridge: Cambridge UP, 1986. 79–136.

England, Eugene. "*Hamlet* against Revenge." *Literature and Belief* 7 (1987): 49–62.

Everett, Barbara. *Young Hamlet: Essays on Shakespeare's Tragedies*. Oxford: Clarendon, 1989.

Farley-Hills, David, ed. *Critical Responses to* Hamlet, *1600–1900*. 2 vols. Hamlet Collection 4. New York: AMS, 1996.

Felperin, Howard. "O'erdoing Termagent." *Shakespearean Representation: Mimesis and Modernity in Elizabethan Tragedy*. Princeton: Princeton UP, 1977. 44–67.

Ferguson, Margaret. "*Hamlet*: Letters and Spirits." Parker and Hartman 292–309.

Fienberg, Nona. "Jephthah's Daughter: The Parts Ophelia Plays." *Old Testament Women in Western Literature*. Ed. Raymond-Jean Frontain. Fayetteville: U of Arkansas P, 2001. 129–43.

Fineman, Joel. "Fratricide and Cuckoldry: Shakespeare's Doubles." Schwartz and Kahn 70–109.

Fleming, Keith. "*Hamlet* and *Oedipus* Today: Jones and Lacan." *Hamlet Studies* 4 (1982): 54–71.

Foakes, Reginald A. Hamlet *versus* Lear: *Cultural Politics and Shakespeare's Art*. Cambridge: Cambridge UP, 1993.

Forker, Charles. "Shakespeare's Theatrical Symbolism and Its Function in *Hamlet*." *Shakespeare Quarterly* 14 (1963): 215–29.

Fox-Good, Jacquelyn A. "Ophelia's Mad Songs: Music, Gender, Power." *Subjects on the World's Stage: Essays on British Literature of the Middle Ages and Renaissance*. Ed. David C. Allen and Robert A. White. Newark: U of Delaware P, 1995. 217–38.

French, A. L. *Shakespeare and the Critics*. Cambridge: Cambridge UP, 1972.

French, Marilyn. *Shakespeare's Division of Experience*. New York: Summit, 1982.

Frye, Northrop. *Fools of Time: Studies in Shakespearean Tragedy*. Toronto: U of Toronto P, 1967.

———. *Northrop Frye on Shakespeare*. Ed. Robert Sandler. New Haven: Yale UP, 1986.

Frye, Roland Mushat. "Ladies, Gentlemen, and Skulls: *Hamlet* and the Iconographic Tradition." *Shakespeare Quarterly* 30 (1979): 15–28.

———. *The Renaissance* Hamlet: *Issues and Responses in 1600*. Princeton: Princeton UP, 1984.

Garber, Marjorie. "'Remember Me': Memento Mori Figures in Shakespeare's Plays." *Renaissance Drama* ns 12 (1981): 3–25.

———. *Shakespeare's Ghost Writers*. London: Methuen, 1987.

Girard, René. "Hamlet's Dull Revenge: Vengeance in *Hamlet*." *A Theater of Envy: William Shakespeare*. New York: Oxford UP, 1991. 271–89.

Goddard, Harold F. "In Ophelia's Closet." *Yale Review* 36 (1946): 462–74.

Goethe, Johann Wolgang von. *Wilhelm Meister's Apprenticeship*. Ed. and trans. Eric A. Blackall in cooperation with Victor Lange. New York: Suhrkamp, 1989. (Excerpts in Furness 2: 272–75.)

Goldman, Michael. *Acting and Action in Shakespearean Tragedy*. Princeton: Princeton UP, 1985.

———. "*Hamlet*: Entering the Text." *Theatre Journal* 44 (1992): 449–60.

———. "Hamlet and Our Problems." *Shakespeare and the Energies of Drama*. Princeton: Princeton UP, 1972. 74–93.

Gottschalk, Paul. *The Meanings of* Hamlet. Albuquerque: U of New Mexico P, 1972.

Grafton, Anthony. *New Worlds, Ancient Texts: The Power of Tradition and the Shock of Discovery*. Cambridge: Harvard UP, 1992.

Granville-Barker, Harley. *Hamlet*. Granville-Barker, *Prefaces* 1: 24–260.

———. *Prefaces to Shakespeare*. 2 vols. 1946. Princeton: Princeton UP, 1974.

Grebanier, Bernard. *The Heart of* Hamlet. New York: Crowell, 1960.

Greenblatt, Stephen. *Hamlet in Purgatory*. Princeton: Princeton UP, 2001.

———. *Renaissance Self-Fashioning: From More to Shakespeare* Chicago: U of Chicago P, 1980.

Greg, W. W. "Hamlet's Hallucination." *Modern Language Review* 12 (1917): 393–421.

Guilfoyle, Cherrell. "The Beginning of *Hamlet*." *Comparative Drama* 14 (1980): 137–58.

Gurr, Andrew. Hamlet *and the Distracted Globe*. Edinburgh: Sussex UP, 1978.

———. *Playgoing in Shakespeare's London*. Cambridge: Cambridge UP, 1987.

———. *The Shakespearean Stage*. 3rd ed. Cambridge: Cambridge UP, 1992.

Hall, Kim F. *Things of Darkness: Economics of Race and Gender in Early Modern England*. Ithaca: Cornell UP, 1995.

Hardy, Barbara. *Shakespeare's Storytellers*. London: Own, 1997.

Hartwig, Joan. "*Hamlet* and Parodic Polonius." *Shakespeare's Analogical Scene*. Lincoln: U of Nebraska P, 1983. 153–70.

Hattaway, Michael. "Christopher Marlowe: Ideology and Subversion." *Christopher Marlowe and English Renaissance Culture*. Ed. Darryll Grantley and Peter Roberts. Aldershot: Scolar, 1996. 198–223.

———. *Hamlet*. Critics' Debate. London: Humanities, 1987.

Hawkes, Terence, ed. *Alternative Shakespeares*. Vol. 2. New Accents. London: Routledge, 1996.

———. Introduction. Hawkes, *Shakespeares* 1–15.

———. "Telmah." *That Shakespeherian Rag: Essays on a Critical Process*. New York: Methuen, 1986. 92–119.

Heilbrun, Carolyn G. "The Character of Hamlet's Mother." *Hamlet's Mother and Other Women*. New York: Columbia UP, 1990. 9–17.

Helgerson, Richard. "The Land Speaks: Cartography, Chorography, and Subversion in Renaissance England." *Representing the English Renaissance*. Ed. Stephen Greenblatt. Berkeley: U of California P, 1988. 327–61.

[Henry, Matthew]. *An Account of the Life and Death of Mr. Philip Henry, Minister of the Gospel, near Whitchurch in Shropshire. Who Dyed June 24, 1696. in the Sixty Fifth Year of His Age. with Dr. Bates's Dedication*. 2nd ed. London, 1699.

Hinman, Charlton. *The Printing and Proof-reading of the First Folio of Shakespeare*. 2 vols. Oxford: Clarendon, 1963.

Hirsh, James E. "Shakespeare and the History of Soliloquies." *Modern Language Quarterly* 58 (1997): 1–26.

———. "The 'To Be or Not to Be' Scene and the Conventions of Shakespearean Drama." *Modern Language Quarterly* 42 (1981): 115–36.

Hodgdon, Barbara. "The Critic, the Poor Player, Prince Hamlet, and the Lady in the Dark." McDonald 259–93.

Hoeniger, F. David. *Medicine and Shakespeare in the English Renaissance*. Newark: U of Delaware P, 1992.

Holland, Norman N. *Psychoanalysis and Shakespeare*. New York: Octagon, 1966.

Homans, Peter. *Jung in Context: Modernity and the Making of a Psychology*. Chicago: U of Chicago P, 1979.

Honigmann, E. A. J. *The Stability of Shakespeare's Text*. Lincoln: U of Nebraska P, 1965.

Howard, Jean E. *Shakespeare's Art of Orchestration: Stage Technique and Audience Response*. Urbana: U of Illinois P, 1984.

Hunter, Robert G. "Hamlet." *Shakespeare and the Mystery of God's Judgment*. Athens: U of Georgia P, 1976. 101–26.

Irace, Kathleen. "Origins and Agents of Q1 *Hamlet*." Clayton 90–122.

Jackson, Russell, and Robert Smallwood, eds. *Players of Shakespeare 3*. Cambridge: Cambridge UP, 1993.

Jardine, Lisa. *Reading Shakespeare Historically*. London: Routledge, 1996.

Jenkins, Harold. Introduction. *Hamlet*. Arden Ed. Ed. Jenkins. London: Methuen, 1982. 1–159.

Jones, Emrys. *Scenic Form in Shakespeare*. 1971. Oxford: Oxford UP, 1985.

Jones, Ernest. *Hamlet and Oedipus*. 1949. New York: Norton, 1976.

Joseph, Miriam. *Shakespeare's Use of the Arts of Language*. New York: Hafner, 1966.

Kastan, David Scott, ed. *Critical Essays in Shakespeare's* Hamlet. New York: Hall, 1995.

———. "'His Semblable Is His Mirror': *Hamlet* and the Imitation of Revenge." *Shakespeare Survey* 19 (1987): 111–23.

Keller, Arthur, Oliver Lissitzyn, and Frederick Mann. *Creation of Rights of Sovereignty through Symbolic Acts, 1400–1800*. New York: Columbia UP, 1938.

Kermode, Frank. Introduction to *Hamlet*. Evans et al. 1183–88.

Keyishian, Harry. *The Shapes of Revenge: Victimization, Vengeance, and Vindictiveness in Shakespeare*. Totowa: Humanities Intl., 1995.

Kirsch, James. *Shakespeare's Royal Self.* New York: C. G. Jung Foundation, 1966.

Kott, Jan. *Shakespeare Our Contemporary*. New York: Doubleday, 1966.

Krutch, Joseph Wood. "The Tragic Fallacy." *The Modern Temper*. New York: Harcourt, 1957. 79–97.

Landis, Joan. "Shakespeare's Poland." *Hamlet Studies* 6 (1984): 8–17.

Leavenworth, Russell E., ed. *Interpreting* Hamlet: *Materials for Analysis*. San Francisco: Chandler, 1960.

Leithart, Peter J. "The Serpent Now Wears the Crown: A Typological Reading of *Hamlet*." *Contra Mundum* 11 (1994). 19 Jan. 2001 <http://www.visi.com/~contra_m/cm/features/cmll_hamlet.html>.

Lerner, Lawrence, ed. *Shakespeare's Tragedies: An Anthology of Modern Criticism.* Harmondsworth: Penguin, 1963.

Leverenz, David. "The Woman in *Hamlet*: An Interpersonal View." Schwartz and Kahn 110–28.

Levin, Harry. *The Question of* Hamlet. London: Oxford UP, 1959.

Lidz, Theodore. *Hamlet's Enemy: Madness and Myth in* Hamlet. New York: Basic, 1975.

Liebler, Naomi Conn. *Shakespeare's Festive Tragedy: The Ritual Foundations of Genre.* London: Routledge, 1995.

Low, Anthony. "*Hamlet* and the Ghost of Purgatory: Intimations of Killing the Father." *English Literary Renaissance* 29 (1999): 443–67.

Lupton, Julia Reinhard, and Kenneth Reinhard. *After Oedipus: Shakespeare in Psychoanalysis.* Ithaca: Cornell UP, 1993.

Lyons, Bridget Gellert. "The Iconography of Ophelia." *ELH* 44 (1977): 60–74.

———. "Melancholy and *Hamlet*." *Voices of Melancholy: Studies in Literary Treatments of Melancholy in Renaissance England.* New York: Barnes, 1971. 77–112.

Mack, Maynard. *Everybody's Shakespeare: Reflections Chiefly on the Tragedies.* Lincoln: U of Nebraska P, 1993.

———. "The World of *Hamlet*." *Yale Review* 41.4 (1952): 502–23. Rpt. as "'The Readiness Is All': *Hamlet*." Mack, *Everybody's Shakespeare* 107–27.

Maguire, Laurie E. *Shakespearean Suspect Texts: The "Bad" Quartos and Their Contexts.* Cambridge: Cambridge UP, 1996.

Mahoud, M. M. *Shakespeare's Wordplay.* London: Methuen, 1968.

Mander, Raymond, and Joe Michenson, comps. Hamlet *through the Ages: A Pictorial Record from 1709.* 2nd ed. Ed. Herbert Marshall. Freeport: Books for Libs., 1971.

Mangan, Michael. *A Preface to Shakespeare's Tragedies.* London: Longman, 1991.

Marks, Robert. Hamlet: *Another Interpretation.* Mahanoy City: Raven, 1980.

Maslen, Elizabeth. "Yorick's Place in *Hamlet*." *Essays and Studies by Members of the English Association* 36 (1983): 1–13.

Maus, Katherine Eisaman. *Inwardness and Theater in the English Renaissance.* Chicago: U of Chicago P, 1995.

McAlindon, Thomas. "Hamlet." *Shakespeare's Tragic Cosmos.* Cambridge: Cambridge UP, 1991. 102–25.

McDonald, Russ, ed. *Shakespeare Reread: The Texts in New Contexts.* Ithaca: Cornell UP, 1994.

McElroy, Bernard. "*Hamlet*: The Mind's Eye." *Shakespeare's Mature Tragedies.* Princeton: Princeton UP, 1973. 29–88.

McGee, Arthur. *The Elizabethan* Hamlet. New Haven: Yale UP, 1987.

McLuskie, Kathleen. "The Patriarchal Bard." *Political Shakespeare.* Ed. Jonathan Dollimore and Alan Sinfield. Manchester: U of Manchester P, 1985. 88–108.

McMillin, Scott. *Henry IV, Part One.* Shakespeare in Performance. Manchester: Manchester UP, 1991.

Mehl, Dieter. "Hamlet." *Shakespeare's Tragedies: An Introduction.* Cambridge: Cambridge UP, 1986. 30–56.

Mills, John A. *Hamlet on Stage: The Great Tradition*. Contributions in Drama and Theatre Studies. Westport: Greenwood, 1985.

Mowat, Barbara A. "The Form of *Hamlet*'s Fortunes." *Renaissance Drama* 19 (1988): 19–126.

Mulryne, J. R., and Margaret Shewring, with Andrew Gurr, eds.. *Shakespeare's Globe Rebuilt*. Cambridge: Cambridge UP, 1997.

Murfin, Ross, "What Is Psychoanalytic Criticism?" Wofford 241–55.

Nardo, Anna K. "Hamlet, a Man to Double Business Bound." *Shakespeare Quarterly* 34 (1983): 181–99.

Neely, Carol Thomas. "Documents in Madness: Reading Madness and Gender in Shakespeare's Tragedies and Early Modern Culture." *Shakespeare Quarterly* 42 (1991): 315–38. Rpt. in *Shakespearean Tragedy and Gender*. Ed. Shirley Nelson Garner and Madelon Sprengnether. Bloomington: Indiana UP, 1996. 75–104.

Newell, Alex. *The Soliloquies in* Hamlet: *The Structural Design*. Rutherford: Fairleigh Dickinson UP, 1991.

Nuttall, A. D. "Freud and Shakespeare: *Hamlet*." *Shakespearean Continuities: Essays in Honor of E. A. J. Honigmann*. Ed. John Bachelor, Tom Cain, and Claire Lamont. London: Macmillan; New York: St. Martin's, 1997. 123–37.

Oakley, Francis. *The Political Thought of Pierre d'Ailly: The Voluntarist Tradition*. New Haven: Yale UP, 1964.

O'Brien, Ellen J. "Mapping the Role: Criticism and the Construction of Shakespearean Character." *Shakespeare Illuminations: Essays in Honor of Marvin Rosenberg*. Ed. Jay L. Halio and Hugh Richmond. Newark: U of Delaware P, 1998. 13–32.

———. "Revision by Excision: Rewriting Gertrude." *Shakespeare Survey* 45 (1992): 27–35.

Orgel, Stephen. "Shakespeare Imagines a Theater." *Shakespeare, Man of the Theater*. Ed. Kenneth Muir, Jay L. Halio, and D. J. Palmer. Newark: U of Delaware P, 1983. 34–46.

Ornstein, Robert. *The Moral Vision of Jacobean Tragedy*. Madison: U of Wisconsin P, 1960.

Padilla, Diomaris. "Comments on Hamlet's Dilemma." Online class notes for the course Shakespeare. New York Inst. of Technology. Fall 1998.

Pagden, Anthony. *Lords of All the World: Ideologies of Empire in Spain, Britain, and France, c. 1500–c. 1800*. New Haven: Yale UP, 1995.

———. *Spanish Imperialism and the Political Imagination*. New Haven: Yale UP, 1990.

Paris, Bernard J. "Hamlet." *Bargains with Fate: Psychological Crises and Conflicts in Shakespeare and His Plays*. New York: Insight-Plenum, 1991. 35–61.

Parker, Patricia. "*Othello* and *Hamlet*: Dilation, Spying, and the 'Secret Place of Woman.'" McDonald 126–46.

Parker, Patricia, and Geoffrey Hartman, eds. *Shakespeare and the Question of Theory*. New York: Methuen, 1985.

Patterson, Annabel. *Shakespeare and the Popular Voice*. Cambridge: Blackwell, 1989.

Pennington, Michael. Hamlet: *A User's Guide*. London: Hern; New York: Limelight, 1996.

Poster, Mark. *The Mode of Information: Poststructuralism and Social Context*. Chicago: U of Chicago P, 1990.

Rabkin, Norman. *Shakespeare and the Common Understanding*. Chicago: U of Chicago P, 1984.

Righter, Anne. *Shakespeare and the Idea of the Play*. London: Chatto, 1962.

Robson, W. W. *Did the King See the Dumb Show?* Edinburgh: Edinburgh UP, 1975.

Rose, Jacqueline. "*Hamlet*—the *Mona Lisa* of Literature." *Critical Quarterly* 28 (1986): 35–49. Rpt. in Barker and Kamps 104–19.

———. "Sexuality in the Reading of Shakespeare: *Hamlet* and *Measure for Measure*." *Alternative Shakespeares*. Ed. John Drakakis. London: Methuen, 1985. 95–118.

Rose, Mark. "*Hamlet* and the Shape of Revenge." *English Literary Renaissance* 1 (1971): 132–43.

Rosenberg, Marvin. *The Masks of* Hamlet. Newark: U of Delaware UP, 1992.

Saccio, Peter. "*Hamlet* and the Perplexing World." *Comedy, Tragedy, History: The Live Drama and Vital Truth of William Shakespeare*. Super Star Teachers. Audiotape and videotape. Teaching Company, Springfield, VA. 1991. Lecture 7.

Sacks, Claire, and Edgar Whan, eds. Hamlet: *Enter Critic*. New York: Appleton, 1962.

Schlegel, August Wilheim von. *Lectures on Dramatic Art and Literature*. 1808–11. London: Bell, 1902.

Schleiner, Louise. "Latinized Greek Drama in Shakespeare's Writing of *Hamlet*." *Shakespeare Quarterly* 41 (1990): 29–48.

Schwartz, Murray M., and Coppélia Kahn, eds. *Representing Shakespeare: New Psychoanalytic Essays*. Baltimore: Johns Hopkins UP, 1980.

Scott, Mark W. "*Hamlet*." *Shakespeare for Students: Critical Interpretations of* As You Like It, Hamlet, Julius Caesar, Macbeth, A Midsummer Night's Dream, The Merchant of Venice, Othello, *and* Romeo and Juliet. Detroit: Gale, 1992. 72–163.

Shakespearean Criticism: Excerpts from the Criticism of William Shakespeare's Plays and Poetry, from the First Published Appraisals to Current Evaluations. Ed. Laurie Lanzen Harris. Detroit: Gale, 1981–.

Showalter, Elaine. "Representing Ophelia: Women, Madness, and the Responsibility of Feminist Criticism." Parker and Hartman 77–94. Wofford 220–40.

Shurgot, Michael. "'Get You a Place': Staging the Mousetrap at the Globe." *Stages of Play: Shakespeare's Theatrical Energies in Elizabethan Performance*. Newark: U of Delaware P, 1998. 199–213.

Smith, Rebecca. "A Heart Cleft in Twain: The Dilemma of Shakespeare's Gertrude." *The Woman's Part*. Ed. Carolyn R. S. Lenz, Gayle Greene, and Carol Thomas Neely. Urbana: U of Illinois P, 1983. 194–210.

Spurgeon, Caroline F. E. *Shakespeare's Imagery and What It Tells Us*. 1936. Cambridge: Cambridge UP, 1988.

Stallybrass, Peter. "Worn Worlds: Clothes and Identity on the Renaissance Stage." de Grazia, Quilligan, and Stallybrass 289–320.

Stanton, Kay. "*Hamlet*'s Whores." Burnett and Manning 167–88.

States, Bert O. Hamlet *and the Concept of Character*. Baltimore: Johns Hopkins UP, 1992.

Styan, J. L. *The Shakespeare Revolution: Criticism and Performance in the Twentieth Century*. Cambridge: Cambridge UP, 1983.

Summers, Joseph. "The Dream of a Hero: Hamlet." *Dreams of Love and Power: On Shakespeare's Plays*. Oxford: Clarendon, 1984. 45–67.

Swander, Homer. "In Our Times: Such Audiences We Wish Him." *Shakespeare Quarterly* 35 (1984): 528–40.

Teague, Frances. "*Hamlet* in the Thirties." *Theatre Survey* 26.1 (1985): 63–79.

Thompson, Ann, and Neil Taylor. *William Shakespeare:* Hamlet. Writers and Their Work. Plymouth, Eng.: Northcote, 1996.

Trewin, J. C. *Five and Eighty* Hamlets. New York: New Amsterdam, 1987.

Trousdale, Marion. *Shakespeare and the Rhetoricians*. Chapel Hill: U of North Carolina P, 1982.

Urkowitz, Steve. "'Well-Sayd Olde Mole': Burying Three *Hamlets* in Modern Editions." *Shakespeare Study Today*. Ed. Georgianna Ziegler. New York: AMS, 1986. 37–70.

Vendler, Helen. "Hamlet Alone: A Celebration of Skepticism." *New York Times Magazine* 18 Apr. 1999: 123.

Vickers, Brian. *Appropriating Shakespeare: Contemporary Critical Quarrels*. New Haven: Yale UP, 1993.

———. "Shakespeare's Use of Rhetoric." *A New Companion to Shakespeare Studies*. Ed. Kenneth Muir and S. Schoenbaum. Cambridge: Cambridge UP, 1971. 83–98.

Videbaek, Bente. *The Stage Clown in Shakespeare's Theatre*. Contributions in Drama and Theatre Studies. Westport: Greenwood, 1996.

Warren, Michael. "Quarto and Folio *King Lear* and the Interpretation of Albany and Edgar." *Shakespeare's Pattern of Excelling Nature*. Ed. David Bevington and Jay L. Halio. Newark: U of Delaware P, 1978. 95–107.

Watkins, Ronald, and Jeremy Lemon. *In Shakespeare's Playhouse*: Hamlet. Totowa: Rowman, 1974.

Watson, Robert N. "Giving Up the Ghost in a World of Decay: *Hamlet*, Revenge, and Denial." *Renaissance Drama* 21 (1990): 199–223.

Watson, William Van. "Shakespeare, Zeffirelli, and the Homosexual Gaze." *Literature/Film Quarterly* 20.4 (1992): 308–25. Rpt. in Barker and Kamps 235–62.

Watts, Cedric Thomas. *Hamlet*. Boston: Twayne, 1988.

Webster, Richard. *Why Freud Was Wrong: Sin, Science, and Psychoanalysis*. New York: Basic, 1996.

Weimann, Robert. "Mimesis in *Hamlet*." Parker and Hartman 275–91.

———. "*Platea* and *Locus*." *Shakespeare and the Popular Tradition in the Theater: Studies in the Social Dimension of Dramatic Form and Function*. Ed. Robert Schwartz. Baltimore: Johns Hopkins UP, 1978. 73–84.

———. "Representation and Performance: The Uses of Authority in Shakespeare's Theatre." *Materialist Shakespeare: A History*. Ed. Ivo Kamps. New York: Verso, 1995.

Weiss, Larry. "10.0349 the Riverside Shakespeare." *Shaksper: The Global Electronic Shakespeare Conference*. 2 Mar. 1999. 30 Apr. 2001. <http://ws.bowiestate.edu/archives/1999/0363.html>.

Weitz, Morris. Hamlet *and the Philosophy of Literary Criticism*. Chicago: U of Chicago P, 1964.

Wells, Stanley, ed. *The Cambridge Companion to Shakespeare Studies*. Cambridge: Cambridge UP, 1986.

———. *Royal Shakespeare: Four Major Productions at Stratford-upon-Avon*. Manchester: Manchester UP, 1977.

Wells, Stanley W., and Gary Taylor, with John Jowett and William Montgomery. "*Hamlet*." *William Shakespeare: A Textual Companion*. Oxford: Clarendon; New York: Oxford UP, 1987. 396–420.

Werstine, Paul. "The Textual Mystery of *Hamlet*." *Shakespeare Quarterly* 39 (1985): 1–26.

West, Robert H. "King Hamlet's Ambiguous Ghost." *Shakespeare and the Outer Mystery*. Lexington: U of Kentucky P, 1968. 56–68.

Wheale, Nigel, "'Unfold Your Selfe': Jacques Lacan and the Psychoanalytic Reading of *Hamlet*." *Hamlet*. Ed. Peter J. Smith and Nigel Wood. Buckingham: Open UP, 1996. 108–32.

White, R. S. *Natural Law in English Renaissance Literature*. Cambridge: Cambridge UP, 1996.

Williams, George Walton. "With a Little Shuffling." "*Fanned and Winnowed Opinions*": *Shakespearean Essays Presented to Harold Jenkins*. Ed. John W. Mahon and Thomas A. Pendleton. London: Methuen, 1987. 151–59.

Wilson, John Dover. *What Happens in* Hamlet. 1935. 3rd ed. Cambridge: Cambridge UP, 1986.

Wofford, Susanne L., ed. Hamlet: *Case Studies in Contemporary Criticism*. New York: Bedford–St. Martin's, 1994.

Wood, Robert E. *Some Necessary Questions of the Play: A Stage-Centered Analysis of Shakespeare's* Hamlet. Lewisburg: Bucknell UP, 1994.

Woodhead, M. R. "Deep Plots and Indiscretions in 'The Murder of Gonzago.'" *Shakespeare Survey* 32 (1979): 151–61.

Woolf, Virginia. *A Room of One's Own*. 1929. San Diego: Harcourt, 1981.

Wright, George T. "Hearing Shakespeare's Dramatic Verse." *A Companion to Shakespeare*. Ed. David Scott Kastan. Oxford: Blackwell, 1999. 256–76.

———. "Hendiadys and *Hamlet*." *PMLA* 96 (1981): 168–93.

———. *Shakespeare's Metrical Art*. Berkeley: U of California P, 1988.

Young, Bruce. "Parental Blessings in Shakespeare's Plays." *Studies in Philology* 89 (1992): 179–210.

Zitner, Sheldon P. "Hamlet, Duelist." *University of Toronto Quarterly* 39.1 (1969): 1–18.

Aids to Teaching

Works on Teaching

Beck, Charles R. "The Poet's Inner Circle: Gaming Strategies Based on Famous Quotations." *English Journal* 87.3 (1998): 37–44.

Coursen, H. R. *Teaching Shakespeare with Film and Television: A Guide*. Westport: Greenwood, 1997.

Elbow, Peter. *Writing without Teachers*. 1973. New York: Oxford UP, 1998.

Epstein, Norrie. *The Friendly Shakespeare: A Thoroughly Painless Guide to the Best of the Bard*. New York: Viking, 1993.

Freire, Paulo. *Pedagogy of the Oppressed*. Trans. Myra Bergman Ramos. New York: Continuum, 1970.

Gilbert, Miriam. "Teaching Shakespeare through Performances." *Shakespeare Quarterly* 35 (1984): 601–08.

Hale, David G. "More than Magic in the Web: Plagiarism for the Shakespeare Class." *Shakespeare and the Classroom* 6.1 (1998): 30–33.

Hapke, Laura. "Deciphering Shakespeare: Some Practical Classroom Techniques." *English Record* 25 (1984): 11–13.

Herz, Sarah K. *From Hinton to* Hamlet: *Building Bridges between Young Adult Literature and the Classics*. Westport: Greenwood, 1996.

Hirsh, James. "Picturing Shakespeare." *Teaching Shakespeare Today*. Ed. James E. Davis and Ronald E. Salomone. Urbana: NCTE, 1993. 140–50.

Hodgdon, Barbara. "Making Changes / Making Sense." *Focus: Teaching Shakespeare II* 12.1 (1985): 2–11.

Howe, Allie, and Robert A. Nelson. "The Spectogram: An Exercise in Initial Analysis." *Shakespeare Quarterly* 35 (1984): 632–41.

Howlett, Kathy M. "Team-Teaching Shakespeare in an Interdisciplinary Context." Salomone and Davis 112–119.

Hunt, Maurice, ed. *Approaches to Teaching Shakespeare's* The Tempest *and Other Late Romances*. New York: MLA, 1992.

MacCary, Thomas W. Hamlet: *A Guide to the Play*. Greenwood Studies in Shakespeare. Westport: Greenwood, 1998.

Marcus, Leah. "Teaching Textual Variation: *Hamlet* and *King Lear*." *Teaching with Shakespeare: Critics in the Classroom*. Ed. Bruce McIver and Ruth Stevenson. Newark: U of Delaware P, 1994. 115–51.

O'Brien, Peggy, Jeanne Addison Roberts, Michael Tolaydo, and Nancy Goodwin, eds. *Shakespeare Set Free: Teaching* Hamlet, Henry IV Part 1. Teaching Shakespeare Inst. Folger Lib. New York: Washington Square, 1994.

Ponsot, Marie, and Rosemary Deen. *Beat Not the Poor Desk: Writing: What to Teach, How to Teach It, and Why*. Montclair: Boynton, 1982.

Potter, A. M. "A Confrontation with the Text: Approaches to the Problem of Teaching *Hamlet*." *Crux: A Journal on the Teaching of English* 20 (1986): 19–36.

Ray, Robert H., ed. *Approaches to Teaching Shakespeare's* King Lear. New York: MLA, 1986.

Riggio, Milla Cozart, ed. *Teaching Shakespeare through Performance*. Options for Teaching. New York: MLA, 1999.

Robinson, Randall. *Unlocking Shakespeare's Language: Help for the Teacher and Student*. Theory and Research into Practice. Urbana: Eric Clearinghouse on Reading and Communication Skills; NCTE, 1988.

Rozett, Martha Tuck. *Talking Back to Shakespeare*. Newark: U of Delaware P, 1994.

Saeger, James P. "The High-Tech Classroom." Salomone and Davis 271–83.

Salomone, Ronald E., and James E. Davis, eds. *Teaching Shakespeare into the Twenty-First Century*. Athens: Ohio UP, 1997.

Stewart, Patrick. Personal interview with Mary Judith Dunbar. Santa Clara Univ. 9 Nov. 1979.

Swart, Marieken. "Cracking the Code: Approaches to the Teaching of *Hamlet*." *Crux: A Journal on the Teaching of English* 22 (1988): 31–43.

Voss, Tony. "Viva *Hamlet!* Viva!; or, The Prince of Denmark as Topical-Historical-Actual-Universal Drama." *Crux: A Journal on the Teaching of English* 28 (1994): 3–14.

Wheale, Nigel. "Scratching Shakespeare: Video-Teaching the Bard." *Shakespeare in the Changing Curriculum*. Ed. Lesley Aers and Wheale. London: Routledge, 1991. 204–21.

Wheeler, Richard P. "Psychoanalytic Criticism and Teaching Shakespeare." *ADE Bulletin* 87 (1987): 19–23.

Wiggins, Grant. "Creating a Thought-Provoking Curriculum: Lessons from Whodunits and Others." *American Educator* 11 (1987): 10–17.

Shakespeare on Screen

Aspden, Peter. Rev. of *Rosencrantz and Guildenstern Are Dead*. Dir. Tom Stoppard. *Sight and Sound* ns 1.2 (1991): 58.

Ball, Robert H. *Shakespeare on Silent Film: A Strange Eventful History*. London: Allen, 1968.

Barton, John. *Playing Shakespeare*. London: Methuen, 1984.

Birringer, Johannes H. "Rehearsing the Mousetrap: Robert Nelson's *Hamlet Act*." *Shakespeare on Film Newsletter* 9.1 (1984): 1+.

Boose, Lynda E., and Richard Burt, eds. *Shakespeare, the Movie: Popularizing the Plays on Film, TV, and Video*. London: Routledge, 1997.

Branagh, Kenneth. Hamlet: *Screenplay and Introduction*. New York: Norton, 1996.

Buhler, Stephen M. "Antic Dispositions: Shakespeare and Steve Martin's *L.A. Story*." *Shakespeare Yearbook* 8 (1997): 212–29.

———. "Double Takes: Branagh Gets to *Hamlet*." *Post Script: Essays in Film and the Humanities* 17.1 (1997): 43–52.

———. "Text, Eyes, and Videotape: Screening Shakespeare Script." *Shakespeare Quarterly* 46 (1995): 236–44.

Bulman, J. C., and H. R. Coursen. *Shakespeare on Television: An Anthology of Essays and Reviews*. Hanover: UP of New England, 1988.

Burnett, Mark Thornton. "The 'Very Cunning of the Scene': Kenneth Branagh's *Hamlet*." *Literature/Film Quarterly* 25.2 (1997): 78–82.

Coursen, Herbert R. "A German *Hamlet*." *Shakespeare on Film Newsletter* 11.1 (1986): 4.

———. "*Hamlet*." *Shakespeare on Film Newsletter* 5.2 (1981): 5+.

———. *Watching Shakespeare on Television*. London: Assoc. UP, 1993.

Crowl, Samuel. "Fragments." *Shakespeare on Film Newsletter* 13.1 (1988): 7.

———. "*Hamlet*." *Shakespeare Bulletin* 15.1 (1997): 34–35.

———. "*Hamlet*." *Shakespeare Bulletin* 18.4 (2000): 39–40.

Davies, Anthony. *Filming Shakespeare's Plays: The Adaptations of Laurence Olivier, Orson Welles, Peter Brook, and Akira Kurosawa.* Cambridge: Cambridge UP, 1988.

Donaldson, Peter S. "Ghostly Texts and Virtual Performances: Old Hamlet in New Media." Multimedia presentation. Meeting of the Shakespeare Assn. of Amer. Atlanta. 2 Apr. 1993.

———. *Shakespearean Films / Shakespearean Directors.* Boston: Unwin, 1990.

Felperin, Leslie. "*Hamlet*." Rev. of *Hamlet.* Dir. Kenneth Branagh. *Sight and Sound* 7.2 (1997): 46–47

Floyd, Nigel. Rev. of *L.A. Story.* Dir. Mick Jackson. *Sight and Sound* ns 1.1 (1991): 53.

Griffin, Alice. "Shakespeare through the Camera's Eye." *Shakespeare Quarterly* 4 (1953): 33–34.

Guntner, Lawrence. "Expressionist Shakespeare: The Gade/Nielsen *Hamlet* (1920) and the History of Shakespeare on Film." *Post Script: Essays in Film and the Humanities* 17.2 (1998): 90–102.

Halio, Jay. "Three Filmed *Hamlets*." *Literature/Film Quarterly* 1.4 (1973): 317–18.

Holderness, Graham. "Shakespeare Rewound." *Shakespeare Survey* 45 (1993): 63–74.

Huffman, Clifford. "The RSC *Playing Shakespeare* Tapes in a College Classroom." *Shakespeare on Film Newsletter* 14.2 (1990): 3.

Impastato, David. "Zeffirelli's *Hamlet* and the Baroque." *Shakespeare on Film Newsletter* 16.2 (1992): 1+.

———. "Zeffirelli's *Hamlet*: Sunlight Makes Meaning." *Shakespeare on Film Newsletter* 16.1 (1991): 1+.

Jackson, Russell. "Film Diary." Branagh 175–208.

Jays, David. Rev. of *In the Bleak Midwinter.* Dir. Kenneth Branagh. *Sight and Sound* ns 5.12 (1995): 47.

Jorgens, Jack J. *Shakespeare on Film.* Bloomington: Indiana UP, 1977.

Kell. Rev. of *Hamlet Goes Business.* Dir. Aki Kaurismäki. *Variety* 30 Aug. 1989.

Klass, Perri. "A 'Bambi' for the 90's via Shakespeare." Rev. of *The Lion King.* Dir. Roger Allers and Rob Minkoff. *New York Times* 19 June 1994, sec. 2: 1+.

Klein, Holger, and Dimiter Daphinoff, eds. Hamlet *on Screen. Shakespeare Yearbook* 8. Lewiston: Mellon, 1997.

Kliman, Bernice W. "Chabrol's *Ophelia*." *Shakespeare on Film Newsletter* 3.1 (1978): 1+.

———. "'Enter Hamlet': A Demythologizing Approach to *Hamlet*." *Shakespeare on Film Newsletter* 15.1 (1990): 2+.

———. Hamlet: *Film, Television, and Audio Performance.* London: Assoc. UP, 1988.

Maher, Mary Z. "Kevin Kline: 'In Action How like an Angel.'" *Modern Hamlets and Their Soliloquies.* Iowa City: Iowa UP, 1992. 175–200.

———. "Kevin Kline's American *Hamlet*: Stage to Screen." *Shakespeare on Film Newsletter* 15.2 (1991): 12.

———. "Stage into Film Doesn't Go." *Shakespeare on Film Newsletter* 13.1 (1988): 7.

Mahon, John W. "Editor's View." Rev. of Branagh's *Hamlet*. *Shakespeare Newsletter* 46.3 (1996): 66+.

———. *"Hamlet* on Video." *Shakespeare Newsletter* 46.4 (1996): 80+.

Mallin, Eric S. "'You Kilt My Foddah'; or, Arnold, Prince of Denmark." *Shakespeare Quarterly* 50 (1999): 127–51.

Manvell, Roger. *Shakespeare and the Film*. 1971. New York: A. Barnes, 1979.

McKellen, Ian, and Richard Loncraine. *William Shakespeare's* Richard III: *A Screenplay*. New York: Overlook, 1996.

McKernan, Luke, and Olwen Terris. *Walking Shadows: Shakespeare in the National Film and Television Archive*. London: British Film Inst., 1994.

McMurtry, Jo. *Shakespeare Films in the Classroom: A Descriptive Guide*. Hamden: Archon, 1994.

Mullin, Michael. "Tony Richardson's *Hamlet*: Script and Screen." *Literature/Film Quarterly* 4.2 (1976): 123–33.

Myers, Caren. Rev. of *The Lion King*. Dir. Roger Allers and Rob Minkoff. *Sight and Sound* ns 4.10 (1994): 47–48.

Newman, Karen. "Chabrol's *Ophelia*." *Shakespeare on Film Newsletter* 6.2 (1982): 1+.

Norman, Marc, and Tom Stoppard. *Shakespeare in Love*. Filmscript. London: Faber, 1999.

Osborne, Laurie. "Poetry in Motion: Animating Shakespeare." Boose and Burt 103–20.

Pall, Ellen. "Kevin Kline Discovers There's a Rub in TV." *New York Times* 28 Oct. 1990: H35.

Pendleton, Thomas. "And the Thoughts of the Other Editor." Rev. of Branagh's *Hamlet*. *Shakespeare Newsletter* 46.3 (1996): 60.

Perret, Marion D. "Kurosawa's *Hamlet*: Samurai in Business Dress." *Shakespeare on Film Newsletter* 15.1 (1990): 6.

Quinn, Edward. "Zeffirelli's *Hamlet*." *Shakespeare on Film Newsletter* 15.2 (1991): 1+.

Romney, Jonathan. *"Hamlet."* *Sight and Sound* ns 1.1 (1991): 48–49.

Rothwell, Kenneth S. "Akira Kurosawa and the Shakespearean Vision: *The Bad Sleep Well* as a 'Mirror up to Nature.'" *Shakespeare Worldwide: Translation and Adaptation*. Vol. 14–15. Ed. Yoshiko Kawachi. Tokyo: Yushodo, 1995. 168–85.

———. *"Elizabeth* and *Shakespeare in Love."* Rev. of *Shakespeare in Love*. Dir. John Madden. *Cineaste* 34.2–3 (1999): 78–80.

———. *"Hamlet* and the Five Plays of [BBC] Season Three." *Shakespeare Quarterly* 32 (1981): 396.

———. *A History of Shakespeare on Screen: A Century of Film and Television*. Cambridge: Cambridge UP, 1999.

Rothwell, Kenneth S., and Annabelle Henkin Melzer. *Shakespeare on Screen: An International Filmography and Videography*. London: Neal, 1990.

The Shakespeare Plays: Hamlet. London: BBC; New York: Mayflower, 1980.

Simmons, James R., Jr. "In the Rank Sweat of an Enseamed Bed: Sexual Aberration and the Paradigmatic Screen *Hamlets*." *Literature/Film Quarterly* 25.2 (1997): 111–18.

Skovmand, Michael, "Mel's Melodramatic Melancholy: Zeffirelli's *Hamlet*." *Screen Shakespeare*. Ed. Skovmand. Aarhus: Aarhus UP, 1994. 113–31.

Spaul, Richard, Charlie Ritchie, and Nigel Wheale. Hamlet: *A Guide*. Cambridge: Cambridgeshire Coll. of Arts and Technology, 1988.

Sterne, Richard L. *John Gielgud Directs Richard Burton in* Hamlet: *A Journal of Rehearsals*. New York: Random, 1967.

Taranow, Gerda. *The Bernhardt* Hamlet: *Culture and Context*. New York: Lang, 1996.

Taylor, Neil. "The Films of *Hamlet*." *Shakespeare and the Moving Image: The Plays on Film and Television*. Ed. Anthony Davies and Stanley Wells. Cambridge: Cambridge UP, 1994. 180–95.

Terris, Olwen. *Shakespeare: A List of Audio-visual Materials Available in the UK.* 2nd ed. London: British Universities Film and Video Council, 1987.

Thompson, Ann. "Asta Nielsen and the Mystery of *Hamlet*." Boose and Burt 215–24.

Wayne, Valerie. "*Shakespeare Wallah* and Colonial Specularity." Boose and Burt 95–102.

Wheeler, Elizabeth. "Light It Up and Move It Around: *Rosencrantz and Guildenstern Are Dead*." *Shakespeare on Film Newsletter* 16.1 (1991): 5.

Wilds, Lillian. "On Film: Maximilian Schell's Most Royal Hamlet." *Literature/Film Quarterly* 4.2 (1976): 134–40.

Willson, Robert F., Jr. "Lubitsch's *To Be or Not to Be*." *Shakespeare on Film Newsletter* 1.1 (1976): 2+.

———. "*To Be or Not to Be* Once More." *Shakespeare on Film Newsletter* 8.2 (1984): 1+.

Special Editions, Comic Books, School Guides, Audio Performances

Andrews, Richard, and Rex Gibson. *Hamlet*. Cambridge School Shakespeare. Cambridge: Cambridge UP, 1994.

Beale, Simon Russell. Hamlet: *A Fully Dramatized Recording*. Arkangel Complete Shakespeare. 2 audiocassettes. Penguin, 1999.

Behrens, Franklin A. "Meanwhile, Back at the Castle: Audio Recordings of the Shakespeare Plays." *Shakespeare Bulletin* 17.2 (1999): 41–43.

Branagh, Kenneth. *Hamlet*. BBC Radio, 1992.

Burton, Richard. *Hamlet*. LP. Columbia Masterworks, n.d.

Chamberlain, Richard. *Hamlet*. LP. Hallmark Hall of Fame, n.d.

Doyle, John, and Ray Lischner. *Shakespeare for Dummies*. Foster City: IDG, 1999.

Durband, Alan, ed. and trans. *Hamlet*. Shakespeare Made Easy. Woodbury: Barron's, 1986.

Gibson, Rex. *Teaching Shakespeare*. Cambridge School Shakespeare. Cambridge: Cambridge UP, 1998.

Gibson, Rex, and Janet Field-Pickering. *Discovering Shakespeare's Language: 150 Stimulating Activity Sheets for Student Work*. Cambridge School Shakespeare. Cambridge: Cambridge UP, 1998.

Gielgud, John. Hamlet: *Old Vic Company*. 2 audiocassettes. RCA, 1957. Listen for Pleasure, Can., 1981.

Hamlet. By William Shakespeare. Classics Illustrated 5. Artist Tom Mandrake. Adapt. Steven Grant. Comic book. New York: Berkeley, 1990.

Hamlet. By William Shakespeare. Classics Illustrated 99. Artist Alex A. Blum. Adapt. Sam Willinsky. Comic book. New York: Gilberton, 1952.

Lamb, Sidney, ed. Hamlet: *Commentary, Complete Text, Glossary*. Complete Study Guide. Lincoln: Cliff's Notes, 1967.

Lowers, James K. *Cliff's Notes on Shakespeare's* Hamlet. 1971. Lincoln: Cliff's Notes, 1996.

Muller, Frank, narr. *Hamlet*. 3 audiocassettes. Recorded Books, 1990.

Scofield, Paul. *Hamlet*. Shakespeare Recording Soc. 4 audiocassettes. Caedmon, 1979.

Shakespearean Coloring Book: Hamlet. Octagon, 1980.

Journals

Hamlet Studies. Ed. R. W. Desai. "Rangoon Villa," 1/10 West Patel Nagar, New Delhi 100,008, India.

Literature/Film Quarterly. Salisbury State U, Salisbury, MD 21801. Spec. issues on Shakespeare: 1.4 (1973), 4.2 (1976), 8.4 (1980), 11.3 (1983), 14.4 (1986), 20.4 (1992), 25.2 (1997), 28.2 (2000), 29.2 (2001).

Shakespeare and the Classroom. Ohio Northern U, Ada, OH 45810.

Shakespeare Bulletin. Incorporating *Shakespeare on Film Newsletter.* Lafayette College, Easton, PA 18042.

Shakespeare Magazine. Georgetown U, PO Box 571006, Washington, DC 20057-1006.

Shakespeare Newsletter. Iona College, New Rochelle, NY 10801.

Shakespeare on Film Newsletter. (1976–92, with index, available from *Shakespeare Bulletin*.)

Shakespeare Quarterly. Annual Bibliography. Folger Shakespeare Lib., Washington, DC 20003. Spec. issues on teaching: 25.2 (1974): 151–271; 35.5 (1984); 41.2 (1990): iii–v, 139–268; 46.2 (1995): iii–iv, 125–251.

Shakespeare Studies. U of Maryland, Baltimore, MD 21250.

Shakespeare Survey. The Shakespeare Centre, Henley Street, Stratford-upon-Avon, Warwickshire CV37 6QW, England. Spec. issues on *Hamlet*: 9, 30, 45.

Upstart Crow. Clemson U, Clemson, SC 29634.

Web Sites

These sites, unless otherwise noted, were accessed or reaccessed 27 February 2001.

Actors of the London Stage. (Formerly ACTER.) U of Notre Dame. 1 Feb. 2001 <http://www.nd.edu/~aftls/>.

Annotated Webliography of Literary Resources. Comp. Sherry Mashburn and Joseph
Thomas. Georgia Southern U.
<http://www2.gasou.edu/facstaff/dougt/weblio. htm>.

Century Dictionary. 3 May 2001 <http://216.156.253.178/CENTURY/>.

Clary's Class: Furness NV Hamlet. 3 May 2001
<http://academics.smcvt.edu/clary_class/>.

Concordances—Shakespeare: Works. Ed. William A. Williams Jr.
<http://www.concordance.com/shakespe.htm>.

The Early Modern English Dictionaries Database (EMEDD). Ed. Ian Lancashire.
Dept. of English, U of Toronto. 15 Oct. 1999
<http://www.chass.utoronto.ca/english/emed/emedd.html>.

Edsitement Websites. NEH.
<http://www.edsitement.neh.gov/websites.html>.

Enfolded Hamlet: *Enfolded Texts of the* Second Quarto *and* First Folio. Ed. Bernice
W. Kliman.
<http://www.global-language.com/enfolded.html>.

Folger Shakespeare Library. 30 Apr. 2001
<http://www.folger.edu/Home_02b.html>.

Gateway to Library Catalogs. Lib. of Congress. 23 Feb. 2001
<http://www.lcweb.loc.gov/z3950/gateway.html>.

Hamlet on the Ramparts. Massachusetts Inst. of Technology.
<http://www.shea.mit.edu/ramparts2000/>.

The Internet Movie Database.
<http://www.us.imdb.com/>.

Internet Shakespeare Editions 10 Feb. 2001
<http://www.web.uvic.ca/shakespeare/index.html>.

Mr. William Shakespeare and the Internet. Ed. Terry A. Gray. 15 Feb 2001
<http://daphne.palomar.edu/shakespeare/>, click on "Best Sites";
<http://daphne.palomar.edu/shakespeare/playcriticism.htm#Hamlet>.

The Perseus Digital Library. Ed. Gregory Crane. Tufts U. 5 Apr. 2001.
<http://www.perseus.tufts.edu/>.

*Renaissance Forum: An Electronic Journal of Early-Modern Literary and Historical
Studies.* 21 Dec. 2000
<http://www.hull.ac.uk/renforum/index.html>.

Shakespeare: A Magazine for Teachers and Enthusiasts. 27 Oct. 2000
<http://www.shakespearemag.com/>.

Shakespearean Prompt-books of the Seventeenth Century. Ed. G. Blakemore Evans.
<http://etext.virginia.edu/bsuva/promptbook/>.

Shakespeare at Clemson
<http://virtual.clemson.edu/caah/shakespr/>.

Shakespeare on Screen. Ed. Mark Andre Singer. School of Information and Lib. Studies, State U of New York, Buffalo. 12 May 1999
<http://www.folger.edu/institute/visual/sh_pathfinder.htm>.

Shakespeare's Language Bibliography: ENG 2503Y: Shakespeare's Language (1996).

By Ian Lancashire, Dept. of English, U of Toronto. June 1996
<http://www.chass.utoronto.ca/~ian/2530bib.html>.

Shenandoah Shakespeare. 14 May 2001
<http://www.shenandoahshakespeare.com/>.

Surfing with the Bard. Ed. Amy Ulen. 12 Feb. 2001
<http://www.ulen.com/shakespeare/>.

Tools for Studying Shakespeare and Contemporaries.
<http://parallel.park.uga.edu/shaxper/>.

The Works of the Bard. Ed. James Matthew Farrow.
<http://www.gh.cs.su.oz.au/~matty/Shakespeare/>, click on "Hamlet."

Resources for Comparison and Illustration

Achebe, Chinua. *Things Fall Apart*. African Writers. London: Heinemann Educ., 1988.

Amos, Tori. "Mother." *Little Earthquakes*. CD. Atlantic, 1991.

Andreas, James R. "Signifyin' on Shakespeare: Gloria Naylor's *Mama Day*." *Shakespeare and Appropriation*. Ed. Robert Sawyer and Christy Desmet. London: Routledge, 1999. 103–18.

Ashizu, Kaori. "A Japanese Anticipation of Modern *Hamlet* Criticism."

Bambara, Toni Cade. "The Lesson." *The Bedford Introduction to Literature: Reading, Thinking, Writing*. Ed. Michael Meyer. 5th ed. Boston: St. Martin's, 1999. 179–84. <http://sunset.backbone.olemiss.edu/~jmitchel/class/ banara.htm>.

Beard, Henry. "Hamlet's Cat's Soliloquy." *Poetry for Cats*. New York: Villard, 1994. 8.

The Bhagavad-Gita. Trans. Barbara S. Miller. New York: Bantam, 1986.

Blessing, Lee. *Fortinbras*. New York: Dramatists Play Service, 1992.

Bohannan, Laura. "Shakespeare in the Bush." *Natural History Magazine* Aug.–Sept. 1966: 28–33.

Cervantes, Miguel de. *The Ingenious Gentleman Don Quixote*. Trans. Samuel Putnam. New York: Viking, 1949.

Chuanxiang, Ji. *An Orphan in Zhao's Family. One Hundred Yuan-Dynasty-Play*. By Jing Shu. 1616. *Stories of Classic Chinese Plays*. By Wu Dakuei. Jiangxi: People's, 1992. 119–20.

Chaucer, Geoffrey. *The Riverside Chaucer*. Ed. Larry D. Benson. 3rd ed. Boston: Houghton, 1987.

Curtis, Richard. *The Skinhead Hamlet*. 23 Feb. 2001 <http://www.frc.ri.cmu.edu/ ~mcm/hamlet.html>.

de Bary, William Theodore, ed. and introd. *Self and Society in Ming Thought*. New York: Columbia UP, 1970.

Deller Consort. "How Should I Your True Love Know" and "Willow Song." *Shakespeare Songs*. CD. Harmonia Mundi, 1987.

Douglass, Frederick. *Narrative of the Life of Frederick Douglass, an American Slave*. Berkeley Digital Lib. Sunsite. 14 May 1997. 23 Feb. 2001 <http://sunsite. berkeley.edu/Literature/Douglass/Autobiography/>.

Fleming, William. *Arts and Ideas.* New York: Holt, 1955.

Gombrich, E. H. *Art and Illusion: A Study in the Psychology of Pictorial Representation.* Princeton: Princeton UP, 1969.

Hegi, Ursula. *Tearing the Silence: On Being German in America.* New York: Simon, 1997.

Ishiguro, Kazuo. *The Remains of the Day.* New York: Knopf, 1987.

Jewel. "Innocence Maintained." *Spirit.* CD. Atlantic, 1998.

Langer, Susanne. *Feeling and Form: A Theory of Art.* New York: Scribner's, 1953.

Laroque, François. *The Age of Shakespeare.* New York: Abrams, 1993.

Marlowe, Christopher. *Dido, Queen of Carthage. Christopher Marlowe: The Complete Plays.* Ed. Mark Thornton Burnett. London: Dent, 1999. 242–93.

McLachlan, Sara. "Elsewhere." *Fumbling toward Ecstasy.* CD. Arista, 1993.

Merchant, Natalie. "Ophelia." CD. Indian Love Bride, 1998.

Montaigne, Michel de. *The Complete Works of Montaigne.* Trans. Donald M. Frame. Stanford: Stanford UP, 1957.

Muller, Heiner. Hamletmachine *and Other Texts for the Stage.* New York: Performing Arts Journal, 1984.

Myers-Briggs, Isabel. *Introduction to Type.* Palo Alto: Consulting Psychologists, 1987.

Plaks, Andrew. *The Four Masterworks of the Ming Novel.* Princeton: Princeton UP, 1987.

———. *The Journey to the West: Masterworks of Asian Literature in Comparative Perspective.* Ed. Barbara Stoler Miller. Armonk: Sharpe, 1994.

Rudnick, Paul. *I Hate Hamlet.* New York: Dramatists Play Service, 1992.

Shiga Naoya. *Shiga Naoya Zenshû* (Collected Works of Shiga Naoya). 22 vols. Tokyo: Iwanami-Shoten, 1998–2001.

Stoppard, Tom. *Dogg's Hamlet [The Fifteen-Minute Hamlet]. Dogg's Hamlet, Cahout's Macbeth.* Inter-Action Playscript. London: Inter-Action, 1979. 27–40.

———. *The Fifteen-Minute Hamlet.* London: French, 1976.

———. *Rosencrantz and Guildenstern Are Dead.* New York: Grove, 1967.

Updike, John. *Gertrude and Claudius.* New York: Knopf, 2000.

Waley, Arthur, trans. *Monkey: A Folk Novel of Ancient China.* 1943. New York: Grove, 1958.

Young, Alan R. Hamlet *and the Visual Arts, 1709–1900.* Newark: U of Delaware P, forthcoming.

Yu, Anthony. *The Journey to the West.* 4 vols. Chicago: U of Chicago P, 1977–84.

Zhang, Hsiao Yang. *Shakespeare in China: A Comparative Study of Two Traditions and Cultures.* Newark: U of Delaware P, 1996.

INDEX OF NAMES

Aasand, Hardin, 38, 65
Abbott, Edwin, 10
Achebe, Chinua, 37
Adelman, Janet, 83
Aeschylus, 136
Allen, J. W., 207, 210
Allen, Michael J. B., 3, 57, 58, 61
Alleyn, Edward, 10
Almereyda, Michael, 12, 235
Altman, Joel, 158
Amos, Tori, 156
Anderson, Randall, 38
Andreas, James R., 12, 35, 36, 38, 165
Andrews, John F., 5, 10
Anthony, Trevor, 204
Aristotle, 10, 214, 215
Armstrong, Philip, 176
Ascham, Roger, 10
Ashizu, Kaori, 127
Ashton, Geoffrey, 12
Asimov, Isaac, 10
Astrana Marín, Luis, 66, 68, 69, 71

Babcock, Weston, 176
Bacon, Delia, 53
Bacon, Francis, 159, 207, 216
Bakhtin, Mikhail, 201
Bambara, Toni Cade, 165, 169
Barber, Deirdre, 197
Barber, Frances, 176, 178
Barnet, Sylvan, 4, 173
Barrymore, John, 241, 242, 243
Barton, Anne, 5
Battenhouse, Roy, 37, 38, 113, 114
Beard, Henry, 240
Beck, Charles R., 33
Beckerman, Bernard, 12, 38, 84, 86
Behrens, Franklin A., 12
Bell, John, 125
Belleforest, François de, 4, 5
Belling, Catherine, 4, 32
Berggren, Paula S., 37
Bergman, Ingmar, 124
Bertram, Paul, 3, 34, 54, 57, 58, 85, 232
Bevington, David, 4, 8, 9, 164
Blessed, Brian, 78
Blessing, Lee, 241
Bloom, Claire, 202
Bloom, Harold, 174
Bocchi, Achille, 208
Bodin, Jean, 10, 208

Boethius, 214
Bohannon, Laura, 11
Booth, Stephen, 157
Borgia, Cesare, 208
Boris, Edna Zwick, 31, 37
Bowers, Fredson, 52
Boyce, Charles, 10
Bradbrook, Muriel, 138
Bradford, John, 110
Bradley, A. C., 11, 114, 117, 119, 123, 174
Bradshaw, Graham, 11, 31, 35, 37, 38, 127
Branagh, Kenneth, 4, 7, 12, 35, 77, 78-79,
    82, 83, 84, 122, 128, 136, 138, 171, 175,
    176, 191, 193, 194, 195, 202, 212
Bright, Timothy, 5
Brower, Reuben Arthur, 37
Brown, Lyn Mikel, 177
Buchanan, D., 38
Buhler, Stephen M., 12, 38
Bullough, Geoffrey, 10
Burton, Richard, 194

Callaghan, Dympna, 31
Calvin, John, 234
Camden, Carroll, 177
Camden, William, 10
Capell, Edward, 70, 74
Carter, Helena Bonham, 84, 202
Carter, Jimmy, 142
Cartwright, Kent, 12
Castiglione, Baldassare, 10, 36
Cervantes, Miguel de, 134, 135, 137
Césaire, Aimé, 154
Charcot, Jean Martin, 128
Charney, Maurice, 38, 39, 138
Chaucer, Geoffrey, 214
Ch'en Hsien-chang, 129
Chuanxiang, Ji, 37, 224
Church, Tony, 191
Cinthio (Giovanni Battista Giraldi), 217
Clark, William George, 3-4
Clary, Frank Nicholas, 10, 36, 37, 65
Close, Glenn, 202
Coke, Edward, 10, 159
Coldewey, John C., 9
Coleridge, Samuel Taylor, 119, 225
Collins, Michael J., 33, 35, 38
Columbus, Christopher, 208
Comfort, Mary S., 37
Corum, Richard, 10
Coursen, H. R., 12, 37, 177, 178

Coye, Dale, 10
Coyle, Martin, 5
Cressy, David, 112
Crowl, Samuel, 12
Crystal, Billy, 212
Cummings, Peter, 34
Curren-Aquino, Deborah T., 36, 37
Curtis, Richard, 153, 242
Custodio, Alvaro, 66, 67, 68, 71

Dalí, Salvador, 158-59
Davies, Anthony, 12
Davis, Paul, 129-30
Dawson, Anthony, 12, 84, 85, 122, 125, 126, 242
de Bary, William Theodore, 129
Dee, John, 10
Deen, Rosemary, 12
de Grazia, Margreta, 11
Dench, Judi, 138
Depardieu, Gerard, 138
De Witt, Johannes, 10
Dickason, Olive, 210
di Grassi, Giacomo, 191
DiMatteo, A., 36, 37, 38, 209
Dollimore, Jonathan, 11
Doloff, Steven, 35
Donaldson, Peter S., 12, 13, 77
Donne, John, 127, 234
Doran, Madeline, 214
Douglas, Claire, 177
Douglass, Frederick, 166
Doyle, John, 10
Drakakis, John, 31, 38
Draper, John W., 116
Drayton, Michael, 208
Dubrow, Heather, 8
DuLaurens, Henri-Joseph, 10
Dunbar, Mary Judith, 38
Duplessis-Mornay, Phillipe, 10
Durband, Alan, 6
Dürer, Albrecht, 137

Edwards, Philip, 7, 51, 54, 55, 66, 70, 71, 85
Elbow, Peter, 12, 218
Eliot, T. S., 97, 146, 147, 149, 151, 152, 221
Elizabeth I, 10, 143, 153, 208
Elyot, Thomas, 10, 206
Elze, Karl, 70
Emerson, Ralph Waldo, 234
Engar, Ann W., 37
England, Eugene, 110
Epstein, Norrie, 10
Escher, M. C., 158
Essex, Robert Devereux, Earl of, 10, 140

Evans, G. Blakemore, 7, 47, 61, 62, 63, 64, 65, 76, 101, 112, 117, 191, 196, 205, 215, 216, 224, 230, 232, 234
Evanthius, 214
Farnham, Willard, 106
Fernández de Moratín, Leandro, 66, 68, 69, 70, 71
Fienberg, Nona Paula, 37
Fiennes, Ralph, 159
Figgis, John Neville, 210
Fortescue, John, 10
Foster, Donald W., 37
Freire, Paulo, 9, 12
French, A. L., 127
Freud, Sigmund, 78, 120, 128, 146-47, 148, 149, 152, 174, 175, 176, 178, 179
Fromm, Erich, 104, 174
Frye, Northrop, 11, 141, 191
Frye, Roland Mushat, 11, 119, 191
Funaki Shigeo, 122, 126
Furness, Horace Howard, 4, 10, 56, 62, 63, 64-65, 68, 69, 70

Galileo, 234
Gandhi, Mohandas Karamchand, 143
Garber, Marjorie, 178, 191
Garner, Shirley Nelson, 176, 178
Garrick, David, 7, 182
Gataker, Thomas, 108, 109
Gates, Henry Louis, Jr., 165
Gates, Joanne E., 37, 38
George, David, 38
Gibson, Mel, 78, 84, 171, 202, 204, 220, 221
Gielgud, John, 138, 139
Gilbert, Miriam, 74, 85
Girard, René, 110
Glover, John, 3-4
Goddard, Harold, 176
Goldman, Michael, 12, 232
Gombrich, E. H., 206
Goodwin, Nancy, 12
Gordon, Christine Mack, 33
Grafton, Anthony, 208
Granville-Barker, Harley, 11, 69, 82, 85
Grant, Steven, 161
Grebanier, Bernard, 115
Greenblatt, Stephen, 8, 11, 57, 80, 85, 123, 156, 157
Greg, W. W., 85, 122, 127
Guilfoyle, Cherrell, 114
Gurr, Andrew, 8

Hadfield, Andrew, 209, 210
Hale, David G., 36, 37
Hall, Kim, 140
Hall, Peter, 83, 122, 125, 126, 127
Hapgood, Robert, 7
Hardy, Barbara, 90

Hartman, Geoffrey, 85, 177
Hattaway, Michael, 138
Hawkes, Terence, 174
Hazlitt, William, 225
Hegi, Ursula, 104
Helgerson, Richard, 208
Henry VIII, 109
Henslowe, Philip, 10
Herbst, Karl, 203
Heston, Charlton, 138
Hibbard, George R., 7, 54, 55, 70, 85, 128, 179
Hinman, Charlton, 3, 83, 85
Hirsh, James, 12, 37, 38
Hodges, C. Walter, 7, 10
Holinshed, Raphael, 140
Holland, Norman N., 178
Hollar, Wenceslaus, 10
Holm, Ian, 124
Homans, Peter, 177
Honigmann, E. A. J., 4
Hook, Sidney, 121
Hooker, Richard, 10
Hopkins, Anthony, 202
Hopkins, Lisa, 32, 37
Horney, Karen, 174
Hoskyns, John, 10
Houlbrooke, Ralph, 109, 112
Howard, Jean E., 11
Howe, Allie, 35
Howlett, Kathy M., 4, 12
Hoy, Cyrus, 5
Hubler, Edward, 4, 94, 183
Hull, Suzanne W., 75
Hyde, Henry, 142

Ingleby, Clement Mansfield, 64
Irace, Kathleen, 55
Ishiguro, Kazuo, 104

Jackson, Glenda, 83
Jacobi, Derek, 6, 124, 126, 128, 138, 159, 171, 202
Jacobus, Lee, 9
James I, 10
Jardine, Lisa, 11
Jenkins, Harold, 6, 54, 55, 69, 82, 85, 89, 114, 115, 140, 152, 184, 190, 191, 192, 210, 222
Jennens, Charles, 4, 64
Jewel [Kilcher], 156
John, Elton, 79
Johnson, Samuel, 57, 61, 117, 225
Jones, David E., 35
Jones, Ernest, 11, 119–20, 175, 242
Jonson, Ben, 127
Jorgens, Jack. J., 12
Julius Caesar, 114

Jung, Carl Gustav, 174, 176, 177, 178

Kant, Immanuel, 206
Kantorowicz, Ernst, 207, 208
Kastan, David S., 10
Keller, Arthur, 210
Kermode, Frank, 216–17
Kincaid, Arthur, 38, 39
Kinney, Arthur, 38
Kirkpatrick, Rob, 33
Kirsch, James, 175
Kittredge, George Lyman, 7, 145
Kliman, Bernice W., 3, 12, 31, 34, 54, 57, 58, 65, 85, 122, 124, 175, 232
Kline, Kevin, 4
Kökeritz, Helge, 3, 57, 58, 61
Kott, Jan, 141
Kozintsev, Grigori, 124
Kurosawa, Akira, 12, 154
Kyd, Thomas, 37

Lacan, Jacques, 121, 147, 149, 152, 178
Laing, R. D., 177
Lamb, Sidney, 6
Landis, Joan Hutton, 11, 32, 38, 110
Langer, Susanne, 73
Las Casas, Bartolomé de, 208
Lavater, Johann Caspar, 5
Lemmon, Jack, 138, 212
Lerner, Lawrence, 214
Leverenz, David, 106
Levin, Carole, 208
Levin, Harry, 11
Lidz, Theodore, 175, 176
Limon, Jerzy, 52
Lischner, Ray, 10
Lissitzyn, Oliver, 210
Liston, William T., 8
Lockyer, Roger, 10
Loncraine, Richard, 139
Looney, Thomas, 53
Louiso, Todd, 220, 221
Lupton, Julia Reinhard, 11, 31, 35, 149
Lyth, Ragnar, 179

MacCary, Thomas, 10
Macfarlane, Alan, 112
Machiavelli, Niccolò, 10, 208, 234
Mack, Maynard, 4, 11, 97, 100, 101, 129, 134, 136, 137, 213
Macpherson, Guillermo, 67, 68, 71
Maguire, Laurie E., 4, 37, 38, 39
Malone, Edmund, 64
Mander, Raymond, 12
Mandrake, Tom, 162, 163
Mann, Frederick, 210
Marcus, Leah, 12
Marks, Robert, 175

Marlowe, Christopher, 10, 138-39, 231
Mary (Stuart), Queen of Scots, 153
Maslen, Elizabeth, 191
Mason, Brewster, 123
Maurer, Margaret, 9
Mazer, Cary, 84
McDonald, Russ, 10
McElroy, Bernard, 176
McLachlan, Sara, 156
McLean, Andrew M., 113
McLuskie, Kathleen, 177
McMillin, Scott, 86
McQuade, Thadd, 203-04
Melzer, Annabelle Henkin, 12
Merchant, Natalie, 156
Meyer, Michael, 165, 169
Michelangelo, 237
Michenson, Joe, 12
Mogubgub, Fred, 32
Molina Foix, Vicente, 67
Montaigne, Michel de, 5, 10, 36, 134-35,
    136, 137, 234
Mowat, Barbara A., 4-5
Muir, Kenneth, 57, 58, 61
Muller, Heiner, 153
Mullins, Denise M., 37
Munday, Anthony, 53
Munro, John J., 64
Murfin, Ross, 178

Nardo, Anna K., 177
Nashe, Thomas, 116
Nazareth, Ralph, 11, 37
Neely, Carol Thomas, 176, 178
Nehru, Jawaharlal, 143
Neill, Michael, 5
Nelson, Robert A., 35
Neuman, E., 177
Nielsen, Asta, 202
Nietzsche, Friedrich, 141
Nuttall, A. D., 120, 121

Oakes, Elizabeth, 4
Oakley, Francis, 210
O'Brien, Ellen J., 11, 34, 38
O'Brien, Peggy, 12
Olivier, Laurence, 12, 32, 35, 38, 77, 78, 82,
    84, 122, 123, 124, 130, 136, 171, 174-75,
    191, 193, 194, 195, 202, 242
Onions, Charles Talbut, 10, 68, 83
Orlova, Natalia, 191, 194
Orwell, George, 34

Padilla, Diomaris, 210
Pagden, Anthony, 207, 210
Paine, Thomas, 238
Papp, Joseph, 241
Parker, Patricia, 84, 85, 177

Paul, 209
Pendleton, Austin, 220-21
Pennington, Michael, 127-28, 175
Perkins, William, 108
Perret, Marion D., 6, 38
Pico della Mirandola, Giovanni, 134
Pinciss, Gerald, 10
Pitcher, John, 216
Plaks, Andrew, 130, 131
Plotnik, Meta, 32, 36, 38
Plowright, Joan, 77
Pollock, Linda, 109
Pompey the Great, 206
Ponsot, Marie, 12
Poster, Mark, 206
Potter, A. M., 12
Pritchard, Thomas, 110
Prosser, Eleanor, 114, 115, 116
Puttenham, George, 10

Quayle, Anthony, 125
Quilligan, Maureen, 11

Rasmussen, Eric, 65
Ray, Robert H., 4, 7
Rees, Roger, 176
Reilly, Terry, 37
Reinhard, Kenneth, 11, 149
Rhymer, Thomas, 10
Ribner, Irving, 7
Rice, Tim, 79
Richardson, Tony, 35, 77, 78, 191, 194, 202
Righter, Anne, 191
Roberts, James, 143
Roberts, Jeanne Addison, 12
Robinson, Randall, 12
Robson, W. W., 87, 88, 127
Rocklin, Edward L., 38
Rommen, Heinrich, 207
Ronan, Clifford J., 101
Rosenberg, Marvin, 12, 124, 242
Rothwell, Kenneth S., 12, 32
Rowe, Katherine, 85
Rozett, Martha Tuck, 12, 31
Rudnick, Paul, 153, 241, 242
Ruth, Dr., see Westheimer, Ruth

Saeger, James P., 77
Saviolo, Vincentio, 191, 192
Saxo Grammaticus, 5, 114
Schell, Maximilian, 35
Schlovsky, Victor, 103
Schmidt, Alexander, 10, 83
Scholes, Robert, 103
Schwarzenegger, Arnold, 32
Scofield, Paul, 78
Scot, Reginald, 10
Scott, Maria M., 37

Scott, Mark W., 36
Shattuck, Charles, 8
Shiga Naoya, 37, 122, 126-27
Showalter, Elaine, 84, 177, 178
Shoyo Tsubouchi, 126
Shuger, Debora, 110
Shurgot, Michael, 38, 87
Sidney, Philip, 10
Silver, George, 191, 193
Simmons, Jean, 84, 175
Sirofchuck, Mike, 12, 32
Skinner, Quentin, 208, 210
Smith, Henry, 108
Smith, Thomas, 10
Sophocles, 129, 148
Speght, Rachel, 108
Spencer, T. J. B., 5, 229
Spenser, Edmund, 231
Spevack, Marvin, 8, 10, 235
Sprengnether, Madelon, 176, 178
Stallybrass, Peter, 11
Stanley, Audrey, 84
Stanton, Kay, 218
Stanyhurst, Richard, 140
States, Bert O., 11
Steevens, George, 64
Sterling, Eric, 36
Stewart, Patrick, 81, 82, 84, 124, 126, 202
Stone, Lawrence, 108, 112
Stoppard, Tom, 32, 37, 219, 220, 240
Streitberger, W. R., 9
Strout, Nathaniel, 37
Styan, J. L., 12
Swaggert, Jimmy, 142
Swander, Homer, 84, 89

Taylor, Gary, 4, 7
Terence, 214
Thompson, E. P., 112
Tieck, Ludwig, 127
Tillyard, E. M. W., 11, 103
Tolaydo, Michael, 12
Tourneur, Cyril, 37
Trevelyan, G. M., 108, 110
Tschischwitz, Benno, 70
Tuck, Richard, 210

Ulpian, 208
Updike, John, 241, 242
Urkowitz, Steve, 4
Valverde, José M., 66, 67, 68

Vergil, 129
Vickers, Brian, 5, 178, 217
Videbaek, Bente, 38
Vogel, Paula, 154
Voltaire, 159
Voss, Paul J., 12
Voss, Tony, 33

Waley, Arthur, 129, 130, 132
Wallace, William, 202
Ward, Lalla, 84, 175
Warren, Michael, 4, 84
Webster, Richard, 128
Weimann, Robert, 204
Weiss, Larry, 8
Wells, Stanley, 4, 84, 203
Werstine, Paul, 4-5
Westheimer, Ruth, 142
Wheale, Nigel, 174, 178
Wheeler, Richard P., 12
White, R. S., 207
Whitworth, Paul, 85
Wiggins, Grant, 12
Williams, George Walton, 191-92, 195-96
Williams, Robert A., 210
Williams, Robin, 212
Williamson, Nicol, 171, 194, 202
Wilson, John Dover, 11, 69, 85, 87, 113, 119-20, 123, 124, 127, 184, 191, 192, 193
Wilson, Thomas, 10
Wing, John, 108
Winslet, Kate, 84, 175
Wirth, Peter, 124
Wofford, Susanne L., 5, 85, 178, 243
Woodhead, M. R., 88
Woolf, Virginia, 108, 110
Worthen, W. B., 9
Wright, George T., 34, 38, 47, 51, 67
Wright, William Aldis, 3-4

Yonge, Charlotte, 178
Young, Alan R., 12, 32
Young, Bruce, 32, 37, 110
Young, Jack, 204
Young, Michael W., 38
Yu, Anthony, 129, 130

Zeffirelli, Franco, 12, 35, 77, 78, 79, 84, 122, 124, 125, 136, 191, 194, 195, 204, 220, 221
Zhang, Hsiao Yang, 130
Zhiye, Luo, 33, 37

INDEX OF SCENES IN *HAMLET*

Act 1
Scene 1
34, 35, 44, 46, 47, 69, 70, 74, 90, 92, 97–98, 105, 114, 115, 160, 208, 234
Scene 2
34, 35, 68, 69, 71, 74–75, 83, 91, 98, 102, 103, 108, 146, 150, 160, 185, 195, 209, 223
Scene 3
33, 34, 38, 46, 47, 74, 103, 110, 116, 154, 166, 170–73, 175, 217, 219, 227
Scene 4
38, 42, 46, 47, 113, 114, 115, 117, 135, 160, 166, 167, 185, 209, 215, 223
Scene 5
38, 41, 43, 45, 46, 47, 77–80, 91–92, 93, 100, 107, 100, 111, 114, 116, 117, 119, 131, 132, 160, 162, 182, 185, 195, 216, 223, 227, 231, 233, 234, 235, 236

Act 2
Scene 1
42, 46, 47, 55, 74, 75, 92, 103, 117, 138, 168, 174–79, 195, 219
Scene 2
6, 8, 42, 47, 49–50, 58, 59–60, 66, 74, 86, 91, 93, 98, 99, 107, 108, 109, 117, 138–40, 147, 154, 162, 167, 180, 186, 204, 212, 214, 215, 221, 223, 234

Act 3
Scene 1
6, 35, 42, 43, 44, 58, 60, 66–67, 82–84, 91, 92, 93, 96, 98, 127, 129, 154, 159, 160, 161, 162, 177, 192, 204, 219, 222, 223, 234, 240
Scene 2
8, 34, 36, 38, 43, 46, 54–55, 60, 67, 82–83, 86–89, 90, 96, 99, 108, 113, 117, 119, 121–28, 135, 139–40, 155, 159, 160, 162,

163, 180, 181, 190, 213, 215, 217, 227, 230
Scene 3
41, 47, 91, 93, 111, 117, 120, 122, 124, 127, 147, 160, 163, 167, 180, 187, 195, 208, 209, 212, 231
Scene 4
34, 35, 38–39, 43, 47, 57, 63–64, 91, 93, 96, 99, 104, 110, 113, 124, 131, 150, 151, 160, 162, 167, 171, 176, 180, 181, 182, 183, 186, 187

Act 4
Scene 1
74, 104
Scene 3
44, 109–10, 156
Scene 4
43, 46, 55, 65, 99, 103, 104, 105, 115, 135–36, 150, 191, 215, 217, 234
Scene 5
34, 35, 46, 47, 58, 93, 137, 154–55, 156, 166, 176, 177, 184–90, 196, 219
Scene 6
99, 100, 126, 151, 160, 225
Scene 7
39, 40, 45, 46, 47, 93, 100, 109, 126, 151, 155, 156, 159, 160, 193, 225

Act 5
Scene 1
33, 39, 46, 91, 93, 100, 108, 117, 121, 155, 159, 160, 177, 178, 189, 203, 209, 232, 241
Scene 2
34, 39, 46, 57–58, 60–61, 75, 76, 79, 92, 93, 100, 104, 105, 111, 114, 132, 136, 145, 189, 191–96, 197–200, 209, 214, 215, 217, 223, 227, 233, 234, 239

INDEX OF CHARACTERS IN *HAMLET*, OTHER THAN HAMLET

Barnardo, 130, 219, 241

Claudius, 34, 36, 37, 41, 45, 47, 54, 57, 61, 68, 69, 74, 75, 79, 82, 86, 87, 88, 91, 92, 93, 95, 99, 100, 103, 104, 107, 109, 110, 111, 113, 116, 117, 120, 122–23, 124, 125, 126, 127, 128, 131, 133, 138, 146, 147, 148, 149, 150, 152, 154, 155, 158, 159, 160, 161, 162, 163, 167, 169, 180, 181, 182, 183, 184, 185, 186, 187, 188–89, 190, 192, 193, 194, 195, 196, 197, 198, 202, 204, 208, 209, 211, 212, 213, 215, 219, 220, 231, 233, 236, 241

Cornelius, 103

Fortinbras, 7, 79, 93–94, 99, 105, 110, 114, 115, 135, 136, 145, 199, 206, 208, 209, 212, 213, 217, 227, 239, 241

Gentleman, 184, 186

Gertrude, 11, 33, 34, 35, 36, 38–39, 41, 47, 57, 60–61, 63, 74, 75, 80, 82, 83, 87, 88, 91, 93, 96, 98, 99, 103, 104, 107, 108, 109–10, 111, 113, 116, 122, 124, 125, 126, 127, 131, 132, 135, 144, 146, 147, 148–51, 152, 155–56, 158, 159, 160, 162, 166, 168, 176, 177, 180, 181–83, 186, 187, 188, 193, 194, 197, 198, 199, 202, 203, 204, 215, 219–20, 230, 233, 234, 236, 242

Ghost of Hamlet's Father, 33, 38, 39, 41, 44, 47, 63, 70–71, 76, 77–80, 91–93, 95, 96, 97, 98, 99, 105, 108, 109, 110, 111, 113–17, 118–19, 120, 127, 128, 130, 131, 135, 141, 146, 147–48, 158, 159, 160, 161, 162, 163, 167, 176, 178, 180, 182, 185, 186, 187, 189, 195, 204, 208, 209, 212, 214, 215, 217, 218, 220, 223, 227, 231, 232, 233, 234, 235, 236

Gravediggers, 33, 39, 91, 100, 203

Guildenstern, 98, 99, 104, 113, 117, 124, 126, 136, 190, 202, 215, 219, 229, 230, 240

Horatio, 60, 69, 70, 71, 76, 82, 87, 88, 90, 91, 92, 93, 94, 98, 99–100, 103, 114, 115, 119, 120, 124, 131, 132, 135, 136, 160, 166, 167, 177, 184, 189, 193, 195, 199, 204, 209, 215, 225, 230, 231, 239, 241, 243

Laertes, 33, 34, 45, 46, 47, 57, 58, 75, 91, 93, 95, 103, 110, 111, 114, 117, 136, 154, 155, 166, 168, 169, 170, 171, 172, 174, 176, 184, 185, 187–88, 189, 190, 192–93, 194–95, 196, 197, 198–99, 212, 213, 215, 217, 220, 227, 228, 232, 234, 241

Marcellus, 69, 70, 71, 90, 98, 114, 115, 130, 138, 167, 241

Norwegian Captain, 65

Ophelia, 6, 32, 33, 35, 36, 38, 39, 41, 47, 60, 66, 67, 75, 82, 83, 84, 85, 87, 92, 93, 98, 100, 103, 107, 108, 110, 113, 114, 117, 120, 122, 125, 137, 153, 154–56, 158, 159, 160, 161, 162, 166, 168, 170, 171, 172–73, 174–78, 179, 181, 184, 185, 186, 187, 189, 190, 202, 203, 204, 206, 209, 210, 215, 217, 219, 220, 225, 230, 232, 233, 234, 236, 241

Osric, 104, 192, 193, 194, 195, 198, 199, 217, 225

Players, 59–60, 86, 87, 88, 90, 91, 107–08, 122, 124, 128, 139–40, 155, 159, 188, 190, 215, 217, 220, 227, 240

Polonius, 33, 46, 57, 75, 76, 82–3, 87, 90, 92, 93, 100, 103, 104–05, 110, 117, 124, 126, 154, 159, 161, 162, 168, 169, 170, 171, 172–73, 174, 175, 176, 177, 180, 182, 184, 185–86, 191, 195, 196, 199, 204, 206, 211, 212–13, 214, 215, 217, 218, 220, 227, 230, 233

Reynaldo, 75, 92, 103, 138, 174

Rosencrantz, 98, 99, 104, 113, 117, 124, 126, 136, 190, 202, 215, 219, 229, 230, 240

Voltimand, 103

Yorick, 33, 91, 158, 178

Modern Language Association of America
Approaches to Teaching World Literature
Joseph Gibaldi, series editor

Achebe's Things Fall Apart. Ed. Bernth Lindfors. 1991.
Arthurian Tradition. Ed. Maureen Fries and Jeanie Watson. 1992.
Atwood's The Handmaid's Tale *and Other Works*. Ed. Sharon R. Wilson,
    Thomas B. Friedman, and Shannon Hengen. 1996.
Austen's Pride and Prejudice. Ed. Marcia McClintock Folsom. 1993.
Balzac's Old Goriot. Ed. Michal Peled Ginsburg. 2000.
Baudelaire's Flowers of Evil. Ed. Laurence M. Porter. 2000.
Beckett's Waiting for Godot. Ed. June Schlueter and Enoch Brater. 1991.
Beowulf. Ed. Jess B. Bessinger, Jr., and Robert F. Yeager. 1984.
Blake's Songs of Innocence and of Experience. Ed. Robert F. Gleckner and
    Mark L. Greenberg. 1989.
Boccaccio's Decameron. Ed. James H. McGregor. 2000.
British Women Poets of the Romantic Period. Ed. Stephen C. Behrendt and
    Harriet Kramer Linkin. 1997.
Brontë's Jane Eyre. Ed. Diane Long Hoeveler and Beth Lau. 1993.
Byron's Poetry. Ed. Frederick W. Shilstone. 1991.
Camus's The Plague. Ed. Steven G. Kellman. 1985.
Cather's My Ántonia. Ed. Susan J. Rosowski. 1989.
Cervantes' Don Quixote. Ed. Richard Bjornson. 1984.
Chaucer's Canterbury Tales. Ed. Joseph Gibaldi. 1980.
Chopin's The Awakening. Ed. Bernard Koloski. 1988.
Coleridge's Poetry and Prose. Ed. Richard E. Matlak. 1991.
Dante's Divine Comedy. Ed. Carole Slade. 1982.
Dickens' David Copperfield. Ed. Richard J. Dunn. 1984.
Dickinson's Poetry. Ed. Robin Riley Fast and Christine Mack Gordon. 1989.
Narrative of the Life of Frederick Douglass. Ed. James C. Hall. 1999.
Eliot's Middlemarch. Ed. Kathleen Blake. 1990.
Eliot's Poetry and Plays. Ed. Jewel Spears Brooker. 1988.
Shorter Elizabethan Poetry. Ed. Patrick Cheney and Anne Lake Prescott. 2000.
Ellison's Invisible Man. Ed. Susan Resneck Parr and Pancho Savery. 1989.
Faulkner's The Sound and the Fury. Ed. Stephen Hahn and Arthur F. Kinney. 1996.
Flaubert's Madame Bovary. Ed. Laurence M. Porter and Eugene F. Gray. 1995.
García Márquez's One Hundred Years of Solitude. Ed. María Elena de Valdés and
    Mario J. Valdés. 1990.
Goethe's Faust. Ed. Douglas J. McMillan. 1987.
Hebrew Bible as Literature in Translation. Ed. Barry N. Olshen and
    Yael S. Feldman. 1989.
Homer's Iliad *and* Odyssey. Ed. Kostas Myrsiades. 1987.
Ibsen's A Doll House. Ed. Yvonne Shafer. 1985.
Works of Samuel Johnson. Ed. David R. Anderson and Gwin J. Kolb. 1993.
Joyce's Ulysses. Ed. Kathleen McCormick and Erwin R. Steinberg. 1993.

Kafka's Short Fiction. Ed. Richard T. Gray. 1995.
Keats's Poetry. Ed. Walter H. Evert and Jack W. Rhodes. 1991.
Kingston's The Woman Warrior. Ed. Shirley Geok-lin Lim. 1991.
Lafayette's The Princess of Clèves. Ed. Faith E. Beasley and Katharine Ann
    Jensen. 1998.
Works of D. H. Lawrence. Ed. M. Elizabeth Sargent and Garry Watson. 2001.
Lessing's The Golden Notebook. Ed. Carey Kaplan and Ellen Cronan Rose. 1989.
Mann's Death in Venice *and Other Short Fiction*. Ed. Jeffrey B. Berlin. 1992.
Medieval English Drama. Ed. Richard K. Emmerson. 1990.
Melville's Moby-Dick. Ed. Martin Bickman. 1985.
Metaphysical Poets. Ed. Sidney Gottlieb. 1990.
Miller's Death of a Salesman. Ed. Matthew C. Roudané. 1995.
Milton's Paradise Lost. Ed. Galbraith M. Crump. 1986.
Molière's Tartuffe *and Other Plays*. Ed. James F. Gaines and
    Michael S. Koppisch. 1995.
Momaday's The Way to Rainy Mountain. Ed. Kenneth M. Roemer. 1988.
Montaigne's Essays. Ed. Patrick Henry. 1994.
Novels of Toni Morrison. Ed. Nellie Y. McKay and Kathryn Earle. 1997.
Murasaki Shikibu's The Tale of Genji. Ed. Edward Kamens. 1993.
Pope's Poetry. Ed. Wallace Jackson and R. Paul Yoder. 1993.
Shakespeare's Hamlet. Ed. Bernice W. Kliman. 2001.
Shakespeare's King Lear. Ed. Robert H. Ray. 1986.
Shakespeare's Romeo and Juliet. Ed. Maurice Hunt. 2000.
Shakespeare's The Tempest *and Other Late Romances*. Ed. Maurice Hunt. 1992.
Shelley's Frankenstein. Ed. Stephen C. Behrendt. 1990.
Shelley's Poetry. Ed. Spencer Hall. 1990.
Sir Gawain and the Green Knight. Ed. Miriam Youngerman Miller and
    Jane Chance. 1986.
Spenser's Faerie Queene. Ed. David Lee Miller and Alexander Dunlop. 1994.
Stendhal's The Red and the Black. Ed. Dean de la Motte and Stirling Haig. 1999.
Sterne's Tristram Shandy. Ed. Melvyn New. 1989.
Stowe's Uncle Tom's Cabin. Ed. Elizabeth Ammons and Susan Belasco. 2000.
Swift's Gulliver's Travels. Ed. Edward J. Rielly. 1988.
Thoreau's Walden *and Other Works*. Ed. Richard J. Schneider. 1996.
Voltaire's Candide. Ed. Renée Waldinger. 1987.
Whitman's Leaves of Grass. Ed. Donald D. Kummings. 1990.
Woolf's To the Lighthouse. Ed. Beth Rigel Daugherty and Mary Beth Pringle. 2001.
Wordsworth's Poetry. Ed. Spencer Hall, with Jonathan Ramsey. 1986.
Wright's Native Son. Ed. James A. Miller. 1997.